ROY ELDRIDGE,
LITTLE JAZZ GIANT

ROY ELDRIDGE

LITTLE JAZZ
GIANT

JOHN CHILTON

continuum
LONDON • NEW YORK

Continuum

The Tower Building, 11 York Road, London, SE1 7NX

370 Lexington Avenue, New York, NY 10017-6503

First published 2002

British Library Cataloguing-in-Publication Data
A catalogue record for this book is available from the British Library.

ISBN 0-8264-5692-8 (hardback)

Library of Congress Cataloging-in-Publication Data
Chilton, John, 1932–
    Roy Eldridge, little jazz giant / John Chilton.
      p. cm. —
    Includes bibliographical references (p.) and index.
    ISBN 0-8264-5692-8
    1. Eldridge, Roy, 1911–1989 2. Trumpet players—United States—Biography.
    3. Jazz musicians—United States—Biography. I. Title. II. Series.

ML419.E37 C54 2002
788.9′2′2165′092—dc21
[B]   2001047750

Typeset by BookEnds Ltd, Royston, Herts
Printed and bound by MPG Books Ltd, Bodmin, Cornwall

CONTENTS

ACKNOWLEDGMENTS

Especial thanks to Charles Graham, Phil Schaap (W.K.C.R.-F.M.), Ray Bolden, Alyn Shipton, and Ira Berger.

Grateful thanks (in some cases, posthumous) to: Walter C. Allen, Jeff Atterton, Jean Bach, Bob Bain, Ovid "Biddy" Bastien, Louie Bellson, Claude Bolling, Billie Bowen, Jack Bradley, John Bray, Michael Brooks, Lennie Bush, Tom Chilton, Buck Clayton, Bill Coleman, Derek Coller, Graham Colombé, Ian Crosbie, Bill Crow, Helen Oakley Dance, Stanley Dance, Spanky Davis, Buddy DeFranco, Carole Eldridge, Chuck Folds, Kenny Gordon, David Griffiths, Kitty Grime, Scott Hamilton, Herbie Harper, Jack L. Higgins, James Hogg, Peter Ind, Institute of Jazz Studies, Franz Jackson, Jonah Jones, Nancy Reed Kanter, Dick Katz, Miriam Klein, Jack Kleinsinger, Eddie Locke, Humphrey Lyttelton, Matty Matlock, Dennis H. Matthews, Alun Morgan, Joe Muranyi, David Nathan (National Jazz Foundation), Art Pilkington, Michael Pointon, Fosco Redeghieri, Howard Rye, Loren Schoenberg, Ed Shaughnessy, Dave Shepherd, Tony Shoppee, Johnny Simmen, Ken Vail, Françoise Venet, Steve Voce, Laurel Watson, Laurie Wright, Trummy Young.

For my good friends Brian Peerless and Dan Morgenstern;
their help has been invaluable.

SMOKETOWN

During the 1920s, before jazz magazines existed, touring musicians spread the word from state to state about young, up-and-coming players who possessed extraordinary musical talent. In this way Roy Eldridge received widespread acclaim before he ever recorded. Everyone who heard the young Eldridge's trumpet-playing found that it left an indelible impression in their memories—his speedy fingering, technique, and commanding range were unforgettable.

By 1930, jazz musicians far and wide were talking about the short, lightweight kid from Pittsburgh, Pennsylvania, whose combative attitude toward other trumpeters was as marked as his musical skills. Even the ace trumpeters of that era never forgot where they first heard Roy play. Jabbo Smith could recall the details of their original meeting, Jonah Jones could cite the venue where he first encountered the young whirlwind, and Bill Coleman had no problem in recollecting his initial brush with Roy:

> He could have only been about 17 years old when I first heard him, but he seemed completely grown-up and so assured. He was very nifty, and his playing was very fast. I commented on his speed and he said, in a very matter-of-fact way, "Well, I've taken the tops off my valves and now they really fly."[1]

Off the bandstand all these notable trumpeters found the young Roy chirpy and restless, cocky but affable. However, playing on stage with Eldridge was a different matter; they were soon made aware that he was doing his utmost to play higher, faster, and more dynamically than they were. Musical combat and blowing the trumpet were inseparable in Roy's mind. He was an ebullient youngster whose dazzling playing was the perfect outlet for his natural competitiveness. Looking back over his career, Roy said:

> All my life I've loved to battle. And if they didn't like the look of me and wouldn't invite me up on the bandstand I'd get my trumpet out by the side of the stand and blow at them from there.[2]

Roy's uncompromising attitude to competitors developed during the hundreds of hours he spent practicing the trumpet during his teens. He adopted a self-imposed regime that involved long periods of solitary blowing. He liked having fun with his pals, but that was lower on his list of priorities than mastering the trumpet. Roy became obsessional about the need to practice morning, noon, and night, and remained so for much of his life. Roy's relentless schedule seems to have created a reservoir of intensity within him, which provided his solos with a cutting edge. He said: "I used to spend eight, nine hours a day practising every day. Get out of bed and start playing, play until I got hungry, go out and eat and come back and play some more."[3]

Roy never lost his competitive attitude, even during his later, mellower years. By then he was a famous trumpeter who thrilled (and entertained) his listeners by trying his hardest at almost every performance. He always appeared to be enjoying himself on stage, but beneath Roy's cheerful manner and his affable responses to his listeners' congratulations, there lurked a broodiness that was prone to hark on old grievances. He was aware of this and sometimes prefaced the polishing of an old grudge by saying, "You may think I'm being paranoid, but... ." I once wrote that Roy liked to make sure that any potential friendship was thoroughly tested. He read this, smiled, and said, "I guess so." Having suffered many disappointments in his dealings with the business side of the music world, he gave his trust slowly and with great care. Photographer Jack Bradley said, "He was a little aloof when you first met him. I would say he was a very private person."[4] Drummer Eddie Locke, a close friend (Roy was godfather to his sons), said, "He had a lot of complexes and was much more insecure than people realized, but I never worked with anyone who so loved to play."[5] Another drummer, Ed Shaughnessy, said, "I found him terrific as a player and as a person."[6] Writer Max Jones described Roy as "a man with a sensitive if taut nervous system."[7] Even so, the word most commonly used to describe Eldridge was "feisty," yet he was often capable of flashing what writer Whitney Balliett called "a 200 watt smile." Pianist Chuck Folds, with admiration in his voice, said, "I can't imagine anyone more competitive than he was in the 1970s. I've never met anyone scrappier than Roy, ever, ever, ever."[8]

Reed-player and long-time colleague of Roy Joe Muranyi said, "He was a moody, difficult little bird. He was very complex and had a fierce temper."[9] Pianist Dick Katz modified this by saying, "Roy had a temper, but you never felt it was hostile."[10] But beneath the conflicting aspects of Roy's personality there existed a warm, kindly, emotional man who could be marvelous company. He was ultra-sensitive, but if he felt at ease he added more than his share of humor to any conversation, often providing, unasked, revealing background information about various jazz events. He could be stubborn, prickly, and easily agitated, but he could also be charmingly courteous in an almost old-fashioned way. The anomalies in Roy's character may well have stemmed from the fact that he encountered racism throughout his life, suffering indignities when he worked with white bands that almost broke him in two. Nevertheless, this book is strewn with examples of Roy helping and advising white musicians. Not that he was, even in the slightest degree, Uncle Tom-ish. If he sensed the merest hint of what he called "a draft" (the chill wind of racism), Roy would instantly bristle with overt antagonism. Writer Dan Morgenstern observed, "Roy could read in people's eyes whether he was being accepted or not. In all things he was completely honest, a rare thing."[11] When I first met Roy in 1958 he was taciturn and guarded. A couple of years later he was friendlier without being effusive. The association stayed at that level. Then, in 1973, his manner suddenly relaxed, and I was delighted to share his company on many occasions throughout the 1970s and 1980s. In general, as he grew old, he became almost jovial with strangers who approached him, providing they didn't have a trumpet in their hands.

Surprisingly, Roy's romance with the trumpet was slow to start. As a young child he had no ambition to become a musician. His early dreams were of working for his father, driving one of the several haulage trucks that formed the basis of Alexander Eldridge's business. Alexander had originally used horses for conveyancing, but switched enthusiastically to mechanization. This line of business was a departure from the Eldridge family tradition: Alexander, like all of his brothers, was by trade a master carpenter. Home for the Eldridge family was on Pittsburgh's North Side, close to the Pennsylvania Rail Road workshops. David Roy Eldridge was born there on January 30, 1911. At an early age he made it clear that he preferred to be called Roy, but even so he continued to use the name David Roy Eldridge on his address labels into the last years of his life.

Because of the success of his father's enterprises, Roy was well provided for during his childhood. He described his father (who was originally from Petersburg, Virginia) as a "good businessman who didn't drink or smoke."[12] Alexander was religious, and made sure that Roy went to church regularly. Besides working as a haulage contractor he also ran a construction business, and managed to convert the top story of what had formerly been the family home into a dormitory for railroad workers, with a restaurant on the ground floor (which was run by his wife and a cousin). Alexander made sure that his two sons (Roy, and Joe—born in October 1907) played their part in the family endeavors by putting them to work at weekends on a shoeshine stand, which was also equipped with a steamer for cleaning hats. The two boys were given other tasks. Roy recalled, "We had one T-model and it had a brass rail, me and Joe used to have to shine it every Sunday."[13] During the summer school vacations Roy's father let him carry water and shovel sand on his building projects. By this time the family had moved a few blocks to Irwin Avenue, one of the main thoroughfares of the area. This substantial dwelling-house was one of several properties that Alexander Eldridge bought over the years.

At an early age, despite not being interested in becoming a musician, Roy showed that he possessed a genuine talent for music. His piano-playing mother (originally from Winston-Salem, North Carolina) gave him every encouragement and often sat him at the keyboard, delighted that her younger son was able to produce coherent music. Roy gave the background:

> My first music was made on piano. You know the old sayings about black people all got the blues in them, well, that can be a load of shit, but I will say that when I was about five years of age I could sit down at the piano and play a blues sequence with all the right bass notes. Even as a kid, before I was playing music, I remember guys around there playing harmonicas, guitars, and mandolins. They could really play the blues. My mother played piano by ear. When I was about six years old we used to go to the movies, that's when they used to have a piano playing for the silent movies. She'd hear all those classical things and she'd come home and play them, and I had a little set of drums and I'd play with her. I took piano lessons for a while, but I didn't like the teacher, so that didn't work out. He was always slapping my knuckles. I also took some violin lessons, but I was mad about the drums, and took lessons to learn to play them.[14]

The violin lessons were an attempt by Roy's parents to set him on the same path his elder brother Joe was treading with some success. Joe (who later picked up the nickname "Don") had begun on violin and soon became proficient on it. He then took up alto-saxophone and clarinet and made rapid progress on both these instruments. Roy hero-worshipped Joe, but showed no interest in playing the violin or the reed instruments. Instead he took to the drums. Looking back,

> I loved the drums. I used to play them in a local kids' band. I was so keen I'd get up early in the morning and get up on the roof of our garage so that the sun would catch the skins of my snare drum and dry them in such a way to let me get just the sound I wanted. Then they put me on bugle, and on Decoration Day I was asked to play "taps" at a church parade out in the open air. Four of us boys were posted at each corner of the cemetery, and we had to echo "taps" one after the other. Out in the cold air I got to feeling nervous and I worried that I would miss the notes. Several of our neighbors had come along to hear me and that made things worse. I was real scared. I was shaking, and I've never forgotten the experience. Ever after, when I got ready to play, I always tried to make sure I was warmed up properly before I played for the people.[15]

This daunting experience didn't put Roy off brass instruments for ever, but he was still far from being fanatical about playing one. He did just enough practice on the bugle to retain his place in the band. Joe listened to Roy's efforts, and soon realized that his younger brother had a natural talent for producing a good tone on the bugle. In addition, Roy possessed an *embouchure* that allowed him to play high notes with ease. But, as the bugle has no keys or valves, it is only capable of producing basic harmonics. Joe reasoned that Roy would find playing the valved trumpet more interesting, allowing, as it did, a performer to blow melodies and scales not possible on the bugle. But Roy wasn't at all excited by this prospect, so, for the time being, the idea was shelved. All of Roy's musical interest was focused on the rhythms he could produce on the drums, and, whereas he found practicing the bugle quite irksome, he loved playing the drums. Joe was impressed by the young percussionist's progress and decided to use him in a band that he organized, which consisted of local young musicians keen to play in public. It was with this group that the young Roy (on drums) played his first gig—a New Year's Eve private party.

Years later, Roy liked to kid interviewers by saying that he was only 6 years old when this engagement took place, but from the description of the tunes the group played (*Whispering, Margie,* etc.) the gig couldn't have taken place before December 31, 1921, when Roy had almost reached the grand old age of 10. Whatever the date, the occasion proved too much for the little lad's stamina. The band began playing at 11 p.m. and by 1 a.m. Roy had fallen fast asleep, but, as he had played so well during his two hours of activity his colleagues forgave him. Before dozing off, Roy said he vividly remembered a couple of female dancers stripping naked, but in recounting the experience he was always quick to point out that tiredness caused him to close his eyes, not a lack of curiosity. Roy continued to be part of Joe's band, along with Norman Sampson on cornet, Clarence Tatum on piano, Henry Tatum on mellophone (neither related to Art Tatum), and Joe Eldridge on violin, who didn't feel quite ready to play the alto-sax in public. During intermissions Roy used to blow on Norman Sampson's cornet, achieving effective results. This reinforced Joe's idea that Roy should begin playing the trumpet. He pointed out to Roy that he was always going to be small in stature, and that carrying a drum kit (with a huge, heavy bass drum) would be a taxing experience when Joe wasn't around to help. Finally, Roy agreed to Joe's suggestion, and as a result his parents obligingly bought him a second-hand trumpet (made by Buescher). They then arranged for him to have lessons from a local musician, P. M. Williams, who supplemented his earnings as a barber by playing the trumpet and teaching music. Roy's interest in playing the trumpet remained lukewarm:

> I was very lazy. I barely learned my solfeggio and couldn't read music. When my teacher and I had to play duets in

church I had to pretend to read my part and there were often curious results. One thing is for certain, Mr Williams was a powerful player, you could hear him ten blocks away.[16]

Because he possessed such a good musical ear, Roy made no real effort to learn to read music. His natural talent even fooled Mr. Williams: "If I heard it I could play it. He thought I was reading."[17]

Tragedy entered Roy's life when he was 11 years old. His mother died, and in order to gain help in raising Roy and Joe, Alexander Eldridge married again. The enormous sense of loss seems to have provided the catalyst for Roy's musical ambitions, and from this point onward he practiced the trumpet relentlessly, exasperating neighbors and family alike. To avoid complaints about the continual blowing, Roy softened the sound of his trumpet by pushing a glove tightly into the bell of the instrument. This made it difficult to pitch notes accurately, but Roy accepted this as a challenge, and taught himself to blow the muffled sounds exactly in tune; in doing so he stretched his upper range beyond the register given in most trumpet manuals of that period. To further develop stratospheric sounds Roy blew phrases he'd heard Joe perform on the clarinet, gradually producing high notes that Mr. Williams regarded as being freakishly beyond the trumpet's normal range. Roy's intensive practice regime also gave him a fast fingering technique. He explained, "Well, if you practice eight or nine hours every day you've got to get speed or get paralysed."[18]

There was no question of a cruel stepmother making Roy's life a misery. The atmosphere at home was generally supportive, but Roy felt happiest when he was left alone to practice the trumpet. The trumpet provided a safety-valve for Roy, who, during his boyhood, often got into fights at school. By the time he was 14, the instrument had virtually taken over his life. He was a bright kid, but one who was unwilling to study hard at school. His stubborn streak led him to avoid the chance to join the school band, something he later regretted: "It was very stupid of me because there was so much music I could have known years ago."[19] Roy could, at a pinch, "spell" out printed music, but he was no nearer to becoming a proficient sight-reader. He spoke of his natural ability:

> From my mother I developed an ear. Anything I heard, classical music or anything I could automatically play. I didn't know what key I was playing in or nothing. Later, all the trumpet-players, like Dizzy Gillespie, would say, "I don't see how you finger things like that," but I never knew the legitimate way.[20]

By this time, brother Joe was proficient on saxophone and clarinet (as well as being a competent violinist). Unlike Roy, he could sight-read with ease and was consequently much in demand, which led to his gradually moving further afield to play with established bands. Roy himself began picking up local evening gigs, including a series of dates where he was one of a band of youngsters who played at basketball games. Some of these games were between white teams, but all of Roy's young colleagues in the band were African-Americans. Roy was often late getting back from these engagements and this led to arguments with his father. Roy was also often in trouble with teachers at his racially mixed school because of his unpunctuality, his absenteeism, and his general attitude toward discipline. At that time, the African-American population of Pittsburgh was around 50,000, just below the 10 percent mark. Segregation was easily encountered— in most of the local theaters African-Americans were only allowed to sit in the rear six rows. With its considerable number of inhabitants of Italian, Polish, Irish, and German descent, the city had a distinctly cosmopolitan feel. Because of the labor demands of the many steel mills, coal yards, and glass factories there were no severe unemployment problems, but Roy had no desire to join the manual workforce. He saw many of his friends leave school and go straight into grimy jobs that ensnared them for the rest of their lives. In those days most of the fuel for the Pittsburgh steel mills' furnaces was coal, and the resulting umbrella of smoke and fumes meant that black roofs and sooty curtains were common in most households. Roy's comment about getting up early to let the sunshine fall on to his drum heads was a necessary maneuver—the sun often disappeared for the day, even in summer-time. As a schoolboy, Roy developed the habit of staying up until very late. Even when there was no chance of sitting in, he'd slip out to hear as much live music as possible, visiting various clubs in "The Hill" district, usually managing to talk his way into being allowed to listen from the back of the hall. If his pleas failed, he'd stand outside to hear what he could of the band.

In the late summer of 1925, after playing a two-month season in North Wisconsin (in a band with saxophonist Greely Walton and others), Joe Eldridge returned home to Pittsburgh and began organizing a band that later became known as The Elite Serenaders. It says something for Joe's skill that he was able to persuade two top-line players, saxophonist Benny Carter and cornettist Rex Stewart, to rehearse with the band at the Eldridge family home. Carter (whose playing became a model for Joe's style) had been working in Pittsburgh with Billy Paige and Lois Deppe (and Earl Hines) at the Paramount Inn. Joe allowed Roy to sit in alongside Rex Stewart for part of these practice sessions, and Roy, much impressed by Rex's playing, was delighted. "My first major influence on my horn was Rex Stewart. I liked his speed, range and power. Rex was the first trumpeter to show me breaks."[21] Rex, scholarly and articulate, was also, by his own definition, "as temperamental as a greyhound." He did all he could to help the young tyro, but was not best pleased when Joe encouraged Roy to take a solo at a band rehearsal, which was couched in phrases that might well have come from the bell of Rex's instrument. Roy spoke of the incident:

> I'll never know why Joe did this. I guess he was proud of my progress, but he set Rex up and got me to blow against him, they used to call it "signifying." There was no point to it because I was too young to tour with The Elite Serenaders. [Roy pronounced Elite as E-light.][22]

Sincere though Roy was in his admiration for Rex Stewart's playing, he couldn't resist trying to outblow him. Over the coming years "master and pupil" were to engage in several epic musical combats, embracing fierce blowing, fusillades of very high notes, and flurries of fast fingering. The Elite Serenaders' regular trumpeter Archie Johnson (born in Mississippi but raised in Pittsburgh) also much impressed Roy. Years later he said, "Archie Johnson was playing awful good in those days."[23] Roy's precocious skills registered favorably with Benny:

> I first played with Roy Eldridge in the Elite Serenaders back in Pittsburgh in 1925. Roy was only 14 years old, playing full time [sic] in his brother Joe Eldridge's Band. Roy was starting to wail then, developing his chops.[24]

Through Benny Carter's recommendation The Elite Serenaders played a residency at New York's Renaissance Casino (known to musicians as "The Renny"). During a school vacation Roy was invited to visit New York to hear the band in these prestigious surroundings. He enjoyed the experience, particularly when Joe invited him to sit in; the thrill of the trip served to increase his desire to become a professional musician. Rex Stewart's unorthodox style of playing continued to appeal to Roy, but later he also felt a strong need to find a way of improvising on trumpet that was based on the jazz phrases played by two great saxophonists, Coleman Hawkins and Benny Carter. By playing along with their recordings, Roy gradually developed his legato-phrasing to the formidable speed required for such an enterprise to sound convincing. Late in his career he said:

> The two men who have been my favorites ever since I began playing music are Benny Carter and Coleman Hawkins. They really inspired me. I'd listen to them and be stunned. I didn't know the right names for anything at first, but I knew what knocked me out. They'd do eight bars and then play what I called a "turn around." Chord changes I dug. Trumpet players

didn't play enough of the harmony for my money, while the saxes used to run through all the chord changes. So I resolved to play my trumpet like a sax.[25]

With all the practicing, rehearsing, playing gigs (some with Harry Turner's Ritz Club Orchestra), and late-night patrols around the clubs, Roy was seeing less and less of the inside of a school classroom. His truancy was further increased when, for a brief while, he became one of a group of young black extras: "I was in a stage play at one of the theaters downtown—a bunch of us kids, naturally shooting craps. What else?"[26] His continual absences caused an official from the David B. Oliver High School to send word to Roy's father saying they were considering expelling the errant youngster, but another event caused the school's administrators to take immediate action. Roy gave the background:

> I got kicked out of school. There was this little white girl, and right from babies we'd been tight. We'd never really got into it, but we started getting close, and it was getting to that stage where it was about to jump off. We got caught in the cloakroom in the wrong position, so they expelled both of us. But we were supposed to go back, but the day my father was supposed to come from work and take me back, that's the morning I left home.[27]

While Roy was deliberating about what would happen when he returned to school, he heard of a musical opportunity offered by a traveling show, and as a result his formal education ended at the ninth grade. He quickly rounded up several of the young musicians with whom he had worked locally, the eldest of whom was 16. They were Charlie Lee (tenor-sax), Chuck Jefferson (piano), Ben Garrison (banjo), and Alvin Burroughs (drums). Somehow Roy talked the show's organizers into booking the band without hearing it; he left home carrying a suit, a pair of shoes, and his trumpet.

The people who hired us didn't know that none of us could read music.

We only knew four numbers, three foxtrots and a waltz. For the overture of the show a blues singer gave us her arrangement saying "Just hit it!" The curtain opened and we couldn't get a sound out. She turned around and asked what was going on. We confessed we couldn't read music. So we played a blues and it worked out.[28]

Roy sometimes revamped the story of this juvenile disaster, adding to the drama by describing how all the kids broke down weeping, unable to continue. It was unusual for Roy to vary an anecdote. He was not given to wild exaggeration and possessed an excellent memory, but the excitement of the debut meant that the event wasn't clear in his memory. What happened next remained vividly in his mind. Soon after the traumatic opening the show folded, and the promoter abandoned the troupe in Sharon, Pennsylvania, some seventy miles from Pittsburgh. They were stranded there without any money, and such possessions as they had were held because the rent hadn't been paid. The performers decided to move a few miles south to Farrell, Pennsylvania, where the show's one-legged dancer, Mr. Fox, attempted to make some money by getting the band to play in an empty store front. The admission price was set at 10 cents, but there were no takers. The young musicians managed to get a lift to nearby Youngstown, Ohio, where a $5-a-musician dance gig awaited them. But Roy, not having eaten for a while, took advantage of an offer of free hot dogs and soda-pop to such an extent that he was too full to blow the trumpet: "I was so full I couldn't hit a note. I sat there all night fixing my valves."[29] Nevertheless, the band got paid. Still in Youngstown, the band attended a hotel party that had been organized to greet the arrival of a traveling carnival show. Roy's new girlfriend played a part in getting the band invited to the gathering: "I hooked up with this chick, we were supposed to be married I guess, and she knew these people on a carnival."[30] At the party, the boss of the carnival, Captain John Sheesley, heard Roy play a version of *The Stampede* in which he copied the solo that Coleman Hawkins (on tenor-saxophone) had recorded with Fletcher Henderson in May 1926; Roy had learned the solo by playing a 78 r.p.m. disk over and over again. The carnival chief had never heard anyone play the trumpet like that, nor for that matter had anybody else. Roy's revolutionary approach enabled him to play long, smooth lines throughout his formidable range, replicating the saxophonist's style. The young trumpeter had by this time developed the ability to articulate his phrases cleanly, inspired by the white cornettist Loring "Red" Nichols, whose 1926 recordings had become readily available. But Roy's style wasn't simply an amalgam of the efforts of Coleman Hawkins, Benny Carter, Rex Stewart, and Red Nichols. There was also the work of a trumpeter whom Roy often talked about when the subject of influences came up. This was Theodore "Cuban" Bennett, born 1902, who was a first cousin of Benny Carter (Carter's mother was born Sadie Bennett). Bennett hailed from McDonald, Pennsylvania, some seventeen miles from Pittsburgh. Apparently Bennett (who never recorded) devised a harmonically bold trumpet style that was also saxophonic. Roy described him as "the living end," adding:

> He played more like a saxophone did. He was really making his changes way back in those days. You could call him one of the first of the moderns. He wouldn't hold a steady job. He drank a lot and never made any records.[31]

Roy's blending of these disparate influences produced a remarkable individuality that instantly appealed to Captain Sheesley, who added Roy to an already large musical entourage: a 32-piece band, five of whom were trumpeters. Roy had to work very hard for his salary of $12 a week. The Greater Sheesley Carnival traveled extensively, sometimes playing as many as 36 shows a week, and these performances were prefaced by five "ballyhoos" each day, which meant the band took on the task of marching around town in order to advertise the show's next performance. Traveling by Pullman car, Roy enjoyed seeing various states he had never visited before, but things were not going smoothly within the band. As a youngster and new to the ensemble, he was regarded as something of a utility player, and was, for a spell, given the job of playing a tuba that was almost as big as he was. The band's lead trumpeter was irritated that Roy still couldn't read music. Roy later confessed, "I got away with it for a while because if he hummed it I could play it."[32] The trumpeter was probably envious of Roy's technique, and of his ability to construct an appealing harmony part within the ensemble without recourse to a written band part. But it seems that it was the band's pianist who was Roy's arch-enemy. He told Roy, "You'll never be a musician. Don't you see you're taking the place of a real musician?"[33] Roy retained unhappy memories of these exchanges for many years:

> The older cats were a little salty with me. So they set me up. They called a rehearsal. I'll never forget this as long as I live. The name of the tune was "Hello Bluebird" [a 1926 pop song]. So the cat handed me that first part. Now, he might as well have handed me some Chinese writing. So he started the band of 32 pieces and the band played about eight bars. "What's the matter, Eldridge?" I said, "It don't seem like they're playing that right." He said, "Never mind about that, just play your part." So I said, "Well, I can't read no music," and now the older cats are satisfied, and boy, they really laid on me.[34]

The writing seemed to be on the wall for Roy's career in the band:

> What kept me in the show was that I switched to drums. The drummer had left and we were playing in Aurora, Illinois. Guys from Chicago were coming over every day to audition. I knew the drum part by heart, so I told them to rent some drums, and that's how I stayed with the show.[35]

Roy was never accepted by the older members of the band, but it wasn't the insults and derision that caused Roy to leave the carnival; it was a racial incident: "The first time I really knew about this prejudice thing was when we got to Cumberland, Maryland. We were playing a fair date and something happened there that really shook me up."[36]

It seems that some locals were unhappy about the site where a black vendor had positioned his stand. Words were exchanged, after which the black stand-owner was assaulted. Captain John Sheesley entered into the argument and hit a white trouble-maker over the head with his cane. A fight broke out, but when the police arrived they forcibly arrested the black victims and let the white offenders go free. Roy was not directly involved but was very upset by the incident: "That night I was on the train back to Pittsburgh."[37] Soon after Roy arrived back home a great chance came for him to lead a small band for the traveling Rock Dinah show, which was headed by a recording duo, Wesley "Kid Sox" Wilson and Leola "Coot" Grant. This married couple (both born in 1893) had plenty of touring experience–Coot's stage debut was as an 8-year-old "pickaninny." Leola was only in her mid-thirties when Roy's juvenile outfit began working with her, but in deference to her seniority they were encouraged to call her "Auntie." The show was contracted to play a series of bookings on the touring circuit run by the Theater Owners' Booking Association (usually referred to as T.O.B.A.) which provided entertainment for theaters that catered mainly for African-American audiences. The Association was not black-owned; it was run by a mixed (black and white) consortium, which operated principally out of Tennessee. Its origins (in 1909) owed much to the organizing skills of the black comedian Sherman H. Dudley, entrepreneur A. Barrasso, and business manager Sam Reevin.

Pay was never high for the performers on the Rock Dinah tours, and a thrice-daily performance schedule was not unknown. Not without reason, the T.O.B.A. circuit was nicknamed "Tough On Black Asses," but years after the enterprise folded (in the 1930s) those who had taken part in T.O.B.A. tours developed a sort of pride in having been part of them, almost like veterans of a spectacular battle. The organization utilized about forty theaters, covering a vast area that took in (among other cities) Memphis, Tennessee, Little Rock, Arkansas, and Atlanta, Georgia. It was always a joy to hear former T.O.B.A. troupers reminiscing about the various acts that were featured on the circuit. They included jugglers, contortionists, comedians, blues singers, bands, dancers, and celebrity acts noted for their unusual physical appearance, such as the tiny Princess Wee Wee. After the T.O.B.A. ceased to function, New York's Apollo Theater in Harlem operated (from January 1934) a similar tradition for many years, albeit with top class acts and none of the grotesques. Roy Eldridge's eyes lit up when he spoke of the wild personalities he encountered during his T.O.B.A. days, none more eccentric than the drummer in the pit orchestra at a Memphis theater, who literally caused a riot:

> In those days *Tiger Rag* was a popular number, everybody knew it and played it. There was a lot of competition to find new ways of filling in the breaks on the tune—the whole band would stand up and shout, or growl, or someone would tap-dance for two bars, or bang a gong, but this drummer in Memphis attracted a hell of a lot of attention by firing off blanks from a pistol during the breaks. Well, one night when we were there, he found out he'd run out of blanks. It was Friday late show, house full, and he couldn't bear the thought of letting down the public so he put real bullets in his gun! When the band stopped to let him have his big moment he fired live bullets into the ceiling. It was a crazy thing to do. Naturally no one was in the line of fire but the bullets brought down small sharp pieces of plaster and these hit people in the front rows on the head. No one was seriously hurt, but people further back in the audience thought that the blood on the people meant they had been shot, so they made for the exit pronto. There was nearly a riot as people fought to get out. The manager tried to explain but he was swept aside. They

refunded the admission money and canceled the show. There was some talk of the drummer going to jail, but in the end I think they just fired him. I never saw him again.[38]

The shadows of segregation and racism crossed a good deal of the territory covered by the Rock Dinah show. One act in the production consisted of a vocal duet on stage between Johnny Briggs and Baby Hines. Briggs wore a smart smoking-jacket and Baby Hines a negligé, but they were separated by a curtain that went down the center of the stage. Thus kept apart, they sang *If I Could Be With You One Hour Tonight* to each other via mock telephones. This was too much for the theater-goers in Pritchard, Oklahoma. Briggs, who was light-skinned, was told to black up and wear overalls when he sang this number, and Baby Hines was forced to wear a plain dress. The show continued its trek through the South and Midwest and on one occasion went into Canada. Wherever the tour went, Roy's exciting playing attracted favorable comments and left a durable impression. He celebrated his sixteenth birthday while the Rock Dinah show was playing at the 12th Street Theater in Kansas City: the cast arranged a party at the Yellow Front Café. During this tour of the Midwest the show played at the Aldridge Theater in Oklahoma City, where, for the first time, Roy met the Texas trumpeter Oran "Hot Lips" Page, who was to become one of Roy's favorite players. Page, after his initial hearing of Roy's trumpet-playing, said candidly, "Goddam, where did this cat come from playing like an ofay?" ("ofay" was Pig-Latin for a white person). But Roy's work on this tour made a more favorable impression on pianist Count Basie, who recalled:

> It was while I was in Oklahoma City that a show came through called Rock Dinah, and they had a little young cat in the band playing the greatest trumpet I'd heard in my life. His name was Roy Eldridge. That's where I first heard him.[39]

Until I read this in Count Basie's 1985 autobiography *Good Morning Blues*, I had no idea that Roy and Basie had known each other for that long. Roy had never mentioned that fact in various conversations we'd had about Basie. I made a comment to that effect and received a grouchy reaction from Roy, who said testily:

> Oh, sure. But I've never forgotten that Basie stole my musicians. He was working with the Gonzelle White show and he persuaded Hildred Humphries and Reuben Lynch to go with him then and there. I woke up and was told they had gone. I was mad about this for a long time.[40]

The Rock Dinah show brought Roy some publicity, including an item in the *Chicago Defender* of November 5, 1927, which mentioned that he was leading his band in the show at the Washington Theater in Indianapolis. Roy was never to forget that engagement. During the preceding months, Roy had partnered the girl who was responsible for his joining the Great Sheesley Carnival Band. She was also probably the link between him and the Rock Dinah job, she being a singer and dancer in the show, but Roy's interest in her waned as he became increasingly involved with an older woman (he was still only 16!). The spurned girl, wild with jealousy, took a razor-blade and slashed at Roy, cutting his back so badly that he needed twenty-six stitches; he carried the scars for the rest of his life. He recalled the trauma:

> It wouldn't have been so bad if it had been in New York or somewhere like that; instead of taking me to the hospital the cat sewed me up and then put her behind bars. The judge said, "Well, how much time do you want her to have?" I said, "Oh turn her loose. I love her." He said, "You're a damn fool. Thirty days." Well, see, that thirty days strands her, because we'd be long gone. So I used to get these pleading letters... she wanted to come back, and I said "No way."[41]

While recuperating from his wounds Roy found himself stranded in St. Louis, Missouri, with only his drums and his trumpet. His traveling trunk arrived empty, all the contents stolen. He and a pianist picked up some work playing at the Grand Central Hotel on Pine Street, but Roy soon found out that he was a sitting target for several of the fine trumpeters based in St. Louis, who attended the hotel's Sunday afternoon jam sessions.

> Until that point I had never come across a whole posse of really good trumpeters, one here, two there, yes, maybe, but not a whole gang of good players in the same place. They ambushed me, I was like "the kid from back East."[42]

Roy elaborated on this situation in an interview with Nat Hentoff:

> Every Sunday five trumpet players came down and tore me apart. I was about 16 and I was playing smooth. They played with a guttural kind of sound. They were more or less on a Louis Armstrong kick, the way Louis used to play, but more guttural. I was playing what could be called cool then, and I wasn't familiar with that other style. I couldn't understand how they got around to playing like that—the lip vibrato, trills, etc.[43]

Years later Roy could still remember his adversaries, naming them as Dewey Jackson, Charlie Creath, Andrew "Big Baby" Webb, Baby James, and Cookie (not Cookie Mason). Despite Roy finding their approach to blowing unattractive, it still had an effect on his playing. He told Phil Schaap, "I played straight notes with a vibrato, but not with a raspy "frog tone" sound. Later I learned how to do that."[44] The abundance of fine trumpeters in St. Louis meant that work was scarce for interlopers like Roy. After about three weeks he ran out of money and was turned out of his hotel. With no other option he joined another carnival and was soon on the move again, this time with an organization headed by C. A. Worthen. The prospect of resuming a life that guaranteed regular meals and comfortable travel appealed to Roy: "Those carnivals in those days were first class. They had their own Pullman Cars, they had their own privilege car where you ate, they had the gambling car. It was really a first-class operation."[45]

However, there was a snag, it being that the musicians were poorly paid. Roy explained, "The stars made money, but the musicians didn't, the musicians were nobody. I finally quit that show down in Little Rock, Arkansas."[46] One suspects that Roy left the troupe impetuously after some unrevealed incident had taken place. He could scarcely have chosen a worse time to arrive in Little Rock. Not long before his arrival it had been the scene of an infamous lynching in which the burnt body of 18-year-old John Carter had been dragged through the streets. Roy spoke of this infamy:

> I came there the week after it happened. And I asked a policeman where I could get an express truck to haul my stuff into town. Boy, he went off! He said, "You're from up there where the niggers cuss the white folks, eh? If I catch you out after twelve o'clock I'm gonna lock you up." Then a wagon came and trucked all of my stuff, because I had the drumset.[47]

So Roy found himself broke and alone in a town where old Southern traditions were rigorously upheld; fortunately he still had his instruments: "Man, I was really hungry, but with nothing to eat. I tried to pass the time by noodling around on my horn, then one of these cats walked in and offered me a job."[48]

Roy's savior had a curious nickname: Big-To-Do. Roy began working for this bandleader in a five-piece line-up which featured a girl pianist:

> We used to travel in Big-To-Do's car and play over in Mississippi. We'd go there Saturday night. Then I joined the best band down there, Oliver Muldoon's. But the only thing about that band was that they didn't work enough.[49]...We played about two of them seven dollar gigs a week until I finally got enough to get home to Pittsburgh.[50]

But, late in his life, Roy admitted to Dan Morgenstern that despite his best efforts, he couldn't earn enough money to get himself out of Little Rock and, in the end, had to ask his dad for the rail fare:

> The trains were a black, muddy green. Naturally they had a Jim Crow car…and when we got to St. Louis I changed trains. I saw that red Pennsylvania train and it was like seeing a letter from home. I was so happy I was crying and laughing.[51]

Roy's father was so pleased to see him again that he dispensed with the reprimands he had planned to deliver. Within days of getting back, Roy had rounded up several of the cohorts who had previously worked with him, and they began operating as the Nighthawk Syncopators, and then (at the behest of a local booking agent) as Roy Elliott and his Palais Royale Orchestra. "He thought it more classy," said Roy—the agent also billed the band as being "from New York." As part of the promotion, Roy built up a new specialty by using a tin-can as a mute on his performances of Duke Ellington's recent success *East St. Louis Toodle-oo* (accompanying his blowing with some comic "camel walking"). But Roy's attempts at bandleading in and around Pittsburgh were only moderately successful. He kept his "chops" in shape by following relentless practice routines, supplementing these efforts by "sitting in" wherever he could. This trait remained with Roy for many years. He couldn't bear to be unemployed, not principally because of the loss of income but because he dreaded "losing his lip," being well aware that the spectacular nature of his playing demanded that his *embouchure* was kept strong and supple. Trumpeter Bill Coleman, playing a season in Pittsburgh (in a band led by drummer Lloyd Scott), elaborated on his first meeting with Roy:

> One night I went to a club and was jamming with the musicians when a young boy came in and took out an old trumpet. He didn't have any experience, but what he played had plenty of fire in it and I could tell he was trying to play Rex Stewart's style. We started talking and he told me his

name was Roy Eldridge. He said he was only 17 and he was married. I don't know if it was true, but after I got to know Roy better I believed he could have been married because he was wild enough to do many things that most boys of his age would not think of doing.[52]

2

TERRITORY
BAND TRAVELS

Roy found that work was scarce in Pittsburgh, so, in order to get some money, he did a brief spell of carnival touring with the Beckman & Garrity show, but soon returned home. Instead of becoming down-hearted, Roy increased his practice routines. Before they had been remarkable; now they became demonic. In order to toughen his lip further, he cut small grooves in his mouthpiece rim and then rubbed the mouthpiece on a hard stone surface. This flattened the rim and broadened it, thus spreading the pressure he used to produce a note over a larger area of his lips. It was not an uncommon strategy in those days, usually producing a scar on the lips, which Roy said he felt quite proud of, thinking he now resembled a veteran trumpet-player. He supplemented the hours he spent blowing at home by sitting in with any sort of band that he could find, padding through the streets at night trying to detect the sounds of live music so that he could make a bee-line for its source. Roy was welcomed at some places, but not by the incumbent trumpet-players who didn't enjoy the antics of the young whipper-snapper who burst in and nonchalantly blew phrases an octave above their highest notes. Roy's pal, tenorist Henry "Hen Pie" Gerold, knowing that Roy was short of work, suggested he audition for

Horace Henderson (the younger brother of the famed bandleader Fletcher Henderson); Horace (who played piano) had brought a band to Pittsburgh for a summer booking. The bandleader was so impressed by Roy's playing that he sacked one of his trumpeters to make room for the youngster. Roy joined the band, became a member of the Pittsburgh Union Local 471, and moved off with his new colleagues to their next engagement.

Roy regarded joining Horace Henderson as the first important move in his career. Horace gave Roy lots of advice that proved useful when he eventually moved to New York—Roy described him as "a great influence." Roy also spoke to Dan Morgenstern about him: "I give that cat all the credit in the world. Because he brought me in his band, and I told him, 'I can't read.' He said, 'You'll be alright.'"[1]

The band was sometimes billed as Horace Henderson's Collegians, but more often they worked as The Fletcher Henderson Stompers, Under the Direction of Horace Henderson, playing engagements that Fletcher's own band was too busy to fulfill. Roy, having spent so many hours listening to, and learning from, Fletcher Henderson's recordings (featuring Coleman Hawkins and clarinettist Buster Bailey, whose speedy technique impressed Roy), now felt that by joining Horace he was half-way toward playing with Fletcher's celebrated ensemble. Certainly some of the arrangements were identical, as Jonah Jones, one of Horace's trumpeters, explained: "Horace would go to Fletcher's pad of arrangements and lift one out so he could copy it out for his own band. He did this without asking Fletcher, knowing that his brother wouldn't take any action."[2]

Horace Henderson was a fine musician, but it wasn't easy to find people, other than Roy, who spoke warmly of him. Despite his denials, it seems that he was envious of his elder brother's successes. Later he had grounds for discontent when arrangements that he had written were attributed to Fletcher and widely praised, but even as a young man he regarded the quietly spoken Fletcher as a rival. I well remember trombonist Dicky Wells saying that whenever Horace learned that Fletcher had enjoyed a friendship with a girl while on tour, he tried his hardest to find her and seduce her. Dicky thought that Horace was a better pianist than Fletcher, but he didn't like him as much. Others preferred Fletcher's playing and his personality; nevertheless, Roy always remained grateful that Horace's offer of work ended a very uneasy period of his life, though he was aware that Horace had a reputation for dropping projects before giving them a chance to develop, moving on just when it suited him, regardless of the feelings of the musicians who lost their jobs as he went off to follow a new whim. Jonah Jones said, "He would leave anyone stranded if something better came along."[3] Horace formed his first band while studying at Wilberforce College in Ohio. During each of the summer vacations (except for the year when he graduated) he took a band on tour. He also briefly led his band at New York's Savoy Ballroom during the spring of 1928. Not all the members of his bands during these early years were students at Wilberforce, but future stars such as Benny Carter, Rex Stewart, and trumpeter Freddie Jenkins (later to feature with Duke Ellington) lived on the campus, experiencing the sort of privileged lives that young track stars enjoyed. Freddie Jenkins explained: "During the school year we played weekend dates, and during the summer we'd go on tour."[4]

Horace, having again recently disbanded, was leading a new line-up when Roy Eldridge joined. In order to whip this outfit into shape, Horace organized a rigorous schedule of rehearsals in Columbus, Ohio, where they were joined by a trumpet ace from Indianapolis, Raymond "Syd" Valentine, who took over most of the first trumpet parts. Roy was given the task of playing third trumpet parts, which were usually allocated to a jazz soloist. Valentine couldn't help but notice that the trumpet that Roy had was old and battered, and looked out of place alongside the other musicians' gleaming instruments. For the sake of appearances Henderson bought Roy a new trumpet, which he accepted with reluctance, being quite happy with what he had got. Valentine recalled the situation in a conversation with Duncan Schiedt: "Roy sat and fidgeted on the stand and obediently played the section parts with the new trumpet, but when his solos came, he reached down for his old horn, as a golfer would for a favourite putter."[5]

Valentine was by nature peripatetic and soon left the band, but Roy never forgot him and always described him as a "very good player." Valentine played specialty numbers on a tiny "pocket" trumpet during his brief stay with Horace Henderson. Twenty years later Roy "flirted" with a pocket trumpet, causing one journalist to suggest that Roy was the first jazz musician to use this novelty instrument, but Roy shunned a chance of free publicity by immediately pointing out that Syd Valentine had used one in the 1920s.

Matthew "Red" Harlan (from Louisville), who enjoyed a reputation as a fine lead trumpeter, came into Horace Henderson's Band and took over the first chair for a while. Thus the line-up was as follows: Roy Eldridge, Matthew Harlan, Bernice Morton (known to all as "Jack Sprat') on trumpets, Guy Jackson, Cleo Good, Alfred Gibson on reeds, William Howard on drums, Luke Stewart on guitar, Sylvester Turpin on bass, and Horace Henderson on piano.

Sylvester Turpin and Luke Stewart later worked with Stuff Smith's Sextet, as did trumpeter Jonah Jones, who eventually replaced Matthew Harlan. Jonah, who joined in Cleveland, recounted the details to Stanley Dance:

> I played first, Bernice Morton second and Roy took all the jazz stuff. Oh, Roy was blowing! Of course he was playing a lot of Louis Armstrong's stuff then. He could play *Beau Koo Jack* note for note. He was serious, about 17 years old, a fantastic trumpeter, one of the naturals. I don't think he could read too good then, but he could play so well that he could put his own third part to the stuff.[6]

Young though he was, Roy knew what he wanted, and became increasingly aware that he didn't like the style of drumming that was the norm in jazz ensembles at that time (even within the line-up he was working with). He told Dan Morgenstern: "There was a cat on drums named Bill. I used to pay him a quarter to play the top cymbal for me, because I wanted to get away from that press roll."[7]

One cannot exaggerate the influence that Louis Armstrong's playing had on almost every black trumpeter in America during the 1920s—some of them even earned their living by learning his solos and playing them by rote. Countless musicians paid homage to Louis by incorporating his ideas into their solos, and even those who wouldn't admit to an influence couldn't hide the fact that Armstrong's genius was a shaping force in their style. Roy Eldridge was in this category. For years he was reluctant to say that he was one of the many who had fallen under Louis' spell. On various occasions Roy maintained that he hadn't really listened closely to Armstrong until he heard him in New York in 1932, but Jonah Jones' comment about *Beau Koo Jack* (recorded in December 1928) makes a mockery of this, and so too did something that the white clarinettist "Matty" Matlock told me. When he was a young man, Matlock (born in 1907) supplemented his musical earnings by working in a general store that sold everything from string to sausages. On display at the store was a large consignment of Okeh recordings that an inspired salesman had persuaded the store-owner to take on "sale or return," but the records didn't sell and the traveler never returned to collect them. So, each Saturday, Matlock took some of the jazz records as part of his wages. Thus he built up a fine collection of Okeh recordings, including a whole batch by Louis Armstrong. Later, when he became a pro-fessional musician, he usually took some of these disks on his travels, along with a small portable gramophone. In Omaha, Nebraska, he ran across Roy Eldridge (during the period when Roy was working in the Rock Dinah show). They got talking about music and Matty told Roy about the Armstrong recordings he carried with him, and when Roy heard them his reaction was one of wonderment. Roy always maintained that he heard Red Nichols on record before he listened to Louis, and this is borne out by what Matlock said. However, there's no doubt as to which of the two, Nichols or Armstrong, played the bigger part in influencing Roy. Quite late in his career, Roy confirmed the details of that early meeting with Matty Matlock:

> In a music store me and the piano-player were humming orchestrations. Matty came up and said he was a musician from Chicago and asked us did we have any place where he could play some records of Louis Armstrong? So I had a girlfriend there and I said, "Yes." So he went and got his little wind-up box and his records of Louis. It was the first time I heard Louis. First time I ever smoked "pot" too.[8]

On another occasion, Roy amplified the details of this inauguration:

> First record of Louis' he played was *The King Of The Zulus*, and I can play that song to this day. So, I'd seen him roll his own cigarettes. So I said, "Man, take one of my Luckies." He said, "No, I prefer this." I said, "Damn, that smells strange," so he said, "Try it." So we tried it, and I didn't pay much attention to it, but he played *Wild Man Blues*, and those things stuck in my head, I couldn't get them out of my head.[9]

Marijuana never became a vital crutch for Roy, more like a handy walking stick to be used on random occasions. He never became a habitual user like Louis Armstrong, and never got involved in what he called "pills or needles." Roy had no knowledge of Louis' smoking habits at the time of the Omaha incident, but he knew (even if he was slow to admit it) that he had listened to music that was dramatically inspirational. Benny Carter certainly believed that Louis Armstrong played an important part in shaping Roy's style, but pointed out, "The early followers of Louis Armstrong didn't remain in his mold. Look at Roy Eldridge, he went on to grow up with his own personal style. Sure the influence is there, but it's not a copy of Louis."[10]

It was to be some years before Roy blew alongside Louis, but during the stay with Horace Henderson he became involved in a "cutting contest" with his early hero, Rex Stewart. Jonah Jones recalled the details:

> Roy would go anywhere to play against anyone and one night when he was with Horace Henderson, Roy ran up against Rex Stewart at a jam session. Rex was by then a famous player, but Horace Henderson got him drunk and then called Roy up to play *Nobody's Sweetheart*, a number he was featured on in Horace's Band. Rex was by this time quite stoned so Roy blew him all over the place, but Rex was wily and said, "Same time, same place tomorrow night." Roy said, "Sure thing," but Horace said, "You ain't going back there," and he made sure that his brother Fletcher got to know that one of his star players had been carved by young Roy Eldridge.[11]

Horace Henderson prevented Roy from taking part in an immediate "return match," but there were to be several epic encounters between Eldridge and Stewart during the years to come. The one trumpeter who Roy couldn't begin to challenge was Joe Smith, who never played high and never played fast. Joe's "secret" lay in the beauty of his open tone, and his skills with a plunger mute, which enabled him to produce a sound that was like a human voice. Roy said that as a young man he actually felt hatred for the mild-mannered Joe, whose trumpet-playing gathered him an army of female fans. Roy spoke to Val Wilmer about Joe:

> He had the most beautiful tone on trumpet that I've ever heard. You talk about some of the other cats, Charlie Spivak and Billy Butterfield, who, incidentally had beautiful tones, but nothing like this cat. He reminded me of a good singer. I dreaded the time the doors opened and Joe Smith would walk in. The minute he came in I was finished for the night. He used to always open up with *If I Could Be With You One Hour Tonight* and the chicks would say "Yeah Joe." I'd go outside because I couldn't stand to hear him play. I'd get so hot you could fry an egg on my head.[12]

The work of cornettist Bix Beiderbecke, a white contemporary of Joe Smith, never won Roy over, and throughout his life he could never be more than lukewarm about Bix's playing. In 1943 he said:

> Bix Beiderbecke has become a historical personality and some people rate him right up there with Louis Armstrong. I heard Bix a couple of times in Detroit [May 1928]. I thought he had a very pretty tone but I wasn't greatly impressed otherwise, and when I found out later about his great reputation I was surprised.[13]

Thirty-four years later (in 1977), Roy hadn't changed his assessment: "He didn't get to me, no kinda way. I much prefer Bobby Hackett's playing."[14]

The young sidemen in Horace Henderson's Band sometimes had a problem in earning enough money to eat properly or to pay for a hotel. They were paid pro rata on the number of engagements they played, $30 a week was their top salary, and during a slack period they earned nothing at all. Money for new clothes or any luxuries was out of the question. Saxophonist Billie Bowen recalled the disheveled appearance of the band when they arrived in Detroit: "The band looked as rough as field mice, but they could all play."[15] The bookings in Detroit sowed the seeds that brought about Roy's departure from Horace Henderson's Band. Billie Bowen recalled that Roy's brother Joe had been working for some while in Detroit: "He was part of Earl Walton's Band who were very popular in Detroit; they could pick and choose where they wanted to work for fifty-two weeks a year."[16] Despite this busy schedule, Joe managed to hear Horace Henderson's Band when Walton's Band battled it out at a Detroit dance-hall. To Roy's chagrin, instead of Joe being delighted by his brother's progress, he was appalled that the young trumpeter still hadn't learned to read music accurately. Bowen said, "Roy certainly wasn't much of a reader at this time, but he played good solos."[17] This wasn't nearly enough for Joe, who had Roy's long-term interests at heart. Bowen continued, "Joe was a quieter fellow than Roy. Joe liked to drink but he was more relaxed than Roy, who could never, even as a youngster, sit down for more than a few minutes, he was always restless."[18]

Joe didn't pull Roy out of Horace Henderson's Band by the scruff of his neck, but he made it clear that he felt Roy had fallen into a comfortable groove where he was never likely to become a proficient reader. Roy recalled the situation:

> I broke it up there in Detroit, and I thought I was really something, but my brother said, "Put your notice in. You don't know anything about music." He tried to get me a couple of jobs with good bands around there, but I couldn't play the music at auditions. So he started schooling me then, how to read, chords and all that.[19]

Roy briefly pondered on this as Horace Henderson's Band started another tour. He then handed in his notice and returned to Detroit. Soon after this, Horace lived up to his reputation by leaving his musicians to fend for themselves so that he could work with Sammy Stewart's Band in Chicago. Benny Carter temporarily led the forsaken musicians in Detroit, and when these bookings were completed he took some of the group to New York. Because of his deficient sight-reading, Roy didn't put himself forward for the Detroit engagements and heeded Joe's advice that he was not yet ready for New York. Horace Henderson duly returned to Detroit and formed a new band, which Roy chose not to join (his place being taken by William Grainger). Roy never regretted that decision, since the new band soon folded in Buffalo. Roy picked up a few gigs in Detroit leading his own quartet. He also spent time studying with Joe before joining a local Nighthawks Band (directed by Jimmy Tisdale). Many different bands used this name during the 1920s following the radio successes of the Coon–Sanders Nighthawks. Soon after Roy joined this Detroit version of the Nighthawks, they decided to accept an offer to be managed by Jean Goldkette, who also represented the famous

McKinney's Cotton Pickers. The Nighthawks, renamed McKinney's Chocolate Dandies, continued to play a long-running residency on Detroit's Hastings Street.

During this period, Roy had a musical encounter in Detroit that he often spoke of in later years:

> I heard this very good trumpet-player, and I stood outside the club getting high and listening. They took an intermission, so I walked into the club, had a taste, and looked around to find the bandstand so that I could sit in. Sitting up at the bar was a girl wearing a long gown, holding a trumpet across her lap. I said, "I guess you're holding that for your boyfriend. When does the band come back?" She gave me a cool look and said, "I'm the trumpet-player," and she started to blow hell out of the trumpet; then she motioned me to sit in. Her name was Dolly Jones and she really gave me a battle, it went on and on; when we finished we were so excited we fell on one another. She was married, so nothing developed, but we moved on to a club in the Valley and played there until nearly three in the afternoon. Years later she worked in New York as Dolly Armenra, and one night in the 1970s she came into Ryan's with her trumpet, but she had teeth trouble, and couldn't play much anymore. With the right agent she could have made a fortune, she was better than Valaida, though I know Valaida could curse better. When she was in Chicago, Valaida got stuck in an elevator on her way up to a radio studio, and when she finally got out she did some of the best cursing I've ever heard, anytime, anywhere.[20]

Joe Eldridge continued to work in Detroit with Earl Walton's Band, on hand to coach Roy and to monitor his musical progress. He approved of his brother's next move, which was to join Zach Whyte's Chocolate Beau Brummels, a successful territory band operating out of Cincinnati, Ohio. This proved to be a short stay for Roy. He later estimated that he was only with the band for "one week."[21]

I didn't stay with anybody too long in those days. It wasn't that they were hard to get along with but nobody was paying any money. If I wasn't getting any money I'd tear out in a minute. I had a funny reputation in those days, they'd say "That little kid can play, but he won't stay with nobody long." For some reason bandleaders didn't want to pay you. The leaders used to have a great habit in those days of having a crowded house and telling you the man ran off with the money.[22]

Zach Whyte led a good band, with several talented youngsters in its ranks including trumpeter Melvin "Sy" Oliver, who became one of the leading arrangers of the Swing Era. Oliver never forgot how combative Roy was when they worked together in Whyte's brass section, but he was friendly enough off the bandstand, and the two young trumpeters happily shared a hotel room. Roy's most enduring memory of his stay in Whyte's Band was the playing of Herman Chittison, whom he considered to be the first of the "modern" stylists. One factor that may have prevented Roy from settling in with this band concerned the ease with which the lead trumpeter Henry Savage played some exceedingly high notes, although finances certainly affected Roy's decision to leave. Saxophonist Al Sears (later with Duke Ellington) recalled his own days with Whyte's Band: "You had one-nighters and maybe you'd have three in a week. If you got a real good week you got five. For a night you'd make about ten dollars or less. Back then you could get a room for 2 or 3 dollars a week."[23]

Through the musicians' grapevine, Roy was offered a job with a band led by Lawrence "Speed" Webb. Roy accepted this opportunity with Joe's blessing, but an immediate physical problem needed to be resolved, namely the removal of several of Roy's bad teeth. Billie Bowen recalled Roy's appearance at this time: "His front teeth were all decayed and green. It not only spoilt his appearance; it also must have been hell for his style of high-note trumpet-playing."[24] Speed Webb's Band was based in Indiana, and it was there, in the town of Peru, that Roy underwent extensive dental treatment: several extractions were made and Roy was fitted with dentures. Speed Webb advanced the money for the dentistry. He could well afford to do so because he was director of a large funeral company as well as being a successful bandleader. Roy had to change his *embouchure* slightly to accommodate the contours of the dental plate, but after some marathon practice sessions he was again climbing fearlessly into the top register of his trumpet. Roy soon forgot that he was wearing false teeth, but found that he had swiftly but minimally to alter the position of the mouthpiece when he played extremely high notes. Then, just as quickly, he had to alter it back when he moved into the low register. Roy followed this unorthodox practice throughout the rest of his career, and although the strategy would not have been encouraged by a conservatory professor, the results were sublime.

Prior to Roy's arrival, Speed Webb's Band had played in California where they appeared in various movies, including the "talkie" *On With The Show* (featuring Ethel Waters). Speed (who sang and occasionally played drums) and his musicians eventually returned to Fort Wayne, Indiana, and disbanded. Webb soon formed a new band, eager to capitalize on the publicity generated by the movie appearances. He gathered his personnel shrewdly; several of the newcomers became world-famous jazzmen, including pianist Teddy Wilson, trombonist Vic Dickenson, and Roy's cousin Reunald Jones (whose trumpet-playing was later featured with Count Basie). Roy knew that he would be working in stimulating musical company. Besides having a strong team of soloists, the band also had eight good arrangers within the line-up, one of the best being trombonist Gus Wilson (brother of Teddy). The personnel was as follows: Reunald Jones, Steve Dunn, Roy Eldridge (trumpets); Vic Dickenson, Gus Wilson (trombones); Ben "Smoke" Richardson, Leonard Gay, Clarence "Chuck" Wallace (reeds); Sam Scott (drums); Teddy Wilson (piano); William Warfield (guitar/banjo/vocals); Melvin Bowles (tuba/double-bass/vocals).

Speed Webb, billed as "The Little Giant of Geniality," fronted the band, and Angelus Babe danced and sang with the group; Roy

Eldridge was usually billed as "trumpet-entertainer." Webb usually paid his musicians promptly, but as Roy noted, "If ever you asked for a loan he'd go to a pocket that had a great roll of money in it and somehow pull out two dollars."[25] Despite the Webb Band's success in the movies, it had no recordings on the market. Before Roy joined, the band did at least two recording sessions, but nothing was issued. Webb was disappointed by this but did his best to make capital out the situation by having his advertising posters proclaim "We don't make records, we break 'em." By now Roy could read music accurately. He was usually given the third trumpet parts, allowing him to devote his energies to fulfilling the role of "hot soloist." Apparently there was no jealousy between Webb's trumpeters. Roy used to say to Steve Dunn, "You cut 'em sweet, and I'll cut 'em hot."[26] But away from the band Roy never shirked a musical skirmish. Trombonist James "Trummy" Young recalled this period:

> I first heard Roy when he played with Speed Webb, and he was so competitive. He was only young but he would take anyone on. A guy called Dan Brashear used to really test him. Brashear had a mouth full of green teeth, almost like he painted them, and he wore a white shirt that had a full black ring of grease around the collar, but he could blow.[27]

Arranger and saxophonist Jimmy Mundy also remembered the duels that took place between Eldridge and Brashear (known to his fellow musicians as "Georgetown"): "When Roy Eldridge came to Washington, D.C. for the first time he was already an exciting trumpeter but "Georgetown" went home, got his trumpet, and ran Roy right out of the Crystal Caverns."[28]

The first engagement played by Speed Webb's new band was a residency at Forest Park, Ohio, which ended in October 1929. They then played in Buffalo, Cincinnati, Indianapolis, Columbus, Lexington, and through New England, where, to their surprise, they lost a "battle of the bands" to a white group led by Mal Hallett (from

Roxbury, Massachusetts). Mal Hallett never forgot Roy Eldridge's spectacular playing, and ten years later became the first white bandleader to employ him. Pianist Teddy Wilson commented on the Webb Band's extensive touring schedule: "As a result of the movie publicity Speed Webb went out on tour with a show band. We toured the Middle West, Indiana, Ohio, Massachusetts, Wisconsin and Nebraska. We played mostly one night stands for dances."[29]

Some of the distances the band traveled to play a single booking were awesome. Roy recalled one trip that involved a journey close to a thousand miles: "We went from Boston in a raggedy bus all the way to Wisconsin, and we was about ten minutes late. We got there and the man had hired a local band."[30] Roy always felt that Speed Webb's big mistake was in not taking the band to New York. He stressed that he thought the band was "as good as Jimmie Lunceford's."[31]

Despite being extremely competitive, Roy never liked to see outstanding musical talent being hidden away, and for much of his life he made it a practice to recommend promising young players to bandleaders who could offer them better prospects. He did this for Teddy Wilson by visiting Benny Carter (then playing in Providence, R.I., with Fletcher Henderson), and advising him to visit nearby Woonsocket in order to hear Wilson playing in Speed Webb's Band. Carter did this and was favorably impressed; Wilson later made his recording debut with Carter.[32] During Speed Webb's stay in Cincinnati Roy met up with his ex-colleagues in Zach Whyte's Band, including Sy Oliver, who said:

> We were all living at the Sterling Hotel there. Roy, Reunald Jones and the other fellows would be in their rooms blowing all day long and I was sitting in my room trying to write arrangements. They used to tease me all the time, "Get out that horn, you'll never be able to play."[33]

Roy and his cousin Reunald Jones were inseparable at this time, and during a Speed Webb lay-off period they worked in Cincinnati with a local band called The Brown Buddies. Webb's Band fulfilled a booking at Walrose Park near Pittsburgh during the summer of 1930, by which time John Nesbitt (formerly of McKinney's Cotton Pickers) was on trumpet, taking over from Steve Dunn. Joe Eldridge and Budd Johnson had joined the saxophone section alongside Leonard Gay, supported by an unchanged rhythm team. Altoist Hildred Humphries, who had worked with Roy in the Rock Dinah show, briefly joined the band. During a period of further widespread touring, further personnel changes occurred, with Raymond "Syd" Valentine again working briefly alongside Roy. Eli Robinson joined and made the trombone section into a three-man unit. Chick Gordon became one of the saxophonists, and a new bassist, Bert Summers, joined. Trombonist "Doc" Wheeler then replaced Gus Wilson; Gus' departure meant the band lost its best arranger, whose orchestration of *Clementine* was the group's most requested number.

In the fall of 1930, trumpeter John Nesbitt left for New York City to arrange for various big bands. Trombonist Vic Dickenson decided to go with him and, soon after arriving in the Big Apple, made his recording debut, singing on Nesbitt's arrangement of *Honey That Reminds Me* with Luis Russell's Band. Vic and Roy were to record together dozens of times in later years, but I never got the impression that they ever became close friends; they seemed to have a guarded relationship. The laconic Vic had seen Roy get ruffled too often. Roy, for his part, greatly admired Vic's ability to play the blues. In his turn, Vic was impressed by Roy's dedication, and cited an occasion when, after a gig had ended, Roy went off to enjoy some female company and missed the Webb Band's bus, which was driven off to the next engagement. Roy apparently woke up the next morning "clipped," his nocturnal companion having walked off with all of his money. He was left without a cent, but mercifully his "hostess" had left his trumpet. Roy went around this Midwestern town trying to borrow money, without success. Eventually he had to pawn his trumpet to rustle up the rail fare needed to rejoin the band. After a long journey he arrived at the band's hotel and borrowed enough money to return to the town he had just left in order to reclaim his beloved trumpet as soon as possible.

Roy certainly had an eye for the ladies, and until late in his life made keen efforts to charm his way into their affections on the briefest of acquaintances. Someone once said, "He's always been a remarkably quantitative worker with women. No one else I know has his capacity."[34] Certainly I have never forgotten seeing him take the boldest of approaches after breaking the ice by praising a waitress's perfume or complimenting a stranger on the way she did her hair. Such was his cheeky charm that he was rarely rebuffed.

Several of the arrangements that Speed Webb's Band played were based on recordings made by white bands, such as those led by Jean Goldkette, Red Nichols, and Paul Whiteman. Whiteman's version of *Sweet Sue* provided the basis for a Teddy Wilson arrangement in which the Webb trumpet section re-created Bix Beiderbecke's celebrated solo. Roy stored the contents of that solo in his mind and quoted it on a recording of *Sweet Sue* that he made some thirty years later. Reunald Jones said, "The Webb Band copied quite a bit from the Red Nichols recordings, Frankie Trumbauer and all. It may seem odd to have been influenced by a white band."[35] The band enjoyed considerable success, but this was not reflected in the wages that Speed Webb paid. Webb was proud to be parsimonious: "I used to be known as fairly tight with a dollar in those days. Whenever I offered to buy a drink for the guys someone would always shout 'Hey bartender, a half pint and twelve glasses over here.'"[36]

The main problem for the musicians was that Speed Webb couldn't decide whether he wanted to be a mortician or a bandleader. He frequently canceled band engagements while he went back to Fort Wayne, Indiana, to supervise some aspect of his funeral business. The musicians became disenchanted by the stop-go progress of the band and dissension grew. After a booking at the Market Auditorium in Wheeling, West Virginia, Teddy Wilson, Roy Eldridge, Reunald Jones, and Leonard Gay decided to form a new unit that was to be fronted by Roy. Others in Webb's Band fell in with the idea, which meant that the line-up that fulfilled a booking in Flint, Michigan, was virtually the Speed Webb Band. The engagement turned out to be simply a one-night stand; Roy, his brother Joe, and Reunald Jones decided to stay in Flint, and found work playing in a Chinese restaurant called the Tico Inn. "The bread wasn't too good, but we wanted to eat," said Roy. While at the Tico Inn, Roy encountered the pianist who had made his life so unhappy in the Greater Sheesley Carnival Band:

> He was destitute. He was hungry, he didn't have no money. I never told him about the misery he put me through. I gave him five dollars and took him back in the restaurant's kitchen and fed him. He actually cried. Well, that did me some good, but I never brought up how mean he was to me when I was younger.[37]

But Roy's stay in Michigan was brief. He told Charles Fox in a 1977 B.B.C. radio interview, "I got run out of Flint. They gave me orders to leave town. I was a pretty bad young cat. We won't get into that."[38] However, in a 1982 interview with Dan Morgenstern (for the Institute of Jazz Studies), Roy said:

> Me and Jonesy [Reunald Jones] used to jack cars and steal wheels. Well, they did that to us, you know. So we'd go into a good neighborhood and jack up a car and the wheels to fit our car. Then Jonesy was entangled with some little girl there, where we used to stay, and the father was looking for him with an ax. We hid until we got out of town.[39]

Roy and Jonesy moved on to Milwaukee where they worked in Johnny Neal's Midnite Ramblers. Within Milwaukee at that time, one of the most adept trumpet-players of the era was being featured at the Wisconsin Roof Gardens. This was Cladys "Jabbo" Smith, an ex-member of the Jenkins Orphanage Band of Charleston, South Carolina. Jabbo's speed and range had already been well featured on recordings (with Charlie Johnson, his own Rhythm Aces and others) and he was being talked about as a contender for Louis Armstrong's crown. It was inevitable that this talented, established trumpeter would meet up with Roy Eldridge, the combative young tyro. Their approach to playing had certain similarities, and bassist Milt Hinton observed, "Roy must have been influenced by Jabbo Smith." Roy always denied this, despite expressing a long-lasting admiration for Jabbo's spectacular playing; he had no hesitation in saying that after hearing Jabbo in person he went off and bought Jabbo's August 1929 recording of *Boston Skuffle* and attempted to learn it note for note. "I started collecting his records and found out where he was at, and he was mean, and he was mean on the trombone too."[40] Roy gave details of their first meeting:

> Jabbo came into where I was playing and noticed that I was getting a nice hand from the people. Now, Milwaukee was his territory, so he thought he'd teach me a lesson. He asked if he could borrow my trumpet, which he did, and blew *I'm Confessin'* on it. I know he played it very well, but it just wasn't my kind of trumpet-playing, and I think he was expecting me to jump up in the air when I heard him play. He could see I wasn't that impressed and I guess I made this obvious by asking for my trumpet back. I was young and fly so I said, "Go home and get your trumpet," which he did, so we met up in a place called Rail's about an hour later. Word must have spread that something was going to happen because a whole gang of people, musicians, and singers turned up there—and Jabbo washed me out of the place.[41]

A half-century after this battle, Roy and Jabbo (by then jovial veterans) often laughed about that celebrated cutting contest, but one night, when Roy was in a reflective mood, he spoke again about that first encounter with Jabbo.

These days Jabbo is a nice, easy-going old cat, but when we

first met he acted like a big-time star, as though I was a youngster way beneath him. My determination got me through the first few numbers that we played, but gradually Jabbo's experience and speed took over and he washed me away, blew me every way but loose. It wasn't really a contest, but I must have done OK because he didn't speak to me for two weeks, then we became friends. In fact, four of us, Jabbo, myself, Reunald Jones, and Stomp Ellis had the wild idea of starting a group that featured four trumpeters and a rhythm section; this was years before anyone did this. We rehearsed some good routines, but the idea was way ahead of its time and no one would book it, so we forgot all about it. People may have thought I left Milwaukee because of Jabbo, but that definitely wasn't so. I soon realized that some of the Chicago mob used Milwaukee as a base when they wanted to get out of Illinois in a hurry, and if you had success there or built up a following in one of these guy's clubs then you'd be there for life, or at the least a long, long time, and you'd play on their terms. That didn't appeal to me at all.[42]

Fate stepped in as Roy was considering how he could quit Milwaukee without treading on anybody's toes. While singing on a broadcast from a night-club he let alcohol cloud his judgment and inserted a mildly obscene line into a popular song. The show was immediately cut off, and the following night the wires for broadcasting were removed. The manager of the club was vexed over this, and extremely concerned as to how the tough owners of the venue would take the news. He called Roy into the office and said, "All the fellows like you, you're a nice little fellow, but I don't know how they are gonna take that when they find out what happened. So I'm going to give you two weeks' salary and you'd better take it out of town." Roy needed no time to make up his mind. He said, "That's when I left. I went to Indianapolis, sold the car, went to Minneapolis for a while, then home to Pittsburgh. From Pittsburgh I went to New York."[43]

3

A BITE AT THE
BIG APPLE

Roy joined Cecil Scott's Band soon after arriving in New York. It was a move that had its origins in Pittsburgh, where, during the summer of 1930, Speed Webb's Band had played a residency at the Crystal Ballroom. At that same time Cecil Scott's Bright Boys (usually based in New York) were also playing a season in Pittsburgh. Scott heard Roy play and offered him a job should he ever come to New York. Roy let this opportunity pass, but later mentioned it to brother Joe, who, hearing of the problems that Roy had encountered in Milwaukee, advised him to join Scott. So in October 1930, just before Hallowe'en, Roy moved to New York and began working with Cecil Scott at the Renaissance Casino (situated at 138th and Seventh Avenue); Scott's Band was also temporarily playing shows at the Douglass Theater. This was the sort of busy schedule that Roy thrived on, but he still found time to seek out any after-hours clubs that encouraged jam sessions, and played at them before wending his way home to Edgecombe Avenue, where he lodged with his aunt. Roy spoke of his early days in New York: "Around Thanksgiving the gigs were very good. For the first time in my life I was making good bread. About a hundred dollars a week—I used to get the money and spread it all over my bed and think, 'wow.'"[1]

In Cecil Scott's Band, Roy linked up with trumpeter George "Buddy" Lee, a capable improviser who was quite content to play lead trumpet, leaving Roy to improvise the musical fireworks; Roy always had the utmost respect for lead players and spoke of the good ones with reverence. Cecil Scott himself played robust tenor-sax and agile clarinet, but made no attempt to hog the proceedings, giving plenty of feature spots to a young tenorist, Leon "Chu" Berry (from West Virginia). "Chu" (so named because he resembled the plump, mustachioed figure in *Chu Chin Chow*, a popular musical show) and Roy Eldridge hit it off immediately. Chu was a disciple of Coleman Hawkins, but was eager to develop his own style. To this end he sat in at various clubs on every possible occasion, blowing energetically throughout the night. Here was someone whom Roy immediately recognized as a musical soul mate, a musician, who, despite playing for seven nights a week (plus a Sunday matinée) still had the energy and enthusiasm to "jam" for hours on end–Roy and Chu became inseparable. However, both Chu and Joe Eldridge knew that, from the moment Roy arrived in New York, his attitude would make him a natural target for established trumpeters who were prone to gang up on any newcomer and test him by playing tunes in every possible key and to improvise on recent songs of which a new arrival might never have heard. Chu and Joe didn't want these musical heavyweights to make Roy "punch drunk" before he had a chance to fulfill his enormous potential, so the two mentors spent time coaching Roy and running through tricky chord sequences that he might encounter: "For two weeks, Chu and my brother and a piano player named Panama kept me in a house and taught me all the tunes before they took me to the Rhythm Club to play against people."[2]

Roy duly played at the Rhythm Club, a musicians' hangout situated near the Lafayette Theater. Roy held his own, but the blasé New York musicians took his arrival coolly; it took time before Roy understood why:

> I was playing fast and I could get all over the instrument, but I wasn't saying anything. I had to play everything fast and I

even doubled up on any ballad I played, making it into a fast number. No one played as fast, but the other trumpeters got more attention. I couldn't play blues. I didn't like ballads either then. And I think the reason I didn't like them was because I couldn't play them.[3]

It took Roy some while to realize that speed and range were not the only attributes a jazz soloist needed to be highly regarded. Roy had previously created a sensation almost wherever he had played, so he was reluctant to change his approach. However, with Chu Berry at his elbow he began to develop maturity, each man spurring on the other by creating daring solos that often left their accompanists bewildered. Roy and Chu began taking the sophisticated pianist Garland Wilson with them (until he moved to Europe in November, 1932) so that they got the sort of backing that was in sympathy with their harmonic explorations. Later Clyde Hart fulfilled the same role for Eldridge and Berry:

> Me and Chu used to get off work at 3 or 4 in the morning, and we'd play perhaps until one that afternoon. We never seemed to get tired. Many a time I'd get out of bed, get dressed and go out again. It seemed like I never put the horn away.[4]

Rex Stewart, Roy's mentor, who later became his tormentor, was present at one late-night New York gathering where Roy gained revenge on Jabbo Smith. The session began as a "grudge" match between Jabbo and Reuben Reeves, previously rivals in Chicago:

> Reuben Reeves challenged Jabbo Smith to see which of them could play fastest, but Roy cut them both. Roy had a way of lurking in the doorway while the other men were vying for the championship, and he'd come in blowing.[5]

But all these combats were incidental to Roy's main employment with Cecil Scott, whose band was enjoying a successful season at New York's Savoy Ballroom. The Savoy catered for a racially mixed audience who were critical of any band that failed to produce a highly rhythmic beat. Both Roy and Chu found this attitude stimulating, as did Cecil Scott: the band swung and the dancers responded. It seemed that Scott was about to make a big breakthrough, but he got involved in a serious wrangle while taking part in a dice-game. Scott, who was married with thirteen children, explained the background:

> There was a girl at the Savoy. She had a man who was taking care of her, but she made quite a play for me. One night she asked me to a "rent party," there was a crap game going on and I started to win. Then her boy friend came in and there was some kind of misunderstanding...I had a big name. I had to get out of there.[6]

But both the front and back doors were locked, so Scott's only escape route was via a window. In his eagerness to leave, Scott didn't take into account that he was three stories up. In the fall he broke his right ankle; gangrene set in and his right leg was amputated. Roy was genuinely upset by the news of Scott's predicament. The bandleader had always been helpful, and had recommended Roy to Clarence Williams who organized pick-up bands for freelance recording sessions. Roy earned a few bucks for playing an unobtrusive part on one of these dates, but even his good memory couldn't provide hard-and-fast details. He thought the titles were *Papa De Da Da* and *Baby Won't You Please Come Home?*, both sung by Williams' wife, Eva Taylor. But when Phil Schaap questioned Roy further he conceded that the date might have been some sort of a rehearsal session, saying, "It was an audition really, but later it turned out to be a record."[7] A confused picture emerged involving the band and Eva Taylor going to three different studios on the same day.

Chu Berry attempted to keep Cecil Scott's Band together while Scott recuperated, but bookers were not interested in the unit without its leader. Fortunately, Roy was soon offered regular work with another outfit. This was the band led by Elmer Snowden, a former employer of Duke Ellington, who played banjo, guitar, and saxophone. Trombonist Dicky Wells had recommended Eldridge to Snowden, who had just left New York's Hot Feet Club in the Village to take up residency at one of Harlem's most celebrated night-clubs, Smalls' Paradise, which flourished in a big basement on the corner of 135th Street and Seventh Avenue. Joe Eldridge (who had worked with Snowden at the Nest Club) approved of Roy joining the band, as did Dicky Wells, who said, "Snowden was a good guy and a wonderful leader."[8] At first Roy had trouble with Leonard "Ham" Davis, who was the lead trumpeter in Snowden's Band for a while. Davis didn't seem to want Roy to solo, but Roy overcame the problem by not giving way when Davis tried to butt into his feature numbers.

Smalls' took its name from a South Carolinian, Edwin A. Smalls, who managed this entertainment landmark for the major part of the sixty years it existed. The club comfortably held 250 people, who could choose from a menu that included Chinese (and American) food. There was a bandstand and a stage on which cabaret artistes performed, and a dance floor surrounded by small banquettes. Usually there were two shows a night: one at midnight, the other at 2 a.m., but the band also played for dancing, so the schedule often lasted from 9 p.m. until almost 4 a.m., and this was augmented by Sunday matinées which lasted from 3 p.m. to 7 p.m. An evening session followed, which in turn gave way to a weekly breakfast dance lasting from 6 a.m. to 11 a.m. Monday morning. This strenuous schedule suited Roy, but various other trumpeters, including Bobby Stark (whom Roy always praised), Buddy Lee, and Gus Aiken became exhausted from the workload. By spring 1932 the regular members of the band were: Roy Eldridge, Matthew "Red" Harlan, and Leonard Davis (trumpets); Dicky Wells and George Washington (trombones); Otto "Toby" Hardwick, Al Sears, and Wayman Carver—who had taken Garvin Bushell's place (reeds); and Dick Fulbright (bass and tuba), Sid Catlett (drums), Don Kirkpatrick (piano), and Elmer Snowden (banjo, guitar, and saxophone).

A similar line-up appeared in a 1932 nine-minute Vitaphone movie, entitled *Smash Your Baggage* (directed by Roy Mack), which also featured the cast of Smalls' revue. The band (in keeping with what was then the general attitude of the film world towards African-Americans) was dressed as Pullman porters; the players performed zestfully in front of the cameras and played brief versions of four tunes, one of which, *Bugle Call Rag*, had a four-bar solo from Roy. *Variety* (of November 15, 1932) described the movie as "One of those hectic song-and-dance melanges, ringing in a flock of colored talent."

Not long after taking part in *Smash Your Baggage*, Toby Hardwick left Elmer Snowden's Band to rejoin Duke Ellington, but not before he had bestowed the nickname of Little Jazz on Roy Eldridge, a sobriquet that was to remain with the trumpeter for the rest of his life. Roy gave the background details:

> At Smalls' I'd be playing the trumpet all the time; we'd finish a set and take an intermission and I'd start practicing—if I couldn't find anywhere else to practice I'd go in the men's room. Well, one day Otto Hardwick said, "I'm going to call you Little Jazz, because you've always got that horn in your face." The name stuck and I didn't mind. At that time I only weighed 118 pounds, soaking wet.[9]

Howard "Swan" Johnson took Hardwick's place, and for a while trumpeter Bobby Cheek augmented the brass section. While Roy was working with Elmer Snowden at Smalls', Louis Armstrong came to New York (for the first time in some while) in order to play at the Lafayette Theater for the week commencing February 20, 1932. Roy decided to visit the show, but he wasn't overly excited or enthusiastic about the prospect. As was common in those days, the show featured a star orchestra (on this occasion Louis Armstrong's Band) sharing the billing with a feature film, which that week was *Charlie Chan's Chance* starring Warner Oland. After sitting through Louis' first house performance Roy was only mildly impressed, but decided to stay for another helping. He recalled the ensuing events:

> You see, to me, Louis was the best of what I called "Southern

Trumpeters," and I wasn't too keen on them. I had heard a lot of them, and that wasn't the direction I wanted to go. Even after I heard Louis at the first show I wasn't "wowed," but I thought, "Well, as this is the first show of the day he hasn't warmed up." So I stayed for the second show, then the third then the fourth, and by then he was blowing in a way that I'll never forget. He played *Chinatown, My Chinatown* and he made every note count. He made his solo into a story. All the time building up the plot of that story. When he finished, the atmosphere was electric, everybody was standing and clapping and I was on my feet applauding as loudly as anyone. I went out next day and bought Louis' record of *Chinatown*, to hear what he did on it. That's when I started changing. I could hit those high notes but I couldn't put them together to make a solo that developed. It came to me there and then in the Lafayette and I never forgot the lesson.[10]

Thus Louis Armstrong provided Roy with inspiration and guidance. The combination of Armstrong's ingenious thematic developments and the fast-flowing lines that Roy had based on the saxophone-playing of Coleman Hawkins and Benny Carter, plus the hard-won instrumental virtuosity and a natural sense of harmonic daring, all jelled, and formed the basis of the Eldridge trumpet style. Based on these foundations Roy created improvisations that were increasingly full of what were then considered (in jazz) to be advanced harmonies, often using chromatic substitute chords, thus pioneering an approach that others developed into "modern" jazz. John "Dizzy" Gillespie, hailed as one of the originators of "be-bop," never denied Roy's enormous influence, but, as Alyn Shipton pointed out in his book *Groovin' High*, Dizzy (like Roy) didn't readily acknowledge the impact that Louis Armstrong's playing had on his early trumpet work. *Chinatown, My Chinatown* became a big number in Roy's repertoire, and remained so for many years. It was often performed when visiting trumpeters shared a bandstand with him.

From this point on it seems that Roy gradually matured, and, whereas listeners had gasped in amazement at his spectacular runs and stratospheric excursions, they now began to nod their heads in solid approval as the young trumpeter blew phrases that linked technique with emotion. Previously Roy's critics had inferred that he was all speed and no substance. One of these was the bandleader Chick Webb. Joe Eldridge, learning of an impending vacancy in Webb's trumpet section, asked Webb to audition Roy. He did so, but didn't accept what was on offer, dismissing Roy's efforts curtly, saying, "Sure he's fast but he ain't saying anything." Roy later admitted that Webb had a case: "I had lots of technique, but no heart.[11]...So I knew what would have to happen, and I started to listen to Coleman Hawkins again, you know, them ballads he was playing."[12]

Louis Armstrong was not yet aware who Roy Eldridge was. However, before his booking at the Lafayette had ended he called into Smalls' Paradise (only three blocks away from the Lafayette) and was so impressed by what he heard of the young trumpeter that he asked Elmer Snowden, with a touch of incredulity in his voice, "Where did you find him?"[13] According to Roy, he then said, "Little Jazz, you're going to be all right."[14]..."He gave me some salve, that salve that he used to put on his lip. I put that shit on my lip and I couldn't play for a week! It was good for him but it didn't work for me."[15] Roy would try anything if he felt it would help his playing, and was continually striving to eliminate what he considered were his stylistic weaknesses. The one aspect of his performances that he felt he never truly mastered concerned his ability to play the blues. Through to the last part of his life he'd hark on this, despite the efforts of friends and fans to convince him that some of his blues solos were masterly, but he couldn't be swayed, insisting:

> I'm not really a good blues player. I play things I heard a thousand years ago. Me and Chu Berry would be skating through these things and Ben Webster and Lips Page [visiting New York with Bennie Moten's Band] would get right in that blues socket. Here we were flying all over the horns and I'd

hear a cat say "Yeah, baby, play it" about another cat's playing and I'd think, "Why don't they say that when I'm playing?" So I turned around and took another look at it. I started listening to the blues singers and I found it was hard to play the blues. You'd be surprised how many people can't play the blues.[16]

Elmer Snowden's Band was a favorite with John Hammond, a wealthy college graduate who was soon to become a successful record producer. At the time of his visits to Smalls' Paradise he was writing for various European music magazines including *Gramophone* and *Melody Maker*. In the December 1931 issue of *Gramophone* he commented on Snowden's "two fine cornetists," but the object of his praise throughout the early months of 1932 was tenorist Al Sears, referred to then by Hammond as "second only to Hawkins." Hammond's lofty assessment disintegrated as the years passed, and in his 1977 autobiography he described Sears as "a wild and woolly player."[17] However, his admiration of Roy Eldridge was more durable. In his book he wrote of Snowden's Band: "Most of the evening they played head arrangements while Roy Eldridge would dream up riff after riff that sent Eastern musicians into raves." Al Sears left the band after contracting pneumonia and his place was taken by Teddy McRae. Roy stayed put, enjoying the hard-blowing regime. For him the two stars in Snowden's Band were drummer Sid Catlett and trombonist Dicky Wells. Looking back, Roy described the group to Phil Schaap as "a real stomping band. When they set out to play they played."[18] However, after becoming involved in a dispute with the Musicians' Union in New York, Elmer Snowden announced that he was disbanding. He did so temporarily, and later led a smaller line-up at New York's Torch Club. Happily Roy wasn't thrown out of work: the management at Smalls', observing Roy's popularity night after night, made it clear to the in-coming bandleader Charlie Johnson that they expected him to find a place for Eldridge within his line-up. He agreed to their request with alacrity.

During his stay with Charlie Johnson, Roy continued to blow at jam sessions whenever possible. At one such gathering he got involved in a tremendous battle with Rex Stewart. The contest started at the Rhythm Club but moved on to a venue with the unappetizing name of Greasy's (on 129th Street). Roy remembered it well:

> So we went down there, and...before you know it, that joint was packed. There was Gus Aiken and Red Allen and some other trumpet player...all of Fletcher Henderson's cats were in there...I made a mistake by coming in on [Rex's] chorus. I screamed a G and the whole house fell out...he jumped in and caught my ass. Hit a B-flat and I ain't *never* heard a B-flat that high and that loud and big, in my life!...I took my horn and put it in the case...I had tears in my eyes. I went home and sat on the side of the bed and said..."He only screamed that note, but he didn't play up to it or back down...so, if I could play up to B-flat and back down, make that part of my natural range, then I'd have him. So that's what I did. It took me two years and I *played* up there, I didn't just scream...so that was my round.[19]

The audiences at Smalls' Paradise always responded to Roy's playing, but, for social rather than musical reasons, Roy didn't greatly enjoy his "transfer" to Charlie Johnson's Band. He sensed that Johnson's musicians didn't like having a youngster transplanted into what was already a successful outfit. Roy could never prove it, but he felt that a friend of Johnson's trumpeter Sid De Paris went to the management at Smalls' and complained that Roy was playing too many high notes.[20] Roy decided it was time to move on, so he readily accepted an offer to join Teddy Hill's Band. Hill, who had formerly been a tenorist with Luis Russell's Band, was never in the front rank of jazz soloists, but he was an efficient organizer and a competent bandleader. Roy enjoyed the glamor of playing again at the Savoy Ballroom, and wasn't fazed by the seven nights a week (plus Sunday matinée) schedule, but he was distinctly disappointed that he was now earning considerably less than he had at Smalls' Paradise. He soon left Teddy Hill, and filled in by gigging with Vernon Andrades at the Renaissance Casino (where he had worked with Cecil Scott). He then played briefly in the San Domingans' Band for a production of *Connie's Hot Chocolates* of 1933, a revival of a show that had featured Louis Armstrong in 1929. Roy went out on tour at a time when he was again having problems connected with the opposite sex, and he felt it would be unwise for him to return to New York for a while. He told Charles Fox, "I got into a little trouble," but later elaborated:

> I was on the road and I got a wire from my brother telling me "Don't come back to New York." They were waiting for me at the station, at the airport, anywhere I could come in. It was something to do with a chick. So I went to Pittsburgh.[21]

Joe also made his way to Pittsburgh, where the two brothers formed a band that consisted of local musicians. Joe took charge of rehearsals and admin, and Roy fronted the band on stage. Roy gave details to Stanley Dance:

> It was called the Eldridge Brothers' Rhythm Team, and we had four saxophones, five trumpets and three trombones. Outside of my brother the only guy I can remember was Kenny Clarke on drums. The band lasted about six months.[22]

Roy's dedication to Louis Armstrong was well in evidence according to Kenny Clarke, who described Roy as "Playing and singing like Louis Armstrong."[23] Roy didn't deny this and said, "I got so indoctrinated with Louis that for a while I was goin' around tryin' to talk like him."[24] Clarke added that Roy was a stern taskmaster: "When I was with Roy Eldridge I would make 50 cents a night and I'd be yelled at and scolded. But it gave me the incentive to play better and earn more."[25]

Roy was younger than most of his sidemen, the notable

exceptions being Kenny Clarke, three years Roy's junior, and tenorist Henry "Hen Pie" Gerold. Several of the new band had been part of a group previously led by pianist George Hornsby, who lived close to the Eldridge home, and who had known the brothers for years. Hornsby became devoutly religious and had given up band work, allowing Roy and Joe to take over what was almost a ready-made orchestra. Joe, who was featured on alto-sax and violin in the new enterprise, also became its principal arranger. The senior musicians in the band tended to grumble their way through the band's tours, which took them into West Virginia and Ohio, pointing out to Roy and Joe how expensive it was "on the road" when they could make just as much money playing local gigs in Pittsburgh, saving on hotel and subsistence expenses. They may have had a case: Roy recalled that the band got $8 a week.

The *Pittsburgh Courier* mentioned some of the band's engagements, including dates at the Pythian Temple in May 1933 where, for a Decoration Day dance, they played from 4 p.m. until 8 p.m. and then again from 9 p.m. to 3 a.m. At the Mapleview park in August 1933 they played to a large, enthusiastic crowd, but by then Roy and Joe were fed up with the problems that went with leading a band:

> Most of the guys in the band developed "star eyes." I had another nine bandleaders in the group, and none of them ever wanted to leave the bar. We had some nice work lined up, but it wasn't worth the hassle. In those days word soon spread, and next thing Joe and I got an invite to join McKinney's Cotton Pickers. The band had just fired McKinney. We joined them at Carlin's in Baltimore. Billie Bowen was the organizer and leader, and drummer Cuba Austin was "the star," I guess you'd say. He'd been with McKinney since the beginning, so too had Dave Wilborn on banjo and Prince Robinson on tenor-sax and clarinet. Billie Bowen was the overall boss, he could rehearse a band just like Don Redman did.[26]

The move, in the late summer of 1933, tested Roy's reading abilities, but he triumphed. All the chiding by Joe paid off, and Roy could now sight-read with ease. Billie Bowen recalled Roy's arrival:

> Just before we went for Roy and Joe I had asked George "Buddy" Lee, who had been playing third trumpet, to go on lead, but he didn't want to. I don't know why, because he was a great trumpeter, with a marvelous range and excellent control—I never heard him miss. So Roy Eldridge arrived and sat down on his first night and played the first trumpet book straight off, in a way that upset the other trumpeters, because he was so full of confidence.[27]

Roy was pleased to be in such a talented musical ensemble: "We found that it was a very good band. In fact, that particular band was as good, if not better, than the best of the old group's recordings, but it made no records, so who is to know?"[28]

The new band, billed as "The Original Cotton Pickers," suffered because of a dispute with William McKinney which meant they were not allowed to use his name. They made the best of the situation by giving Cuba Austin and The Eldridge Brothers star billing. After finishing his first night's work with the Cotton Pickers at Carlin's Park, Roy made it his first task to find out where in Baltimore he could "jam" after hours. He discovered a suitable, local night-spot on Pennsylvania Avenue, and, together with altoist Eddie Barefield (who had recently joined the Cotton Pickers), he went there and blew until dawn. The two of them made this a nightly ritual, even though they had been playing for five hours with the Cotton Pickers; they came straight from that gig and didn't even bother to change out of their red Eton band jackets. A local saxist, Chauncey Haughton, greatly impressed Roy at the late-night gatherings. One of these informal sessions shaped Barefield's career. He and Roy were standing on chairs to play, so that people at the back of the club could see them. Among the onlookers was the famous black bandleader Cab Calloway, who had just finished his nightly appearance at the Baltimore Hippodrome. Cab offered Barefield the chance to join his band immediately. Eddie hesitated but, at Roy's urging, agreed to the move. The following night Barefield told his colleagues in the Cotton Pickers that he was leaving town next day to join Cab Calloway. The consensus of opinion was that Barefield had to give more notice than that; a heated discussion erupted into a fight. Barefield described the free-for-all: "Everyone jumped on me but Roy Eldridge and another fellow."[29] Despite some bruising, Barefield left then and there to join Calloway, and was soon being featured with him in New York.

A bigger problem than Barefield's departure occurred soon after the alto-player had left. While in transit from one booking to the next, the band's entire library of arrangements, uniforms, and instruments was stolen. Billie Bowen described the resultant consternation:

> When we got to the next job all the band had to play their parts from memory. We were able to borrow instruments for everyone except for Joe Eldridge, who had been playing baritone sax—we had to buy a baritone sax from a second-hand store. The irony was that the manager of the hotel where we were booked to play somehow felt cheated that we didn't use music. He felt that he shouldn't be asked to pay as much for a band that played by ear. So I explained all over again that the parts were lost, but he didn't believe me and went out and bought a printed arrangement of a waltz, which, of course, everyone played at sight, and this pacified him.[30]

Roy felt the loss of his trumpet very keenly, but he was even more concerned by the fact that his mouthpiece had been stolen. His trumpet was a standard model that could be easily (albeit expensively) replaced, but his mouthpiece was unique. It had started out as a stock model, available in most music stores, but over the years, Roy's restless nature (and his quest for perfection) had persuaded him to having minute alterations made to it: the mouthpiece's rim had been broadened, the throat widened, and the cup made deeper. All these personalized adjustments meant that there wasn't another mouthpiece in the world that had exactly the same dimensions. The loss meant a long period of trial and error with new mouthpieces, until Roy finally settled on one that had been rejected by its maker, Rudy Muck, as being imperfect and unplayable. Something about this reject suited Roy (even though he later ordered a long-running series of alterations), and he used it for much of his career. At the time that his original mouthpiece had been stolen, Roy took a decision that he had pondered on for a while. This involved him again altering his *embouchure*, finding a new place on his lips for the new mouthpiece, one that offered him more flexibility. He began playing less on the inside of his bottom lip, and instead tucked both lips well into the mouthpiece. It took Roy a while to adjust to his new approach, but after several hours of daily practice he soon began to produce spectacular results again.

As the Cotton Pickers moved from state to state and town to town Roy became acquainted with every night-spot that encouraged jam sessions. Roy's companion on most of these outings was the band's new pianist, Clyde Hart (from Baltimore). Harry Edison, then a young trumpeter (who later starred with Count Basie's Orchestra), recalled his first encounter with Roy:

> I never forgot when the Cotton Pickers came to Cleveland. Roy Eldridge came in one night and carried us from place to place. He almost made me want to quit. What chops he had, and how he could play! He and Pops (Louis Armstrong) were the only two people I ever heard who could play continuously like that. The longer they played, the stronger they got.[31]

There was a feeling of mutual admiration. While in Cleveland, Roy made friends with a teenage bassist, George "Red" Callender, and advised him to visit Mamie Louise's Chicken Shack to hear Harry Edison play. Roy and Red fancied themselves as fashion-plates, and wore long overcoats that dragged along the ground. However, they considered the wearing of hats to be "sissified."[32]

During the visit to Cleveland, Roy, Joe, and Prince Robinson took a taxi out to Val's In The Alley, a club that featured the wonder pianist Art Tatum. The resultant jam session was memorable for Roy, as was the aftermath: all four musicians (including the partially sighted Tatum) indulged in a snowball fight. Despite his severely restricted vision, Art took careful note of the sounds his adversaries made in the frosty night air and aimed hard and true, invariably hitting the target. Roy and his pals made return visits to Val's. Tatum, realizing the visitors were short of money, treated them to a meal in the adjacent diner. Roy's voice took on a special tone of admiration when he talked about Tatum:

> I used to hear him on the radio when he was still very young, and even then his playing was just incredible. He was so fast, but he wasn't just gliding over the keys; he could hit a single note with such power that it sounded like the crack of a pistol shot.[33]

Roy, who had first met Art Tatum in Toledo, Ohio, got to know him better when the pianist came to New York in 1932 as accompanist for singer Adelaide Hall:

> We used to go to one joint; it was called The Devil's Kitchen, between Lenox and Fifth. The piano had very few keys on it, but he could play it. He played on any of them pianos, ones that only had four keys on it.[34]

During the summer of 1934, the Cotton Pickers fulfilled a booking at the Kentucky Club in Atlantic City, where trumpeter George "Pee Wee" Erwin (later to be featured with Benny Goodman) first heard Roy Eldridge: "I got an awful big kick out of Roy. He was blowing up a storm and he was a cute little guy. His identification was a fez cap he always wore, and sometimes would stick it over the end of his trumpet."[35]

Whenever the Cotton Pickers played in Baltimore Roy made a point of taking part in the after-hours sessions. At one of these sessions (at Ike Dixon's Comedy Club) he first played with the legendary tenorist Lester Young, then in the middle of a brief and unhappy stay in Fletcher Henderson's Orchestra, dealing with musicians who made him feel unwelcome. Roy explained:

> Lester wasn't enough like Coleman Hawkins for them, but I sure dug his playing. He was so glad to get out somewhere and play. So I used to meet him and we'd go to a joint and play all night long, and we were friends ever after.[36]

Although Roy was getting all the blowing he wanted, he gradually came to realize that being with this version of the Cotton Pickers was like treading water. The band was good, but it could still only be advertised as the Cotton Pickers, and to make matters worse McKinney had decided to resume leading with a new band, naturally billing it as McKinney's Cotton Pickers. Roy's wage packet rarely topped $30 a week, but because he liked the musical ambience he stayed on. However, after more than a year with the Cotton Pickers he found himself hanging around Baltimore waiting for the next job to come in and knew it was time to move on. Roy sent word to his former sidekick Chu Berry, telling him he was looking for work. Obligingly, Chu (who was then in Teddy Hill's Band) mentioned this to his leader, who immediately invited Roy to rejoin the band, which was playing at the Ubangi Club in New York, in preparation for another residency at the Savoy Ballroom. Meanwhile, Joe Eldridge had also left the Cotton Pickers to join Blanche Calloway's Orchestra, depriving Roy of his brother's guardianship for this stay in New York. Nevertheless, Roy made the move, and took Bernard Flood's place in the Teddy Hill trumpet section. Bill Coleman, on third trumpet, who had been taking most of the jazz solos, watched Roy's arrival with interest, but there was never any trouble between these two wonderful players, because Roy now reveled in playing in a section and reading trumpet parts accurately. Later Bill said, "It was an exciting pleasure to work with Roy and be in a position to hear him night after night."[37] Roy soloed often, always parading spectacular ideas. When work was done, Roy and Chu invariably ended up at a jam session. Between 1934 and 1935, their haunts included Reuben Harris' Club on West 130th and the Log Cabin (formerly Pod's and Jerry's) on West 132nd, where they backed a young singer called Billie Holiday. For Roy, these informal sessions with Billie were a reunion. He said he first met her when she was a precocious teenager in Baltimore. He had gone there to visit Billie's mother Sadie, but she was away in New York, so Roy spent the evening with Billie.

A favorite "hang-out" for Roy and Chu was the Subway Club on Seventh Avenue, but any place that encouraged "jamming" was on their itinerary. Guitarist Danny Barker often saw them going from club to club, describing them as being "on the rampage." During this period Barker worked with Roy and Chu for two nights in a band led by his uncle, drummer Paul Barbarin, at the Strollers' Club, where they accompanied the blues diva Clara Smith. Before they could begin their third night at the venue a violent dispute between rival gangsters took place, and the police promptly padlocked the premises. Roy never seemed to need sleep, and a devil-may-care attitude marked his outlook on life. On one occasion he and Teddy Hill's trombonist Dicky Wells tried out a Chinese drink which (according to Wells) left them "high for six hours."[38] Teddy Hill's line-up at this time was: Bill Dillard, Roy Eldridge, and Bill Coleman (trumpets); Dicky Wells (trombone), Russell Procope, Howard "Swan" Johnson, and Chu Berry (saxes); Sam Allen (piano), John Smith (guitar), Dick Fulbright (bass), and Bill Beason (drums).

It was this line-up that recorded four titles in February 1935; Roy always regarded this as his official recording debut. His startling high-note playing and adventurous phrasing on *Here Comes Cookie* made an immediate impact on listeners. Although he is featured only briefly, what he plays is unforgettable.

The Teddy Hill Band occasionally worked outside of New York City, and one such booking took them to the Lincoln Theater in Philadelphia. Duke Ellington's Orchestra was also working in the

Philadelphia area, and Roy got to hear that Duke's musicians (including his old rival Rex Stewart) planned to visit the Rendezvous Club for a late-night jam session. A young Dizzy Gillespie, who had recently moved to Philadelphia, was at the gathering, and witnessed the inevitable musical collision between Roy and Rex. According to Gillespie, Eldridge overwhelmed Stewart so decisively that Rex wept. Looking back years later, Rex said, "Roy developed another dimension of his own, which was faster and better than mine."[39] For Roy, the two years of stretching his working range beyond Stewart's had paid off. There was to be one further musical confrontation between Roy and Rex, but, according to Eldridge, this final contest proved to be the damp squib that ended the series: "Each of us was waiting for the other to strike—nobody struck."[40]

Some of the most exciting music to be heard in New York City during the 1930s emanated from the Savoy Ballroom. This vast structure, which occupied almost an entire block at Lenox Avenue, first opened in 1926. It achieved instant success by providing continuous dance music every evening, employing a series of bands working from adjacent stands in the long, narrow ballroom. When one band finished a set, its counterpart immediately struck up with a number, so that there was no interruption for the dancers. The Savoy was managed by an African-American, Charles Buchanan; most of the bands that played there regularly were represented by the Moe Gale Agency. Wages at the Savoy ($32 a week in 1935) were never beyond the basic union scale, but most bandleaders were wily enough to realize that fulfilling a successful residency at the Savoy (called "The Track" by musicians) brought their outfit publicity, plentiful radio exposure, and live audiences of thousands. At this stage of his life Roy didn't worry unduly about money matters. He adopted an easy-come-easy-go attitude, and said: "I made $32 a week at the Savoy, and every two weeks I bought a suit, and all of them went out of style."[41]

Numerous band battles took place at the Savoy Ballroom, including one between orchestras led by Count Basie and Benny Goodman, while another involved groups led by Gene Krupa and

Chick Webb. Webb, a diminutive, misshapen drummer, was generally recognized as the "King" of the Savoy. He played with amazing skill and zest, and if he sensed competition he inspired his band to outblow and outswing anyone who played on what he considered to be his home territory. Teddy Hill had faith in the skills of his musicians, but something in his nature caused him to avoid band battles whenever possible. He probably realized that most of his band arrangements were unremarkable; there were few "killer-diller" (an expression of the period) charts in his library. Hill was not an effective showman, but he was a good organizer who paid his men on time—and wisely refrained from featuring himself on the tenor-saxophone. Roy Eldridge succinctly summed up Teddy Hill's abilities by saying, "Nice cat. No soloist."[42] Hill's Band also occasionally played at Connie's Inn, where wages were $50 a week, considerably more than the Savoy paid, but playing at "The Track" definitely kept musicians on their toes. The dancers were inspirational, as were those who came solely to hear the jubilant music. In the summer of 1935, London-based writer Leonard Feather, on his first visit to New York, heard Teddy Hill's Band at the Savoy and wrote in *Melody Maker* about "a young trumpeter, Roy Eldridge, who is really great."[43] By this time Roy was one of the stars in Hill's Band. Besides his ultra-inventive trumpet-playing he was also contributing ideas for the band's arrangements; riffs he devised for the band's version of *Between The Devil And The Deep Blue Sea* were supremely effective (Dicky Wells later used them on his own recording).

Roy and Chu continued to supplement their nightly blowing by sitting in all over Manhattan after they had finished work at 2.30 a.m. They were now recognized as a team, and as such were booked to accompany the cheerful vocals of Louis "Putney" Dandridge (who also played some piano) on a 1935 recording session that produced three satisfying but not sensational tracks: *When I Grow Too Old To Dream*, *Nagasaki*, and *Chasing Shadows*. The two young musicians acquitted themselves well as accompanists, and in their solos gave a good indication of why their talents were the envy of so many other jazz musicians. A month after the date with Putney Dandridge, Roy was featured on two recording sessions organized by his former colleague pianist Teddy Wilson, who organized a pick-up sextet to accompany singer Billie Holiday, whose reputation as the most individual of all jazz vocalists was rapidly growing. The results are sublime, with the musicians (including Benny Goodman) producing solos and backing phrases that exactly dovetail with the moods of Billie's remarkable singing. Roy's work covers a wide range of emotions ranging from his scorching interpretation of *What A Little Moonlight Can Do* to the tender approach he shows on *I Wished On The Moon*. At about this time Roy and Billie had a brief affair, which Roy said ended "When Billie found herself in love with a girl friend."[44] He wasn't heart-broken because he knew that she had broad sexual preferences. Years later he said:

> I loved her. She had something of her own, different. She could *sing*. She always had it, even as a girl, before she recorded. Me and Chu used to go and sit in with her at the place called the Hot-Cha (uptown at West 134th Street). She was what you'd call a natural. She was no tragedy queen. She didn't have to study.[45]

4

CHICAGO
BANDLEADER

Teddy Wilson nursed an ambition to become a full-time bandleader, and during the summer of 1935 it seemed as though the opportunity for him to do so had presented itself. He was offered the chance to bring his own sextet to audition for a residency at the French Casino at Times Square and Seventh Avenue. He decided to employ a personnel similar to a line-up he had used on various recordings, namely Roy Eldridge on trumpet, Chu Berry on tenor-sax, bassist John Kirby (from Chick Webb's Band), and drummer Cozy Cole (who had been working alongside Teddy Wilson in Willie Bryant's Band). This array of talented musicians passed the audition with flying colors and a starting date was arranged for them to begin work at the French Casino. By this time Roy and Chu felt they needed a change from Teddy Hill's Band, and both had received hints that they would be invited to join Fletcher Henderson's Band for a proposed booking in Chicago in a few months' time, so the chance to work with Teddy Wilson during the interim sounded ideal. They both handed in their notice to Teddy Hill and prepared to join Wilson.

The management and owners of the Savoy Ballroom followed the plans of the French Casino with great interest, and soon became aware that several young jazz stars who regularly graced their stands (with various bands) were about to begin working for a rival organization. The locale of the French Casino, in mid-town Manhattan, was unlikely to draw away the clientele of the Savoy, up in Harlem, but what irked the Savoy's bosses was the fact that the new venue was offering musicians considerably more than the Savoy ever paid. Roy was earning $32 a week at the Savoy, but was offered $125 a week at the French Casino. It looked as though the rigid wages' policy that the Savoy ruthlessly maintained was about to be broken by another venue. They learned to live with the fact that Connie's Inn paid musicians more than they did, but they determined to stop anyone offering what was almost a 400 percent increase.

Teddy Wilson and Roy Eldridge were the two "stars" picked out to be made examples of in dissuading other musicians from moving downtown for a wages bonanza. Enter Hyman "Feets" Edson (on whom it is said Damon Runyon based one of his tough-guy characters). Edson was, for a long time, the manager of film star and dancer George Raft (both of whom were close friends of the noted mobster Ownie Madden). Later, Edson also managed Erskine Hawkins' Band. Apparently, "Feets" Edson was asked to explain to Wilson and Eldridge that it would not be a good idea for them to work at the French Casino. He did so, allegedly, by threatening to shoot off their fingers if they did—not surprisingly, Teddy and Roy decided not to perform at the French Casino.[1] The November 1935 issue of *Down Beat* magazine gave a brief report of events: "As a result of the enthusiastic reception by the French Casino management both Roy Eldridge and Chu Berry left Teddy Hill on the same day for the new job, which promptly washed up for unprintable reasons."

Roy spoke about it years later:

> The people all got together who were in charge of these things to stop us taking the gig. They even offered me a job at the Cotton Club with Claude Hopkins. I liked Claude but I didn't want to work at the Cotton Club; I'd rather be down there with Teddy Wilson. I never would work the Cotton

Club. I didn't like the fact that this was the place where black people couldn't go in...you had to go in the back door. Well, what would I want to work up there for?[2]

On another occasion, Roy elaborated further about the French Casino offer: "We signed the contracts and were rehearsing to go into the Casino when Teddy Wilson received a threat: if he played the Casino the place would be stink-bombed. I believe to this day it was some of those darkies at the Savoy."[3]

Roy didn't remain unemployed for long: he soon accepted an offer to take a small band into the Famous Door on 52nd Street for a residency beginning in September 1935. Roy had to audition for the job but couldn't locate Clyde Hart, the pianist whom he intended to use at the club, so bassist Ted Sturgis played the piano at the audition, and did so with such skill that the band were offered the job. Hart was eventually located, and played the piano for the residency, with Sturgis reverting to the double-bass. The rest of the group that opened in the upstairs section of the Famous Door on September 29, 1935 consisted of Roy, Joe Eldridge on alto-sax, and Jimmy McLin on guitar (a drummer wasn't used). Roy's band played only brief sets; the group that played downstairs was the main attraction. For the first part of the run the top spot was taken by Red Norvo's Sextet, which was succeeded by Wingy Manone's Quartet on November 18, 1935. Roy recalled, "We played until people came in the place. They kept us upstairs, feeding us until everybody went home and then they called us to close the joint."[4] Frustrated by this lack of blowing time, Roy made sure that he found plenty of places to jam until dawn and beyond. He even took part in Sunday afternoon sessions at the Hickory House, playing alongside Artie Shaw, Tommy Dorsey, Benny Goodman, and Joe Marsala. Marsala, who played clarinet in Wingy Manone's Quartet, managed to work Roy into what turned out to be an exciting record date in December 1935. Marsala gave the details: "We had a chance to make a record for Decca but Wingy was recording for Vocalion at the time, so we got Roy Eldridge. That was one of the great sessions.[5]

Marsala wasn't exaggerating. The exciting playing on *Farewell Blues* and *Swingin' On The Famous Door* (featuring Roy, Joe, Carmen Mastren on guitar, and Sid Weiss on bass) played a big part (especially with European jazz fans) in establishing Roy's reputation as one of the most important of the emerging young jazz-players. On one occasion, when Roy was asked about this session, he gave dark hints that Wingy Manone had curtailed the session after hearing the thrilling results of the two tunes recorded. But when Roy was in a better mood he gave a different story: "We only made two sides. Wingy talked for the rest of the time so we didn't get the chance to make any more. We still owe Decca two sides."[6] Anyone familiar with Wingy Manone's ability to talk the hind leg off a donkey will find this explanation plausible. More often than not, Roy chuckled when Wingy's name was mentioned: "Wingy was a funny cat. The first time I saw him was in the 1920s, working as a single trying to play like 'Pops.' Later he guested with Speed Webb's Band."[7]

During his stay at the Famous Door, Roy took time out to play some dates with Fletcher Henderson's Band at the Roseland Ballroom, and in Massachusetts. On these dates Roy was reunited with Chu Berry, who had joined Henderson as soon as the French Casino deal fell through. At first Roy felt unable to negotiate the tricky, seldom-used keys in which Fletcher Henderson wrote his arrangements, and told the bandleader, "I can't make it." He replied reassuringly, "You'll be all right," then, quite suddenly, while the band was playing at the Spanish Gables near Boston, everything dropped into place and Roy was never again bothered by "difficult" keys.[8] Soon after this, Henderson asked Roy to join the band for its forthcoming residency at the Grand Terrace Ballroom in Chicago. With his immediate future settled, Roy decided to take a brief vacation when the stint at the Famous Door ended. By this time Roy had abandoned his habit of buying a new suit every two weeks, and had thriftily put away a regular amount each week in a Post Office account, but, revealing a trait that was to remain with him throughout his life, he drew out all his savings in order to go on a wild spree:

> I told Fletcher Henderson I had to go home, but I didn't get
> no farther than Philadelphia. I went over there with $500 and
> got stranded, with gambling, and taking all my buddies out
> when I'd go to jam, and buying drinks. I only had a silver
> dollar left, and I pawned that to wire my aunt here in New
> York to get $5 to get home—it only cost $2 and something on
> the train. So that's when I joined Fletcher.[9]

By joining Henderson, Roy achieved one of his big ambitions, but the prospect of being away from New York vexed him because it meant being a long distance from his steady girlfriend Viola Lee (whose mother was Chinese); they met when "Vi" was working as a dance hostess at the Savoy. Roy asked her to accompany him to Chicago. She said that she would—but only if he married her. Roy immediately agreed to this solution and made the necessary arrangements for the couple to be married in New York on January 24, 1936. This was on the very day that Henderson's Band set out for Chicago, where it opened two days later. Fletcher Henderson and his wife Leora attended the City Hall ceremony. Roy forgot the ring but Mrs Henderson obligingly loaned hers, then the newly weds boarded a train for Chicago to begin a marriage that lasted until Vi's death in 1989. The train conductor, on being told about the couple, made a special gesture which Roy never forgot: "He gave us one of those staterooms and didn't charge for it, which I thought was very nice."[10]

Roy and Vi spent their honeymoon at the Grand Hotel in Chicago, later moving (with their dog Wiz) into a third-floor, $40-a-month one-room-and-kitchenette apartment in the Ritz Building on East Garfield Boulevard at 55th and South Parkway—Roy's salary with Henderson was $70 a week. The bride didn't have much time alone with her husband. Roy's hours at the Grand Terrace were long and arduous, and, of course, Roy had to do some "jamming" before he made his way home. The building that housed their apartment had a night-club on the first floor (which was known at various times as Dave's Café, Swingland; and the Rhumboogie). Roy soon became good friends with his next-door neighbor Bob Redcross, a keen and knowledge-able jazz fan who later became Billy Eckstine's manager. Via a Silvertone recording machine, Redcross was able to capture lots of the marvelous jazz that was broadcast on Chicago radio stations. One of Roy's nocturnal ports of call was the Annex Club on 23rd and State, where trumpeter Jimmy Cobb (brother of multi-instrumentalist Junie Cobb) led the resident band. Roy sat in at breakfast dances there and usually blew rings around Jimmy, much to his dismay, but, years later, in Ohio, Jimmy thanked Roy for "carving" him so effectively, saying that these musical "hidings" convinced him to quit full-time trumpet-playing in order to study law—he triumphed at this and became a successful attorney.

By now, Roy loved the challenge of playing Fletcher Henderson's "difficult" arrangements:

> We used to call Fletcher "the sharp king," everything had sharps on it. I remember one arrangement that was written in eight sharps. That band was a great school. Fletcher Henderson was really "it" and Duke Ellington was considered "corny."[11]

The Grand Terrace, at 3955 South Parkway, opened in 1928 under the management of Ed Fox. The site of the ballroom was owned by Joe Glaser, later a world-famous booking agent (and Louis Armstrong's long-time manager). Glaser and Fox had previously been partners at the Sunset Cafe, 35th and Calumet, the scene of some of Armstrong's early triumphs. Fox and his associates spent a lot of money decorating and furnishing the Grand Terrace Ballroom, installing expensive mirrors, sophisticated lighting, a swish bar, and a handsome raised bandstand, but (like many other club-owners) they were reluctant to buy a good piano. This was particularly galling for pianist Earl Hines, the long-time resident bandleader there. The place was said to have "syndicate" backing: when Earl Hines said he would like to play at New York's Cotton Club he was told by Ralph Capone (brother of Al) that the only way Hines would leave the Grand Terrace was in a pinewood box. Hines got used to having a resident "tough-guy" platoon, installed as part of a protection deal. He was allowed to take "outside" engagements occasionally, but only after these bookings had been vetted and approved by Ed Fox. When Hines did go on tour, an out-of-town band (usually from New York) came in to replace him temporarily; thus Henderson's Band arrived in Chicago early in 1936. The final night of Hines' stay coincided with Henderson's arrival, so both bands played at the Grand Terrace on January 26. Roy said with some pleasure: "We played a battle of music the first night against Earl Hines. Tore him up, Tore his group up."[12]

Metronome magazine commented on the excitement created by Henderson's arrival: "We have been waiting a long time here for Fletcher, and everybody is talking about it."[13] But the band's initial broadcasts from the Grand Terrace brought disappointment to George T. Simon, who wrote in the March 1936 issue of the same magazine:

> Fletcher Henderson is not running broadcasts that do him much credit. True, there are some excellent arrangements, the band does swing at times, and Chu Berry's tenor and Roy Eldridge's trumpet are very worthwhile. But the slip-shod attack of the band is discouraging.

Yet the same issue also contained a review of the band's live performance, and was headed: "Fletcher Henderson A Sensation At Grand Terrace." After commenting on the huge crowds the band was drawing, and noting the large number of musicians who came to hear the aggregation, it pointed out:

> The band is suffering under a great many disadvantages. The Terrace is very bad acoustically and the pick-up for the air couldn't be worse. The balance on the broadcasts is so bad that the worth of the band is almost unrecognizable and the piano is so bad that it is impossible to tune the band to it. It

doesn't seem as though Ed Fox is making any effort to give the band much of a break.

Metronome of March 1936 contained a further mention of the band's activities, commenting that Roy Eldridge, after finishing his long stint at the Grand Terrace with Fletcher, took a short break, then appeared at 5 a.m. at the Three Deuces Club to take part in a nightly jam session held there, noting that he cut everybody. After putting in a couple of hours' blowing, he and several of his pals from Henderson's Band (Chu Berry, Sid Catlett, Buster Bailey, and John Kirby) left the Three Deuces to sit in at the Club De Lisa's 7 a.m. breakfast dances. The stamina required for Roy's self-imposed regime had to be colossal, because his work with Fletcher involved playing at the Grand Terrace seven nights a week from 9.30 p.m. until 3.30 a.m. (Saturdays 10 p.m. to 5 a.m.). Admittedly, Roy was playing third trumpet parts, but he was taking most of the improvised solos and was regularly featured on numbers that were potential lip-busters. Like the rest of Henderson's musicians, Roy was stimulated by the success they were achieving at the Grand Terrace, and their regular broadcasts from there also won them many new fans. On almost all of these radio transmissions the band featured a catchy riff-tune *Christopher Columbus* (composed by Chu Berry on the chords of *I Got Rhythm*). Lyrics were added by Andy Razaf and the piece gradually achieved national fame—crowds began to flock to the Grand Terrace to hear Henderson play it. The increased audiences were racially mixed, and by March 1936 it was reported that "black patronage was twice what it had been." The success of *Christopher Columbus* brought forth claimants who said they had written the catchy little theme. Trumpeter Paul Bascomb was one: he said that during his stay in Erksine Hawkins' Band they played a riff-tune called *A Rhythm Cocktail* that Chu Berry and Roy Eldridge heard them play at the Savoy Ballroom before the markedly similar *Christopher Columbus* was launched. However, a four-bar excerpt of the main theme formed the concluding phrase on a recording that Roy and Chu had made with Billie Holiday (*Yankee Doodle Never*

Went To Town) in October 1935. Subsequently Roy piped up to say, in an aggrieved fashion, that he had devised the snappy trumpet figure that answered the main theme, but had never received any of the considerable royalties that the song earned: "No credit. No bread" was how he put it.[14] Worse still, there were to be instances when Roy felt that an entire composition of his had been appropriated by someone else.

Roy and Chu remained friends, despite the "misunderstanding" over *Christopher Columbus.* Chu was a very popular member of the band, and was featured extensively by Fletcher Henderson, who raved over his tenor-playing: "He's one of the fastest, most inventive and creative minds that has ever been in my band. He doesn't set his choruses, he's continually bobbing up with something he hasn't done before."[15]

Fletcher also gave some solo space (mainly on ballads) to the band's other tenorist Elmer "Tone" Williams, of whom Roy said appreciatively, "He could play pretty."[16]

Discipline was not Fletcher Henderson's strong point, and Joe Thomas, Roy's colleague in the trumpet section, told Albert McCarthy that on one occasion the bandleader became so annoyed by the casual attitude of his trumpet trio, Thomas, Eldridge, and Dick Vance, that he sardonically observed that these three would be as well occupied going back to bed, whereupon the culprits packed up their instruments and left the bandstand with one set still to be played.[17] Apparently Henderson never referred to this temporary defection, thus demonstrating his unwillingness to reprimand errant musicians, which, combined with his practice of accepting rude and unjustified criticisms from agents and manager, built up his reputation as a milksop bandleader (but one who had enormous gifts as a musical arranger). In *Down Beat* of July 1936, John Hammond publicly castigated Henderson for his unwillingness to stand up for himself or for his musicians. Hammond called Ed Fox "a dictator," and cited one of Fox's outlandish acts:

He fired Fletcher's male vocalist, Teddy Lewis, in an abusive tirade before a large crowd of onlookers. Fletcher's refusal to stand up for the elementary rights of his band and himself will land him again in the same mess from which he has been painfully extricating himself. It is certainly tragic that colored performers are so subject to exploitation, but it is even sadder when they are themselves to blame.

However, despite Henderson's musicians regarding their leader through jaundiced eyes, Roy's stay with the band provided him with what he later described as the most exciting gig of his life. The event was a Swing Concert held in the Joseph Urban Room of the Congress Hotel in Chicago on Sunday afternoon, March 8, 1936. It was organized by a young Canadian writer Helen Oakley and a noted jazz fan Squirrel Ashcraft, under the auspices of the Chicago Rhythm Club. The full Henderson Band participated, and there was also a jam session featuring Benny Goodman (whose band was playing a residency at the Congress Hotel), his star drummer Gene Krupa plus Roy Eldridge, Chu Berry, Fletcher Henderson, and bassist John Kirby. Roy said later: "This concert was one of the greatest things I ever experienced. That session stands out in my mind. The Henderson Band played so good I literally sat down and cried."[18] No recordings were made of the concert, but we can get some idea of the excitement engendered during the jam session from four sides recorded a few days earlier featuring some of the principals: Goodman, Eldridge, Berry, and Krupa (together with pianist Jess Stacy, guitarist Allan Reuss, bassist Israel Crosby, and singer Helen Ward). Billed as Gene Krupa and his All Star Swing Band, the group produced four magnificent sides. The music the sextet recorded was red hot, as was Roy's temper when he discovered that one of his compositions (recorded on the date) had not been credited to him. This was *Swing Is Here*, which Roy had written under the title *At The Rugcutters' Ball* when he was in Teddy Hill's Band:

After I wrote the tune I gave it to the publisher and he said,

"I'll send you a contract," and he never sent any contract. Then, when I went down to ask him about it, he said, "That's not yours, that's Benny Goodman's tune." And it was my tune. I wrote the lead-sheet! I'd been playing it on the piano for years.[19]

The ensuing contretemps didn't help Roy and Goodman to be easy companions, particularly as none of the royalties of *Swing Is Here* reached Eldridge. During this same period Roy and Benny had another disagreement, over the merits of drummer Sid Catlett. Looking back, Roy said:

I knew Sidney for a long time. We played a lot together. We were with Fletcher Henderson's Band in 1936. Benny Good-man didn't like Sidney. He came over to hear us at the Grand Terrace and asked me, "How do you like that drummer?" I said "He's great." He answered, "Man, in about three or four weeks you ain't gonna be playing nothing with that drummer." I just told him, "Nobody can tell me about Sidney, because I've worked with him before. I'll probably be playing better the longer he stays around."[20]

On another occasion Roy went out of his way to stress his admiration for the great drummer: "I loved Big Sid Catlett. He was so smooth. He had that weight without being noisy."[21]

In May 1936, Billie Holiday, by then regarded as an up-and-coming recording star, was added to Fletcher Henderson's personnel. This was not at Ed Fox's instigation, but was a move engineered by Billie's manager Joe Glaser (who was still the owner of the Grand Terrace). Ed Fox felt that he'd been pushed into accepting this deal, and reacted by making spiteful remarks about Billie's appearance and her vocal style from the moment they met. Billie, knowing that Glaser had pulled strings to get her the booking, remained unusually taciturn, but when Fox banned her from singing on the Henderson Band's broadcasts she stormed into his office and, in a fit of fury, rearranged

Fox's furniture and threatened to do the same to his features. This ended the association. Fletcher Henderson, much to the annoyance of his sidemen, had simply stood by and watched Fox's deplorable behavior without making any comment. Billie Holiday moved back to New York, doubly disappointed. She'd lost her job and she also had to say goodbye to pianist Teddy Cole (brother of drummer Cozy Cole) with whom she was having an intense love affair. Cole was then playing in Zutty Singleton's Band at the Three Deuces, the club Roy visited almost every night.

Surprisingly, Ed Fox made no move to ban Roy from sitting in regularly at the Three Deuces after he'd finished his stint at the Grand Terrace. It seems likely that the powerful forces that ran most of the Chicago entertainment scene had decided not to make an issue of late-night jamming. Ed Fox and Sam Beers (the owner of the Three Deuces) knew one another: they had both been entrepreneurs throughout the rough-and-tumble years of Prohibition. Beers opened the original Three Deuces in 1927, so named because of its address at 222 North State Street (but also as an "in" joke that tilted at Chicago's most notorious whore-house, The Four Deuces, at 2222 South Wabash Avenue). The Three Deuces rapidly became a nocturnal gathering place for musicians, song-writers, and actors, all of whom had a thirst. Jazz musicians liked "jamming" in the informal surroundings of the club. Like many other club-owners, Beers encouraged the practice, realizing that he often had a twelve-piece band on stage, of which only four or five needed paying.

The club flourished during the late 1920s, ignoring the Prohibition laws and various other regulations, but after one particular burst of flagrant whoopee-making the police stepped in on December 28, 1928, raided the night-spot, and virtually wrecked it.

Sam Beers took a breather but soon reopened a club on Lake Street which he named "My Cellar." Beers was a part owner of this enterprise. The organization that controlled the club used it as a gambling joint during the day and a 150-seater cabaret at night-time. At first, Beers featured various white musicians, including Wingy

Manone and Art Hodes; then he brought in Louis Armstrong. The club adopted a more highbrow name, as noted in *Orchestra World* of May 1931: "Louis Armstrong and his Orchestra are packing them in at the Showboat Cafe, which may I remind you is My Cellar re-named." When Louis left to go on tour, Beers brought in Jabbo Smith to front a band, but Jabbo, whose unpunctuality irked Beers, was soon on the move back to Milwaukee, his place as leader being taken by pianist Cassino Simpson. During these various changes the blatant law-breaking at the Showboat became too prolific for the Prohibition agents to ignore; Beers saw the warning signs and decided to retire temporarily from club management.

It wasn't until Prohibition was repealed in December 1933 that Sam Beers felt the urge to resume being a club-owner. He opened up again at his old address in the Loop district, 222 North State Street, and installed (in the basement) a band led by the New Orleans drummer Arthur "Zutty" Singleton. The club's press adverts billed Zutty as "King Of The Drums," and proclaimed itself as "The Musicians' Hang-Out In Chicago."[22] Zutty played a long residency there using various line-ups which included, at various times: Vernell Yorke, Lee Collins, and Jimmy McClary (trumpets); Horace Eubanks and Gordon Jones (reeds), Zinky Cohn, Henry Gordon, and Bill Smith (piano); Everett Barksdale and Mike McKendrick (guitar), and Milt Hinton and Leonard Bibbs (double-bass). At the time of Roy Eldridge's regular visits, the personnel was pretty well stabilized as Vernell Yorke (trumpet), George "Scoops" Carry (alto-sax), Teddy Cole (piano), Charles "Truck" Parham (double-bass), and Zutty Singleton (drums). The club was open from 10 p.m. until 4 a.m. and, besides its musical fare, it was noted for its barbecued ribs cooked over hickory wood. Music in the upstairs bar was provided by pianists such as Cleo Brown (who sometimes used drummer Baby Dodds) and the great Art Tatum. There was certainly a free-and-easy atmosphere at the Three Deuces, and bassist Milt Hinton recalled that during the intermissions there was always an opportunity to smoke pot: "All the guys in our band used reefers. For a while it seemed like the thing to do.

Practically every time we had a break, a group of them would go to the boiler room and light up."[23]

Zealous government officials, feeling that Sam Beers had slipped through the weave of regulations for too long, conducted a rigorous survey of the club and found that safety laws were not being observed; thus, during the late summer of 1936, the Three Deuces was closed for restructuring and redecoration. Zutty Singleton went off to guest with Carroll Dickerson's Orchestra at Benny Skoller's Swingland during August and September 1936, and Roy Eldridge found other places where he could blow his trumpet until daybreak. Sam Beers was no fool; he had been dealing with jazz musicians for years, and recognized that Roy's trumpet-playing was extraordinary. He was also aware that Roy's skills and personality vocals appealed both to his regular customers and to devoted jazz fans. Through a long-term association with James Petrillo, then head of Chicago Musicians' Union, Beers learned that there was to be a crack-down on sitting in. For years, the American Federation of Musicians had occasionally collected token fines from club-owners who encouraged sitting in, but now they were threatening stronger action. Beers reasoned that the best thing he could do to keep his customers happy was to offer Roy the leadership of the Three Deuces' Band. Roy accepted without hesitation, and became leader when the club reopened in September 1936. Zutty Singleton needed no persuasion to change his status from bandleader to sideman, and he become Roy's drummer, a move that satisfied Roy, who said, "Zutty's time was always good." Scoops Carry, Teddy Cole, and Truck Parham remained from the "old" line-up, and were joined by Dave Young on tenor-sax and a friend of Scoops Carry, guitarist John Collins.

There was no financial gain for Roy in the move. Beers paid him the same salary ($70 a week) that Henderson had done. But by this time Roy was tired of working with Fletcher, especially at the Grand Terrace, to which they had recently returned after a successful tour:

When he got back, Ed Fox's son, who was in the music

publishing business, started getting tunes in that he was publishing, to get them on the air. Well, we had a lot of good music that I wanted to play, and we stopped playing it. So that turned me into Peck's Bad Boy, and I used to sit on the end, smoking pot, or drinking and getting off whenever I wanted to. So finally I couldn't take it no longer and I put in my notice.[24]

Roy was also dissatisfied with Fletcher Henderson's strategy, particularly because he had sold arrangements to a "rival" bandleader:

If it had been me, Benny Goodman wouldn't have been broadcasting the same book. Don't forget that Henderson didn't spend as much time rehearsing the band as Benny did. Horace Henderson was the guy that took care of business, worked the band into shape. I really dug Horace.[25]

Fletcher Henderson wasn't heart-broken to see Roy go. Over the years he had survived the departure of Louis Armstrong, Tommy Ladnier, Joe Smith, Rex Stewart, Bobby Stark, and Henry "Red" Allen from his orchestra. He held no grudge against Eldridge, but later uttered what were (for him) some unusually candid words:

Roy Eldridge is another man with a highly creative mind. When it comes to ideas on trumpet he's just about as fickle as a fellow who doesn't know which girl he wants. But he never tires. He's got an iron lip. Often times he's great, but it is his weakness that he can't maintain that level at all times.[26]

So began what Roy later described as the happiest period of his musical life. The band he led at the Three Deuces soon achieved an amazing rapport, spontaneously creating ingenious head arrange-ments (musical routines that didn't use written parts), with each man able to improvise exciting solos, and to create ingenious riffs and counter-melodies. Roy would suggest a standard tune, and this provided the harmonic sequence for the framework of an entirely new, spontaneously conceived composition. The band developed an almost telepathic understanding, with Roy leading the way by creating strong new themes out of unlikely material; he said, "We thought like one person."[27] Bassist Truck Parham, in a conversation with Alyn Shipton, spoke of the band's almost devil-may-care attitude:

> I've heard about playing *avant-garde*, I guess we were doing that a long time ago on the air. Roy would say, "Let's go into the symphony bag." He'd start off, then we'd all end up with one theme. He'd do it on the air while we were broadcasting. At first the cats started getting all nervous. Roy said, "No, just blow, just end up together." It went down so beautiful, we had a great time.[28]

The radio station's copyright administrators needed to know the names of these instant creations. Roy obliged by improvising such titles as *Gee Jake, What A Snake* and *Roaches And Incense*. At the Three Deuces Roy produced dozens of compositions including *Little Jazz*, which he adopted as his signature tune (years later, Roy recorded a different *Little Jazz* with Artie Shaw's Band). The band's nightly broadcasts were aired at 1.15 a.m. Central Standard Time on Station W.B.B.M.-C.B.S., a 720-kilowatt transmission that went out (via a land-line) every night except Saturday, reaching a large catchment area and doing a lot to build Roy's reputation. The program was particularly enjoyed by musicians who had just finished work. Roy commented on this: "Most bands that traveled had a radio in the bus, and we came on late at night, when they were traveling."[29] The broadcasts were also enjoyed by many jazz fans and members of the general public. Hearing Roy on the radio prompted a young blind pianist Lennie Tristano (later to be the guru of a new school of jazz improvisation) to visit the Three Deuces. He became a regular there and occasionally sat in. In doing so he established a lifelong friendship with Roy, and often cited him as one of his major influences. In 1949 Tristano selected two records featuring Roy, (*Rockin' Chair* with Gene Krupa, and *Sittin' In* with Chu Berry) in his

"Top Ten All-time favorite jazz recordings."[30] Helen Oakley visited the Three Deuces regularly:

> That's where I first heard Roy Eldridge, and knew right away that something was going on. He had a terrific lip from the word go, and he was on fire to play at every opportunity. Roy and I hit it off from the beginning, because, in those days, there were not too many people who knew what they were listening to. And Roy was one of those little guys always eager to show what he could do and he really appreciated anyone aware of his talent. He was very likeable, and what was nice was that we came up together and were always special friends. It was an exciting time, and some of us knew we were watching and enjoying the development of a great talent.[31]

Roy's growing eminence meant that his photograph was used in the advertisements for Martin trumpets; this in an era when few African-Americans were shown endorsing any products. Roy played a Martin Committee-model trumpet for many years, alternating between that and a custom-built trumpet made by the ex-Chicago Symphony Orchestra virtuoso Eldon Benge. Years later he also played a Le Blanc trumpet and flugel horn. Late in his life Roy donated one of his Martin trumpets to the Institute of Jazz Studies at Rutgers University.

Sam Beers (and his new partner Frank Friefield) were intent on keeping their customers and their resident band happy, so there was virtually no interference with Roy's style of music-making. To keep the overflow of customers happy, Beers rebooked Art Tatum to play again in the upstairs section of the club. For the final part of Tatum's sets he liked to be accompanied by a bassist, which meant that Roy's bassist Truck Parham dashed upstairs with his instrument to fulfil a task he proudly remembers. Milt Hinton did the same thing when Tatum had played there in 1935. Tatum did several stints at the club, then moved on to richer pastures, allowing pianist-singer Cleo Brown to return to the upstairs section. Behind the main bar, Gladys Palmer (originally from Jamaica) sang and played the piano. Usually the downstairs section featured a cabaret interlude. It also had what one musician described as "a postage stamp dance floor."

Although Roy could, from his middle years onwards, put away a considerable quantity of alcohol without getting drunk, he was, when not working, a light "social" drinker. His input of intoxicating drink at the Three Deuces was moderate, except when trumpeter Shorty Sherock visited the club and, as a mark of respect and admiration, lined up ten glasses of whiskey for Roy to drink. Usually, such stimulation as Roy needed came from marijuana. Like Louis Armstrong, he did not classify this as a drug, saying on many occasions that he didn't use drugs (meaning "hard drugs"); he vowed he was never likely to, since he had a morbid fear of hypodermic needles. Tenorist Dave Young told writer Dempsey J. Travis about the part marijuana played in the band's life:

> On pay day most of the guys would buy a shoe-box full of marijuana. A size 13 shoe-box full of the stuff cost only five dollars. The cats stayed high while they played the gig. They always played well because they knew their instruments. The radio network had to clear the popular tunes before they could be played on the air. So Roy would get high and make up the lists of tunes while he was closetted with his tea. He had hallucinations from the pot and came up with titles for tunes we never heard of.[32]

Roy loved reminiscing about his broadcasts from the Three Deuces, and confirmed Young's recollections:

> That was a crazy band—the most flexible. There was nothing those cats couldn't do. And you never knew what they were coming up with. We could be doing *Limehouse Blues* way up in tempo, look at the clock, and do a direct segue into the theme.[33]

Amazingly, Roy still continued to go out jamming when the Three Deuces closed for the night. He knew all the clubs that simply ignored the Union rules about sitting in, so when Count Basie's Band came to Chicago to play a residency at the Grand Terrace, he called for tenorist Lester Young and drummer Jo Jones in his new Ford roadster and took them on a tour of the free-blowing night-spots. Jo Jones never forget these sessions: "Roy Eldridge would pick us up in front of the Grand Terrace after work every night and we'd jam from four until ten or eleven in the morning. We'd often wind up with just the three of us playing."[34]

Roy filled in the details:

> I'd be in my car and we'd go around different places and play. We'd play until way into daytime. We'd go to the De Lisa and to Martin's Chicken Shack, or to Martin's on the West side (1900 West Lake Street). At these sessions Lester was always building. Those weren't cutting sessions and they never left you hung up, there was no animosity at all, we just went out to play and have a ball.[35]

Another Count Basie sideman, trumpeter Buck Clayton, first met Roy at the Three Deuces. He said, "He was the most streamlined trumpet player I'd ever heard, barring none."[36] Musically and socially, Roy and Lester Young always enjoyed each other's company, and in January 1938, when Lester recorded *Every Tub* with Count Basie, he sent a subtle, coded musical communication to Eldridge: "He put in one chorus of my theme song *Little Jazz*, but he played it backwards, like sending me a message."[37] But much as Roy admired Lester's playing, he still retained a hero-worship of Coleman Hawkins, and Roy's friend Bob Redcross remembered Roy specially ordering records from England that Hawkins made during his long stay (1934 to 1939) in Europe.

During the 1930s a great many night-clubs in Chicago had connections with organized crime, and, as Roy visited many of these places to sit in, he quickly came to recognize a lot of the city's infamous gangsters. Some of them acknowledged Roy with a nod, others made jocular but not unfriendly comments; an onlooker said of Roy at this time, "He had a big perpetual smile and was very jovial."[38] One night, while doing his sitting-in "rounds," Roy discovered that he had lost his wallet, which happened to be full because he had just been paid. He felt certain that he had been the victim of a pickpocket, and hurried to Dave's Café (situated below his own apartment) where he explained the situation to Sam "Golf Bag" Hunt (who allegedly got his nickname through always carrying a shotgun with him, hidden in a golf bag). Hunt, who was the overseer of most of the South Side's gambling, told Roy not to worry, as he would do his best to locate the missing wallet. Roy, in a state of agitation, went upstairs to his apartment to calm down. He said he felt he had been home for only a matter of minutes when one of Hunt's aides knocked on the door and returned the wallet, which not only contained all the missing money but also an extra $100 bill.

The only thing that irked Roy at the Three Deuces was having to bother himself with the administrative duties that went with bandleading: booking substitute musicians if someone was ill, sorting out the wages, making sure the musicians were punctual, and so on. Roy's wife Vi gave him some help, but, in the late fall of 1936, Roy decided that the answer would be to add his brother Joe to the band, and delegate these tasks to him. Joe agreed to leave his well-paid job with Blanche Calloway in order to join Roy in Chicago. When Joe arrived at the Three Deuces his hero was still Benny Carter, whose alto-playing had provided the main inspiration for his solo style for over a decade. However, in Chicago, he soon came under the influence of Roy's incumbent altoist, George "Scoops" Carry (a former University of Iowa student who later became a lawyer). The change was so dramatic that players who had worked with Joe in earlier bands didn't recognize the "new" Joe Eldridge when recordings of Roy's Chicago band were first released. In an age when individualism was highly prized the similarity could have been unwelcome, but it proved an asset for the band (and a talking point for listeners). Joe and Scoops combined beautifully in the section and continually stimulated each other's soloing ability. Roy always had a great admiration for Joe's playing: "He was the schooled musician of the family; I was just the 'jive cat.'"[39] At the Three Deuces Joe's ability to write down any music he heard was very useful: a spontaneously created theme could easily float away once the session had ended. Joe saw to it that it didn't by making a quick, shorthand-like sketch of the phrases, which later formed the basis of a new arrangement.

A contemporary report glowed with enthusiasm for Roy's playing. It also encapsulated what he was actually up to by perceptively noting, "He almost plays sax on trumpet. He hits 'em higher and faster than Louis."[40] *Down Beat* of October 1936 noted that he was also developing an impressive coherence, adding: "Roy's only bringdown before has been his over indulgence in screaming on his horn and reaching for high "C's" in the excitement of trying to impress the cats. More mature now, his taste is revealed in the sparing use of tricks."

Roy's *embouchure* was in tiptop shape and his upper range was extraordinary. In 1937 he told a *Down Beat* reporter, "When my chops are right I can pop-off a B flat above high 'C' like nothing." Roy gradually increased this prodigious blowing to embrace a high "G" (above altissimo "C") which was an octave and a half above the top "C," given as the highest note on a trumpet in the manuals of that era. But Roy never claimed to be the pioneer of stratospheric trumpet-playing and pointed out that Tommy Stevenson, the trumpeter in the early Jimmie Lunceford Band, could play as high as anyone. Even the non-jazz press began to notice Roy Eldridge. The *New York Age* of August 15, 1936, said, "He follows the Armstrong tradition, can probably make the weirdest hot licks in captivity and also has a distinctive style." Roy always said that the basis of his expansive range had been achieved by developing his diaphragm and always wearing a belt as well as suspenders (braces).

5

SETTLING IN
NEW YORK

Benny Goodman's successes in 1935 heralded the beginning of the "Swing Era," a period when highly rhythmic music was all the rage in ballrooms, on record, and on the radio. But Roy Eldridge's repertoire at the Three Deuces was never crammed full with popular Swing themes or highly commercial arrangements. It was as if Roy were bypassing the banalities of the movement, yet still creating the excitement that figured in the best of the "Swing" performances. Despite Roy's growing maturity he was still sometimes carried away by the need to impress. Apparently this happened at another of the Congress Hotel's concerts, held on April 18, 1937. This was a benefit show organized by Carl Cons (the editor of *Down Beat*) and Gil Rodin (head of Bob Crosby's Orchestra) for the ailing pianist Joe Sullivan. Some 877 people, all seated at long tables, attended the concert, which featured Bob Crosby's Orchestra plus an all-star cast of musicians including three jazz legends: Johnny Dodds, Baby Dodds, and Natty Dominique. Show-business celebrities Jimmy Durante and Ethel Merman were also there, as were jazz notaries John Hammond and Helen Oakley. Roy was a late addition, as *Down Beat* of May 1937 explained:

Jack Teagarden couldn't make the concert because of a Paul Whiteman engagement and Roy Eldridge, Teddy Cole and Zutty Singleton kindly substituted. They were magnificent on the first two numbers, but something went wrong on *Nagaski*. Zutty drummed like a freight train and Roy could think of nothing but reaching for high notes which was too bad because he didn't get a lot of them convincingly. I wish he had some more discipline or played less extravagantly, for when he's right he has no rivals.

In another review of the same event, George T. Simon wrote in *Metronome*: "Roy's a vastly improved musician, who, when he isn't showing off on high notes, plays some really grand stuff on his instrument."[1] A bonus for the listeners occurred when Roy sat in with Bob Crosby's musicians on *Spinning Wheel*. This fleeting interlude was later to present Roy with a tantalizing invitation.

On Sundays, their day off from the Three Deuces, Roy's band often played at Chicago's Savoy Ballroom (47th and South Parkway). On these occasions the press advertisements were not afraid to offer "Dancing To The World's Hottest Gang." These weren't the only "outside" engagements that Roy's Band played. Tenorist Dave Young maintained that the most exciting gig Roy's Band played was when they battled with Benny Goodman's Orchestra at a dance held at the Eighth Regiment Armory in Chicago. This took place on June 22, 1937, the night Joe Louis defeated James J. Braddock to become heavy-weight champion of the world. This victory sparked an incredible atmosphere at the dance, where Roy's Three Deuces line-up (with Harold "Doc" West on drums for this occasion) held their own against Goodman's considerably bigger line-up. The event was just too much for pianist Teddy Cole. Roy said simply, "He flipped and I had to get another pianist called "Gabby," I don't know what Gabby's last name was."[2]

Roy showed the restrained side of his playing when the Three Deuces band (with tenorist Herbie Haymer in place of Dave Young) made their first recordings in January 1937 as accompanists for singer Mildred Bailey. The band's main task was to provide scored backgrounds for the singer, which they did admirably on all four tracks. Roy's one solo of any length—his sixteen bars on *Where Are You?*—is a model of ingenuity, without fireworks of any kind. However, four days later, the full Three Deuces line-up, with Dave Young back on tenor-sax and Joe Eldridge on alto-sax, went to the studio and recorded three of the most exciting sides of that era, with Roy at his spectacular best, pouring emotion into every phrase he played on *Wabash Stomp*, *Florida Stomp*, and *Heckler's Hop*, creating a landmark in the development of jazz trumpet-playing. This was no fluke: various "airshots" taken from the band's radio transmissions prove that the band consistently performed with excitement and inspiration. A few days later the band returned to the studio and brought with them Gladys Palmer, the singer-pianist from the Three Deuces, who took the vocals on *Where The Lazy River Goes By* and *After You've Gone*. This latter piece was a feature of Roy's daredevil playing. The brilliance of his performance here meant that for the rest of his career he was constantly being asked to play the number. Looking back, he said, "*After You've Gone* was made to make people applaud."[3] The other title from the date, *That Thing*, is a somber number that shows that the band, and Roy in particular, could create a wide variety of moods.

In September 1937 Sam Beers followed his usual custom and briefly closed the club while he took a short summer vacation. As a result of Roy's radio shows, several ballroom operators throughout the Illinois region wanted to book the Three Deuces Band. Accordingly, a brief tour of one-night stands was organized, but before this could be completed Roy was taken ill, pneumonia was diagnosed, and on September 24, 1937 he was admitted to the Passavant Hospital in Chicago. Happily, Roy's health soon improved, and he returned to the reopened club blowing as powerfully as ever. However, in the interim, Zutty Singleton became fidgety waiting for Roy to return (so he said) and decided to move with his wife Marge to

New York. But the background to Zutty's departure was a little more complicated than onlookers were led to believe. While Roy was in hospital, Zutty assumed that he would lead the band at the Three Deuces (as he had done before Roy's arrival), but the rest of the sidemen didn't see it like that and a bad atmosphere developed which culminated in Zutty and Marge leaving Chicago. Roy liked Zutty but had mixed feelings about his departure; as he told Dan Morgenstern:

> I just really could never figure him out. He had problems with Louis Armstrong too. He always thought somebody was plotting against him. Like he would tell me to watch Truck Parham and John Collins because "they've got black hearts, they're evil." I know when I came out of hospital he was gone and Harold West was there, but Harold couldn't read. He was a good swinger, though, so I said, "Look, Harold, you've got the gig, take some lessons, because you might have to play something outside of *I Got Rhythm*." So we had a gig in Stony Island, Illinois and we had to play for an adagio dancing act, and West couldn't get it, so I had to end up playing the drums.[4]

Roy's absence from the Three Deuces sparked off a series of moves. Zutty Singleton left, as did Scoops Carry (whose place was taken by Billie Bowen), Dave Young departed, and in came Franz Jackson (previously an alto-sax specialist) on tenor-sax. The new personnel soon settled in and things went on as successfully as before at the Three Deuces, but the restlessness that marked Roy's life began to assert itself, and in early 1938 he mentioned to Sam Beers that he would like to work outside of Chicago for a while. His need for change had been stimulated by a managerial offer from Bing Crosby's brother Everett, who wanted Roy to work out in California. Everett's interest had been sparked by the glowing reports of Roy's recent guest spot with Bob Crosby's Orchestra. Everett, who wanted to expand his booking agency, had observed how smoothly Louis Armstrong had worked with Bing Crosby in Hollywood. He couldn't prise Louis away from Joe Glaser, but he thought he might persuade Roy Eldridge to try his luck in California. Sam Beers immediately vetoed the idea, and Roy was left wondering what might have happened if he had made the trip West. It was something he often mentioned late in his life.

Roy was increasingly aware of the enthusiasm the huge crowds at Chicago's Savoy Ballroom showed when his band played there, and he became keen to know if big ballroom audiences in other cities would similarly react. Roy did not want to return to New York just yet, being mindful of the problems that had prevented him from working at the French Casino; however, he felt willing to travel anywhere else. But Sam Beers could see only one city on Roy's itinerary and that was Chicago. Roy discussed this problem with Gordon Kibbler, who had worked as a publicity man for Fletcher Henderson, as well as being involved in radio production. Kibbler (from Detroit) suggested that his home city would be the ideal place for Roy to launch his bid for national success. Kibbler had led his own band in Detroit during the 1920s and had recently set up a booking agency with Mike Falk as his partner: the Falk–Kibbler Agency operated out of offices at 552 Book Building, Detroit, Michigan. Roy was impressed by the agency's plans and decided to work with them.

It was possible for a band to achieve national fame while being based in Detroit. The success of McKinney's Cotton Pickers had proved that, as had the achievements of Jean Goldkette's Orchestra. So Roy looked to the future optimistically, but, when he announced his decision to leave, Sam Beers dug his heels in and insisted that the contract Roy had signed in 1936 gave him jurisdiction to veto Roy working for any new management until five years had elapsed. Nevertheless, Roy decided to take a chance. He moved to Detroit (a city he knew well), taking with him a few of the musicians who had worked with him in Chicago, augmenting them with local players. With this line-up he played his first engagement in Detroit, which was a party to launch a new Detroit-based magazine called *Swing*. Dressed in a white suit and sporting an elegant necktie, he fronted his tuxedo-clad band looking very sharp. A few local bookings came in during the early summer of 1938, including playing at a private party for Miss Frances Dodge (of the famed automobile family) which took place near Royal Oak, Michigan, and a booking at a Detroit theater.

Otherwise engagements were few and far between, and it became increasingly obvious to Roy that he would be better off moving to New York. The band left Detroit, and *en route* to New York played some bookings in Ohio, first in Columbus and then at Buckeye Lake (near Zanesville) where they were involved in a dramatic incident. Roy was driving a big Buick, with several musicians on board (the rest of the band were traveling with Billie Bowen). Roy stopped at a gas station, which was also a sub-post office, and there, unbeknownst to Roy, pianist Gabby dipped his hand into the till and took the contents; apparently a little boy saw him do this. Roy drove off but was soon aware that he was being followed by police cars. He pulled over and, within seconds, felt the barrel of a lawman's Winchester rifle pressed firmly against his head. Roy said:

> A crowd gathered around and I couldn't get an explanation for what had happened. Plus, we had a jar full of pot all rolled pretty for us. They put us in the patrol car, and I said, "Well, what about my car?" He said, "Don't worry, we're going to search your car." When we got to the courthouse, this little boy came out and pointed to Gabby, so Gabby was the only one they took away. They didn't search the car. Oh, was I relieved![5]

The band made its way to New York, arriving without a pianist, but Roy contacted his old friend Clyde Hart, who immediately filled the vacancy. Any misunderstandings that Roy had with the management of the Savoy Ballroom were smoothed over, since the Falk–Kibbler Agency negotiated a deal that led to Roy and the band beginning a four-week engagement there, starting on August 6, 1938. The event was noted by *Swing* magazine, which in its September 1938 issue commented, "Roy is doing great business at the Savoy." That same month *Orchestra World* said that the band "laid the cats in the aisle." Roy also guested on the popular radio show *Saturday Swing Session*. It seemed as though he was being recognized as a successful bandleader, but the dispute over his contract still clouded the air, with Sam Beers threatening an injunction that would prevent the band from working. In September 1938 *Orchestra World* reported: "Roy Eldridge is in the midst of a legal tangle over management, and is trying to avoid a legal trial over a previous contract." At this point the all-powerful booking agent Joe Glaser (who had come to some sort of deal with his old Chicago associate Sam Beers) entered Roy's life, having apparently brushed aside any claims that the Falk–Kibbler Agency had. Roy recalled:

> Joe Glaser came in to the Savoy one night to listen to me...[He] told me to be at his office at ten o'clock one morning, and I told him "I won't be there. I don't want nobody to book me." He said, "You be there, or you won't work around New York."[6]

Rather than make an immediate decision about Glaser's "offer," Roy took an eight-piece band to play some dates in Massachusetts for the Shribman Brothers, who were prominent band-bookers in New England. Among these engagements was a performance at a Harvard freshmen's "Smoker," which led to the students suggesting that Roy be awarded a "Doctor of Jazz" degree, an idea that the University administrators opposed.[7] While playing the engagements in Massachusetts (some of which were opposite Vaughn Monroe's Band), Roy was contacted by Mal Hallett, whose band had "cut" Speed Webb's Band years earlier. Hallett, who had never forgotten Roy's amazing playing, was leaving New England temporarily to play some dates in New York. Realizing that Roy's presence would greatly strengthen his personnel, he offered him the chance to guest with his band. Roy jumped at the opportunity, and got Max Kaminsky to front the octet for the remainder of their New England dates. Thus Mal Hallett became the first white bandleader to employ Roy Eldridge. It was only a temporary arrangement, but one that Roy looked back on with pleasure. However, soon after they reached the Palace Theater in New York, Roy received a wire from the Musicians' Union saying that if he didn't sign up with Joe Glaser (who had apparently bought Roy's contract from Sam Beers) he wouldn't be allowed to work. The threat was "They'd tear up my card, well, that's politics, you know," said Roy.[8] The ultimatum meant that he had to leave Mal Hallett.

Roy was so disheartened by this turn of events that he seriously thought of quitting the music business in order to become a radio engineer. He had always been fascinated by the insides of radio sets and had shown himself adept at repairing them. He enrolled in a correspondence course run by the National Radio Institute and achieved good marks on the initial test papers, but the pull of playing the trumpet eclipsed Roy's need for security and he gave up the radio studies, a decision he said (in later years) he always regretted. Through all the uncertainties Roy managed to keep his chops in shape by playing at jam sessions and at the Sunday morning breakfast dances held at Smalls' Paradise. He was certainly in top form on recordings he made in November 1938 with his former sidekick Chu Berry for the Commodore label. During that same month Roy met the noted French jazz critic, Hugues Panassié, who was visiting New York. Panassié heard Roy play, but was only partially impressed, saying he either played numbers too fast or too slow. The two men conversed about jazz, with Roy denigrating New Orleans jazz and mounting his hobby-horse about not liking Southern trumpet-players. Some days later, Roy (taking pianist Clyde Hart with him for moral support) visited Panassié's New York hotel, taking with him a batch of new recordings that he felt supported his argument. Forty years later, Roy could still recall the heat of the ensuing discussion, which was fueled by the arrival of Sidney Bechet who enthusiastically took the Frenchman's side. Neither party would give way, and Bechet concluded his side of the argument by growling, "And Louis Armstrong can play some too!"[9]

As 1938 ended Roy realized there was no chance of him selecting his own agent, so he signed a seven-year contract with Joe Glaser's Consolidated Radio Artists of 30 Rockefeller Plaza, New York (the company later became the Associated Booking Corporation). Through working in Chicago, Roy knew a lot about Joe Glaser's activities in that city, well aware that when Louis Armstrong returned from Europe in 1935 it wasn't long before Glaser became his manager and, in so doing, severed most of his direct connections with the Chicago and ballroom scenes before moving to New York. Glaser represented Armstrong for the next thirty-four years, during which period Glaser's empire grew until eventually he represented many of the jazz world's top attractions (as well as boxers such as Sugar Ray Robinson and cabaret star Noël Coward). By signing Roy Eldridge (and Hot Lips Page), Glaser effectively controlled the destiny of two contenders for Louis Armstrong's trumpet "crown"; Glaser already had Henry "Red" Allen working in Armstrong's Big Band. When people attempted to book Armstrong on dates that he was working, Glaser did his best to sell them the services of one of the younger stars, but Roy saw a more sinister motive: "Joe Glaser signed both me and Hot Lips Page, but I swear he did it to keep us under wraps and away from Louis, who was having a little lip trouble then."[10] For all the dislike that Glaser engendered, he remained a very skillful agent and booker, and through his services Roy soon signed a contract to take his own ten-piece band into a residency at New York's Arcadia Ballroom (at 53rd and Broadway) which began in January 1939.[11] The Arcadia didn't threaten the Savoy's scale of pay, or its musical policy; it was more staid than the Harlem ballroom, its air-cooled atmosphere being a far cry from the vibrancy of "The Track," but at least the residency kept the band together, even if they were expected to play tangos, Viennese waltzes, rhumbas, and slow foxtrots. The only time that unrestrained improvising was tolerated at the Arcadia was on Sunday nights, and these sessions were usually transmitted on N.B.C. radio. But those jazz fans who heard the torrid side of Roy's band on the Sunday broadcasts and then visited the ballroom on a week-night were in for a disappointment, unless they also liked novelty dances and old-time ballroom favorites. The Arcadia's regulars were confused by the Sunday offerings, and Roy wryly observed, "Nobody danced when we played jazz."[12]

Roy's ten-piece line-up featured some of his former Chicago sidemen (including his brother Joe) fortified by a few New York-based musicians such as tenorist Ben Webster. But Ben was going through a harum-scarum period of his life which involved dodging the bailiff, so he soon left (and later joined Teddy Wilson's Band). Ben was replaced by Roy's former tenor-man Franz Jackson. Eli Robinson, who had been with Roy in Speed Webb's Band, was on trombone, and another ex-colleague Prince Robinson specialized on clarinet. Bobby Williams was on trumpet and the rhythm section consisted of Clyde Hart on piano, John Collins on guitar, Ted Sturgis on bass, and Bill Beason on drums. Later, the band was augmented by the addition of Reunald Jones. When he left his place was taken by Carl "Bama" Warwick. The band's three principal arrangers were Don Redman, Joe Eldridge, and Franz Jackson (Redman usually also directed rehearsals of the saxophone section). Franz Jackson spoke to Alyn Shipton about his stay at the Arcadia:

> You liked to play for Roy because he was always exciting. It was nice to work with him; he accepted anything that was good. If it was good it stayed in. We all contributed, it didn't make any difference, the thing was—did it work? If someone played a good riff, or did a great ending, Roy would say, "Keep it in." It was good because it encouraged you to play.[13]

Charles Graham, who became a lifelong friend of Roy, first met him at the Arcadia Ballroom during a visit to New York in the summer of 1939. Graham had the foresight to pay the Veritone recording studio on Broadway to take down, on disk, several of the numbers the band broadcast. They show how lively the aggregation was, with Roy's trumpet scorching a path through some zestful arrangements.

Franz Jackson pointed out that Roy developed a technique of playing across the radio microphone (rather than directly into it); and this allowed him to blow as hard as he liked—it being difficult to blow very high notes when playing softly. Jackson said, "He could get all his range out; that was really the key to his playing on air."[14] Although Roy had no problems in thinking up new themes, he never became an arranger. He told Dan Morgenstern:

> I never had any eyes for that. I almost got into that when I was in the Arcadia. I wrote an introduction on something, I used to get high and borrow this (manuscript) paper and I got more four bars or eight bars written down than anybody in the world, but that's as far as I could get.

Roy did have time to sing on some of his radio shows, however, and on one occasion (in a mad moment) decided to warble "Ah. Sweet mystery of life, at last I've found you." This prompted his sister-in-law to send him a cryptic cablegram: "Don't Sing. Play!"[15]

Bill Beason was Roy's original choice as drummer for the Arcadia band, but just as the unit was taking shape the bandleader-percussionist Chick Webb was taken seriously ill, so Bill Beason departed to act as Chick's "sub" and stand-by. Kenny Clarke, Roy's Pittsburgh colleague of early days, helped out, but didn't take the job permanently. Agent-manager Joe Glaser suggested that the vacancy might be filled by Sid Catlett, who was unsettled within Louis Armstrong's Big Band. But Catlett didn't even contact Roy to discuss the issue, so Roy began auditioning various drummers including the young David Francis, whom Roy had heard playing at a jam session (Francis having already gained useful experience with Billy Hicks and his Sizzling Six). Francis reminisced:

> I was asked "Would you like to play with my band?" I said, "What's the name of your band?", and he says "I'm Roy Eldridge." I almost dropped on the floor! Roy was at zenith then. He says "We're playing at the Arcadia ballroom and

rehearsals are Tuesday at one o'clock. Joe Glaser, who was Roy's manager, had hired Sid Catlett to join the band. When Joe Glaser walked in he looked up and asked Roy, "Where's Big Sid?" and Roy says "I don't know." Glaser said "Who's that drummer up there?" and I guess Roy didn't remember my name, but I still had my Panama hat on. He says, "Oh, that's Panama." I was too scared to tell the fellows in the band that wasn't my name, and they started calling me "Panama." One thing that Roy did for me I later much appreciated. During intermissions he made me go in the next room and practice on my practice pad. I wanted to be out there with the rest of the guys and I was angry about it, but I respected him and I practiced. He helped me and showed me a lot of things about the drums, he played very good drums himself.[16]

Surprisingly, Roy buckled down to the Arcadia's highly commercial dictates, and the month's trial blossomed into a six-month residency. Roy continued to sing occasionally, but regularly featured his new vocalist Laurel Watson, who had previously sung with Don Redman's Orchestra. Laurel had her own devoted following, among them the jazz writer Leonard Feather, who said in his 1986 book *The Jazz Years*, "Of all the young singers, Laurel Watson, remains in my memory as one of the most wrongly neglected." Looking back sixty years, Laurel said: "It was a good band and the audience responded to Roy's playing and to his personality. He treated me like a queen, and never got worried if anyone in the band got a lot of applause."[17]

Franz Jackson made the same point: "Roy never got jealous if one of his sidemen got a big hand. Everybody got on fine, it was a good atmosphere and there was no 'I am this, and I am that' so there was no need for a 'straw boss' telling you what to do."[18]

When the band's initial stay at the Arcadia ended it played for a week at Harlem's most celebrated theater, the Apollo. The band received enthusiastic receptions there but long-term prospects were not looking good. The July 1939 issue of *Metronome* noted that the band "had nothing after its Apollo booking." Franz Jackson said, "The trouble was that we just couldn't make a hit record. You only needed one to carry you around for a long time."[19] The recordings that Roy's band made in 1939 were mostly received with indifference; "Gordon Wright," a pseudonym for George T. Simon, reviewing the disks in *Metronome*, said that the band was "sloppy," though he was enthusiastic about the individual talents of Roy, Franz Jackson, and Laurel Watson. Happily, the Arcadia management soon rebooked Roy's band for another residency, which they started after doing some out-of-town dates including two days in Akron, Ohio. Roy and Joe's spirits were boosted when their composition *Pluckin' The Bass* was recorded by Cab Calloway's Orchestra in August 1939; two months later Roy recorded the tune with his own band. The only major personnel change in the band came late that year when pianist Clyde Hart began suffering health problems. His place was taken by Kenny Kersey.

Roy continued to accept the commercial regime at the Arcadia because he was able to make up his quota of jazz-blowing at jam sessions, here, there, and everywhere—being a bandleader didn't alter his willingness to play jazz for nothing.

Trumpeter Jimmy Maxwell (soon to be featured with Benny Goodman) had recently arrived in New York when he paid his first visit to the Arcadia:

> Roy Eldridge was playing at a ten-cents-a-dance ballroom. I introduced myself and he was wonderful to me. He had an hour's break and took me Uptown to the Symphonic Chord Club in Harlem, an after hours club, open from 10 p.m. to 10 a.m. He introduced me to Lester Young and Big Sid Catlett. After his job was over Roy came up to see if I was alright, and to find out if they were letting me play, and we became good friends.[20]

One particular jam session in 1939 placed Roy alongside Coleman Hawkins, who had recently returned to New York after a five-year sojourn in Europe. Roy recalled:

It was the first time I'd played with Coleman, and my he really played; we stayed out until 2 o'clock the next afternoon. Coleman had been my idol since I was 12. He hadn't heard me play live, but he said he had heard records I'd made while he was in Europe. He said he liked what I was doing because I was playing more legato than the other trumpeters around.[21]

The session took place at Puss Johnson's Tavern at 130th and St. Nicholas in Harlem where a number of musicians turned up, either to welcome Hawkins back or to blow against him. Among them was tenorist Lester Young (by then known as Prez—short for the President). Inevitably a battle took place between Hawk and Prez, the outcome of which has always been in dispute. What is certain is that the session marked the beginning of Roy's long and productive association with Coleman Hawkins:

Lester Young and Charlie Shavers stood on one side and myself and Coleman stood the other. There was no big plan, we just stood where we found ourselves, it was that casual, but later on people made it a big deal that we had planned to blow together, but that wasn't so. Coleman took everything out that night. He came up with new things nobody had heard. He liked my playing, so right away we fell in with each other.[22]

By dropping in to jam sessions at many venues, Roy made sure that his lip was always ready for any freelance recordings or radio dates that came his way. He didn't mind how unglamorous the surroundings were. Writer Benny Hoff went with guitarist Teddy Bunn to a back-street club not far from 125th Street in Harlem, where Bunn joined the resident pianist and bassist for an informal session. Hoff reported:

Just as things were getting warmed up, who should walk in but Roy Eldridge. Within minutes of Roy's arrival the police raided the joint, causing the musicians to leave the building. They were soon informed that they could return into the club, and the session resumed as though nothing had happened.[23]

Teddy Bunn was brimful of praise for Roy's skills, and told Hoff that he considered Roy to be the greatest living trumpet-player:

> Sure Louis can play wonderful horn if he wants. But then I guess I have to class him along with King Oliver and those others from New Orleans. Roy has started in where those other guys left off. Both Louis and the King were pioneers and they had to wait a long time for recognition. I guess maybe it'll be the same way for Roy.[24]

Roy never turned down the chance of a jam session and was happy to be part of a get-together for Bud Freeman's opening at Kelly's Stable. Claude Thornhill was on piano and Floyd O'Brien on trombone. Also present was trumpeter Bunny Berigan, for whom Roy had the highest respect. Roy remembered that night:

> Bunny was just about able to stagger on to the bandstand, he was as drunk as I'd ever seen him, but to my amazement he blew his trumpet as well as I ever heard him. Nobody could top what he did that night.[25]

Roy described Berigan as "The best white trumpet player I ever heard. Bunny played with real soul, a fine sense of chord changes and an individual style and tone."[26]

By early 1940 Roy's band was coming to the end of its further stay at the Arcadia, but it was encouraged by an offer to play at the huge, newly opened Golden Gate Ballroom (in late 1939 during the first ten days of its existence this New York dance-hall drew 33,000 people). During the gap between finishing at the Arcadia and playing at the Golden Gate, Roy played on a number of freelance recordings, including dates with Mildred Bailey and with Billie Holiday as well as four sides with the white bandleader Freddie Rich. At this period of his life Roy usually made freelance recordings as a sideman for the normal Musicians' Union scale of $24 for a three-hour session and $12 an hour overtime.[27] If the music was good, the money was incidental to Roy, and he always regarded his sessions with Mildred as among his best. For her part, Mildred was always delighted when Roy was available to play on her sessions, and cited one of the sides she made with him, *Don't Take Your Love From Me*, as her favorite recording. Roy also liked most of the sides he recorded with Billie Holiday, but pointed out that many of Billie's recordings from this period used written arrangements, with the outlines for solos sketched out on paper. However, in May 1940, Roy took part in a session that was a model of spontaneity, the recorded results of which were issued as by The Chocolate Dandies. The music the group produced was some of the most imaginative and scintillating jazz of that era. Roy's colleagues on this occasion were Coleman Hawkins, Benny Carter, Bernard Addison on guitar, Sid Catlett on drums, and John Kirby on bass—all the participants were ex-Fletcher Henderson sidemen. The level of invention is breath-taking throughout, and on *I Can't Believe That You Are In Love With Me*, Benny Carter plays a plus-perfect alto-sax solo. Roy, sharing a front line with his two boyhood heroes, sounds totally inspired.

Unfortunately, Roy's band didn't stay long at the Golden Gate Ballroom. It began there on March 2, 1940 and ended after a month. The ballroom itself didn't last much longer and was taken over by the Savoy "group" in May 1940. Roy's memories of his final days there consisted of his collecting the band's wages in coins. The audience's response to Roy's band at the Golden Gate was never overwhelming, one of the reasons being that the group was midway between a big band, usually fourteen pieces, and a small combo. In this era almost every bandleader was being urged by ballroom operators to adopt a bigger-the-better strategy (though few of these bookers showed any inclination to pay for the extra musicians employed). Roy pondered on whether to gamble everything on increasing the size of his band, but decided against it, being well aware that several top jazz instrumentalists (including Bunny Berigan and Jack Teagarden) had bankrupted themselves in trying to pay for the arrangements, publicity, uniforms, music stands, agency fees, and transportation costs involved in the running of a big band. Roy left New York and played briefly with his usual line-up at the Grand Terrace in Chicago before deciding to disband. He told Joe Glaser of this decision. Glaser simply shrugged and promptly fixed Roy with a small band booking at Kelly's Stable, New York (a club then situated at 137 West 52nd Street)–there was no Kelly: the club was named after a successful Chicago night-spot.

Roy opened at Kelly's on April 25, 1940, opposite Billie Holiday, whose recently successful recording of *Strange Fruit* had further enhanced her career. Leo Watson, a celebrated, zany singer, was also on the bill, but, even so, the club was packed only at weekends. Kelly's operated without a cover charge, with a $1 minimum charge (a beer there cost 50 cents). Roy recalled the quiet nights:

> Sometimes when it got a little slow, me and Billie would get in my car and we'd go around to different joints. Billie would say, "Come on, little brother, let's go." And the cat says, "Well, wait a minute, you've got another set to play."[28]

Blues singer Joe Turner was briefly added to the bill at Kelly's and rehearsed with Roy's band at the Eldridge home. Joe was one of the blues singers who impressed Roy. He particularly liked his sound, but when Roy spoke of Jimmy Rushing, he said, "I love him, but I didn't think he was a real blues singer."[29] A blues singer who Roy greatly admired was James "Kokomo" Arnold, whom he had regularly heard in Chicago. Billie Holiday temporarily moved out of Kelly's to play other engagements fixed for her by Joe Glaser, allowing pianist-singer Una Mae Carlisle and her Trio to make up the bill. But even in the "Golden Era" of New York club life there were many nights when business was slow. Writer Leonard Feather visited Kelly's on one such occasion in June 1940 and found Roy playing piano while pianist

Kenny Kersey blew some "swell trumpet."[30] The full line-up of Roy's band at Kelly's was Roy, Joe Eldridge, Kenny Kersey, Ted Sturgis on double-bass, John Collins on guitar, and Kenny Clarke on drums. White tenorist George Auld sat in so often with the band that people thought he was part of the group. During his stay at Kelly's, Roy was regularly asked if he was related to vocalist Jean Eldridge (who recorded with Teddy Wilson and Duke Ellington). He was not: Jean hailed from Buffalo, New York.

Musicians who wanted to sit in at Kelly's were not automatically encouraged to do so, but certain illustrious players were always welcome, including two young men who were then in the forefront of jazz developments: guitarist Charlie Christian and bassist Jimmy Blanton. In describing an occasion when both these brilliant musicians sat in together, Roy said, "They swung so much. I felt so good I had to stop playing."[31] However, despite the inspired music that was played at Kelly's, the money available for the performers' wages was negligible. Packed to capacity, the club held only a hundred customers. Much as Roy enjoyed the atmosphere at Kelly's he was well aware that financially he was worse off than he had been when working with Cecil Scott when he first arrived in New York, almost ten years earlier. The white bandleader Charlie Barnet became aware of Roy's situation and made him an attractive financial offer that Eldridge decided to accept. As a result, several newspapers published news items during the summer of 1940 hinting that Roy was about to join Barnet. The *Chicago Defender* reported, "Eldridge and Barnet both confirmed that as far as they were concerned the deal was all set."[32] But Joe Glaser intervened, pointing out forcibly that Roy was still under contract to him. So Barnet (a pioneer in breaking down racial barriers, who had hired trumpeter Frankie Newton years before) left New York to go on a tour that he had hoped would feature Roy Eldridge. Another opening was offered to Roy by Cootie Williams, who was about to leave Duke Ellington to join Benny Goodman. He suggested to Duke that Roy should take his place, but Roy declined the opportunity. He spoke of this later:

I had my own little band in Kelly's. I was pretty happy with them, so I didn't make it, yet I would have loved to have played with Duke. Of course I've played with Duke in joints and clubs and places, but not with the band. It's a ball to play after-hours with Duke behind you, he gives you a wonderful background. I dig him as a person. Play with him and you don't need drums, for he really knows how to back a cat.[33]

This was truly the age of the all-star jam session. The keenness of players (many of them already famous) to blow jazz for nothing was a feature of that romantic era. Several big impromptu sessions took place on stage at New York's Apollo Theater, none more illustrious than the line-up that gathered to commemorate Coleman Hawkins' Big Band opening there. Roy, Bunny Berigan, Gene Krupa, Pete Brown, Tommy Dorsey, Jack Jenney, Count Basie, Joe Marsala, and Carmen Mastren all turned out for the daytime clambake. Harry James arrived late, and, according to a contemporary report, "had to step forward before the curtain and play about six choruses unaccompanied."[34] The participants were so delighted to be in this jam session that they accepted an invitation from D.J. Martin Block to reassemble at the W.N.E.W. radio studios and begin blowing again for his *Make Believe Ballroom* show. Airshots were recorded of that gathering, and although they were not hi-fi they show that Roy was the star of the event—accordingly his reputation moved up a notch or two. Roy maintained that he was ultra-nervous on big occasions, but no one could have guessed this by the way he played at a W. C. Handy Tribute Concert held at Carnegie Hall in 1940, when, according to *Swing* magazine, he drew "six encores for his sensational solos." He was equally outstanding at a New York Hippodrome "Swing Concert." As a result of Roy's growing eminence, he was invited by E. B. Marks Music in New York to record his improvisations on half-a-dozen old standards, including *Jazz Me Blues* and *Ida, Sweet As Apple Cider*. What he played was then transcribed and published (in 1940) as "Special arrangements by Roy Eldridge, The All-American Trumpeter."

Roy's long stay at Kelly's ended on September 11, 1940. A couple of weeks later the band did a week at the Apollo as part of a bill that included Billie Holiday and Butterbeans and Susie. The band left New York to play a series of one-nighters through the Midwest, also playing a booking at the Regal Theater, Chicago. When the musicians returned to New York, most of them were eager to relax, but not Roy. He had no immediate work for the band so he played, as he had done in the past, anywhere he could. To keep his chops in shape he took a job with his former sideman, drummer Zutty Singleton, who was leading a trio at the Village Vanguard (with Don Frye on piano). This sort of behavior exasperated Joe Glaser. He was doing his best to build Roy into an up-and-coming star bandleader, but Roy negated Glaser's efforts by being willing (and indeed eager) to play as a sideman for a few bucks a night in what Glaser called "some crummy tavern." Roy even tried going out as a "single," playing trumpet, drums, piano, and tenor-sax in a sort of cabaret act, but Glaser wisely pointed out that this would in no way help get bookings for the band. So the experiment ended, but I got the impression that Roy really enjoyed this interlude: he cheerfully recalled, "I could only play the sax in B flat, but I could swing."[35] Glaser's publicity department did its best to elevate Roy's status by getting him mentioned in various magazines. This led to him being asked by *Music and Rhythm* such riddles as: "Which is more important, showmanship or musicianship?" (Roy chose musicianship.) The same magazine asked Roy and several others: "What do musicians think of the Communists?" Roy (in January 1941) replied: "It's got a veil over it. It doesn't come out in the open. How can I tell you anything about Communism when I don't know anything about it. For all I hear it's un-American, and if it is, I'm against it."

6

CRUSADING
WITH KRUPA

By 1941 there were many young trumpeters who modeled their playing on Roy Eldridge's style, but none came anywhere near creating a perfect copy, except for Dizzy Gillespie, who openly admitted learning Roy's recorded solos note for note after they had been written out for him by saxophonist Howard "Swan" Johnson—Dizzy enthusiastically started each day by listening to Eldridge's recording of *After You've Gone*. Roy first became aware of the skillful young copyist when he heard recordings that Gillespie made with Teddy Hill's Orchestra; Dizzy said, "When I joined Teddy Hill's Band I could play all of Roy's solos exactly as he had played them."[1] On *Hot Mallets*, a side that Gillespie made in 1939 as part of a Lionel Hampton small group, Roy initially thought it was a recording that he himself had forgotten making, so convincing was Dizzy's imitation. Later, Roy said, "Dizzy used to play exactly like me, so too did Charlie Shavers. When I came back from Chicago there'd be four or five of them cats, all of them knew my records."[2] On another occasion Roy named the quintet of disciples as Gillespie, Carl "Bama" Warwick, Bobby Moore, Joe Guy, and Charlie Shavers. Countless other trumpeters were inspired by Roy's revolutionary approach, even if they didn't directly copy his phrases. Count Basie's trumpeter

Shad Collins was particularly influenced by Roy's playing at this time, as was Emmett Berry, and Joe Newman (who worked with Lionel Hampton and Count Basie), who said: "I idolised Roy Eldridge so much that when I first played with Lionel Hampton I had Roy's picture pasted on the bell of my horn, where I could look at it while I was playing."[3]

Roy's ideas formed the foundations of a new style of "modern" trumpet-playing. Trumpeter Bernard "Buddy" Anderson told Frank Driggs of a 1941 meeting with Fats Navarro (destined to be one of the leading be-bop trumpet-players): "Roy Eldridge was Fats Navarro's idol then, and his own style was based on Roy's to some extent. I told him that Dizzy Gillespie was soon going to run Roy out of the picture, and Fats turned away from me in utter disgust."[4]

Joe Wilder, who starred with Lionel Hampton, told Ed Berger, "I think we should all bow our heads to Roy because he's the one that made us take risks playing the trumpet. He did things that nobody would ever dare to do." Pianist-arranger Milt Buckner recalled the influence Roy had on Clark Terry's early career: "I saw Clark in Illinois in 1940 when he was playing everything that Roy Eldridge played, in fact I wrote out some solos for him that Roy Eldridge played."[5] Others who regarded Roy as a musical hero included Snooky Young (of Jimmie Lunceford's Band), who said, "I thought a lot of Roy Eldridge," and Joe Gordon, who confirmed, "My first real influence was Roy Eldridge." Kenny Dorham cited Roy as a role model, and Maynard Ferguson, then a 13-year-old in Montreal, Canada, featured a transcribed version of Roy's recording of *After You've Gone.*

But it wasn't only trumpeters who were inspired by Roy's playing. Two musicians who became important figures in the development of jazz spoke of Eldridge's influence: trombonist J. J. Johnson said, "My original influences were Prez and Roy," and tenorist Dexter Gordon revealed, "I used to get almost the same thing listening to Roy as I did listening to Lester Young."[6] The series of advertisements for Martin trumpets, complete with a photograph of Roy, helped stoke up the interest that Eldridge was creating among fellow musicians. The advertisements contained some bold copy: "Roy is the one-man phenomenon of the music business. Musicians hearing him for the first time invariably come away mumbling, 'It isn't true. You just can't do those things on a trumpet.'"[7]

But despite this adulation and the widespread counterfeiting of his phrases, Roy's prospect of becoming the leader of a successful big band were no nearer. He returned to Chicago where he led his own small group (from December 1, 1940) for a residency at the Capitol Cocktail Lounge (run by Milton Schwarz and Al Greenfield). The Capitol was thought of by the Loop locals as being the successor to the Three Deuces, though it was slightly more formal, with the band dressed in tuxedos. Certainly many of Roy's old fans from the Three Deuces came to hear him at the Capitol, and they liked what they heard, which was a five-piece line-up consisting of Roy, his former sideman tenorist Dave Young, John Simmons on double-bass, and two young musicians who had recently been in Walter Fuller's Band, pianist Rozelle Claxton and drummer Kansas Fields. For part of the residency, Ray Walters took Rozelle Claxton's place. Kansas Fields described the management's attitude at the Capitol:

> They would tell you what you could do and couldn't do in regards to association—associating with the white section of the clientele. It was a good band. Roy wanted to take us to New York, but he couldn't get the money straight.[8]

The booking at the Capitol was extended into 1941, but Roy's long-term prospects looked no better than they had a year earlier. However, Roy's old friend drummer Gene Krupa was about to offer him a life-changing opportunity. Krupa had finished his stint with Benny Goodman almost three years earlier and was now one of the foremost bandleaders of the era. Krupa's Band played at the Hotel Sherman in Chicago during late 1940 and Gene often visited the Capitol (with his wife Ethel and manager Frank Verniere) after he'd finished his sets. Sometimes Roy went off with Gene to find a night-spot on the South Side where they could jam and eat ribs. During this Chicago stay Roy, as ever, was always game for an "after-work" blow, and when Cab Calloway's Band was in town he greatly enjoyed jamming at the Du Sable Hotel with his old sidekick Chu Berry (sadly, not long after these sessions, Chu lost his life in an automobile accident). Roy took no rest on Sundays; he usually played at jam sessions organized by Harry Lim. During Krupa's Chicago stay, his trumpeter Clarence "Shorty" Sherock had to miss a couple of dates and Gene was delighted when Roy agreed to deputize. Krupa had always been a fan of Roy's playing, but his admiration increased when he felt the degree of swing that Roy's musical presence brought to the band. Krupa, encouraged by Shorty Sherock's enthusiasm for the idea, decided to offer Roy a permanent place with the band. Roy was thrilled to receive the invitation but pointed out that he was still under contract to Joe Glaser, who would have to approve the deal; Roy had also taken the lease on an apartment at 55th and Michigan. *Metronome* magazine must have been well abreast of the situation: a small news item in its November 1940 issue was headed "Eldridge for Krupa?" Meanwhile, Roy played through to the end of his booking at the Capitol Lounge, prior to beginning a four-week stint at the Blatz Club in Milwaukee (from February 26, 1941). When that was completed Roy disbanded and moved back to New York, prior to playing a split-week in Providence, Rhode Island, as a guest star with Gene Krupa. Things went well, so Roy decided to request formally that Joe Glaser release him from his contract, but Glaser insisted that Krupa would have to pay for the five years that were left on the agreement which Roy had signed with him in 1938. Roy went to the White Rose Bar in New York and relayed this information to Krupa's manager, who told Roy that Gene didn't want to pay for the contract. After further negotiations, Glaser agreed to sell the contract back to Roy for $1000—the amount to be paid in installments from money taken from Roy's wages with Krupa.

Roy was now at liberty to become a full-time member of Gene's Band. He did so by joining the outfit for their six-week residency at

New York's Hotel Pennsylvania, beginning in April 1941. Roy's wages were $150 a week, $25 more than he had been making with his own quintet in Chicago. Roy was happy with the deal, but realistically pointed out, "I turned out to be the big thing for the band."[9] Swing fans were absolutely delighted by Roy's move, as were the musicians in Krupa's Band. According to Canadian trumpeter Graham Young (then only 19 years old) the band had recently been taken apart in a "Battle of the Bands" with Jimmie Lunceford's Orchestra at a ballroom in Baltimore:

> We lost terribly. There had been talk about hiring Roy Eldridge but the officials at M.C.A., who ran the band at the time, were afraid of the public reaction of having a black person sitting in a white band. However, after the Lunceford fiasco, Gene just hired Roy the next day and didn't ask M.C.A.[10]

The only disgruntled note came from the *Chicago Defender*'s columnist Al Monroe, who, under a heading "Roy Eldridge Turns Ofay to Hook up with Gene Krupa," wrote:

> Fletcher Henderson and Roy Eldridge both had bands and broke them up to accept positions with the outfits with which they now travel. This meant that many musicians were thrown out of work. Raiding bands is new to the profession. It means more money, perhaps, for a few musicians, but will this offset the harm it does to our name Negro bands?[11]

At the time, Roy commented, "While I was happy leading my own band, I found I had limitations, and at times it was tough keeping the men together."[12] Graham Young (who became a lifelong friend of Roy) spoke of Eldridge's stay in Krupa's Band:

> Roy was a wonderful man and he said he wouldn't join the band if it meant any of the trumpet players had to get fired, so

he came on as a feature. No arrangements were written for him at that time, he had to take some of the jazz solos that Shorty Sherock had been playing. After a while, Shorty flipped and got mad at Roy (not at Gene), so Shorty was gone. Roy sat next to me, he was a great guy and inventive. Every night was a jazz lesson, and it was like that for a year and a half.[13]

It wasn't only the band's trumpeters who benefited from Roy's arrival; the rhythm section also felt they had been given a huge lift by Eldridge's playing. Bassist Ovid "Biddy" Bastien emphasized this, saying:

Back in 1940, I met Roy through pianist Tony D'Amore: we were both with Gene Krupa and Roy invited us up to his apartment in Harlem for a jam session. We had a great time musically and socially, so it was a pleasure to welcome him into Gene's band. Shorty Sherock was also a real good pal of mine, but he knew he wasn't the jazz trumpeter that Roy was; he tried to play like Roy but to my ears it came out more like Ziggy Elman.[14]

Shorty Sherock was a great fan of Roy's playing, and took his admiration to the point where he had his suits made in the same style as Roy, he ordered the same type of spectacles, and bought the same model of car that Roy drove (a La Salle convertible). He was delighted to have made a private recording with Roy, together with pianist Tony D'Amore and Lloyd Hundling (a trumpeter and vocalist with Charlie Barnet's Band, who lost his life in August 1941 as a result of the car crash that killed guitarist Bus Etri). Roy said the acetate recordings were made at his apartment "just for fun," and the only title he could remember was *The Sheik Of Araby*. Shorty Sherock's then wife was Jean Bach, who said:

Shorty certainly idolized Roy's playing, and took inspiration from it, so much so that trumpeter Bobby Burnet commented on the fact, which led Shorty to say, "When I change, I change all the way." Shorty was very likable, a darling blond teddy bear, and he kept suggesting that Gene hire Roy. But when Roy played in the band Gene found himself thinking, "This is the real thing," and though Gene was a decent, sweet guy he didn't feel like keeping Roy and Shorty, so Shorty left. He was getting $85 a week then, but had already drawn his wages in advance. Roy and Shorty certainly didn't become enemies; in fact their friendship stayed as before. But Roy, who I'd known since Three Deuces days, asked me one day "How's Shorty?" When I told him he was fine, Roy said, to my surprise, "But like all ofays he turned."[15]

At the heart of the problem was the fact that Roy was allocated a lot of what had been Shorty's solo spots, and naturally Shorty, who had less and less to play, became vexed. After suffering for five nights at the Café Rouge section of the Hotel Pennsylvania, Shorty launched into an altercation with Krupa's manager Frank Verniere, and ended his association with the Krupa Band (he left and soon joined Tommy Dorsey). From this point on Roy ceased to be a featured attraction out-front of the band, and instead took his place in the four-piece trumpet section. Roy was still known as "Little Jazz," but his new colleagues admiringly called him "Leather Lip" (a name that Joe Marsala had originally used about Roy) because of his stamina, range, and power. Gene Krupa summed up the esteem that he, and his musicians, felt: "Roy became our spark plug. Every time he played it was like a light going on in a dark room."[16] Roy and Gene shared a relaxed friendship that was apparent both on and off the stage. Critic Barry Ulanov commented on the band's stay at the Hotel Pennsylvania:

> Roy Eldridge is almost singly responsible for making the Gene Krupa Band the fine outfit it is today. His volatile personality and incredibly versatile trumpeting have sparked the band to a point where it can truly be said to be coming on.[17]

But joining Gene Krupa, and playing for long hours in the trumpet section, as well as being extensively featured, didn't mean that Roy gave up sitting in elsewhere; he was still always on the look-out for places to blow after hours. During the Krupa Band's residency at the Hotel Pennsylvania he sat in at various New York clubs including Minton's Playhouse, a club based in the Hotel Cecil at 210 West 118th Street, where Roy's former bandleader Teddy Hill had recently become manager. Until then the club had not been regarded as one of the liveliest music spots. It was described as "a gathering place for old men"; Teddy Hill's arrival changed all that. Henry Minton was a former saxophone-player who became a Musicians' Union official, but despite this he actively encouraged Hill's policy of inviting musicians to sit in. Teddy Hill hired a resident rhythm section of piano, bass, and drums, then asked various of his ex-sidemen to drop in whenever they felt like it, to blow, and to enjoy a few free drinks and a free meal. This wasn't a huge gesture, because drinks were only 20 cents a shot and the DeLuxe dinner could be bought for 60 cents. Nevertheless, the ex-sidemen came, as did young musicians, who liked the new atmosphere at Minton's, and as a result the jam sessions thrived. Among those who appeared there were Roy and the new trend-setter, Dizzy Gillespie. Guitarist Les Paul described a night at Minton's, with Roy playing "like a bat out of hell. Everybody in the joint is going crazy. Dizzy Gillespie came in there to knock off Roy and Roy blew him away, and he said 'Well, I guess I'm not ready yet.' "[18] But Dizzy didn't feel totally vanquished and was soon taking part in further adversarial sessions with Roy. During this period, Roy said in an interview, "Dizzy started out playing more or less in my style, then developed a good personality of his own." Years later he commented, "He found his own thing, like I found my own thing and he made it."[19]

Gradually, Minton's attracted many of the young musicians who were developing the innovative jazz style that later became known as "be-bop." The club's resident pianist Thelonious Monk became a central figure in the movement, as did Roy's former drummer Kenny

Clarke, who acknowledged the help and musical guidance that Eldridge had given him:

> Roy had been important to me in my development in modern jazz. He encouraged me and when I was working out my ideas on modern jazz drumming I wanted to be original. I couldn't see copying any one. With Roy I got everything I'd been trying to do together. This was just before Minton's.[20]

One might think that Minton's would have been a favorite haven for Roy to blow in after hours, but it was not. Although Roy had been in the vanguard of jazz developments in the 1930s and early 1940s, like many other revolutionaries he did not welcome any drastic changes that seemed likely to supersede his achievements. Roy fairly bristled when anyone described him as a regular at Minton's, and said forcibly, "I hardly ever went there. It wasn't my scene, but because there was a photo of me, Monk, Howard McGhee, and Teddy Hill outside Minton's, people later thought I was always there, but I spent more time at Monroe's than I ever did at Minton's."[21] Monroe's was Clark Monroe's Uptown House at 198 West 134th, which stayed open until 9 or 10 a.m. Some musicians played at Minton's until it closed at 4 a.m. and then moved on to Monroe's. Charlie Parker, soon to be recognized as the leading "modernist," spoke of hearing Roy at that venue: "At Monroe's I'd listen to trumpet men like Lips Page, Roy Eldridge, Dizzy Gillespie and Charlie Shavers outblowing each other all night long."[22]

Roy's sensitivity discerned the changing atmosphere at Minton's. Dizzy Gillespie revealed in his autobiography (co-written with Al Fraser) that Roy had mixed feelings about Dizzy's growing eminence, a view supported by bassist Red Callender, who felt that Roy was originally hostile towards the younger Dizzy: "When Louis Armstrong first heard Dizzy, he put him down hard. Roy Eldridge resented Dizzy as well. They thought this guy is doing tricks. The respect came later."[23] Dizzy himself recalled this period:

Roy didn't treat me too well. Sometimes I'd meet him in front of the Three Deuces and say, "Hey, Roy." He'd make like he didn't hear me, and all the trumpeters were trying to play like me, instead of trying to play like him. Roy Eldridge is the most competitive musician I've ever seen. Roy used to come into places, and we're on the bandstand, the younger trumpeters, playing gentlemanly. He'd take out his horn at the door and start on a high B flat.[24]

There's no doubt that Roy's habit of bursting into a club session in order to outblow the trumpeters on stage sometimes caused ill feeling. Dizzy did his best to point this out to Eldridge:

Roy would hurt himself before he'd let you blow him out. One night we were standing outside a club and Roy said, "Come on, let's go inside and blow!" And I told him, "Roy, would you mind if *I* went in by myself and played a while first? 'Cause when *you* get up to play, you don't know how to act!"[25]

Gradually Gillespie's style moved assuredly away from Roy's influence. Drummer Kenny Clarke was on hand to observe the metamorphosis both in Dizzy's style and in the playing of jazz: "One night, after weeks of trying, Dizzy cut Roy Eldridge. It was one night out of many, but I think it meant a great deal. We closed ranks after that. To make things tough for outsiders we invented difficult riffs."[26]

Looking back, Dizzy was magnanimous about his various encounters with Roy:

When I was growing up, Eldridge was my boy. All I ever did was try and play like him, but I never quite made it. I'd get all messed up because I couldn't get it. So I tried something else, and that has developed into what became known as "bop."[27]

The same point was succinctly made by guitarist Steve Jordan: "Dizzy finally gave up trying to cut Roy at his own game (it was no contest) and wisely went on to develop his own distinctive style of jazz trumpet."[28]

It certainly wasn't the "battles" that Roy had with Dizzy at Minton's which turned him against the venue; it was simply that he hated feeling he was on the outside of a clique. Jesse Drakes, then an aspiring trumpeter (who later worked with Lester Young), observed how Roy kicked against the "bop" trends:

> I was born around the corner from Minton's Playhouse and I spent all my young life in that area. Professor Teddy Hill let us sit down as long as we didn't try to get a glass of beer. So I heard Roy Eldridge arguing with Thelonious Monk, trying to make Monk play um-cha comping. Walter Bishop and I would be sitting down in the corner and Monk's looking at Eldridge like he's nuts.[29]

Roy disliked what he considered to be the emphasis boppers placed on certain harmonic "tricks" (as he called them) and their use of the same devices over and over again. He also strongly objected to the bop drummers' use of the bass drum to punctuate the rhythm: "as for 'bombs' they don't belong with my kind of playing."[30] He was irked that one had to know the boppers' themes (usually based on standard chord sequences) in order to be accepted as a participant in their sessions:

> I didn't see why I should have to play like that. The thing I resented most was if you didn't play the licks all the other cats played you weren't "with it," you weren't "on the kick." I resented that, but I never put it down.[31]

Drummer Wilbur Campbell remembered receiving specific instructions from Roy about the type of backing he required:

> In 1947 I was working with Roy Eldridge right down the street from Charlie Parker and Max Roach at the Argyle. I'd go down

to hear Max and then come back on Roy's gig and I'd want to be breaking the rhythm up. One day Roy told me, "You ain't playing with Charlie Parker, you're playing with 'Little Jazz,' so play me some titty-boom, just straight titty-boom." So I played titty-boom.[32]

Bassist Gene Ramey couldn't help but notice Roy's attitude to drummers. He told writer Stanley Dance: "Lester Young, Ben Webster and Roy Eldridge were the only people who were really vocal about the new rhythm sections. They played their solos in phrases, and when a guy dropped a bomb in the middle it killed the phrase."[33] It must be faced that Roy was getting some of his own medicine. As a youngster forging new jazz developments, he liked to establish a degree of exclusivity at jam sessions: "In those early days any cat who wanted to sit in with me (Coleman Hawkins did the same) we'd say 'sure' and then go through all the keys to try to find one the guy didn't use."[34]

Roy also admitted that when he and Chu Berry did the rounds in the 1930s they took their own pianist with them, so that they could immediately drop into a difficult key to get rid of any bandstand passengers. But there was no question of Roy mounting a crusade against the modernists, and on many occasions he said, "You never heard me knock 'bop.' "

But whatever the setbacks Roy encountered at Minton's, his musical contributions to Gene Krupa's Band were always rapturously received by his colleagues. The Hotel Pennsylvania's Café Rouge, described as "staid and luxurious," was not typical of the venues that Gene Krupa's Band played, but even there Roy's playing got good receptions from jazz fans and from the dancers and listeners. His work with Krupa received universal praise from the critics. A *Metronome* reviewer said of the trumpeter's work on Krupa's recording of *Green Eyes*: "It's one of the most freekicking, thrilling bits of blowing waxed by anybody in a long, long time."[35]

When their Hotel Pennsylvania residency ended, the Krupa entourage toured New England before playing in Ohio and Illinois.

Then, in August 1941 they played a series of engagements *en route* to California, where they worked for several weeks. The band spent a large part of each year playing one-night stands, covering vast areas, sometimes traveling 4000 miles in a week. Looking back on his stay with Krupa, Roy said, "We used to work 346 days a year, and for good money."[36] However, despite the financial rewards, conditions were frequently difficult for all of Krupa's musicians, as the leader pointed out:

> In most spots we had to use the men's washrooms for changing in, along with the male patrons. Not that we have anything against them, but we do like a little privacy and peace. And, incidentally, some place to retire during inter-missions.[37]

Like the rest of the band, Roy had to put up with these unsatisfactory conditions, but he had the added indignity of suffering wounding situations caused by racial prejudice—and not only in the Southern states. An incident in York, Pennsylvania made front-page news in the *Down Beat* issue of December 15, 1941. The details were given under a headline that read "Krupa Fined After Fight Over Eldridge":

> Gene Krupa used his fists two weeks ago to subdue the operator of a restaurant here in York, Pennsylvania who refused to allow Roy Eldridge admittance. Gene and his band were playing a one-nighter at the Valencia Ballroom. It was reported that the restaurant man made "unfair" and ungentlemanly remarks about Eldridge, and then asked that Roy leave the place. Finally Krupa and the restaurant man "mixed" with fists flying. Police were called, Krupa was arrested, taken to jail and fined ten dollars. Then he was released. Musicians in the Krupa Band applauded their boss for his action, although both Roy and Gene said they were "sorry as hell" the occasion arose where force was necessary to maintain right.

Another slant on the fracas came from trumpeter Torger Halten:

> One time in York, Pennsylvania, several of us including Roy
> dropped into a small "beanery." The burly cook-waiter
> wouldn't serve Roy, so we all walked out, there wasn't much
> verbal conflict but we were all incensed. After he was told,
> Gene went down there and raised the roof![38]

Out on tour, Roy often encountered problems in trying to stay at
the same hotel as the rest of the band. Segregation reared its ugly
head both in the North and in the South, where many places refused
to accept black guests. However, thanks to some advice from George
"Bon Bon" Tunnell (a black Philadelphian who sang and toured with
a white band led by Jan Savitt), Roy worked out a strategy that
defeated the odious restrictions:

> When the bus pulled up I would take my bags out like I was
> the porter. I'd go up to the desk clerk and say, "Bags for Mr.
> Eldridge, Where's his room?" They'd give me the key and that
> was that. Never paid any attention to me until I came to pay
> the bill.[39]

Roy had enough humor to joke about these situations, saying,
"They always checked to see if the black had come off on the
sheets."[40] These problems apart, Roy was generally happy to be
working with Krupa:

> It killed me to be accepted as a regular member of the band.
> All the guys were nice and Gene was especially wonderful. If
> Gene and I felt good we would really make the music
> happen. I loved playing with that cat.[41]

Years later, when Roy had time to brood over real or imagined
slights, he adopted a different attitude toward musicians with whom
he'd worked in Krupa's Band. In the interviews that Dan Morgenstern
conducted on behalf of the Institute of Jazz, Roy said:

> There were only two guys that I really dug in the band, I mean, as far as being straight on the black-and-white thing: Ray Biondi and Graham Young. If I had to stay across the tracks Ray would go and stay across the tracks with me. Nobody else would do that.

After more thought, Roy added singer Johnny Desmond, trumpeter Norman Murphy, and tenorist Charlie Ventura to the names of those he felt were "straight" on racial issues.

Roy was a star attraction with the band, as trumpet soloist, singer, and as an auxiliary drummer; he played drums when Gene went out front to conduct the band. Roy also shared vocal duets with the band's female singer Anita O'Day, and recordings of their slick duets began to sell in large quantities. The cohesion and rapport that the two created on stage and on record were not matched by any comparable closeness off stage. Roy and Anita were simply acting their roles as a harmonious twosome, but behind the scenes there were some fierce disagreements. One of Roy's gripes about Anita was that during his trumpet solos she danced around the stage, pulling the audience's attention away from him—each accused the other of not sticking to well-rehearsed routines. For a long time, Roy and Anita scarcely exchanged a spoken sentence off stage, but few onlookers knew that, and even Roy's brother Joe was fooled. He said to Roy, "You must be screwing that bitch," and Cab Calloway let Roy know that he felt the same way as Joe. It took years for Roy and Anita to settle into anything even resembling tolerant acceptance of each other, and even then things did not go smoothly. Nevertheless, Anita said in one later interview, "Roy, he's a sweet sincere, swingin' guy. He's the man. For a long time people thought I was Mrs Eldridge. Hah! we were merely co-workers."[42]

Anita had a tough upbringing in the Chicago area, but sang her way out of poverty, gaining an early reputation in the Windy City, where she often worked with pianist and vibes-player Max Miller. Gene Krupa first heard her singing with Max Miller's group in

Chicago in 1940. It became an accepted story that Krupa had discovered Anita while she was singing with Roy's Band, but this was not so, though she had sat in with Roy at the Three Deuces. Anita was what could be described as a fun-loving girl. She said, "Gene didn't pay as much money as Glenn Miller and a few others, but being with his band was more fun."[43] Contrary to rumors, she did not have an affair with Krupa, saying unequivocally, "I never mix business with pleasure."[44] Anita joined Krupa's band on February 14, 1941, two months before Roy arrived. Effective and admirable though her solo-singing was, it was the duets with Roy that really got the fans interested. One of these, *The Walls Keep Talking*, became one of Roy's own favorite recordings, and the twosome's *Let Me Off Uptown* gained a prolific number of radio plays and huge record sales. However, it was a trumpet feature for Roy that produced a recording which remains a masterpiece of jazz. *Rockin' Chair* had been recorded by many artists by the time the Krupa Band put its version on wax at the Liederkranz Hall in New York on July 2, 1941. The song (by Hoagy Carmichael) had settled comfortably into various repertoires as a light-hearted vocal duet, but there was no singing on the Krupa–Eldridge version and it contained some of the most searing and intense trumpet-playing ever recorded, wonderfully show-cased in a Benny Carter arrangement. Krupa underlined the merits of the performance when he said, "If it isn't the greatest Roy Eldridge on record, it's awfully close."

Almost all of Roy's recordings with Krupa were lavishly praised but there were persistent complaints about the merits of some of the band's arrangements. Nevertheless, the popularity of Krupa's outfit rose steadily, so it was inevitable (in this era) that it was invited to appear in a musical movie. Before Roy joined, the band had been filmed in a full-length feature, *Some Like It Hot*, the results of which left Krupa feeling dissatisfied, as he explained:

> I was supposed to be playing the part of Gene Krupa and yet
> the lines I was given were not natural to me—nor to any other

musicians that I know. As long as Paramount hired me to play Gene Krupa it's a shame they didn't let me do it with more honesty.[45]

However, during the 1941 visit to California, Gene agreed that his orchestra (including Roy Eldridge) would take part in the filming of Howard Hawks' movie *Ball of Fire*, starring Gary Cooper and Barbara Stanwyck. Krupa was never enthusiastic about the results, and Roy was utterly disappointed. Although Roy was seen playing the trumpet, in order to ensure that the film was given unrestricted showings all over the U.S.A. (including the Southern states) he felt that he was hastily shunted out of the action as soon as he had finished blowing. He can be glimpsed in a scene where Gene Krupa plays intricate rhythms on a matchbox, but he is not given the prominence that his position as the band's premier soloist deserved. During the early run-throughs of that scene the diminutive Roy was out in front of the crowd of musicians, but the film-makers, perhaps sensing that this shot might cause distribution problems, moved Roy to the back of the gathering. At the time Roy was told that this was done because he was "too tall," which all 5 feet 3 inches of Roy found hard to believe. Happily, Roy was given full prominence when the Krupa Band made three-minute film versions of *Let Me Off Uptown* and *Thanks For The Boogie Ride* for the "soundie" market (soundies being brief movies that could be seen on visual juke-boxes—anyone inserting 10 cents could view (and hear) one musical number).

The Krupa Band's residency at the Hollywood Palladium, on Sunset Boulevard, began on September 12, 1941. During this visit to California, Roy had his first meeting with bassist Charles Mingus, then 19 years of age, who recalled the confrontation:

We had a gig at Jefferson High School to play with Roy Eldridge and a couple of older guys. And I remember I used to think Roy Eldridge had a cocky attitude. Well, I walked in to him and said, "What's the relative minor of B flat?" He looked me over, "I'm gonna tell you something, nigger. You young punks out here, I'm running into you every time I turn around. You don't know nothing about me, you don't know about your own people's music. I bet you never heard of Coleman Hawkins. I bet you never listened to him. I bet you can't sing one of his solos."[46]

Roy also met future impresario Norman Granz for the first time in Los Angeles during the late summer of 1941. Granz was not yet promoting jazz, but was already a devotee of the Los Angeles jazz scene. Roy told Phil Schaap:

> I first met Norman when he was working in the film industry; he was a cutter, I think, something like that. Anyhow, we had a party for Billie Holiday. That's when I first met him. We jammed at the party, Rex Stewart was there, lots of musicians, Duke's Band was in town, they were in the show *Jump for Joy*. We became real tight. He came to New York and we had him out to dinner.[47]

Norman Granz never forgot that party, recalling that singer Marie Bryant, who also appeared in *Jump for Joy*, introduced him to both Billie Holiday and Roy Eldridge during the course of the evening. Granz said, "Imagine what that meant to a young jazz fan."[48]

Roy's dynamic live performances with Gene Krupa won him many fans on the West Coast. When he was temporarily absent from the band through a brief illness *Metronome* magazine noted that there was a fall in attendances. Roy generally enjoyed good health, but occasionally his unrestrained style of blowing caused him painful lip problems. Even so, he never shirked going for the concluding high "F" on *Rockin' Chair*. One night he missed the high note, and Gene Krupa, looking on sympathetically, said, "I could see big tears in his eyes. I could also see his lip, it looked like a hamburger."[49] Roy greatly appreciated Krupa's attitude, saying, "Gene never turns or glares at you if you have a bad lip or hit a bum note. He just lets you play the way you know best."[50]

In 1941, Louis Armstrong, who had had his share of lip problems in the 1930s, expressed admiration for Roy's fortitude: "He has power and a pair of chops that's out of this man's world. And there's no use wondering how high Roy can go on his trumpet, because he can go higher than that."[51] During this same period, another famous trumpeter, Harry James, was unstinting in his praise of Eldridge's playing:

> Roy has an uncanny range and great flexibility. He can play some of the wildest stuff you ever heard, and then chill you with a lovely chorus of *Body And Soul*. Incidentally Roy has one of the toughest set of "chops" in the business.[52]

Harry James' old boss, Benny Goodman, made no effort to contribute toward the almost universal adulation that Roy was getting. In September 1941, when Cootie Williams was preparing to leave Goodman, trumpeter Jimmy Maxwell suggested that Benny should sign Roy Eldridge to fill the vacancy. The idea was immediately quashed by Goodman, who said, "I do all the fast high note playing in this band."[53]

After their successful stay in California, the Krupa Band made their way back to New York, where (on December 31, 1941) they began a season at the Paramount Theater. Proof that their popularity was snowballing was underlined by the huge audiences that queued to hear them there—the eager crowds broke a Paramount attendance record that had stood for six years. Barry Ulanov was on hand to praise Eldridge: "Roy is a wonderful little man on stage. He tips his brass hat over his right eye and struts to the microphone. He kicks off a typical solo and then duets with Anita. Fine. *Let Me Off Uptown* a symphony of solidarity."[54] Everything seemed to be fine, but under the surface Roy was becoming increasingly agitated about not receiving film copyright fees and royalties for *Drum Boogie*, even though the published music listed the two co-composers as Gene Krupa and Roy Eldridge. In those days it was standard practice for a bandleader to take a share of any compositions written by his sidemen, but, as Gene admitted quite willingly, he had received the song before Roy joined the band:

> Roy Eldridge gave this to us before he ever joined the band. I used to go and hear him all the time at the Capitol Lounge in Chicago, it was right next to the stage door of the Chicago Theater, and Roy used to play this thing, only he called it *Rare Back*. I told him I liked it, so he said I could have it.[55]

Despite Roy's everlasting admiration for Krupa he couldn't stop brooding about the royalties. However, I got the feeling that he never seriously discussed this problem with Gene. He certainly mentioned the problem to me in the 1970s, pointing out that it was definitely his tune, but originally called *Won't You Sit In The Rear Back* (referring to the seating arrangement in his car) and not *Rare Back*. Things became cloudier still when Roy said he had also written *That Drummer's Band* (originally *We're Open*) without due reward and also *Ball Of Fire*. In 1983 the issue still bothered Roy as he told Dan Morgenstern: "There was about five or six tunes that I did that have been recorded— and Gene got a lot of play out of them." What Roy usually omitted to say was that he had received $500 from a music publisher to sign away the rights to these compositions.[56] When these compositions began earning big amounts Roy felt aggrieved, but, like many other composers, he had parted with his rights for a "buy-out" payment. His friend Charlie Shavers did the same thing with his much-played tune *Undecided*. But, after twenty-eight years had passed, both Eldridge and Shavers were able to reclaim part of the rights they had signed away. They did so, and this led to Roy being accepted as a member of A.S.C.A.P. (American Society of Composers, Authors, and Publishers), and thereafter he began receiving record royalties and money whenever the tunes were played on radio, television, and in films. Even so, Roy remained disgruntled about all the money the songs had previously earned, and said, "Finally when it was worn out, they decided to give me some bread."[57] Rancor over royalties has caused many a friendship to buckle, but happily this wasn't the case with Roy and Gene, and I think deep down Roy knew that the combined acumen of a music publisher and Gene's manager was at the root of his dissatisfaction.

After their succesful stay in New York the Krupa Band went on tour. Before they did so Norman Granz got the chance to hear Roy play in a jam session:

> In 1942, courtesy of the U.S. Army I spent a couple of months in New York, and I remember the club that used to have the best Sunday afternoon jam sessions–Jimmy Ryan's. I recall once being horrified at Roy playing with blood streaming from his lips, but not lessening his attack one bit.[58]

The Krupa Band's travels involved them in playing a series of mainly ballroom dates before they began another residency at the Panther Room of Chicago's Hotel Sherman. Beginning in February 1942 they began a six-week stay there that did tremendous business, with "Standing Room Only" boards in permanent use. The success brought a lot of contentment to all the musicians. Buddy DeFranco who played clarinet and alto-sax later spoke of the amicable feeling that existed within the band: "Roy was a fun guy, and everybody loved Gene, he really was the nicest sort of person. We had a small band-within-a-band, and Roy, Charlie Ventura, and me used to stand out front to play certain numbers like *Drum Boogie*."[59] One visitor to Chicago was the young drummer Louie Bellson:

> When I was about 17 or 18, every two or three weeks I'd make the 175-mile journey from Moline, Illinois to Chicago to take drum lessons from Roy Knapp (who had taught Gene Krupa) and I'd always got to the Chicago Theater or to the Hotel Sherman to catch various bands. So I saw that Gene and the band, with Roy and Anita O'Day, were at the Chicago Theater and decided to go backstage and introduce myself to Gene, who in turn introduced me to Roy. When I won a

national Gene Krupa contest I saw them often, and that's how I got to know them. But I didn't work with Roy until 1955.[60]

After playing an April 1942 booking in Montreal, Canada, the Krupa band fulfilled dates in Cleveland, Pittsburgh, Detroit, Cedar Point, and so on, establishing a pattern of far-flung engagements that kept them busy throughout 1942. Many of these bookings were co-ordinated to tie in with the showing of the *Ball of Fire* movie, which undoubtedly gave a fillip to an already successful band—their 1942 dates at the Paramount in New York grossed an average of $93,000 a week. But the full coffers didn't produce backstage harmony at the Paramount between Roy and Anita. In fact it was the site of a breaking off of diplomatic relations, as Anita explained in her autobiography *High Times, Hard Times*:

> From Roy's point of view I got to dancing too much during *Thanks For The Boogie Ride* and *Let Me Off Uptown*. One day Roy said to Gene, "Tell that kid to stop upstaging me." I turned to Gene, "Don't you want me to dance while he plays? I thought I was augmenting it. If not, just tell me." Gene wanted to keep Roy and me happy. He couldn't say yes, or I'd have stopped and he couldn't say no or Roy would have flipped out. So he talked about the up side and the down side without committing himself. Neither Roy nor I knew where we stood on the problem. Gene was very good at that. Roy finally got to the place where he stopped talking to me offstage. I didn't care whether he talked or not. In fact I was glad. If he was really pissed off, he'd say out of the corner of his mouth after he finished a solo, "See what I'm talking about." I insisted I was just trying to dance gracefully while he played the best trumpet solos in the world. Finally he must have concluded that he'd never speak to me again—which he didn't for several years. Not even when we worked together.[61]

Usually this sort of rancor is kept from the audience because most professionals leave their animosity in the wings, but in the case of Roy and Anita the split was obvious enough for George T. Simon to comment on it in his review of an October 1942 Paramount show:

> Anita and Roy aren't apparently on speaking terms. They worked separately and at no time did either one approach the grooves they used to get in numbers like *Let Me Off Uptown*. The spirit is missing. Here's hoping Anita and Roy get together again![62]

There was no question of Roy's trumpet-playing showing any lack of spirit. He was as keen as ever to blow anywhere, and he proved this again in late 1942 when the Krupa Band did a theater date in Philadelphia. In Nat Siegel's Downbeat Club, close to the Earle Theater in Philadelphia, a brilliant young trumpeter was making his debut as a bandleader. This was none other than Roy's past adversary at Minton's, Dizzy Gillespie, who had just left Lucky Millinder's Band. Roy couldn't resist making his way there as soon as he had finished his work with Krupa. Dizzy immediately called Roy up to join in the jam session, and thus began a memorably fierce contest between the trumpeters. The tenorist who sat between them was a local musician, then in his twenties, who worked as a clerk in the local Naval Yard and blew whenever he could. His name was Charlie Ventura and he later became a successful bandleader. He never forgot the encounter: "It was great. I blew a little then I just sat there between them and stopped playing for the rest of the night."[63] Although Roy heard Ventura only briefly, he recognized that he was a class player, so he again fulfilled the role of talent-spotter and suggested that Krupa should invite Ventura to join the band. Ventura jumped at the chance and joined almost immediately. Most of the jazz tenor-playing in Krupa's Band was done by Danny Cappi, and although Roy liked Cappi's big tone he prompted Gene to let Ventura take some solos when the band played head arrangements; Ventura's career was launched and he always thanked Roy for the part he played in changing his life.

7

STARRING
WITH SHAW

Wartime restrictions meant that every leader of a touring band faced huge administrative problems. Besides the transportation difficulties brought about by the rationing of gasoline and by a shortage of tyres, there were also the woes and worries of trying to fill every position in a band when there was a steady stream of departures caused by young musicians either enlisting or being drafted into the Armed Forces. Personnel changes occurred regularly in all of the big bands, and finding replacements was a perpetual headache for the various leaders. Despite these problems, the Krupa Band's late 1942 trip to California was just as successful as its previous forays to the West Coast. One of various changes brought in Joe Triscari on first trumpet. By this time Gene had persuaded Anita and Roy to patch up their differences, at least while they were on stage. As a result they resumed working together on their celebrated duets and both gained favorable reviews for their efforts on a November 1942 C.B.S. radio show from the Hollywood Palladium. Roy and Anita continued to portray a degree of closeness that didn't exist off stage. They were so convincingly linked that complaints came from those who disliked seeing their "friendship." Roy recalled, "The church people said I was getting too close to her. And we couldn't stand each other, really."[1]

Roy and Gene Krupa remained close friends, but Roy pondered for years over an incident that happened at the Hollywood Palladium when they played a double bill with Harry James' Band. In 1981 he spoke of this to Arthur Smith:

> Me and Gene were just like brothers—up to a point. Up to a point when we played the battle against Harry James and he didn't let me play nothing that night until the broadcast, and then he turned me on with *Rockin' Chair*. That night he kept me quiet.[2]

But Roy himself agreed that he had a hang-up about playing that piece because during his early days with Krupa, two old ladies dining at the Hotel Pennsylvania had complained that the band was too loud. Roy tried hitting the top "F" softly, and in doing so he said, "I split it in nine million pieces." It may have been that Gene Krupa was solicitously shielding Roy from the faint chance that this sort of mistake might recur on a night when one of the top trumpeters of the era, Harry James, was part of the same radio show. Accordingly he may have decided to keep Roy fresh for the physical demands of *Rockin' Chair*, but Roy couldn't accept that possibility:

> So he waited until the broadcast before he let me play. He didn't let me play solos until *Rockin' Chair*. And he put it way down in the broadcast. I got through with the thing and I hit that top "F" and I felt like it was going away from me, and I don't know where I got the wind from, or the strength, but then I just grabbed an "A" and just screamed that fellow. Then I had to play an encore. We had 6000 in there. So outside that Gene was beautiful.[3]

During the band's six-week stay at the Hollywood Palladium, Gene was briefly out of action through influenza and his place was taken by the young Buddy Rich.[4] Gene soon returned and played out the final part of the run. The next port-of-call was the Golden Gate Theater in

San Francisco. After finishing a show there (on January 18, 1943) Gene walked off the stage and was immediately confronted by two Federal Narcotics investigators (Giubbini and Poleuch) who proceeded to search Gene's dressing-room. Nothing illicit was found there, but back at the St. Francis Hotel, Gene's new band-boy John Pateakos (a 20-year-old who had only been doing the job for a week or so) was apprehended as he left Gene's suite carrying a total of 37 marijuana reefers. No arrest was made that night, and it was agreed that the band could continue at the Golden Gate Theater for one more night in order to complete the contract. Roy Eldridge was not involved at all, but forty years later he admitted saying to Krupa, "Lay some bread on me and I'll take the rap."[5] Anita O'Day was absent during the dramatic events in San Francisco. She had taken leave in order to get married to former golf pro Carl Hoff (who was by that time in the Air Corps).

By the next day (January 19), the celebrated attorney Jacob Ehrlich was working on the defense case, having been hired by Gene Krupa. Gene was charged with a misdemeanor, namely "contributing to the delinquency of a minor." Jacob Ehrlich successfully applied for and was granted bail of $1000, but was dismayed when two days later a felony charge of "using a minor to transport narcotics" was added to the indictment. Judge Foley informed Krupa and Ehrlich that the felony charge would be heard in a superior court but agreed to continued bail—this meant that Gene could resume working with the band which was due to begin another season at the Hotel Sherman, Chicago, on January 29. At the Sherman, business was even better than usual for Gene and the band: the crowds arrived in droves and the coast-to-coast broadcasts continued. On one of these radio shows Gene presented Roy with a *Down Beat* trophy awarded to mark the fact that Roy had been voted "The outstanding trumpet player of 1942" in that magazine's popularity poll (he won the award again in 1946). In order to get the maximum publicity out of the first award it was again "officially" presented on stage at Chicago's Oriental Theater, when the band took time out from the Hotel Sherman to play a show there.

During Anita O'Day's leave of absence her place was taken by Penny Piper but when Anita sent word that she had no plans to return, a new vocalist, Gloria Vann, joined the band in Chicago prior to Dolores Hawkins becoming its regular singer. While these change-overs were taking place the problem of providing the "Anita" vocal rejoinders on *Let Me Off Uptown* was temporarily solved by Gene Krupa singing the part, but this ploy was soon abandoned because the leader's efforts made Roy and the rest of the sidemen helpless with laughter. After Chicago, the band did a string of theater dates in Ohio, and then played for week-long bookings in Pittsburgh and Philadelphia, moving straight on to a residency at Frank Dailey's Terrace Room in Newark, New Jersey, on April 9, 1943. This night-club setting gave the band a chance to rehearse six new musicians who had joined the band during its recent theater tour. Critic Leonard Feather reviewed the band favorably at the Terrace Room, comment-ing, "If you must have drum solos they might as well be Krupa's, for his technique is a wondrous thing." Feather praised Johnny Bothwell on alto-sax, Charlie Ventura on tenor-sax, Buddy DeFranco on clarinet, Mike "Dodo" Marmarosa on piano, and arranger Bert Ross, but his warmest words were for Roy Eldridge:

> A cornerstone in the Krupa Band for two years now, Roy is as indispensable as Gene himself. Broadly speaking every number either has an Eldridge solo or no solo at all. Roy plays in the section, he plays instrumental specialities, he takes semi-straight solos on ballads, and he sings such jive songs as *Big Fat Mama* and *Knock Me A Kiss*, in a manner so disarmingly charming that you overlook his lack of a voice. And Roy even plays drums on some of the ballads when Gene is out front conducting. Good drums too![6]

But storm clouds were gathering over Krupa's long-term pro-spects. Frank Dailey, who also owned the huge Meadowbrook Ballroom (in Cedar Grove, New Jersey) went to the American Federation of Musicians, and, citing the impending court case, tried to cancel the contract he had signed with Gene. Paramount Theater followed suit and expressed doubt about going ahead with their plan to present Krupa's Band in May 1943. During Gene's residency at the Terrace Room, Newark, he was contacted by attorney Jacob Ehrlich who advised him to make plans to fly to the West Coast and plead guilty to the lesser (misdemeanor) charge of "contributing to the delinquency of a minor," which Ehrlich estimated would result in a fine of $500. Consequently, in mid-May 1943, Gene Krupa, after playing at the R.K.O. Theater in Boston, flew from Providence, Rhode Island, to San Francisco and went with Jacob Ehrlich to the Hall of Justice there. To Ehrlich's surprise and Krupa's shock his "Guilty" plea incurred not only a fine of $500, but also a sentence of 90 days in the county jail. Judge Foley agreed that Krupa could serve the sentence in a San Francisco jail while awaiting the second trial on the charge of "using a minor to transport narcotics," which was a federal indictment. Gene, carrying a set of practice drums, surrendered to the local sheriff and began serving his sentence. Six weeks later, on June 28, 1943, he was temporarily let out of prison to face the felony charge. After some almost comic cross-questioning about the effects of smoking marijuana, Gene was asked, "You have smoked it?", to which he replied, "Yes, I have."[7] The jury took a little under three hours to find Krupa guilty and he received a sentence of one to six years in San Quentin Prison, but, as he was still serving the original sentence, a right to appeal was granted. Eventually this was successfully sustained, when (on May 31, 1944) the California District Court reversed the felony conviction on the grounds of "double jeopardy." Contrary to misinformation later published, Krupa himself was never charged with possession or use of drugs.

While the litigation was still in progress a great pall of uncertainty hung over Roy Eldridge and the rest of Krupa's sidemen. In May 1943 the band had all been given ten days' pay to tide them over while Gene went to the Coast; they all agreed to keep together (if at all possible) for eight weeks, but this was on the supposition that Gene would pay his fine and immediately return East. When this didn't happen, Frank Verniere, Krupa's manager, offered Roy the use of the band's arrangements and got the band (under Roy's leadership) to fulfill some of the engagements that Gene had been booked to play, including a week at the Earle Theater in Philadelphia. Anita O'Day declined Verniere's offer to be part of this enterprise. She explained later, "I didn't go back on the band, Roy tried to keep it going, with Harry Jaeger subbing on drums."[8] But Harry Jaeger had commitments that prevented him from doing more than a few jobs with the band, so Roy took over on drums for the final gigs they played. Trombonist Herbie Harper recalled, "We took a lay-off so that Gene could stand trial in California. He was obliged to serve time so the band did a few dates with Roy at the drums then broke up. I think the final date was at Atlantic City's Steel Pier, by that time I was with Charlie Spivak."[9] As Roy recalled it, the band played for two weeks in Atlantic City, two weeks at the Metropolitan Ballroom, Philadelphia, then disbanded. He did not enjoy his brief spell fronting the band because he was approached by different musicians every night, asking, "How come you don't give me more solos?"

Just before the breakup, Frank Verniere told Roy and the rest of the band that it was unlikely that Gene would immediately re-form the band when he was released. Gene was uncertain as to how the general public would react to him now that he had served time. Verniere and the M.C.A. Agency shared this quandary, so the musicians were left with no option but to scatter and find employment. Gene finally completed his stay in the county jail on August 9, 1943 and flew back East, Jacob Ehrlich having posted bail of $5000 on the appeal relating to the second sentence. Krupa recalled his homecoming: "I felt pretty bad. I didn't want to see anybody."[10] He virtually sat about for several weeks, then, surprisingly, in view of the fact that they had never been close friends, Gene's old boss Benny Goodman asked him to rejoin his band. Thus he spent most of the fall playing with Goodman at the Terrace Room of the New Yorker Hotel. When that stint ended Gene joined Tommy Dorsey, and received (according to Buddy DeFranco) a salary of $1500 a week during his stay.

Nothing ever shook Roy's belief that Gene Krupa had been framed, and that the marijuana had been "planted" with the connivance of government agents. Roy looked deeper, suspecting that racism was at the root of Gene being singled out for punishment, because of the obvious success that his employment of a black musician had brought. There is no doubt that Roy's presence in the midst of a white band antagonized bigots, but the scenario he suggested was unlikely. Gene smoked pot regularly and was thus an easy target for the Federal Narcotics agent to bust. Nevertheless, Roy always became grim-faced when the subject of Gene's arrest came up, saying that Gene didn't smoke marijuana, ignoring the fact that Krupa himself didn't deny that he did, and said on one occasion:

> I can only tell you about one part of the scene and that's the marijuana scene, which I was very much involved in. Probably the best thing that ever happened to me was that I got busted for it, because God knows, I might have gone into harder things too, and the guys that did didn't survive.[11]

Anita O'Day gave a matter-of-fact summing up, linking Gene's flirtations with marijuana and the breakup of his romance with film starlet Lana Turner: "After that Gene drank more heavily and used a little pot, which eventually got him into serious trouble but made him a lot easier to work for."[12]

Roy, still unsure of his draft status, made no long-term plans. He was disappointed at no longer working with Gene, and was also feeling a financial pinch caused by a drastic fall in income. In June 1943 he took a five-piece band into the Onyx Club on 52nd Street, New York for several weeks—part of the time working alongside Billie Holiday. Roy used two players there who later became jazz stars: bassist Oscar Pettiford and pianist Charles Thompson, who said, "That was my greatest experience playing with Billie and Roy on 52nd Street."[13] The critics seemed to enjoy what they heard there, and *Down Beat* reported, "Eldridge is putting on a show every night that is sensational."[14] However, the association between Oscar Pettiford and Roy didn't last long. Oscar was a brilliant musician, but after a few drinks he often became belligerent and unpunctual. Within days of joining Roy he began turning up late for the gig. Roy called him to order, but was offered the excuse by Pettiford that the hour hand had dropped off his watch. This incident marked the parting of the ways for the two men, though they worked together on several later occasions. Roy's Quintet's next residency began in August 1943 at a club that was very different from the Onyx. The new venue was the Folies Bergère, a New York club described as a "paradise for swanks." Its clientele were not lovers of jazz and Roy found that the majority of requests he received were for waltzes. He kept smiling, knowing that it was only a stopgap for him, Joe Eldridge on alto-sax, Cyril Haynes on piano, Eddie Robinson on bass, and Harold "Doc" West on drums. *Down Beat* reported that Roy's group "failed to register" with the customers at the Folies Bergère. The quintet next played a brief residency at the Club Kingsway in Toronto, Canada, then began a booking that washed away all the memories of the unhappy stay at the Folies Bergère.

The new residency marked Roy's return to Chicago, this time the venue being the Preview Club on Randolph Street in the Loop district. Roy brought Joe and Harold West with him plus his former sideman, bassist Ted Sturgis, but chose to use the Chicago-based pianist Rozelle Gayle in place of Cyril Haynes. Once again, Roy made a huge impact on the Chicago club scene. Happily, the band, augmented by Andrew "Goon" Gardner on alto-sax and Tom Archia on tenor-sax, recorded a series of transcriptions (playing Joe Eldridge arrangements) that show how wonderfully well Roy was playing at this time. Two of the pieces, *The Gasser* (a reworking of *Sweet Georgia Brown*) and *Stardust*, regularly featured in Roy's own listings of his favorite recordings. While Roy was living in Chicago he gave a detailed interview which was published in the October 1943 issue of *Metronome*. In it he discussed the work of various jazz trumpeters, and on this occasion he let his admiration for Louis Armstrong pour out:

I still believe that nobody has had or ever will have a greater influence on jazz trumpet. His tone, his phrasing, his power and his showmanship are something that nobody was ever able to duplicate. Louis was the first modern musician of all the jazzmen, by which I mean that he played more chord changes than anybody, and his work on those early records still stands up where all the other solos sound dated, and he has the most wonderful tone of all.

The music press shared the Chicago public's appreciation of Roy's performances at the Preview. *Down Beat* of November 15, 1943 commented:

> Roy Eldridge is the standard for the best in trumpet playing. His incomparable ideas are as truly great as they've been for fifteen years, which still doesn't make him an old man. Roy's vocals and comments on tunes bring out all of his terrific personality. He's a fine entertainer as well as musician, and the combination of talents puts him at the top of the small jam-crew leaders.

It seems that *Down Beat* readers shared the enthusiasm for Roy's line-up. In the annual popularity poll (taken in late 1943) they voted it top of the Small Combo section, some one thousand votes ahead of the second-placed John Kirby Sextet. The band continued to do great business at the Preview until its contract ended on January 10, 1944; for the latter part of the booking Joe Eldridge played tenor-sax. Roy was as keen to work as ever, and during their stay in Chicago the band also played Sunday dance dates at Chicago's Parkway Ballroom. Although Roy was saddened by the prospect of leaving the Preview, his disappointment evaporated when he learned that as a result of a draft board medical he had been classified 4F, which meant he would not be required for military service. Roy moved back to his New York home and began mulling over plans to launch his own big band, encouraged by the news that he had won the "Hot Trumpet" category in the January 1944 *Metronome* poll. While biding his time Roy worked in a small band, featuring Ben Webster on tenor-sax and Joe on alto-sax at the New York version of the Three Deuces (on West 52nd Street)—this Three Deuces had nothing to do with Sam Beers, but was run by Irving Alexander and Sammy Kracow.

Besides his club work, Roy also took part in a monumental jam session organized by *Esquire* magazine and held at New York's Metropolitan Opera House on January 18, 1944. This gathering still ranks as one of the most star-studded assemblies of jazz musicians, featuring, as it did, the talents of Louis Armstrong, Barney Bigard, Sid Catlett, Roy Eldridge, Lionel Hampton, Red Norvo, Coleman Hawkins, Art Tatum, Jack Teagarden, and other stellar figures, as well as the vocal artistry of Billie Holiday and Mildred Bailey. But Roy's star shone bright in this constellation and Barry Ulanov wrote in *Metronome*, "Roy Eldridge was easily top man. He blew great horn whenever he was called upon; he pushed the ensemble—he showed just why and how jazz is."[15] Fortunately, recordings of the entire concert were later released, allowing listeners to marvel at the improvised performances of these immortal giants of jazz. Roy demonstrates that his lip was in tremendous shape, but, in retrospect, he was never totally happy when talking about that concert, and said, "The producer didn't let me do the thing I wanted to that night."[16] Roy usually shrugged off any praise that fans offered about recordings from the concert, but during one late-night bar chat he gave the reason for his reaction. Apparently Louis Armstrong's manager Joe Glaser (formerly Roy's agent) called Roy aside at the rehearsal for the concert and pointedly informed him that Louis was suffering a lot of pain from kidney stones and might not be able to blow his best. Glaser pointed out, with no room for negotiation, that it would be appreciated if Roy did not attempt to outblow an ailing Louis. Roy said he decided to heed Glaser's words, but even so, listeners can hear him produce some fearsome trumpet-playing on several of the numbers recorded, and Louis, in turn, also sounds formidable. When I commented on this, Roy managed a smile and said that just as he was getting up steam, Louis without any warning went into the National Anthem, and that concluded the concert.

In early 1944 Roy did a lot of freelance work on the many recording sessions that marked the end of an eighteen-month ban on recording enforced by the Musicians' Union in August 1942 as a move to obtain recompense for musicians who were not getting any money for their recordings being played on the radio and on juke-boxes. When the dispute was settled there was a sudden deluge of sessions; one of these that Roy did was for Harry Lim's Keynote label. It featured Roy in an attractive joust with two fine trumpeters, Emmett Berry and Joe Thomas. Some stimulating, free-wheeling jazz was created, with Roy sounding in fine form. However, his efforts failed to please *Down Beat* reviewer John Lucas, who wrote: "Emmett Berry and Joe Thomas cut him to shreds most of the way. Can Little Jazz explain the meaning of every note he blows, or why he blows so many?"[17] However, there were no complaints about another January 1944 session at which Roy and Coleman Hawkins re-established the rapport they had shown so admirably on the 1940 Chocolate Dandies' sides. The further success of this 1944 date strengthened the foundations of what eventually became a prodigious partnership. In this same period, Roy, as a freelance, recorded with Charlie Barnet's Band, creating pleasing results that make one conjecture what music the thwarted liaison of 1940 might have produced.

Roy continued to sit in wherever he could, keeping in touch with all styles of jazz, blowing one night with young "modernists" and the next night with Max Kaminsky at the Pied Piper Club in Greenwich Village. Roy may not have felt totally at ease on some the jam sessions he participated in during this period, but he was still an influence on young players. Miles Davis, who had recently arrived in New York from Illinois, said, "When I got to New York I thought everybody knew as much as I did and I was surprised. Wasn't nobody playing but Dizzy, Roy and Joe Guy."[18] The New York Three Deuces was smack in the center of what was then called "Swing Street," but the appellation was soon to disappear as young modern jazz musicians were gradually booked into the clubs more often than their veteran counterparts. Dizzy Gillespie gradually advanced his case for being recognized as the new force in jazz trumpet developments, and he too led his own group on 52nd Street. But Roy still had his following, and he enjoyed playing for the crowds who came to hear him. Roy was also wryly amused at the Three Deuces by the peak-capped figure of the doorman Gilbert Pinkus (known as the Mayor of 52nd Street) who continued to chomp on a soggy cigar as he shouted, "Come in folks, the show is just about to start," even if only five minutes were left before the club closed. At the Three Deuces, Roy and drummer Jo Jones stoked a rivalry as to which of them was the better pianist. During intermissions the two made their way to the back of the club where an old piano had been put out to pasture. There they tried their darndest to better one another at the keyboard, sometimes joined by guitarist Tiny Grimes, who also fancied his pianistic skills—no winner was ever declared.

Roy's recording activities were augmented by the various sessions he did that were released on "V Disks"—these Victory Disks were made for the U.S. armed forces and were not for sale. Musicians donated their efforts and enjoyed the freedom and extended playing time that these 12-inch disks allowed. Roy was featured on several occasions, sometimes with his own group or with Benny Goodman, Boyd Raeburn, and so on. Most of the V Disk sessions took place late at night, which perfectly suited Roy's body clock. He knew that his lip would be well and truly warmed up by the time the recordings were made and this seemed to add even more zest than usual to his approach. Roy completed a month's booking at the Three Deuces, then took a group (featuring trombonist Sandy Williams) to play at the Tic-Toc Club in Boston, Massachusetts. Williams later spoke of working with Roy, and described him as "One of the best trumpet players of all time," adding, "He had a great little band at that time."[19] Back in New York, Roy did some radio studio work with Paul Baron, who had recently been appointed musical director of the C.B.S. Studios in New York. Roy, Teddy Wilson, drummer Specs Powell, bassist Al Hall, and guitarist Al Casey played on the *Chesterfield* radio show, but, according to Roy, their introduction into the ranks of studio session men was something of a token act, because they were used only on this one show, whereas resident white musicians played on several regular programs. Even so, according to Roy, there was some picketing by white musicians about the introduction of black players into the New York C.B.S. Studios. Only Specs Powell remained in the studio set-up after the initial series. As for Paul Baron, Roy said, "They called him a Communist for hiring black cats."[20] Roy wasn't disappointed that he didn't enter the studio world permanently:

> I never had trouble in reading in studio work, but it was unusual to have black players in, and you got the feeling that you had to read perfectly and be on time. It's a nice feeling at first to know that you can make it, that you can read well and fast enough. Not having an orchestra of thirty men stopped because of you. Then what do you have? Playing the same thing again and again becomes monotonous. I guess I don't have the temperament for it.[21]

Roy decided this was the time to start rehearsing his own big band which was soon playing casual engagements as well as trial bookings at the Shubert Theater in New Haven, Connecticut, and at Harlem's Apollo Theater. These engagements took place during the final stages of his stay at C.B.S., which meant all his stamina was needed to play theater bookings and do studio work on the same day. Fortunately, he always seemed to have some in reserve. George T. Simon heard the big band at the New Haven date and wrote, "I can't recall Little Jazz in better form."[22] The big band shaped up well and gave Roy the confidence to take it on tour during the late summer of 1944. The line-up featured some fine players, including trombonist Sandy Williams, trumpeters Sid De Paris and Maurice "Shorty" McConnell, plus tenorist Franz Jackson, who, together with Clyde Hart, wrote most of the band's arrangements. Unfortunately, business was only so-so, Roy felt partly because a publicity agent had decided to bill Roy as "the ex-Gene Krupa star," which gave people the idea that it was a white touring band. Most of the men who had been on the tour took part in the recording sessions that Roy did for Decca, under the supervision of Milt Gabler on June 26 and October 13, 1944. The second of these dates produced *Twilight Time* and *Fish Market*. The latter, a stark blues riff (written by Roy but named by Sandy Williams), got a lot of radio plays and sold well. But even this success didn't bring Roy the benefits it should have done, as he explained:

> I had a hit with *Fish Market*–the only thing I ever made a lot of money on. I remember particularly the first big check I got was from England. I put all the money into a Little Jazz music publishing firm, and got swindled out of it.[23]

Roy returned to the Tic-Toc in Boston with the full band, then played a two-week residency in September 1944 at the Club Bali in Washington, D.C. But as the revival of interest in traditional jazz grew so too did various controversies between those who liked big bands and those who did not. One school of thought had it that true jazz could not be played within the confines of a big swing band. Critic Rudi Blesh was one who supported this crackpot theory, maintaining, "Jazz and Swing are two different kinds of music."[24] Such comments were inclined to raise Roy's blood pressure, as he made clear in an interview with a *Metronome* reporter in 1944:

> Difference between jazz and swing? Hell, no man. It's just another name. It's ridiculous to talk about big bands and small bands as if they played two different kinds of music. I play a chorus in exactly the same style with my small band as I did when I was with Gene Krupa's 16 pieces.[25]

Roy's big band played a return date at the Apollo Theater in October 1944, which was reviewed by Leonard Feather:

> A strange thing happened in this show. Roy Eldridge's band

started to play the blues, at medium tempo, and didn't stop until a quarter of an hour later, by which time, Roy, Joe Eldridge and Sandy Williams and guitarist Sam Allen had each taken umpteen choruses. What's even more amazing is that the audience didn't seem to find it too long. Roy called this number *Fish Market*. The other numbers played by the band suffered by comparison and some suffered by being played at all. Maxine Johnson, Roy's vocaliste, did a couple of numbers. Roy provided a kick by playing drums on the last number *Flying Home*, and pretty good drums too.[26]

After this booking Joe Eldridge moved out to California to work with Zutty Singleton. Joe said farewell to his brother, not realizing that in a sudden turn of events Roy himself would move out to California within weeks. The reason for Roy's coast-to-coast journey was to accept an offer to join a new big band that Artie Shaw was forming. This wasn't the first time that Shaw had featured a black trumpeter. In 1941 Oran "Hot Lips" Page was featured with Shaw's band and made several fine records with it. Shaw, who had been deeply troubled by the pressures connected to his earlier successes, led a U.S. Navy band in the Pacific zone during World War II (with the rank of Chief Petty Officer). After receiving an honorable discharge from the Navy, Shaw recuperated then assembled a big band featuring strings. He soon disbanded, paused, then formed a new big band which featured, among others, pianist "Dodo" Marmarosa and guitarist Barney Kessel. Roy Eldridge left New York on October 23, 1944 to become part of this enterprise, which began rehearsing on November 1 at Shaw's luxurious home on Bedford Drive in Beverly Hills, where the ensemble ran through arrangements by Eddie Sauter, Buster Harding, and trombonists Ray Conniff and Harry Rodgers; vocalist Imogene Lynn joined a little later. The rehearsal schedules meant that there was plenty of free time for Roy to sit in at clubs in Los Angeles, or to play local gigs. Thus Roy played his first date for Norman Granz, taking part in an on-stage jam session format as part of a concert held at the Philharmonic Hall, Los Angeles on November 13, 1944. This was the first of many occasions (spanning three decades) that Roy was part of a Norman Granz presentation.

Roy's starting wage with Artie Shaw was said to be $500 a week,[27] a considerable sum in 1944. This meant, once again, that Roy, working as a sideman, was able to earn much more than he did as a bandleader. He was also free of the headaches of leadership, and later said that his 1944 touring big band was beset by drunkenness and unpunctuality: "I never was one of those type of cats who showed up late on the gig, because I liked to play too much. Not starting on time? No, I wasn't like that, I never did play those games." Roy was intrigued by the prospect of working with Artie Shaw. The two men had occasionally taken part in jam sessions together, but had not worked with each other. Reminiscing about Shaw, Roy said:

> Artie took himself seriously, but he had a right to. He was not only a good musician; he was a celebrity, married to famous film stars, making hit records, and hitting the headlines. Some musicians said he was a very good player but not a great improviser, but he could really improvise if the mood took him. I remember when he was with that heiress [Gloria Vanderbilt De Cicco], we were playing at the Strand and he improvised solidly throughout every show. But his best gift was in knowing how to rehearse a band, how to get the best out of musicians, getting them to interpret. He was outstanding at this, whereas Benny Goodman was no good at explaining what he wanted, so a lot of time and effort was wasted at rehearsals, whereas Artie knew exactly what he wanted and could connect with his sidemen. Charlie Shavers always used to tell of the time that Benny Goodman made the full band run through a hard-blowing arrangement fifteen times, to get something right in the rhythm section. Charlie spoke up and said, "Look Benny, do you want it right now and wrong tonight, or wrong now and right tonight?" There was nothing like that with Artie Shaw.[28]

Years later Artie Shaw spoke of hiring Eldridge: "I was color blind and I hired people for what they did. I could hire the musicians, rehearse the band, get it to sound like what I thought it should." But Shaw admitted he could not deal with the antics of some of his fans: "It's one thing being a musician, another thing to be a celebrity."[29] On another occasion Shaw was unreserved in his praise of Roy's contributions to the band: "He was the spark plug. He was marvelous."[30] Guitarist Barney Kessel gave his assessment of Shaw as a bandleader:

> Some of the guys in the band resented Artie's attitude, but you've got to have discipline haven't you? He did everything a leader was supposed to do, stayed sober, got plenty of work and fronted a very musicianly band. We had some Buster Harding arrangements and some beautiful Eddie Sauter things.[31]

Before November 1944 had ended, Shaw's new band had played a couple of trial dates in San Diego in preparation for a long series of theater bookings, involving week-long stints in Minneapolis, Chicago, Detroit, and various cities in Ohio. Gradually the band's performances were honed to the standard that Shaw required it to achieve on its New York debut at the Strand Theater on January 12, 1945. There were extra rehearsals for a small contingent within the band, because Shaw had decided to resurrect his Gramercy Five, the original version of which (in 1940) featured Billy Butterfield on trumpet and Johnny Guarnieri on harpsichord. This time the harpsichord was dispensed with and all the keyboard work was done by Dodo Marmarosa on piano. Roy was on trumpet alongside Shaw on clarinet, Barney Kessel on guitar, Morris Rayman on bass, and Lou Fromm on drums. The swing and precision of the original group were ably recaptured by its successors, whose performances, both on record and in person, greatly pleased both the fans and the critics. In a review of a New York Strand date, Frank Stacy wrote in *Down Beat*: "The new

Gramercy Five brightened the atmosphere with a couple of well-played originals," but he was less pleased with the big band's efforts, which he described as "disappointing on the whole," conceding that "lines at the box-office are still a mile long." Roy's feature number, *Body And Soul*, was evaluated as "fine," and Shaw's clarinet work deemed "matchless."

The release of the big band's first recordings didn't produce any glowing reviews. *Metronome* of January 1945 said of the *Accentuate The Positive/Jumpin' On The Merry Go Round* coupling, "For us ardent Shaw supporters this first record by his new band is a sad letdown. The band plays it with some verve but little musical interest except for Roy Eldridge's four measures." But the same issue carried the news that Roy Eldridge had again won the All Star Poll as the nation's top "Hot Trumpeter." During the period when Roy was working with Shaw at the Strand Theater he managed to fit in a recording session for Decca with a unit that was billed as his orchestra, mainly comprising white New York session musicians (apart from Ted Sturgis on bass and Cozy Cole on drums). The two resultant numbers *Little Jazz Boogie* and *Embraceable You* did nothing to diminish Roy's reputation, and he subsequently put this version of *Embraceable You* high on a list of his own favorite recordings. Although Decca allowed Roy to record for Artie Shaw, his contract with them prohibited the use of his name on the labels of Shaw's recordings. Roy found that making records with Shaw could be an exhausting business:

> He's such a perfectionist. I'll never forget this as long as I live. We were recording one night and I marked it down—one, two, three, four…38 attempts. And Shaw said, "Well, we're going to finish this thing if we have to stay here until eight in the morning. If anybody doesn't like it they can go home." I said, "Well, I'll go home." He says, "I'm not talking to you."[32]

Artie Shaw's persistence in the recording studios was a deliberate strategy, as he acknowledged: "I took more time with the records that band made than I ever did before. I decided I would take the time needed to reach for as close to perfection as I could get."[33]

After the New York bookings ended, the Artie Shaw band wound its way through a cross-country itinerary that eventually got them back to Los Angeles by April 1945. Shaw was again the subject of tabloid publicity concerning his romantic attachments, with the public being asked to make up their minds about whether he loved the film star Ava Gardner more than he did Gloria Vanderbilt De Cicco. Shaw did his best to ignore these intrusions into his private life and continued to strive for musical perfection. He too was finding that personnel changes were being forced on him by the requirements of the draft boards, but he also chose to make changes from musical reasons whenever he felt a position in the band might be improved on. By the time the band reached California in April there were seven changes from the line-up that had played in the East. During the next few months the band played mainly in California: in San Diego, Los Angeles, Ocean Park, San Francisco, Oakland, and Culver City, but it did occasional, brief tours in other states. One of these took them to Phoenix, Arizona, where a teenage trumpeter Art Farmer heard Roy live for the first time:

> He came into the little joint where I was playing—the Shaw band had a night off. I must have been about 15 years old and I knew nothing, but he was such a great guy and he loved to play so much that he came up on the bandstand and he played the drums for about an hour. Then he went to his room and got his horn and came back and played with me. We had a great time.[34]

At this juncture Shaw's band didn't work as often as it could have done because Artie detested theater tours, and said on one occasion, "A guy who plays theatres must hate music."[35] He also preferred to remain on the West Coast partly because he hoped to get the band featured in a prestigious movie (one of his previous bands starred in the 1940 film *Second Chorus*). Several studios broached Shaw with offers, but he turned them down, saying they lacked "a realistic treatment of jazz."[36] Shaw went through one of his periodic detestations of the music business and took time off to visit New York with Ava Gardner. Roy remained in California during this hiatus, and found a lot of pleasure in temporarily fronting a band usually led by tenorist Jack McVea, who (in August 1945) was briefly out of action through illness. By September, Shaw was back in Los Angeles leading his band for a four-nights-a-week residency at the Casa Manana and preparing for his marriage to Ava Gardner (who became Shaw's fifth wife). Roy liked her and stressed, "Ava was great. She's a very fine person, and at this time she and Artie became good friends to me."[37] However, despite the couple's solicitude, Roy found that the racial climate in California caused him perpetual strife: "I had to live out in Los Angeles, while the rest of the guys stayed in Hollywood. It was a lonely life; I'd never been that far away from home before, and I didn't know anybody. I got to brooding."[38]

Speaking of Roy, Artie Shaw said:

> He was a cute little stocky, chunky guy, a feisty guy, in many ways a tragic guy. It was very tough for him racially in my band just as it had been for Billie Holiday, when she was with me in the 1930s. I told him I could handle racial matters when we were on the stand, but there was very little I could do when we were off. He used to carry a gun and I'd try and discourage him, and he'd tell me that he'd rather take his chances with the police than run up against some crazy guy unarmed. He saw himself as travelling through a hostile land and he was right.[39]

Roy found himself in the same sort of situation that had marred his stay with Gene Krupa:

We got to Del Mar. I got in the hotel all right but couldn't eat in the dining room. Some of the guys who knew I liked Mexican food suggested that we go to a little Mexican joint. When they refused to serve me, all the other guys walked out with me, but it still started to put me in that mood again. I went to the place where we were supposed to play a dance and they wouldn't let me in the place, "This is a white dance" they said, and there was my name right outside, Roy "Little Jazz" Eldridge, and I told them who I was. When I finally did get in I played that first set trying to keep from crying. By the time I got through the tears were rolling down my cheeks—I don't know how I made it. I went up to a dressing room and stood in a corner crying and saying to myself, "Why the hell did I come out here again when I know what could happen?" Artie came in and he was real great. He made the guy apologise that wouldn't let me in and got him fired.[40]

Roy later gave further details about the incident:

We were down in San Diego, and my name's up on the marquee, big as life. So we're staying about nineteen miles from San Diego at the hotel out there, the Del Mar. But I'd come into town early on the bus and go over there to eat dinner, had to come to the kitchen, change my clothes. So I walked in that night and the guy says, "Where you going?" and I say "I play in the band." "You?" he said, "This is a white band." I said, "But look out there, there's my name, Roy 'Little Jazz' Eldridge." But I'm still walking, see, and during those times I always carried a pistol, because you never know—you had to. And this man never knew how close he was to getting it.[41]

Roy said he felt too wounded mentally to continue working in Shaw's band. At the time it was said that Shaw (himself no stranger to trauma) readily understood that the trumpeter wanted to return home to New York as soon as possible. *Down Beat* of October 15,

1945 reported: "Roy Eldridge suddenly left the Artie Shaw Band without notice, as they opened at the new Meadowbrook. All contractual commitments and usual notice were apparently waived by both Shaw and Eldridge." Years later Artie Shaw revealed some intriguing background details:

> I tell you why I had to fire him. The racial pressures were getting to him. I did what I could but there were lots of ugly incidents, and one day when he was mad about everything he pulled a knife on me. I said "Roy, if I'm your enemy, who's your friend?" He started to cry and I took the knife away from him. Then I sat him down and told him, "Look at yourself, it's tearing you up. Go to Europe for a while." So I had to let him go. Later he did go to Europe and when I ran into him after he came back, he said, "Yeah, you were right."[42]

Shaw also spoke of the intolerance that Roy encountered: "Droves of people would ask him for his autograph at the end of the night, but later, on the bus, he wouldn't be able to get off and buy a hamburger with the guys in the band."[43]

But just how long Roy would have stayed with Shaw is a matter of conjecture. Roy's contract with Artie was for a year, and he had not sought a renewal. As *Metronome* noted at the time (October 1945 issue), "When Roy Eldridge's contract is up in about two months he'll form his own small combination." But as it happened, Artie Shaw disbanded before the year had ended. Before Roy left California he took part in a Los Angeles concert entitled "The Evolution of Modern American Music," which was a potted history of jazz featuring Kid Ory, Zutty Singleton, Corky Corcoran, and singer Ivie Anderson. After traveling from Los Angeles by train, Roy took a brief rest at his New York home, but by October 24, 1945 he was guesting with Ben Webster's group (Kelly Martin on drums) at the Onyx Club, having turned down an offer to join Woody Herman's Band. Much as Roy liked Woody (they had first met at New York's Rockland Palace in the mid-1930s when Woody was with Isham Jones), he declined the chance to work with him. When his stay at the Onyx ended in mid-November Roy played some casual gigs in the New York area as he mulled over his future. This breathing space allowed Roy to lead a pick-up group (featuring a white line-up plus Specs Powell on drums) on a November 1945 V Disk recording which produced some marvelous music.

At about this time Roy introduced a novelty into some of his sets by occasionally playing a tiny "pocket trumpet" (which had been given to him by Jack Teagarden), but he never made it a regular part of his "armory." After kicking his heels briefly, Roy, temporarily forgetting the woe he'd encountered in his previous attempts to lead a big band, decided that the prospects of glory and financial gain as a bandleader were too attractive to be dismissed. The notion was encouraged by Roy's personal manager, Frank Verniere, who had previously been Gene Krupa's right-hand man. Roy was persuaded to appoint as his booking representatives an agency run by the Fredericks brothers. B. W. and L. A. Fredericks were originally from Shawnee, Oklahoma, where they achieved local prominence in the early 1930s by booking King Oliver and Joe Haymes. George "Pee Wee" Erwin also got work via the brothers (whom he first encountered when they operated out of a disused garage in Kansas City). Gradually the agency expanded and moved from Kansas City to Cleveland, Ohio, before opening their New York offices in 1938 (later they also operated branches in Chicago and Los Angeles).

But before Roy's new big band took shape he played on a late 1945 tour as part of Norman Granz's Jazz at the Philharmonic package show. Norman Granz (b. 1918) began promoting in the early 1940s by hiring Los Angeles clubs in order to present jam sessions to desegregated audiences, paying the musicians involved the union scale. Well-known West Coast jazzmen and other players who were touring California enthusiastically took part in these informal, well-attended sessions, encouraging Granz (in 1944) to present a similar format in concert, first at the Music Town Auditorium, then, from July 1944, at the Los Angeles Philharmonic Auditorium. Over two thousand people attended the first of these Jazz at the Philharmonic shows, which featured Illinois Jacquet on tenor-sax, Nat "King" Cole on piano, Joe Sullivan on piano, Barney Bigard on clarinet, Meade Lux Lewis on piano, and other top-line jazzmen. *Down Beat* of August 1, 1944 commented on the first of these J.A.T.P. (as they became known) presentations, saying that Granz "had rung up a notable achievement both for music and the racial unity so important right now in this city." Granz himself said: "My main reason for starting this thing was to try and improve race relations. It's a subject I was greatly interested in when I was a student at U.C.L.A. and I'm delighted that jazz has given me the chance to do something about it."[44] During the coming years, Granz did a great deal to break down racial barriers, always refusing to allow his concerts to take place for segregated audiences. In his survey of J.A.T.P. from 1944 to 1957, *Let Freedom Swing*, James T. Hershorn wrote:

> Norman Granz had three main aims when he began producing concerts known as Jazz At The Philharmonic in the mid-1940s: to challenge racial discrimination, make money and produce good jazz. The energy and brilliance he brought to bear allowed him to succeed on all three levels.[45]

Norman Granz's second J.A.T.P. presentation (on Sunday, July 30, 1944) was an even bigger success than the first, but soon afterwards the Philharmonic authorities snootily rejected Granz's further attempts to book their venue. Undeterred, Granz went on to promote successfully at major concert halls throughout the world, retaining the J.A.T.P. billing to describe his shows. By 1945 Granz was promoting in several cities on the West Coast, gaining an accolade from writer Leonard Feather, who described him as "A businessman with a strong social conscience." Roy Eldridge, always inspired by jam session situations, was a natural for Granz's enterprises, and in late 1945 he took part in what was to be the first J.A.T.P. tour, working alongside

Coleman Hawkins, Thelonious Monk, Denzil Best on drums, Al McKibbon on bass, Tom Archia on tenor-sax, Helen Humes on vocals, and Meade Lux Lewis on piano. Throughout the next quarter of a century, Roy was to play in innumerable concerts organized by Norman Granz, and for much of that period Granz usually provided the major source of Roy's annual income.

8

JAZZ AT THE PHILHARMONIC

When that first brief J.A.T.P. tour ended, Roy returned East and guested with various bands, fitting in these engagements with rehearsing his new nineteen-piece band and also finding time to play on more of the V Disk sessions. The official debut date for Roy's band was February 8, 1946, when it was booked to start a residency in Chicago at the Pershing Hotel's El Grotto Club, but before that the band did a string of one nighters at which Roy took the opportunity to audition possible sidemen for his new venture. Roy, wary of facing the indiscipline and unpunctuality he had experienced when using veteran players in his 1944 band, selected as many young musicians as he could, among them baritonist Cecil Payne, altoist Porter Kilbert, and trumpeter Elmon Wright. However, Roy's right-hand man and principal arranger was the veteran pianist Buster Harding, who severed ties with Artie Shaw in order to work with Roy.

Many of Roy's old Chicago fans made their way to the El Grotto Club (at 6412 Cottage Grove), encouraging the management there to extend Roy's contract. The big band also played for two weeks at the Regal Theater in Chicago, where it shared billing with pianist Dorothy Donegan, but despite these emphatic local successes there was little sign that bookers across the country were eager to hire Roy's Band. A successful bandleader usually has a penciled outline of the itinerary he would play a year hence, but for Roy it was a matter of his only knowing where the bookings would be in the immediate future. As a break from bandleading, Roy played at a session organized by the Chicago Hot Club which reunited him with two former sidemen, tenorist Dave Young and pianist Rozelle Gayle. The highlight of the concert was provided by trombonist Jack Teagarden who sat in with Roy's group. The big band returned to New York, and in late April 1946 played for a week at the Apollo Theater before going on the road. Roy told a reporter from the *Pittsburgh Courier* that he was determined to keep the band intact, adding that what he could say about working with a white band would fill a book: "Some people think that it's great, but they don't know."[1] Roy was later to amplify these sentiments in an interview that filled the front page of *Down Beat*. When the band returned from tour it began a residency at New York's Spotlite Club on 52nd Street. There, Clark Monroe (who had run the Uptown House where Roy often blew in the late 1930s) was persuaded by the Fredericks brothers to book the full line-up of nineteen men as well as hiring a group led by Coleman Hawkins.

Roy's big band was suffering the teething problems that most newly formed ensembles encounter, but unfortunately Roy was also being troubled by his own aching molars, and, just before the Spotlite opening, he had to have two of them extracted. Roy had first been fitted with dentures some fifteen years earlier, but the loss of two of his remaining natural teeth meant that his existing plate (which had been so comfortable and conducive to blowing the trumpet) had to be scrapped and a new one made. It was to be many months before Roy felt totally at ease with his new false teeth, and, from this point on, he paid extra attention to warming up before a gig. Roy said, "I never can say all I want to say. For one thing it takes me a long time to warm up."[2] Roy attempted to solve the problem by first blowing into a skeleton mouthpiece (without putting it into the trumpet). These mouthpieces have a normal rim, but instead of having a metal cup they have a series of ribbed struts that allow the air to flow out of the sides immediately; thus very little pressure is used. The purpose of the device was to allow a teacher (or the player himself) to look in a mirror and see if the lips were placed correctly within the skeleton mouthpiece. But Roy found these featherweight mouthpieces ideal for warming up the lips; he'd follow up by buzzing his lips into a standard mouthpiece, still without putting it into the trumpet. When he felt that his lips were vibrating satisfactorily he'd insert the standard mouthpiece into his trumpet and begin blowing soft, long, low notes, gradually moving up step-by-step into a top register that was truly remarkable. On a good night, Roy could hit a "G" above double high "C" (over seven ledger lines above the treble clef stave). In later years, for some reason, Roy became secretive about using the skeleton mouthpiece, regarding it as a "trade secret"; he usually covered the device with his hand prior to slipping it back into his pocket. I felt honored one night in Jimmy Ryan's Club in the 1970s when Roy showed me (and drummer Chuck Smith) this clandestine accessory.

But no matter how thoroughly Roy warmed up, the loss of two teeth and the inconvenience of a new dental plate meant that preparing for the 1946 Spotlite opening was a frustrating experience. Instead of Roy being in top form for what was one of the biggest nights of his career, he was struggling to play both high notes and low notes. Nevertheless, Roy's showmanship and personality, plus the happy spirit that filled the tiny bandstand, carried the day. The band continued its successful run until late September, but Dizzy Gillespie, who heard the band at the Spotlite, was not impressed. When Leonard Feather played Dizzy the Artie Shaw recording of *Little Jazz* (as part of a "blindfold test") Gillespie said, "Roy gets a better sound on records than in person. Fine sound. This can't be the same band he had at the Spotlite." When the Spotlite residency ended, Roy made his way to California to play dates in San Francisco and Los Angeles with Jazz at the Philharmonic; his dental problems were easing, but it was to be months before he felt his old self again. Roy took part in only a segment of that J.A.T.P. tour because he was contracted to take his band into the Paradise Club in Detroit on October 10, 1946. When this booking had been completed he rejoined J.A.T.P. troupe, and received a poor review for his efforts. In *Down Beat* of November 18, 1946, D. Leon Wolff wrote: "Roy Eldridge spent most of his time on long, elaborate intros and codas which showed off his range, technique and poor taste. In between he played riffs with Coleman Hawkins and a couple of solos full of sound and fury, signifying nothing."

This reaction to Roy's playing was almost complimentary compared to Wolff's comments on Rex Stewart's performance: "Norman Granz, if he had the guts, should have yanked him off the stage." Granz was quick to defend the work of both men, saying of Eldridge, "Roy's performance displayed wonderful, tasteful jazz," and added, "Roy and Hawk's duets happen to be examples of the most modern kind of jazz played today."[3] But Wolff wasn't the only one to mete out severe criticism of the J.A.T.P. troupe. Clyde H. Clark, relaying news from the U.S.A. to readers of the Australian magazine *Jazz Notes*, wrote:

> Jazz At The Philharmonic were here on November 5th 1946, and they honked, squealed, screamed, screeched and clowned for hours. I have never before seen or heard such a display of disgusting, revolting, obnoxious, unlistenable and stomach-turning bad taste and exhibitionism.[4]

Yet the line-up was packed with superior jazz talent, including Roy, Coleman Hawkins, Rex Stewart, Dave Tough, Buck Clayton, Trummy Young, Kenny Kersey, Illinois Jacquet, and Chubby Jackson. Granz's continued support of Roy's playing rang out loud and clear in a J.A.T.P. advertisement that appeared in the *Chicago Defender* promoting the concerts at the Chicago Opera House: "Just as Louis Armstrong was the outstanding trumpeter of the past decade, so Roy Eldridge is the greatest trumpeter today."[5] Leonard Feather praised this J.A.T.P. tour, saying, "Musically by far the best thing in the show was the set by Hawk and Roy," but added a note of disappointment: "Many concessions are being made in the interests of box office and applause in these concerts."[6]

Roy's attempts to be a J.A.T.P. star and to lead his own big band had all the appearances of an uncertain balancing act, and the picture became more confused when, after the J.A.T.P. tour ended on Thanksgiving Day, Roy decided to stay on the West Coast to front an all-star group consisting of Trummy Young on trombone, Wardell Gray on tenor-sax, Willie Smith on alto-sax, Jackie Mills on drums, Kenny Kersey on piano, and Charlie Drayton on bass. Most of this line-up, plus Buddy DeFranco on clarinet, played a brief stint at Billy Berg's Club in Hollywood, where they found themselves accompanying Roy's adversary, Anita O'Day. Roy told Phil Schaap about this encounter, which didn't go smoothly—either musically or socially. When Roy complained that she had missed eight bars out of a song, Anita went to the manager and said, "Roy ain't playing my music." Roy explained, "In the first place she had no music." His reaction was to tell the singer, "If you lose eight bars again, you're lost." Trummy Young was amused to note that Roy had lost none of his competitiveness:

> I'd see him sitting down to eat his dinner, and he'd hear another trumpet-player sounding good in front of a receptive audience and although it was our break he'd have to jump up and leave his meal to get out on the stand to start blowing. I used to call him "The Bubbling Gladiator"—he never stopped looking for guys to blow against.[7]

After a few weeks, Roy decided to return to New York, where he attempted to salvage his big band plans; during his absence the group had worked sporadically, fronted by the singer, dancer, and trumpet-player "Taps" Miller. Looking back, Roy always felt he had bad luck with this big band, but it must be said that his strategy of trying to play solo engagements came at a time when he should have been devoting all his energies into establishing the new unit. When Roy first nurtured the idea of forming this big band he received the aid of backers, who realized that a successful big band could, in the long run, earn a tremendous amount of money. These "businessmen" decided to be the guiding force in Roy's musical destiny, whether he liked it or not. However, despite this funding, the band just couldn't get established, and vexingly for Roy's "investors" he continued to go off on wide-ranging tours with J.A.T.P. during the first six months of 1947. On some of the 1947 concerts the troupe was augmented by the presence of Charlie Parker, and at a Carnegie Hall date Roy locked horns with Dizzy Gillespie, an event reviewed in *Down Beat*: "Both played well on *Lady Be Good* with everyone noting a marked improvement in Little Jazz's playing over recent months. Evidently the trouble Roy has had with his teeth is over and he is settling down again.[8]

Many of the J.A.T.P. performances were recorded and issued on Clef, the record label that Norman Granz had started. The enterprise soon prospered, and Granz was able to sign many of his touring stars to an exclusive recording contract. For Roy, news on the dental front was good, but his plans for the big band turned sour when his "sponsors" demanded some financial return for the money they had advanced for arrangements, music stands, microphones, uniforms, and publicity services. Manager Frank Verniere resisted Roy's claims that the music publishing company they had formed (Little Jazz Music, with offices in New York's Brill Building) owed him a considerable amount of money. The dispute caused enmity between Eldridge and Verniere, leading Roy to say, "He hated me. I never saw that money; he bought a couple of farms."[9] Some while later Roy found that all his big band arrangements, music stands, and microphones had mysteriously disappeared. Worse still, it seemed to Roy, back in 1947, that certain club-owners had suddenly developed a reluctance to book him as a single, or as the leader of a small group. Fortunately, he was still being featured with J.A.T.P. and was also playing semi-regularly at the W.N.E.W. radio jam sessions, but he let bitterness take over briefly by inferring, "If I'm supposed to be an important part of jazz history and a link between Louis and Dizzy, how come I'm not getting any gigs?" Despite this attitude, Roy never felt at ease when theorists talked to him about a trumpet lineage, and he was positively brusque when anyone suggested that his playing had been influenced by Henry "Red" Allen's work. When Nat Hentoff raised this point Roy spluttered an unequivocal answer: "I like Red, but *Oh God No!*"[10] Max Jones of *Melody Maker* received a similarly abrupt reply when he asked about Allen's influence: "Red Nichols yes, but *not* Red Allen," an answer that Max described as being delivered with "finality."[11] Roy found it irksome that this trumpet lineage theory was trotted out in most of the articles written about him. As Dan Morgenstern has pointed out, the result is that tyros could easily think that Roy's contribution to jazz was simply in being part of a branch in the jazz tree, whose influence was more crucial than his perfor- mances, whereas, over a long period, Roy created a series of magnificent and dynamic examples of immortal jazz.

Gigs remained scarce for Roy, but in May 1947 he returned briefly to play at Smalls' Paradise (the scene of his early successes with Elmer Snowden and Charlie Johnson), where he led pick-up groups which included clarinettist Tony Scott, tenorist Eddie "Lockjaw" Davis, drummer Sonny Payne, and his vocalist from the stay at the Arcadia Ballroom, Laurel Watson. But the jam session fare didn't exactly suit the clientele at Smalls', so Roy decided to play some dates in Chicago, one of which was a one-night booking at the Argyle Show Lounge. This turned out to be a miserable affair, as reported by Don Haynes in *Down Beat*:

> The Argyle was packed for most of six hours. But the music was something else—Roy struggling against Lee Silvers and his Beboppers. While Roy is far from playing his best today, the support given him by the young cats there would certainly have dragged anyone down. Several musicians from the

Claude Thornhill and Charlie Ventura bands walked out in complete dismay.[12]

But Roy greatly enjoyed his visit to another venue in the same city:

> I went into a joint in Chicago for one night. It was strictly a modern place and I went into training for the job, practising six to seven hours a day for a whole week just to play one night. This was when the modern scene was at its height and I was a foreigner in that club. I had good drums and bass and I blew that night! Wow! I didn't play anything I'd practised. I just played.[13]

A sparsely filled engagement book greeted Roy's return to New York—even allowing for the fact that many New York club-owners were booking groups that played be-bop, his lack of work was mysterious. Roy gladly accepted an offer to take a quintet into the Famous Door in September 1947, but despite the presence of the fine tenorist Ike Quebec, there was no rush by other club-owners (or agents) to book the group. Amazingly, Roy didn't record under his own name throughout the years 1947 to 1949. Gigs almost dried up completely for him, and for two weeks (early in 1948) he went off to Boston to guest with a band led by white saxist Ted Goddard. A comment in *Metronome* highlighted Roy's position: "He has been playing in comparative obscurity."[14] Yet whenever Roy did work, his talents were well received by the public, as was the case when he led for a week at the Apollo Theater during the summer of 1948. But soon after this booking he decided to try his luck on the West Coast. He was encouraged to do this by Charlie Barnet, who offered him guest spots with his band at the Edgewater in San Francisco, so, eight years after they had originally planned to work together, Barnet and Eldridge finally combined to play some live dates. While in California Roy was offered some bookings there in the near future, so after playing some contracted dates at the Pershing Hotel in Chicago, he formed a quintet to play for a four-week booking at Lashio's in San Francisco. The line-up featured Roy's old sidekicks Franz Jackson (on tenor-sax), Kenny Kersey (on piano), and Ted Sturgis (on double-bass), plus the New Jersey drummer Danny Farrar. Roy said at the time that he was grooming this quintet for a New York television show, and to this end booked singer and dancer Dottie Saulters to work with the group; it remained in California to play a three-week season at the Zanzibar Club in Sacramento, which ended in December 1948. After this, Roy again made his way back to New York.

The television opportunities didn't materialize, though Roy was seen occasionally on N.B.C. as part of the *Eddie Condon Floor Show* programs. At the end of 1948, Gene Krupa re-entered Roy's life with dramatic results. Gene had decided to take a three-week rest from bandleading so that he could rethink his strategy. He didn't want to change his personnel drastically but he needed a fillip to lift his band back into favor with the general public, and with bookers, agents, and ballroom operators. The answer he came up with was to offer Roy the chance to rejoin the band. Roy instantly complied with the suggestion and agreed to work for Gene from January 1949, seeing the move as a relief from the despondency that his own efforts at bandleading had created. This time Roy fulfilled the role of fifth trumpeter, playing an easier part in the section than he had during his previous tenure, and this time able to devote all his energies to being featured as trumpet soloist, singer, and bongo-player. This was the period when the inclusion of someone playing the bongo drums became a craze within many bands, both large and small: they featured the exotic percussion sounds on almost every number whether appropriate or not. When Roy rejoined Krupa, Gene was shopping around for a bongo-player, and was quickly told by an enthusiastic Eldridge to look no further—he would take on the job. Roy was soon in his element, skillfully producing swinging rhythms on his new "toy," and playing a bongo feature on *Caravan*. Besides his solo vocals he also shared duets he'd recorded with Anita O'Day with Gene's singer Dolores Hawkins, and on top of this he played his heart out on old features such as *After You've Gone* and more recent successes.

As before, Roy and Gene enjoyed each other's company both on and off the bandstand. Gene's enthusiasm for classical music led Roy to become interested in the works of Frederick Delius and Igor Stravinsky as well as other twentieth-century composers, though Gene never forced his tastes on other people. Trumpeter Red Rodney, who later worked with Krupa, described him as "a very beautiful man, cultured and highly intelligent, who treated everyone just marvellously."[15] Twenty years later Roy looked back on his second stay with Gene Krupa and said, "One of the best periods of my life was with Gene Krupa's big band after the war. It really was never a very good band, but for some reason we all got along together."[16] Krupa's incumbent young jazz trumpeter Don Fagerquist accepted Roy's arrival with equanimity. He told Ian Crosbie, "I still played my usual solos. Roy played all of the super-star solos, and brought the house down. He usually came out front playing and singing his special numbers."[17] Roy made several fine recordings with Gene during this second stay. One of them, *Swiss Lullaby*, was described by critic Barry Ulanov as "one of the handful of genuinely important records of 1949."[18] Roy himself cited *What's This?* as one of his favorites. Roy's own recordings for Decca had failed to achieve satisfactory sales figures, so he was released from his contract with that company and in late 1949 signed for M.G.M. Records.

Successful though the renewed partnership between Roy and Gene was, both men, observing the demise of touring big bands, realized it was not likely to be a long-term arrangement. During late-night chats Gene confided to Roy that he wasn't sure how much longer he would continue to lead a big band—even though his present unit was doing better business than most of his rivals. People had been saying for years that the big band era was about to end, but this time the prophecy seemed to be coming true. Count Basie had cut down to a small group, as had Benny Goodman, and several big names had disbanded their orchestras. Long-term prospects looked uncertain for those who were prepared to soldier on through the crisis. One bizarre plan was mooted which involved Harry James,

Tommy Dorsey, and Charlie Barnet taking it in turns (during the course of an evening) to front the same personnel. Roy was well aware of all this uncertainty and was not displeased to receive an offer from Norman Granz to be part of the J.A.T.P. 1949 fall tour, even though it would probably mean the end of his stay with Gene Krupa, who couldn't be expected to give Roy a long leave of absence at this crucial time. The two friends discussed the outcome, and decided they would both be happy to continue with the present arrangement through the summer of 1949. Accordingly, Roy played a tour that took the Krupa Band out West to huge ballrooms in Denver, Portland, Spokane, Salt Lake City, and Los Angeles. During the visit to California Roy guested on a Gene Norman Just Jazz concert in Pasadena, which also featured tenorist Teddy Edwards. The band then gradually fulfilled a series of one-night stands, eventually playing a week's booking at the Steel Pier in Atlantic City during August 1949. Tenorist John Lucak remembered the last part of Roy's touring days with the band:

> Before he went we were playing in Boston and Gene had to undergo minor surgery, which kept him off the stand for three days. The first night we hired Boston's top drummer, but after one set he was paid off and Roy took over on drums for the rest of the night. He could play the arrangements almost as well as Gene. On the second night we had another "hot shot" who lasted about two numbers and Roy finished the night again. We didn't bother to find another drummer for the third night.[19]

Roy began his J.A.T.P. tour on September 17, 1949, but returned briefly to Krupa's band to fulfill a week's contracted booking at the Apollo Theater from October 14 to 20, 1949. Gene continued to lead a big band for a further eighteen months, after which he formed a highly successful trio. Most of the critics enjoyed Roy's contributions to the Krupa Band, but as soon as he donned the J.A.T.P. mantle it seemed as though he was a sitting target. Playing ultra-high notes was an integral part of Roy's trumpet style, but this strategy didn't please John S. Wilson, reviewing the J.A.T.P. midnight performance at Carnegie Hall. He wrote, "Aside from a breathy solo on *Embraceable You*, Eldridge confined himself to a few shrieks."[20] Roy usually feigned indifference to such reviews, but he became exasperated when any critic attempted to analyze his feelings:

> It's hilarious how some people say, "Eldridge plays with anger." You know, I'm not angry! That's the vitality I've got in me and that's in my playing, that's not anger. I don't buy that shit of reading other things into your playing.[21]

Roy loved the hurly-burly atmosphere of a jam session, and always did his best to create excitement on up-tempo numbers. He was a catalyst, and usually the bigger the event the more he was motivated. He had no trouble in working himself into a combative mood for a big concert at Carnegie Hall. The September 1949 concert there marked the J.A.T.P. debut of the young Canadian pianist Oscar Peterson. It was reported that Peterson was in the audience at Carnegie simply as a guest of Norman Granz, but as the concert progressed, Granz called the young man up on stage to play. Roy always chuckled when this story was trotted out, because he had arrived early for the concert (as was his wont), and found Oscar Peterson already at the keyboard warming up. Ella Fitzgerald was next to arrive, and Roy then introduced them to each other. Later Oscar took a place in the audience from where he accepted Granz's invitation to play. This ploy avoided any retaliatory action by the Musicians' Union and the Bureau of Immigration, which could have demanded to see a work permit if the young Canadian was deemed to have been employed to play at the concert. Roy (and Coleman Hawkins) had first heard Peterson in Canada and had been mightily impressed; over the coming years Roy was to play innumerable sessions with him.

The format for future J.A.T.P. tours was gradually evolving. This

1949 package was something of a prototype for later presentations. Roy, Lester Young, Flip Phillips, and trombonist Tommy Turk (backed by Buddy Rich on drums, Hank Jones on piano, and Ray Brown on bass) played a handful of tunes, often including a ballad medley, then Ella Fitzgerald sang with the rhythm trio prior to an intermission. Coleman Hawkins opened the second set accompanied by Rich, Jones, and Brown; then (at Carnegie) Charlie Parker and Oscar Peterson filled the guest star spot, prior to the entire cast assembling for a *How High The Moon* finale, which was followed by a *Perdido* encore. Business was excellent in most of the major cities where the troupe played, with "house full" notices regularly in use: a capacity attendance of 3600 at the Chicago Opera House was typical. But J.A.T.P. continued to have its critics, one of whom was the brilliant altoist Lee Konitz (a protégé of Lennie Tristano). His candid assessment of the shows was published in *Metronome*: "The whole idea of this thing is not designed to present music as music, but just to knock out a bunch of people with an end-product that is absolutely meaningless."[22] But the musicians working for Granz rarely complained. They were being paid generously and they always traveled first-class and stayed in the best hotels, and these benefits were supplemented by the thrill of playing to huge, abundantly responsive audiences.

The enmity between modern jazz fans and those who liked traditional jazz was beginning to hot up, with insults and disparaging remarks flying in both directions. Modernists Charlie Parker and Dizzy Gillespie regularly did their best to explain how their styles had developed, with Gillespie never failing to acknowledge how much he had been influenced by Roy Eldridge's playing. But some veterans felt the encroachment of be-bop was likely to kill off the general public's interest in any sort of jazz. Louis Armstrong entered the argument, saying, "Bop is ruining music," but trumpeter Miles Davis advocated a broadminded approach: "I don't like to hear someone put down Dixieland. Those people who say there's no music but bop are just stupid."[23] The controversy placed Roy Eldridge in something of an awkward spot. His work had played a part in shaping the improvisations of many young modernists, and he enjoyed the friendship of Dizzy Gillespie and of Howard McGhee (who won the 1950 *Down Beat* trumpet poll). He also had the highest regard for Charlie Parker's genius, but he objected to the obligatory mannerisms that seemingly had to be present in every be-bop performance, and he did not like bop drumming. Howard McGhee spoke of Roy's attitude:

> Roy told me one time, we were going downtown, on a Jazz at the Philharmonic tour, I think it was 1947, 1948, he told me, "You don't like that bebop do you?" and I said, "You're not going to like me for saying it but I like it." He was trying to get me on his side. I couldn't go for that, even though he was my idol a long time ago.[24]

On another occasion, Roy cited what he didn't like about so-called be-bop cliques:

> With a lot of modernists it was often a matter of you having to know the first chorus. I listen to all the records and they rub off on you, and sometimes I'd get with a young group and to keep the peace I had to play a few of the riffs from the opening chorus, and they thought I was wailing because I knew these riffs. They had their set things you had to play to be considered modern.[25]

When Roy selected his ten favorite records for the *Metronome Yearbook* 1950, the only "modern" item was Dizzy Gillespie's *I Can't Get Started*, the rest being a mixed bunch. Three of the selections honored Roy's early idols: Coleman Hawkins (*Yesterdays*), Benny Carter (*Cocktails For Two*), and Chu Berry (*A Ghost Of A Chance*). Louis Jordan's *Saturday Night Fish Fry* was included, as was Duke Ellington's *All Too Soon*, and Illinois Jacquet's *She's Funny That Way*, followed by Morton Gould's *Body And Soul*, David Rose's *Bewitched*, and Mantovani's *The Dream Of Olwen*.

The 1949 J.A.T.P. tour ended, and Roy was again struck by the paucity of available gigs around the New York area, so, for the umpteenth time in his career, he made for Chicago, but he found that in working there as a single he was invariably backed by young (and he felt) unsympathetic bop musicians. This was the case at the Silhouette in December 1949, but when he was invited back to play there in January 1950, he only agreed to return provided he was given suitable accompaniment. The management complied with Roy's request, and as a result he was backed by a group led by the ex-Earl Hines musician George Dixon, containing two of Roy's former sidemen, pianist Rozelle Claxton and drummer Alvin Burroughs, plus bassist Lotus Perkins. Two drum kits were set up so Roy could play percussion duets with Alvin Burroughs. At the Silhouette, Roy engaged in a duet-cum-duel with Henry "Red" Allen, who dropped into the club after playing a Chicago gig. Roy greatly enjoyed this second booking at the Silhouette, but he gradually came to realize that he would increasingly be backed by house bands who wanted to play bop. He later admitted that he got depressed about the situation, thinking that perhaps his style was outdated and not likely to be appreciated by young listeners. He said:

> I had to go away and think. Things were getting so turned round in music I couldn't figure out which way to go. I listened to all the records, but I'd always go back to Hawkins, Carter, Tatum, Teddy Wilson, etc., because they seemed to be playing with more originality, and they seemed to be playing more music all the time than the others. They didn't get so set, so involved with stock things.[26]

By the end of the 1940s Dizzy Gillespie was winning most of the popularity polls organized by various jazz magazines. Roy continued to figure in the top ten placings (well below Miles Davis and Chet Baker) during the coming years, but Roy found no solace in gaining votes in these contests during what was a depressing period for him.

Fortunately, a figure from his past—Benny Goodman—approached Roy via agent Billy Shaw, and asked him to be part of a sextet he planned to take to Europe in April 1950. The offer appealed to Roy, but first he had to face up to a family dilemma: his brother Joe was suffering from a chronic illness that was getting steadily worse, and Roy didn't want to be thousands of miles away if Joe's condition suddenly deteriorated. Roy went to Pittsburgh to ask his father's advice, pointing out to his dad that there was a chance that he might remain in Europe for some time. Alexander Eldridge assured Roy that there was nothing he could do to help Joe, and offered his best wishes for a successful stay in Europe. Roy then confirmed that he was available to be part of the small group that Goodman was organizing, which consisted of tenorist Zoot Sims, drummer Ed Shaughnessy, Goodman on clarinet, and an ex-Skitch Henderson singer Nancy Reed, then 24 years old. Pianist Jimmy Rowles was originally scheduled to make the trip, but other commitments prevented him from doing so, and his place was taken by a brilliant young musician, Dick Hyman. English bassist Charlie Short (with whom Goodman had worked in London in 1949) joined up with the group after it arrived in Europe, as did the Belgian harmonica player and guitarist Jean "Toots" Thielemans (who had been recommended to Goodman by Billy Shaw).

The Goodman group left New York on April 15, 1950 and flew to Europe aboard a Scandinavian Airlines plane, which refueled in Greenland and in Prestwick, Scotland before landing in Denmark. Some sources indicate that before continuing on to Scandinavia the troupe stayed overnight in London and performed there, but that is not so: the plane actually flew straight from Prestwick to Copenhagen. Drummer Ed Shaughnessy was particularly disappointed that England wasn't on the tour itinerary because he had hoped to link up with various British drummers with whom he was corresponding. Nevertheless, Shaughnessy was looking forward to the tour, having been primed about working with Benny Goodman by a musician who had experienced that situation, Lionel Hampton:

A week before we left for Europe, Lionel Hampton called me aside and said, "I hear you're going to Europe with the King of Swing. Well, I want you to know he's weird, but I can tell you how to deal with him. When he gets strange, you get stranger, and that works." And it did![27]

Pianist Dick Hyman has happy memories of that trip. He was newly married and his wife traveled with him:

> There were no written arrangements, but there were enough rehearsals in New York to work things out. We all knew the basic B.G. arrangements and no doubt took our own notes. We all stayed in the same hotel, except for Benny, probably Muriel Zuckerman (Benny's personal assistant) and Nancy Reed. The tour seemed quite smooth to me, but I was so young, inexperienced, and so thrilled to be along, I wasn't critical.[28]

Roy Eldridge needed no advice on how to deal with Benny Goodman. They had known one another for fifteen years, and, despite making various recordings together, they were not good friends. On this tour Roy was quite prepared to bite his tongue rather than have a slanging match with Goodman. However, B.G. was at his most unpredictable at the start of this odyssey and fired Roy as soon as they had completed their opening date in Copenhagen (on April 21). Looking back, Roy said:

> The only run-in we had was right after our first date in Copenhagen. I went over twice as well as Benny at the concert and naturally Benny didn't like that. He complained about my drinking—and I wasn't juiced—but he told me to take the next plane back to New York.[29]

Fortunately, Goodman soon cooled down and rescinded the dismissal almost immediately, and from then on things proceeded fairly smoothly, if guardedly, between the two men. Goodman even vouched for Roy's good character when the trumpeter had been interviewed by local police after some excessive carousing in a Copenhagen club. Harald Grut gave the opening concert a mixed review in the *Melody Maker*. After praising the rhythm section for the way they accompanied Goodman on the quartet numbers that opened the show, he went on to say, "When tenor saxist Zoot Sims augmented the quartet he provided a good example of modern tenor sax playing," but added, "I was not amused by Thieleman's rendering of *Stardust*, but his guitar solos showed him to be a talented performer." However, most of Grut's comments were devoted to Roy's playing:

> Roy Eldridge was the least perfect of the crew, therefore the perpetrator of the happiest moments during the concert. His show-off numbers were frankly awful—a combination of less polished Louis Armstrong, half-digested Dizzy Gillespie (Dizzy is my boy, Roy told me) and a certain amount of Eldridge. But his high-register trumpet playing brought the house down. At other times he swung the band in an incredible fashion. He managed to bring heart into a concert that lacked it most of the time.[30]

All in all, the group played four concerts at Copenhagen's K. B. Halle, and when these shows ended the group (minus Benny Goodman) usually dropped into the jam sessions that were held nearby. The scars of the Goodman–Eldridge contretemps were not visible to the public, and they both arrived in Sweden with smiles on their faces, though one suspects that inwardly Roy was seething because he felt he had been reprimanded for trying his best:

> I went along to Stockholm and all of us were really dragged; nobody played good and Benny missed that last high note on *The World Is Waiting For The Sunrise*. I felt so bad I had to get some schnapps to make it. After that Benny said he didn't mind my drinking on the job. Everything went along fine.

Later on I even had Benny dancing and scat-singing on stage, one time he handed me his clarinet and I blew a little. We had a ball.[31]

Later the group found an after-hours jam session in Stockholm, and Zoot Sims and Charlie Short stayed there until 4 a.m. Zoot welcomed the chance to unwind: his feature had gone so well with the audience that it was withdrawn by Benny from the second house performance. Zoot, like Roy, felt he couldn't win with Benny Goodman. At each of the bookings in Denmark, Sweden, and Norway, the group was warmly welcomed, but although spring had officially arrived, the visitors encountered some sudden bursts of bitterly cold weather. At an outdoor performance in Oslo, Norway, Goodman played the concert in his camel-hair overcoat; Dick Hyman never forgot the way his piano technique slowed down as the frost got to his fingers. Happily there is a permanent memento of the sextet's visit to Sweden in the shape of a C.D., part of which features Nancy Reed sharing a duet with Roy (à la Eldridge–O'Day) on *Let Me Off Uptown*. Reed was a fine singer who also sometimes accompanied herself on piano. In 1999 she looked back on the tour with pleasure:

Roy, Ed Shaughnessy and I were a sort of triumvirate, sightseeing and biking (in Belgium). My nickname for Roy was "Cups," a play on his pronunciation of "merci beau-coups," which came out sounding like "merky bo-cups." One night we were given a party at a jazz club in Basel, Switzerland. The decor was real sharks in a tank and some wild, caged animals. Roy and Eddie played a joke on me, they had the owner (a jazz buff) place a boa constrictor under my seat and it proceeded to wrap itself around my leg. They saw great humor in my shocked face. Roy drank a lot, but it didn't inhibit his performances. He was a smash hit everywhere. Roy was a true character, and original and thrilling soloist who was also very funny and unpredictable.[32]

The group encountered the warmer climate of Italy as they moved south to play further concert dates. Throughout the tour, Roy shared a hotel room with Ed Shaughnessy. Ed found Roy "terrific both as a player and as a person";[33] both of them managed to see the funny side of Benny Goodman's often irrational behavior. Shaughnessy recalls, "Benny was playing great, but he always let his foibles show when he was on tour."[34] In Rome, Eldridge and Shaughnessy were advised by the hotelier not to drink the tap water, so they bought a huge five-gallon straw-covered flask of Chianti and drank that instead. They also used it to clean their teeth, which led Roy to observe, "We're not letting the water get to us and we're starting the day with a nice buzz."[35] Originally the group had been told that, following their bookings in Italy, they would play a series of dates in Switzerland and France, but not all of these engagements materialized. When the musicians asked Goodman about being paid for these cancelations, he simply shrugged his shoulders and said he couldn't see any payment being forthcoming. Dick Hyman recalled, "We threatened to return home, if as Benny suggested, our pay might be docked for the week when there would be no bookings."[36] A major row was averted when Roy was offered the chance to take the outfit, *sans* Benny Goodman, to play for a series of dances at the Odeon in Basel, Switzerland. By playing these dates the musicians were able to fund themselves and have enough money spare to travel on to Paris, where Goodman was resting before the group's next engagements—an eight-day tour of Belgium. In Paris, Roy linked up with his old buddy from Pittsburgh, drummer Kenny Clarke, who was by this time a resident in France. Kenny Clarke was particularly helpful to Ed Shaughnessy, showing him around the city and introducing him to local musicians.

In Paris, Goodman gave an interview in which he summarized what had happened at the concerts:

The old favourites went down best. Nancy Reed's *I Can't Give You Anything But Love, I Would Do Most Anything For You* and *Where Or When* were hot favourites. Roy Eldridge's trumpet brought the house down. European audiences were not very different from the American variety, and I had no trouble with bop fans. Bop? I never think about it.[37]

The group moved into Belgium on Sunday, May 28, 1950 and played the first of two concerts at the Knocke Casino. A series of appearances in various Belgian towns followed, culminating in two concerts in Brussels (arranged by the Hot Club of Belgium) after which they moved back to Paris for two shows at the Palais Chaillot, where Ed Shaughnessy had occasion to use the advice that had been given to him by Lionel Hampton:

> To my horror I found I was about thirty minutes late getting to the rehearsal for the concert; a French taxi driver had taken the wrong route. I entered the hall and saw Benny sitting on stage doodling; he looked at me and gave a fierce stare. I looked back and said, "Hell, Benny, are we going to sit around or are we going to play?" Benny looked amazed and turned to the other waiting musicians and said, "The kid's right, let's start playing." He didn't take any action, but Roy suffered. At the first concert his *Rockin' Chair* was given a tremendous ovation, so Benny cut it out of the second show.[38]

Typically Benny saw to it that the tour ended in acrimony. Goodman's agitation was sparked off by the fact that Roy had accepted an offer to record six titles for French *Vogue* during the stay in Paris, using Hyman, Shaughnessy, and Zoot Sims, with French bassist Pierre Michelot taking Charlie Short's place. Roy later commented on the session, "Everyone was so relaxed, we made six sides in less than three hours, and no master-minds in the control booth telling us what to do. It wasn't like any session I'd ever made."[39] When Goodman got to hear about these June 1950 recordings (issued by King David and his Little Jazz), he refused to pay the musicians for the last five days of the tour, telling them, as Ed Shaughnessy recalls, that he had an exclusive right to their musical services throughout the duration of the tour. Shaughnessy added, "I flew back to the States with Zoot, we were both absolutely broke. We got a taxi from the airport to Charlie's Tavern in New York and got the bartender to loan us $20 to pay the cab fare."[40]

Because bassist Charlie Short hadn't been on the recordings, he emerged unscathed from Goodman's financial penalties. Short's end-of-tour assessment was quite revealing. After acknowledging that there had been some "super sessions" he said:

> Benny? He plays a collection of clichés, which he seems to have accumulated over the years. He plays what you expect him to. It's not particularly exciting, a lot of the same phrases crop up in different numbers. When he plays anything tricky he lifts one foot off the ground. The crowd enjoy that. They seem to think it's terrific for him to play the stuff on one leg. Dick Hyman is a very good pianist, but he rarely gets a chance to get going. Zoot Sims was a good example of modern tenor playing, he's a good tenor player by any standard. He plays more jazz than anyone else in the group. Yes, even more than Roy Eldridge. Roy is exciting because he blows. I wouldn't say he was a great technician, but he really swings.[41]

Roy wasn't enamored of Benny Goodman's behavior on this tour, and even took a swipe at Benny's musicianship by saying, "Sometimes he definitely played the wrong changes."[42]

Goodman briefly remained in Paris when the tour ended, then flew back to the States—not on the same plane as any of his musicians—but Roy decided to carry out a plan he had been considering for some time. He decided to remain in the French capital, making it his base for working throughout Europe. With the help of a letter from a sympathetic doctor, Roy managed to extend his return air ticket to cover a year and a day from the time he had left the U.S.A. in April 1950. Long before Roy went to Europe with Benny Goodman he had received various offers to work as a single in

Europe, but wisely decided to summarize the situation at first hand: "Charles Delaunay had already propositioned me to take some jobs in Paris and I made up my mind to stay."[43] Delaunay himself said, "To be in Paris for Roy was like starting a new life."[44]

9

INTERLUDE
IN PARIS

The motivation behind Roy's decision to remain in Europe didn't concern money. He realized that he would be offered only a small number of well-paid concerts, and that most of his bookings would be as a guest star in small jazz clubs. The idea of enjoying a respite from racial tension greatly appealed to Roy, and this linked with his realization that, in the U.S.A., he was increasingly being thought of as no longer in the vanguard of jazz exploration. The emergence of a steady stream of talented young be-bop players had hit the headlines, and captured the interest of many jazz fans. Roy was still capable of producing extraordinary flights of imaginative playing, embracing rhythmic and harmonic daring, but detractors pointed out that he had scarcely changed his approach to improvising since the late 1930s. His solos were still awesome and exciting, but they could not be mistaken for be-bop, and thus were not what the fans of modern jazz wanted. It was of no significance to them that Roy's work had provided the main struts in shaping the style of many of the heralded bop trumpeters. Roy analyzed the situation: "I felt out of place. My playing didn't seem to fit."[1] Being thought of as "old hat" was, for Roy, almost too painful to be contemplated. Strangely, during the last part of his life, he chose to deny that his sojourn in Europe had anything to do with the encroachment of bop, maintaining that it was entirely because of racial pressures. He told Phil Schaap in March 1987:

> I just got tired of running up problems in these towns. Having a pocketful of money but can't find a place to eat. They've been writing about this thing that when this other music started I got frightened and ran from it. Which is a lie.[2]

However, this viewpoint directly contradicted what Roy had said in several interviews during the 1950s and 1960s, in which it seemed his intention was to work in surroundings where the scorching intensity of his playing wouldn't be thought of as simply a curio from the past. He outlined his thoughts in Paris, during the summer of 1950:

> Progress in music, yes, but no bloody revolution. A lot of people seem to think I'm against bop. I'm not, but it's no use plugging it when so many people just don't catch on. I believe music must have something that the fans can whistle. Sandwich a progressive number between two real tunes. That's the way to get them interested.[3]

During his stay in France, Roy wrote some articles for the *Paris Post*, the first of which was entitled "Is bop dead?" For most of that summer, Roy guested with what would now be called a "mainstream" band (led by tenorist Jean-Claude Fohrenbach) which played at the Club Saint-Germain-des-Prés. Roy, as the featured guest star, came on stage for two sets a night, after the resident band had played a few numbers; he built his program around old favorites such as *I Can't Get Started, I Surrender Dear, Undecided, I'm Confessin', Knock Me A Kiss*, and *Schooldays*. Roy's most requested number was *Rockin' Chair*, which he played only occasionally. The band consisted of Benny Vasseur on trombone, Gerard Bayol on trumpet, Claude Pallier on alto-sax and clarinet, Robert Barnet on drums, various bass players, and J.-C. Fohrenbach on tenor-sax (and occasionally piano). Most evenings Roy sat down at the piano and played some boogie numbers, backed by enthusiastic riffing from the band. The American jazz critic Barry Ulanov, on a trip to Europe, heard Roy in Paris and wrote in *Metronome*:

> Roy Eldridge at Paris's Club St Germain des Pres in 1950 is the Roy Eldridge of Chicago's Three Deuces in 1936. This is not the Roy you may remember from recent appearances with Gene Krupa; this is not even the Little Jazz who presided over his own bands between intermittent appearances with Gene and Artie Shaw. This is a little man with an enormous excitement, who loves being in Paris, adores his audiences, and doesn't mind any of the concessions he makes to the tourist listeners. Roy is blowing his head off and that's welcome music. Undressed by American standards, playing in an open, short-sleeved sports shirt, Roy sings *Schooldays*, *Knock Me A Kiss* and other jazz simples and makes complexes of voice, beat and personality. He winks at the customers, blows a kiss to that one, extends a warm hand, stretches a joyous smile across grappling couples and grasping waiters.[4]

Ulanov's only gripe was about the French rhythm section, which he said, "seems to abide by only one regulation: lose Roy's beat."[5]

Roy was happy and relaxed, and it showed in his playing. He often visited the Paris flea market and bought all sorts of knick-knacks there. He couldn't resist purchasing old broken-down radios, telling himself that it would be fun to get them working again, but he never found the time to do the repairs, and at one point his hotel room (on Rue Washington) looked like a scrap-yard. The concierge made a formal request that he got rid of this detritus, so he and a friend filled up the boot of a car with the radios and took them back to the flea market, where Roy recouped only a fraction of the money he'd paid for the wrecks. This was the era in which the Existentialist movement kindled the imagination and behavior of many young Parisiens. Roy was sympathetic to the new concepts and often sat down on the terrace of the club when he had finished playing, listening to beautiful young women explaining the philosophy to him, prior to becoming involved in things more physical than cerebral. Roy adopted one of the movement's dress codes by rolling up his trousers almost to his knees. At the suggestion of one admirer he took up painting. He also toyed with the idea of writing his autobiography after a French publisher expressed interest in such a project.

Roy met up with various American expatriate musicians in late-night bars, where they reflected on the general absence of color prejudice. Kenny Gordon (from Bermuda) observed that Roy's zest for life was immense:

> I was singing in a vocal trio, *The Three Just Men*, and I regularly met up with Roy after we'd finished work, usually at Morgan's Bar in Pigalle (where they had an upright piano upstairs). He was great company but I made the mistake of trying to keep up with his reveling—I had to quit after four nights without sleep. I crashed out but within a few hours Roy was banging on my door telling me about a party, and I know he hadn't been to sleep. It was a fantastic time in Paris for jazz: you could hear Roy, Bechet, Bill Coleman, Kenny Clarke, Don Byas, and James Moody all within the space of a night. I only saw Roy upset on one occasion and that was when a black guy, an ex-G.I., said to him, "You shouldn't be here playing for peanuts in these clubs, you're a star back in the States." I could see this really annoyed Roy and I said, "Don't pay him no mind. He's only trying to wind you up," but Roy dashed out and went back to his hotel room. He returned within minutes with a great wad of francs clutched in his hand. He walked straight up to this guy, threw all the notes at him, then turned and walked out of the door.[6]

Roy took part in various weekend "All Star" concerts. At one (with Jacques Diéval on piano) Eldridge and Don Byas played (according to a critic) "near bop." The two Americans also took part in the filming of a 21-minute documentary *Autour d'une trompette*. Roy interrupted his Saint-Germain routine by working for a week in North Africa, at the Belvedere Casino in Tunis (with Jacques Diéval's group). Roy enjoyed the Tunisian climate and the food. He'd always been willing to try exotic dishes and had long favored Mexican cuisine, so the spicy dishes of North Africa delighted him; he also acquired a taste for the fierce local red wine.

In late 1950, Roy and French pianist Claude Bolling were featured at the first of the season's Jazz Parade concerts; Bolling's Sextet backed Roy effectively, but not to the satisfaction of critic Henry Kahn:

> Roy came on and started with *The Man I Love*. Playing with a better combination he would have been even better, for he was in great form. He hit a top "A" like an angel. Roy is something of a comedian. He talks no French, but does it very well. At times the audience even understood what he was talking about.[7]

Claude Bolling recalled Roy's struggles with the French language: "We had some hilarious moments when Roy absolutely wanted to sing blues improvisations in French."[8] Roy recorded with Bolling in Paris on a quintet date, with Don Byas on tenor-sax, Guy de Fatto on bass, and Armand Molinetti on drums, and an idea sprang from that session that produced remarkable piano and trumpet duets on two of Louis Armstrong's great successes, *Wild Man Blues* and *Fireworks*. Bolling gave the background:

> At this period I was fond of Earl Hines, and Roy was crazy about Louis Armstrong, particularly on the beauty of *Cornet Chop Suey*. Listening to me practicing in the Hines manner he had the idea of recording a duet, as a remake of the famous Armstrong–Hines one, which was immediately agreed to by the recording company, because it wasn't expensive.[9]

Accordingly the two men rehearsed in the studio and then created superb duets on the two numbers. A second take of *Fireworks* shows how flexible and inspiring the format was for Eldridge and Bolling. Claude looked back with happiness at working with Roy:

> I played with Roy Eldridge at the Club du Vieux Columbier and at the Club St Germain. Some jam sessions (featuring Hot Lips Page, Max Roach, Don Byas and many others) started at the club and overtimed beyond 2 a.m., then they ran on at private homes until dawn. Roy also liked to play drums and at one of our concerts he made a contest with the drummer of the band, and we could not stop him![10]

Roy made guest appearances in various French cities, but Musicians' Union restrictions prevented him from working in Britain. He did, however, play in Frankfurt, Germany, where he was delighted by the reception, saying, "The people here are crazy about jazz—it was amazing."[11] On Roy's wide-ranging tours of Scandinavia he renewed friendships he had recently made during his tour with Benny Goodman. On the first of his visits to Sweden he shared concert dates with Charlie Parker, who was also touring Europe. Both men were represented on this trip by the agent Billy Shaw, but if anyone described Shaw as Roy's manager he quickly corrected them, saying, "booked by, but not managed by." Looking back twenty years later, Roy said:

> Charlie Parker was great. "Bird" had those roots. I'll never forget in 1950, when I was living in Paris and they sent for me to come up to the Scandinavian countries to do a concert tour with Bird. We were playing in Copenhagen, and Bird said to me, "Hey Jazz, let's get some of those Kansas City riffs going." He had those roots, where these younger cats don't.[12]

Pianist-vocalist Cab Kaye heard a concert that Parker and Eldridge shared at the National Hall in Stockholm: "Both were in great form.

Bird was backed by Rolf Ericson and Arne Domnérus. He brought the house down. Roy had the same house rocking with *Schooldays*. His playing was really inspired, though not as clear as when I heard it in 1942, but the enthusiasm made up for that."[13] At Roy's prompting, Parker was invited to appear at the International Jazz Fair, which opened in Paris on December 1, 1950. As a result, Parker left Sweden and duly arrived in Paris on November 28, but then—in one of the many about-turns that marked his career—he left France and flew back to the U.S.A. without appearing at the Jazz Fair. After agreeing with the fair's organizer, Charles Delaunay, that he would take part, he suddenly changed his mind and left for home. During the fair's Sunday night concert (December 3) Parker's voice (relayed by transatlantic telephone) was heard in the Paris Salon. Roy jumped into the conversation, saying, "This is Little Jazz talking. What did you want to leave me for?" Parker replied, "Sorry Roy. I just had to go. I would have loved to have been there." The rest of the message was lost in a swirl of atmospherics. Apparently, Parker had been instructed to leave Paris by agent Billy Shaw, who pointed out that the promoters of Parker's Scandinavian tour had paid the air fares and expenses involved, and they would have to be reimbursed if he played the Paris Fair. Roy couldn't hide his disappointment. Had Roy and Bird played together in France it might have convinced the younger critics that there wasn't an unbridgeable distance between the two men's styles. André Hodeir's observation—"In 1950, Paris fans applauded 'on trust' the great trumpeter, Roy Eldridge, at a time when he was already on the decline"[14]—was a premature assessment considering the huge number of fine recordings Roy made after that was written. Roy also inspired, and taught by example, many of the French musicians he worked with, though he was very matter-of-fact about taking credit: "Certainly some bands seem to be inspired when they are playing with a coloured musician. It may be just the idea, or we may give a real good lead and feeling. But the fact is that most French bands copy the records they have studied, and I doubt whether our arrival has made much difference."[15]

Roy returned to Sweden to fulfill a string of engagements, and in January 1951 took time out to record some neat small band sides with local musicians, including titles issued as being by Roy Eldridge And His Gramercy Five. He returned to France and played at various places, including further dates at the Club Saint-Germain, but he was mindful that almost a year had passed since his first arrival in Paris, and that the extension on his air ticket would soon be reaching its expiry date. Before he left for the U.S.A. he summarized his feelings:

Man, I like living in France, because this country has something most other countries lack. I know people will say, "Ah, that's because you're coloured. You like the free-and-easy atmosphere." Some day the U.S. will be just like France in that respect, but today even the most liberal of us cannot deny that the freedom of being able to pass through any door simply does not exist in the States for coloured folk. A lot of people back home are fighting the colour bar and they're winning. Meanwhile, here in Paris coloured musicians feel free, easy and at home. If I write a tune, I can walk into an office in Paris and say to them, "Take it, play it, and if you like it buy it." I cannot do that in the States, I first have to know someone who knows someone before my tune will get a hearing. As far as music is concerned, there is one great difference between the fans in the States and the fans in France. They make the same noise and they show the same enthusiasm—but the French fans know more about music. The vast majority prefer New Orleans and Dixieland because it is sweet—and it is amazing how this sweet music will soften and sweeten the nerves and the musician feels that he is really listened to. On the other hand, when you grow a bit boppish the enthusiasm is vocal. Is it real enthusiasm? That depends on your audience, for there is a minority with a liking for progressive music. I think it is also right to say that French musicians do not always look on us kindly. More than one has asked me why I do not go off to Sweden where the pay is better. I knew exactly what he was hinting at. It is a mistake to believe that life in France is all honey. It's not, yet I repeat, France is a lovely place to live in. Right now I'm going back to the States for a while. But I'll be back.[16]

If Roy had doubts about his ability to relaunch his career in the States they were dispelled by impresario Norman Granz, who visited France as Roy was preparing to leave. Granz played Roy some recordings (that Eldridge hadn't heard) of the 1949 Jazz at the Philharmonic Carnegie Hall concert featuring Charlie Parker and Roy. To Roy's surprise he heard that he fitted in well with line-ups that had a boppish flavor: "I listened and I couldn't believe it, it sounded good. My playing didn't stick out—it was a statement."[17] Norman Granz used the opportunity to offer Roy a five-year contract to become a regular feature of the increasingly widespread J.A.T.P. tours. Roy said, "He offered me a good contract, and to make it more appealing he showed me some bills. It was good to see real money again."[18] One thing that Roy knew he could rely on was Granz's attitude toward segregation, which the promoter himself outlined:

> When I first formed Jazz at the Philharmonic I never had any trouble playing anywhere in the South with a mixed group, and I mean anywhere. The important thing was that I had a clause in my contract in advance that said I could play with a mixed group and that I would only play before non-segregated audiences, and it was with that point of view that we managed to break down segregation, establishing in many cities a precedent for mixed audiences.[19]

Roy accepted Norman Granz's offer, and at 2 a.m. on April 3, 1951, in the lobby of the Hotel Claridge in Paris, he signed this important contract. Next day he flew back to the U.S.A. bearing lots of presents for his wife Vi and his daughter Carole. The long stay in Europe may have restored Roy's confidence, but it had not eliminated his restless urge to play. He had been back in New York for only a day before he was back in action playing a gig at the Stuyvesant Casino on Second

Avenue at 9th, where promoter Bob Maltz organized a series of Friday
night "bashes." At first, Roy was semi-reluctant to do the engagement,
and made the excuse that his trumpet was still "on the boat," though
in truth Roy hated to travel on water ("I don't even like to go across
the lake in a boat") and had flown from France. However, Maltz told
Roy it would be a "Welcome Home Night," and the trumpeter, having
gone a couple of days without exercising his lip, agreed to play. Roy
later played many gigs for Bob Maltz at the Stuyvesant, or at the
Central Plaza on Second Avenue. On Friday, April 13, 1951 he began
work in earnest, playing a residency at New York's Birdland (opposite
Dizzy Gillespie's group) leading a quintet that featured two of the
musicians with whom he had shared the Benny Goodman "experience" in Europe: tenorist Zoot Sims and drummer Ed Shaughnessy.
Dick Hyman couldn't be considered for the gig because he'd just
started a solo residency at New York's Little Club. Instead, Billy Taylor
played piano, alongside bassist Clyde Lombardi. The group soon
melded into a swinging unit, with Roy and Zoot quickly re-establish-
ing the happy and productive partnership they'd enjoyed in Europe.
The only discordant note that occurred during the residency
concerned an interview which writer Leonard Feather prized out of
Roy.

The saga began during one of disk jockey Symphony Sid Torin's
W.J.Z. radio shows, which was broadcast from Birdland. On this
particular program Roy presented Miles Davis with a *Down Beat*
plaque commemorating his success in that magazine's annual
popularity poll. Roy was never an avid fan of Miles' playing, but
was not displeased when Davis said in a 1950 interview, "When I was
growing up I played like Roy Eldridge, Harry James, Freddie Webster
and anyone else I admired."[20] Knowing that Miles had already
developed a penchant for candor, Roy was pleased to be the first one
mentioned in that listing; however, Miles' outspokenness caught Roy
on the hop during the live radio show presentation. Before the
program began, Roy and Miles had chatted together, with Roy
emphasizing the merits of Europe and the lack of a color bar there.

He then added a few moans about Benny Goodman's madcap behavior. The show started and Roy, projecting his usual public ebullience, began by saying, "I'm sure glad to be back. It's good to see the lights of Broadway again." Whereupon Miles interrupted by saying, "Why don't you tell them what you were just telling me?" Leonard Feather, standing close by, reported Symphony Sid's reaction: "After a moment of embarrassed, dead air, Sid tactfully changed the subject."[21]

Leonard Feather was too adept a reporter not to sense that there was a good story lurking within this brief exchange, and when the transmission had ended he honed in on Roy asking about the background to Miles' comment. On being faced with a journalist's direct questions, Roy often joked his way around anything that seemed too probing, or else gave the questioner a long, hard look and said nothing, but on this occasion he decided to get matters off his chest, and did so in a way that pitchforked his words on to the front page of *Down Beat*. Under a banner headline, "No more white bands for me, says Little Jazz," Roy bitterly compared his trouble-free stay in Europe with the racial problems he had encountered during his touring days with Gene Krupa and Artic Shaw.

> "It was a wonderful year. During that whole time I was never once reminded that I was colored—the only exception was when there were some visiting Americans out to make trouble." Leonard Feather asked if this was the reason for Roy's decision not to work for a white bandleader. Roy replied, "No it goes back way before that. All the way back to 10 years ago when I joined Gene Krupa's Band."[22]

Roy went on to describe the indignities of not being able to stay at the same hotel as his Krupa colleagues, not being allowed to sit with fans (some of them famous people), being asked to travel in a separate car during a rail journey through Virginia, adding that there was no lessening of the problems when he toured with Artie Shaw.

Roy concluded his painful reminiscences by saying, "Man, when you're on the stage you're great, but as soon as you come off you're nothing. It's not worth the glory, not worth the money, not worth anything. It was the trip to Europe that made me really realize that and made up my mind for good. Never again!"[23]

Roy's comments provoked a great deal of discussion in the music profession. One of the first in print about the article was Lena Horne, by then an internationally known film star and singer:

> My opinion is that Leonard Feather just happened to catch Roy in one of his bad moments, moments all of us have known in this business. I love Roy. He is a great musician and one of my best friends. I hope others will not be influenced by his decision, if he really meant what he said, because we can't lick a problem by running away from it.[24]

Roy felt aggrieved at the way Feather had slanted the story, and he remained angry over that article for many years. In 1982 he told Dan Morgenstern, "They thought I was putting the white race down and it didn't have nothing to do with that."[25]

Roy temporarily left New York to play at Lindsay's Club in Cleveland, Ohio, with his own quintet, featuring tenorist Zoot Sims, bassist Ted Sturgis, vibraphonist Teddy Cohen, and a drummer who had worked with him in the 1930s, Harold "Doc" West. Sadly, West, aged 36, suffered a fatal heart attack on May 4, while the quintet was working in Cleveland. Roy was very distressed by this tragedy but decided to carry on with the tour, using Phil Brown on drums as a replacement. They played at Frank Holzfeind's Blue Note Club in Chicago from May 18 to 31, then Roy and Zoot did a two-week residency at the Colonial Tavern in Toronto, Canada. During Roy's stay in Chicago he had a long discussion with Frank Holzfeind about the recent *Down Beat* article, and this talk undoubtedly prompted the club-owner to write in *Down Beat*:

A good headline doesn't put Roy in the position of a crusader. Because he is the great musician that he is, he is asked to play with the best—not because the best is getting big-hearted about the fact that a Negro should be given equal opportunities. These musicians would take a musician like Roy if he were any color. Experiences don't make him bitter. He can overlook the time when he wanted to buy a drink at the bar where he worked only a month before and the bartender "friend" didn't sell him a drink, or when the magazine dedicated to the Advancement, etc., refused to publish pictures of such incidents. I feel that he's doing more for a proper evaluation of the Negro than those who accept the sprinkling of crumbs that fall to the meek if not the humble.[26]

But Leonard Feather was an astute journalist who, in his own view, did what countless other reporters have done in quoting off-the-cuff remarks. However, Roy's problems with Feather didn't end with that article. Soon after this "bombshell" Feather seized upon another comment by Roy and created a controversial feature out of it:

When Roy Eldridge returned after a year in France it seemed to me that some of the French Crow Jim attitude had rubbed off on him. Just as the French jazz fan or critic arbitrarily invents some non-existent types of music such as "Black jazz," "American white jazz," etc. Roy claimed he could distinguish a white musician from a Negro simply by listening to his style. "You wanna bet?" I asked. The result was a unique blindfold test, a challenge to Roy's ability to separate musicians along racial lines. Even the law of chance should have made him 50 per cent correct, yet, as I expected, Roy proved to be wrong or noncommittal more often than he was right.[27]

Roy listened to the records that Feather had selected for the test and recognized performers on five of them: Zoot Sims, Pee Wee Russell, Woody Herman, Bill Harris, and Eddie Miller, but missed various pianists including George Shearing, Tadd Dameron, Billy

Taylor, and a duet featuring Duke Ellington and Billy Strayhorn. Of Miles Davis' *Venus De Milo* he said, "I couldn't tell whether this is white or colored. Most of these guys play with hardly any vibrato. One minute I thought it might be by Miles Davis, but it's not quite his sound." Of Billy Taylor's Quartet, Roy said, "They could be Eskimos for all I know." When the test was over, Roy said to Feather: "I guess I'll have to go along with you Leonard—you can't tell just from listening to records. But I still say I could spot a white imitator of a colored musician immediately. Okay, you win the argument.[28]

But Roy never really forgave Feather for making such a big issue out of what Roy insisted was a misquotation of what he had said in the first place. Roy made his point to Dan Morgenstern, saying, "Boy, that cat really hung me on the wall with that."[29]

Using a line-up of Billy Taylor (piano), Art Blakey (drums), and Curly Russell (bass), Roy played another residency at Birdland (opposite vibraphonist Terry Gibbs). When this ended, Roy, together with Coleman Hawkins and Terry Gibbs, went to work at New York's Embers Club, where the pianist was scheduled to have been Eddie Heywood, Jr. (with whom Roy had worked and recorded years earlier). But in the interim Heywood had enjoyed a great deal of success, so much so that instead of buckling down to rehearse with Roy and Hawk he went to great lengths to rearrange the setting of the stage lights so they shone brilliantly on him. Roy observed this maneuver with some agitation, getting angrier by the minute. Finally Heywood noticed the look on Roy's face, who later described himself as being "fit to be tied," and decided it would not be wise for him to remain within this line-up, a fact he announced by saying, "My manager doesn't want me to play with you." Happily, pianist Marian McPartland was on hand, and told Roy and Hawk that she would be honored to work with them, so a musical disaster was averted and a happy friendship established.[30]

It was soon time for Roy to begin fulfilling his contracted appearances with Norman Granz's J.A.T.P., whose eleventh national tour began on September 14, 1951 in Hartford, Connecticut, then played in Newark, N.J., prior to playing at Carnegie Hall. The full line-up was Ella Fitzgerald (vocals), Lester Young, Illinois Jacquet, and Flip Phillips (tenor-saxes), Bill Harris (trombone), Ray Brown (bass), Gene Krupa (drums), Roy Eldridge (trumpet), and two pianists: Oscar Peterson and Hank Jones (Ella's accompanist). Gene Krupa was a late addition to the troupe; his presence delighted Roy, and Norman Granz was also pleased when Krupa agreed to be part of the package. He said, "I think, honestly that the musicians play better with his beat because they like the guy so much personally."[31] Pundits had expected that the percussionist for this tour would be Buddy Rich, who had often been part of Granz's presentations, but the promoter explained why this was not so: "Finally, I reached the end of my patience with Buddy Rich." The two men later had a reconciliation. Krupa was a model of enthusiasm, both on and off the stage. Relieved at not having the worries of bandleading, he summarized his feelings by saying, "No headaches, no ulcers, fine people, just a ball all the time."[32]

In general a happy, co-operative spirit flourished backstage on this tour, allowing for the fact that once they were on stage each musician tried his or her hardest to be the top performer. Roy thrived in this atmosphere. After playing a coast-to-coast tour that involved almost fifty concerts, the members of the troupe went their own separate ways, knowing that most of them would soon reconvene for the spring 1952 tour. Several of the musicians took time off to rest after completing the grueling schedule, but not Roy Eldridge. Within days of returning home he was guesting with various Dixieland musicians at the Stuyvesant Casino, prior to playing residencies in Boston in November 1951. After working at Boston's Storyville Club in December Roy played for a week at the Colonial Tavern in Toronto, leading his own group, an unusual feature of which (in this era) was the inclusion of a female bassist, Bonnie Wetzel (née Bonnie Jean Addleman), widow of the recently deceased trumpeter, Ray Wetzel. The rest of Roy's personnel consisted of Teddy Brannon on piano and Carl "Kansas" Fields on drums—it was one of the first times that a trumpet and rhythm section line-up had worked regularly as a touring unit. For Roy this quartet was only a short-lived venture, but another departure from routine found him recording for the first time with strings (in December 1951).

In January 1952 Roy took part in a reunion with Anita O'Day (one that neither of them went out of their way to share), but by then each had signed recording contracts with Norman Granz, and it was under his auspices that the studio sessions (with Ralph Burns and his Orchestra) took place. Roy was not called upon to duet vocally with Anita; his task was to play trumpet in what was an all-star septet backing the singer. The most prestigious booking that Roy played during this early part of 1952 was a February appearance at the Apollo Theater where he shared the bill with Erroll Garner and Buddy Rich, but alongside the professional elation caused by his recent successes Roy experienced great personal sadness when his brother Joe died in March 1952. Joe, aged 44, had long been in poor health and hadn't played in public for some while, though he had managed to do some teaching from his New York home during the final year of his life. Choked with emotion, Roy said, "He taught me all I know about music." Twenty-five years later Roy said poignantly of his brother, "He was the musician in the family. I was just the jive cat."[33] The fact that Joe's death was not unexpected didn't lessen the pain for Roy, but he had to continue with his professional schedule, and on March 26 left Idlewild Airport for J.A.T.P.'s first tour of Europe. Although the tour was not a long one (it ended on April 20) the troupe played in seven European countries, and, in most of the foreign cities the show visited, it played two sell-out concerts each evening. Roy and Lester Young were room-mates throughout most of the tour. It was Lester's first visit to Europe, and he was guided on whatever sightseeing there was time for by Roy, who had recently visited many of the same places during his travels with Benny Goodman. Roy told Graham Colombé, "We always had a lot of fun together." When Colombé asked, "Was Coleman Hawkins easier to get to know than Lester Young?", Roy replied, "Neither of them was easy. They liked my playing and I liked theirs. They both inspired my playing. But they weren't close to many other people."[34]

On the occasions that the J.A.T.P. troupe traveled by band-bus, the atmosphere on board engendered the sort of practical jokes that might surface on a school trip. On one journey Charlie Shavers and Roy Eldridge decided to hide Lester Young's bottle of whiskey. He soon discovered his loss, but couldn't ascertain who had taken the booze. He didn't lose his temper, but walked to the front of the bus and solemnly announced, "Whoever has taken my whisky, I'm their mother's best man."[35] On this spring 1952 tour the J.A.T.P. musicians were given a short break in Paris, where Roy happily spent time with local friends, while Oscar Peterson, Flip Phillips, and Norman Granz crossed the Channel to indulge in several hours of shopping and sightseeing in London (the Musicians' Union rule banning performances by foreign musicians was still in force). The tour ended in Frankfurt, Germany, where the musicians played two concerts in addition to making a brief appearance at the General Hospital, where they played for the patients. After the concerts had ended there was what Norman Granz described as an unfortunate incident: "Roy went to a club with friends and was refused service by an American headwaiter."[36] On this, and on all of his subsequent travels with J.A.T.P., Roy usually found time to observe the local music scene, which was sometimes a mixed pleasure, as he recalled:

> Funniest I ever heard was when Gene Krupa and I went to a club in Stuttgart, Germany, and the Dixieland Band there sounded as if they had just picked up their horns a couple of weeks before. As for revivalist bands, I heard one and that got a little too far back. I've been playing for a thousand years but that's about a thousand years before me.[37]

Roy and Gene Krupa shared a considerably more dramatic incident:

> We used to heckle each other when we were travelling. I'd go

to sleep and he'd wake me. I'd wait until he began to snooze and I'd wake him. Well, we were flying to Norman, Oklahoma for a date at the college there. Because we were having a rough trip we declared a truce. Gene gives me the elbow and said, "Hey Jazz, you better wake up." I said, "I thought you weren't gonna start..." He was real serious, "You'd better wake up man, I think the plane's on fire." Half awake I thought it was a put on. Then he pointed out of the plane's window to the wing, sure enough, there was a little fire going on. Ray Brown and Whitey Mitchell came running down the aisle with their basses. They wanted them in the back of the plane in case we crashed. Flip Phillips or Bill Harris, one of the two, started whistling *The High And The Mighty*. Buddy Rich got salty. Then we gathered together, shook hands and said it had been nice doing the tour and all that. We really didn't think we were going to make it. We landed in Garden City, Kansas, with just one engine.[38]

When the J.A.T.P. returned to the States after their spring 1952 trip to Europe, Roy followed his usual procedure and was soon on his way to play a two-week residency at Tootie's Mayfair Club in Kansas City, Missouri. When that booking ended Roy spent a further month in Kansas City working with saxophonist Leo Parker. This was only a temporary pairing, but a small, two-line item in the *Down Beat* issue of July 30, 1952 gave news of a musical partnership that was to become an important feature of Roy's working life throughout the next fifteen years. The initial news announcement simply mentioned that the "newly formed Coleman Hawkins–Roy Eldridge Quintet" would be playing at the Capitol, Chicago in July 1952. Roy's musical partnership with Hawkins produced a great deal of wonderful jazz, but the regular meetings of two such diverse personalities produced a complex relationship.

Much as Roy admired Hawkins, and never failed to say that the origins of his style were founded on the saxophonist's work, he did not like the idea of taking a back seat to his hero, and no matter how many times they worked together this situation never changed. Hawk's dignified and phlegmatic poise contrasted with the impish, impulsive aspects of Roy's nature. They became friends, but never bosom pals. Bassist Peter Ind, who worked with the two men, felt they shared a "love–hate" relationship: the "love" coming from the admiration each had for the other's talent, and the "hate" from the fact that they were ceaselessly competitive. Dan Morgenstern summarized the partnership:

> It was an odd kind of relationship; they were very different people. Roy wore his heart on his sleeve, he reacted emotionally and instantly but Hawk was much more reserved. In spite of his combativeness, Roy was always sure of who he was, he wasn't at all envious, but Hawk had a pretty big ego and wasn't as open as Roy. I think he was slightly jealous of Roy because of Roy's ability to capture an audience. But after all, the trumpet is an aggressive instrument, and no matter how Hawk blew his big sound, Roy was the dominant force. Roy could blow people away, and I think Hawk sometimes felt that Roy was elbowing him out of the way, grandstanding him, but this was simply an instinctive thing on Roy's part.[39]

But during the early 1950s, the Hawkins–Eldridge partnership was the second string in Roy's bow. His main allegiance was to Norman Granz and J.A.T.P. (which provided the major part of his annual income). So, after some brief club residencies alongside Hawkins, Roy resumed working for Granz on the 1952 fall tour, which played in many of America's concert halls as it moved from coast to coast. The itinerary was similar to the 1951 trek, but Norman Granz was always devising ways of adding zest to his line-ups. He did so with a vengeance on these 1952 presentations by featuring both Buddy Rich *and* Gene Krupa on drums. Because of Roy's friendship with Krupa he usually indicated that Gene's playing pleased him more than Buddy Rich's, and on one occasion went as far as to say, "There's no comparison,"[40] though he later conceded that each man had something the other didn't possess. But even after working with Buddy Rich for years in various J.A.T.P. shows, both Roy and Coleman Hawkins felt that Rich, despite his awesome technique and remarkable individuality, didn't willingly drop into the groove of the tempo they required. Oscar Peterson observed the frowns and fall-outs that Rich's attitude caused, as his biographer Gene Lees noted:

> Roy Eldridge and Coleman Hawkins liked tempos at a medium pace that would permit them to show their abilities to best advantage. Buddy however would move them up to where he wanted them, and presumably where they showed him to best advantage. Hawkins and Eldridge, and others, would complain to Norman Granz or Oscar Peterson or both, and finally Oscar confronted Buddy.[41]

Although Eldridge and Rich often engaged in some very salty exchanges, Rich consistently cited Roy as being one of his favorite musicians, and Buddy was always in a list of Roy's favorite drummers. During the 1950s Roy selected his top drummers as Gene Krupa, Buddy Rich, Alvin Stoller, Max Roach, Kenny Clarke, and Sam Woodyard. His two favorite bassists then were Ray Brown and Wendell Marshall.[42] Besides encouraging competition between percussionists, Granz also decided to pit Roy against someone who was just about the fleetest jazz trumpeter of them all: Charlie Shavers. Charlie not only executed his phrases with awesome speed, he could also play them accurately in the highest register of the trumpet, sailing way above top "C" with consummate ease and considerable skill Charlie was plumper than Roy but of a similar height, so when they dueled on stage they resembled a pair of small, fighting bantam-cocks, each determined to make his rival buckle into submission. One night Roy would outblow Charlie, the next night it could well be Charlie's turn to triumph, but, as recordings of their concerts together show, no quarter was given or asked for, and there was never a lack of excitement. Pianist Billy Taylor recalled their perpetual competitive-ness:

Roy had just come in from Chicago and hadn't played in a couple of days, so he came to sit in with Ben Webster, to just kind of get his chops together and he was taking it very easy. Well, Charlie Shavers was at the bar and he hurried out to his car and got his trumpet and came in and challenged Roy very quickly, and you've never heard a guy's chops get together so quickly...so that was a very exciting night, two master trumpet players at the height of their powers.[43]

But off stage, Eldridge and Shavers shared jokes and drinks; neither felt that their "battles" involved any degree of personal animosity. Shavers said, "Roy Eldridge is a great friend. We used to share an apartment and people thought it was because of the trumpet thing, but we never used to talk music."[44] Roy and Charlie invariably stuck up for each other in any dispute that occurred on tour. Roy was absolutely infuriated when he learned that on one trip Ben Webster had lashed out at Charlie in a dressing-room, his blow narrowly missing Charlie's mouth. Roy thought the world of Ben, but knew only too well how the demon grog could alter his personality: "When Ben Webster was sober he was the nicest cat you ever met, but when he was drinking he'd turn rough. Sometimes he'd slap me or something like that, and I'd end up chasing him down the street, big as he was."[45] Soon after the incident with Charlie Shavers, Roy again worked with Ben, and decided to issue a warning to the tenor-saxist. Roy's ultimatum was unequivocal. He placed his pistol on the dressing-room table and told Ben that he wouldn't hesitate to use it if Ben ever made any move to strike him. Ben took this on board and never again attempted to slap Eldridge. In various interviews Charlie Shavers had no hesitation in pointing out that he had based his style on Roy's playing. He told Max Jones of the *Melody Maker*, "It came from Roy Eldridge. So far as inspiration goes. Dizzy, Sweets Edison, Bobby Moore and myself were trying to play like Roy then. Many other trumpet players were. At that time in New York Roy was the man."[46]

When the J.A.T.P. 1952 tour ended, Roy resumed working with Coleman Hawkins. By the end of that year most band-bookers were aware that the Hawkins–Eldridge Quintet was available for engagements and happily a stream of work materialized. Roy and Hawk played a week at the Colonial Tavern in Toronto, then a week at the Times Square Club in Rochester, N.Y. before moving on to California to play at the renowned Blackhawk club in San Francisco. Brief residencies in Boston, Washington, D.C., and Baltimore followed. Playing these contracted dates with Hawkins meant that Roy had to drop out of a five-week J.A.T.P. tour of Europe (which opened in Sweden on February 16, 1953). During this trip, J.A.T.P. made its debut in Britain; the British Musicians' Union waived its rules to allow the troupe to play in London for victims of a flood disaster. The only trumpeter on this tour was Charlie Shavers, and drummer J. C. Heard had taken Buddy Rich's place. Rich, who had joined Harry James, spat out his reason for not being with the show: "I don't want any part of Granz or his Jazz at the Philharmonic. It's not jazz, it's just honking and noise."[47] Granz retaliated by saying, "Buddy Rich is an unmitigated liar. Although Buddy has continued to grow in his playing he has, unfortunately, remained an adolescent."[48]

After his dates with Coleman Hawkins had temporarily ceased, Roy played for ten days in late February 1953 at the Midway Club in Pittsburgh where he worked with the house band, but in April, for a six-week stay at Lou Terrasi's (254 West 47th Street, New York), Roy booked Slam Stewart (bass), Dick Wellstood (piano), and Zutty Singleton (drums) to accompany him. On paper it might appear that these three differing stylists would not jell effectively, but, on airshots taken of Radio W.M.G.M. broadcasts from the club, it's obvious that they were an admirable musical team. But socially things were not totally harmonious, with Zutty grouching about Dick Wellstood and not paying much attention to what Roy said. Things came to a head when Roy (in response to a customer's request) asked Zutty to play his *Tiger Rag* drum feature. Roy recalled the scene:

We played it, and man, he was mad at me, then we had a break. So when it comes time for the broadcast Zutty had a solo on one of the tunes we played, and instead of playing anything, he throws his hi-hat down, dut-dut-dut—it sounded like a clock ticking. So I still didn't say anything. So we got to *After You've Gone* and he's supposed to start it off with a drum break, and he played it like he was playing a waltz, soft, you know…and the next night, Panama Francis was there; Zutty didn't show no more.[49]

The booking ended and Roy left New York to play a concert date with Coleman Hawkins in Montreal, Canada. Although the Hawkins-Eldridge partnership later achieved considerable success, it was not overly busy in 1953 mainly because the two principals had a different approach to quoting fees. Roy very rarely played for "peanuts," but his desire to play as often as possible sometimes led to him working for a bargain price rather than sitting at home. In contrast, Hawkins demanded a top rate and if this was not forthcoming he was content to relax within his salubrious New York apartment, listening to his magnificent collection of classical recordings or playing the piano in solitude. This difference in attitude irked Roy, because it meant that Billy Shaw, who was doing the booking for the quintet, had to turn down work because he couldn't get the fees that Hawkins demanded. When Roy raised this with Hawk he simply shook his head and gave a half-smile which meant that even if his tenor-sax case remained unopened for days on end he wouldn't fret. Thus Roy began working again as a single, and in July 1953 played at the Café Society, 2 Sheridan Square in the Village, alongside the Mills Brothers and Marian McPartland.

Roy was recording regularly for Norman Granz's Clef label; he was also part of a J.A.T.P. personnel that played at a Soldier Field concert in Chicago in August 1953. The line-up was a familiar one, but guitarist Herb Ellis had taken Barney Kessel's place in Oscar Peterson's Trio. The next big J.A.T.P. jaunt was a two-week tour of the Pacific area (including Japan). For this trip Benny Carter and Ben Webster were added, trombonist Bill Harris rejoined, as did altoist Willie Smith and drummer J. C. Heard. Both Roy and Charlie Shavers were on this tour and each girded himself for a succession of fierce trumpet battles. Even those J.A.T.P. musicians who sometimes adopted a blasé attitude to foreign travel were thrilled by the idea of visiting Japan. The troupe's November 1953 arrival in Tokyo was greeted with a ticker-tape welcome; Roy talked of this trip for years afterward. Happily there was enough spare time for sightseeing and opportunities to relax when the evening concerts had ended. On one such occasion, while sitting in a Ginza bar with J. C. Heard, Roy was pleased to hear what he first thought was his recording of *Embraceable You* being played over a loudspeaker system. Every contour of the trumpet solo seemed Eldridge-like, but something was not quite right—slowly Roy realized that it wasn't his own playing but someone copying his recorded performance. He soon met the perpetrator, who announced himself by saying, "I'm Japan's Number One Little Jazz." The two trumpeters became friends, and Roy met up with the skillful imitator on a subsequent visit to Japan. The internal travel in Japan was by train, and although Roy fitted comfortably into the horizontal individual sleepers, some of the larger members of the troupe, notably Oscar Peterson, Ben Webster, and Bill Harris, found them impossibly small. On the whole, the travel arrangements went smoothly throughout this Pacific tour, the only real blip occurring in Honolulu, Hawaii, when Ella Fitzgerald's luggage was lost and she had to sing in her traveling clothes. At the Civic Auditorium in Honolulu, altoist Willie Smith had the misfortune to fall off the stage as he bowed and backed away after his feature number, but fortunately he wasn't seriously hurt. The J.A.T.P. package flew back to the States in late November 1953. Roy was soon on the move again to fulfill bookings in Chicago. He then readied himself for the J.A.T.P. tour of Europe which opened in Belgium on Feburary 6, 1954. Just before he left, Roy was delighted to receive royalties from a recording that Ray Anthony had made of *I Remember Harlem* (composed by

Roy and Bob Astor, who worked for agent Billy Shaw). Anthony was always a fan of Roy's trumpet-playing and said, "He has inspired what jazz music there is in me."[50]

10

TOURS AND
TRIUMPHS

When Roy returned to the U.S.A. after J.A.T.P.'s whirlwind tour of Europe he was happy to learn that Coleman Hawkins had agreed to play some shared dates on the West Coast during the spring of 1954, including another stay at the Blackhawk, San Francisco. Roy was never an early-to-bed type, but in Hawkins he met his match when it came to staying up late: "He never wanted to go to sleep. He used to come to my room. He'd sit there and we'd be talking, next thing I'm gone and he's still talking."[1] When the quintet bookings ended, Roy stayed in California and guested for a while in a trio led by organist-pianist Milt Buckner, which featured drummer Sam Woodyard who had worked briefly with Roy a couple of years earlier. During the interim Woodyard's playing had improved dramatically, so much so that when Roy learned that Duke Ellington was looking for a new drummer he recommended Woodyard for the vacancy. Duke took Roy's advice: Woodyard later joined Ellington and remained with the band for over ten years.

Back in New York, during the early summer of 1954, Roy briefly became part of an unusual sextet that featured him and Charlie Shavers on trumpets, Teddy Charles on vibes, George Duvivier on bass, Ralph Martin on piano, and Louie Bellson on drums. The group played at Basin Street East, with Shavers opening each set, and then being joined by Eldridge for a succession of combative duets. Every number ended in high register playing with competitiveness elbowing artistry out of the way. The mixture was too unvaried for the critics, and George T. Simon wrote despairingly, "Why is it necessary for two trumpets to blow down the house every second or third chorus is something I can't understand."[2] As if to prove that there were no lasting ill feelings toward Ben Webster, Roy worked with Ben for a booking at New York's Café Bohemia where their rhythm section consisted of Johnny Acea (piano), Ted Sturgis (bass), and Shadow Wilson (drums).

The biggest event in the 1954 jazz calendar was the inaugural Newport Jazz Festival (held in Rhode Island) on July 17 and 18, but because of previous commitments neither Roy nor Hawk took part; they made their debut at the 1955 event. After the first year's successes, producer-director George Wein said, "We'll be back next year and for many years to come; this is just the beginning," a statement that proved, happily, to be all too true.

Leonard Feather continued to conduct magazine "blindfold tests," but the feature had been transferred from *Metronome* magazine to *Down Beat*. One of the summer 1954 subjects was Louis Armstrong. For Louis' test, Feather selected a version of *Rockin' Chair* that Roy had recently recorded for Norman Granz's Clef label (accompanied by Oscar Peterson on organ). Louis gave the recording four stars, voicing enthusiasm for Roy's bold use of high notes:

> That ending—the high note—well I know it's Roy Eldridge. You know I'd hit that note, just get right out of bed, give me a cup of coffee, where is it? I'd hit it! But Roy is the only one that's going to have the nerve to hit that note like that. Roy has that musicianship.[3]

Roy was naturally pleased to read such praise from someone who had provided him with so much inspiration, but, soon after those words were in print, another of Roy's trumpet-playing heroes Oran "Hot Lips" Page died of a heart attack, aged 46. Roy was honored to be asked to be a pallbearer at Page's funeral, because Hot Lips held a special place in his esteem. Roy didn't buy many records by other jazz trumpeters, but he always kept abreast of new issues by Page. Some twenty years after Page's death I entered Roy's hotel room in London as he was listening to a recorded cassette of the late trumpeter's work. Roy decided to test me by asking me who was playing. I was able to identify the passionate trumpet work, and Roy, pleased by my response, went on to praise Lips, saying he was definitely the most under-rated of all jazz trumpeters and easily the best blues player of his era. On another occasion, talking of Page, he said, "To really play the blues is no easy task. It's much easier to play something up-tempo like *Cherokee*."[4]

A new J.A.T.P. national tour set out in September 1954 to play from coast to coast and in Canada. One of the first dates on the schedule was at Carnegie Hall, where a combat between Roy and his main adversary on the tour, Dizzy Gillespie, took place. Dizzy never shunned a musical challenge, but looking back he said that the format which incited "battles" between musicians reflected Norman Granz's "weird sense of competition."[5] *Down Beat* reviewed the Carnegie Hall concert:

> The first set combined the powerful presence of Roy Eldridge, Dizzy Gillespie, Ben Webster, Flip Phillips, Bill Harris, Oscar Peterson, Ray Brown, Herb Ellis and Louie Bellson. What was most impressive about the opening was the inventively, illuminating solo of Eldridge (even though he got hung up toward the end of it). Variations on *I Got Rhythm* followed, with Roy, muted and gathering momentum like a tape-busting mile winner, cut Dizzy in their first extended exchange. During that whole first half those two really drove each other to more and more incisive flights and when Dizzy's lip began to warm-up the competition became too keen for this listener to be concerned about a decision.[6]

Such was the demand for tickets at Carnegie Hall that Norman Granz decided, for the first time, to climax the whole tour by playing two further concerts there as a finale to the widespread travels. His strategy paid off, with fans queuing for "returns"; it became "the thing" to attend a J.A.T.P. concert, but a percentage of the show's audience had never heard jazz live and they definitely needed entertaining. As one of the stalwarts of these tours, Roy was well aware of the need for showmanship and the playing of solos that were spectacular enough to entertain the general public. He spoke of this in the mid-1950s:

> Night after night on a stage like that is really difficult, because more or less you have to play to the people. That isn't what Norman tells us to do. He doesn't tell us how to play at all, and that's why I like working for him. But if you want to get those hands, you play to the people. There are certain little things all musicians make that get to the people. They're not great musically but they get to the public. I get in between whether to do one of those things or to do what I really have in mind, and sometimes I wind up doing nothing. One thing about J.A.T.P. is that our choruses never get set.[7]

For younger musicians with J.A.T.P. the benefits of working with experienced veterans were considerable, as Oscar Peterson told Alyn Shipton in 1999:

> I cherish those days because they did a lot for me, playing with great players like Coleman Hawkins, Dizzy Gillespie, Roy Eldridge, Benny Carter, and Ella; that was a great training ground for me. Everybody wanted something different; Prez wanted simple, swinging stuff, but Dizzy wanted the "sock it to me" type of thing. Roy Eldridge was the most aggressive; "Speedy" was always ready for a battle. He used to love strollers—the piano and guitar lay out, just leaving bass and drum.[8]

Roy himself said, "I thought I invented strolling, then I heard an old recording of Louis Armstrong strolling with the banjo player. I guess nothing's new."[9]

Sometimes the night-after-night routine, journeying from one indistinguishable hotel to the next, meant that cities blurred into each other. A sense of ennui developed when musicians, after traveling 500 miles, encountered hotel rooms that were carpeted and curtained exactly the same as the ones they had left that morning. To combat tour boredom some of the musicians devised a "game" involving them trying to detect any sounds of love-making in an adjoining room. If noises were heard, colleagues would be called in to listen: the musician who gave the most vivid description of the unseen exercise was declared the winner. Roy was called into one of these listening gatherings but became bored within two minutes, solemnly announcing that he would only join in the "game" again if he was allowed to be one of the two participants on the other side of the wall. Japes of a more innocent kind also occurred, as Gene Lees related:

> Once during a J.A.T.P. intermission, Oscar Peterson and Bill Harris reversed the mouthpieces on the trumpets of Roy Eldridge and Dizzy Gillespie. The entire ensemble were to assemble onstage for the finale, Roy and Dizzy came on stage, late as usual, after playing poker. Dizzy picked up his horn and blew: nothing. He told Roy to play and Roy came out with this horrible sound. He went crazy and he was yelling "But it wasn't me. I swear it wasn't me."[10]

On another occasion, the running order of a J.A.T.P. concert took an impromptu direction when Roy and Illinois Jacquet each sat behind a drum kit and indulged in a percussion battle. But for dispelling tensions that could build up during a long, tiring tour, nothing eclipsed the "happening" that took place during a San Diego concert when Flip Phillips rode a bicycle across the stage during the finale. Flip was involved in another light-hearted interlude when he and Lester Young rehearsed and performed a dance routine that surprised and delighted their colleagues and the audience. Roy was exasperated (and perhaps a little envious) when saxophonists got the crowds howling with pleasure by simple honking a very low note over and over again. One night he borrowed Coleman Hawkins' tenor-sax and went on stage, loudly blurting out a low B flat, a move that produced an ecstatic reaction from the audience. He attempted the same ploy on the next show but was beaten to the punch by Illinois Jacquet, who nipped out on stage before Roy's entrance and blew exactly what Roy had played in the first house.

As an aftermath to the 1954 J.A.T.P. fall tour, three members of the troupe, Roy, Bill Harris, and Ben Webster, decided to work together as a front line that guested with local rhythm sections. After completing a two-week season at the Blue Note in Chicago, they played brief residencies in Philadelphia, Detroit, and Boston, then saw in the New Year at the River Lounge in River Rouge, Michigan, where their rhythm section included a young musician who later became a jazz star: Barry Harris. Trombonist Bill Harris was a renowned practical joker, and during this booking he saw the opportunity to indulge in a prank involving Roy. Roy was tremendously proud of a magnificent jacket he had bought in Europe, and when they arrived at the River Lounge he put it in to be dry-cleaned, with strict instructions that it had to be delivered to the band's dressing-room by that evening. Bill Harris followed all this in a seemingly detached way, but an hour later he began scouring the town's thrift stores for the oldest jacket he could find. In the end he selected (for 50 cents) one that was frayed and soup-stained. He made sure he got to the club before Roy did, and substituted old for new—hiding the coveted European jacket in the wardrobe. He then got out his trombone and warmed up. Roy duly arrived, eager to see how well his jacket had been cleaned. Pulling off the wrapping that Bill had put around the cruddy, mildewed garment he let out the best string of oaths that Harris had ever heard. "What's up?" asked Harris, keeping a straight face before saying, in mock innocence, "Gee, they haven't made a good job of that, I can see all sorts of stains." "That's not my jacket," roared Roy, who was, by this time, so close to apoplexy that Harris decided to terminate the joke by saying, "Well Roy, you can certainly borrow my spare coat" (which was about ten sizes too big for Roy). With that, Harris opened the wardrobe and solemnly handed Roy the splendid European jacket, perfectly pressed and cleaned. It took Roy some while to appreciate the joke, and one feels that ever after he viewed Bill Harris in a different light.

The breakup of this threesome had nothing to do with the jacket incident. By early February 1955 it was again time for Roy to fly to Europe with J.A.T.P. for what turned out to be a hugely successful tour (at four Stockholm concerts they drew a total of 14,000 people). Drummer Louie Bellson was in the troupe and quickly saw what an important part Roy played in the proceedings:

> I think Norman Granz greatly respected Roy's playing and his personality; I believe that he relied on Roy to add the sparks and to keep everyone on their toes. Roy would try his darndest on every single show; he wasn't exactly a straw boss of the unit, but Norman listened to everything he had to say.[11]

As part of the odyssey, the unit played a couple of dates in Paris, where Roy was delighted to revisit old haunts. Less pleasing for Roy was the reception the show received during the first-house concert at the Théâtre des Champs Elysées. Most of the audience were there to enjoy themselves, but a vociferous minority had come to mock the music—a situation which exemplified the partisan feelings that then existed in France among those who liked traditional jazz to the exclusion of any other style, and were quite prepared to make their point by hooting derision at anything they considered modern. The hostility wasn't directed at anyone in particular, but the tension affected Roy. Local writer Henry Kahn reported:

> Roy was so upset he felt the only way to calm his spirits was to swallow lashings of Arabian food, known as cous-cous, this is principally red-hot millet. When Roy washed this down with

libations of strong red wine he soon felt better. Several of the troupe joined Roy and sampled his antidote to the crowd's reaction, then, when the clock struck 11 p.m. they walked on stage and played "as never before," to quote Norman Granz.[12]

After the second show had ended, Roy and Flip Phillips went to the Vieux Colombier to hear Sidney Bechet play; by then Roy had deliberately dropped his trumpet off at his hotel. For once Roy shunned the chance of a jam session. The evening's concerts had been trying, and tiring, so any attempt to combat the power of Bechet's playing on his "home ground" would be too exhausting. Sidney and all the staff greeted Roy and Flip warmly, but after listening to several numbers they rounded off the night by visiting the Mars Club. While Roy was in Paris he took the opportunity of buying a flugel horn and began doubling on it regularly when he returned to the States. Roy never became a great flugel horn-player, mainly because he insisted on using a trumpet mouthpiece on the instrument, which deprived his efforts of the flugel's mellow tonal qualities. He also attempted to play the flugel in the same manner as he did the trumpet. Naturally his amazingly fleet fingers served him well on flugel, but, when he moved into the high register which he loved to use on trumpet, his tone thinned unattractively and his usually excellent pitching sometimes went awry. Roy said that using the trumpet mouthpiece "felt better," but that didn't mean it sounded better. It was like using soccer boots to play tennis. Roy didn't want to risk affecting his trumpet *embouchure* by using the different dimensions of a flugel mouthpiece, and, as was his nature, he consistently attempted to produce fireworks on an instrument more suited to creating filigree effects.

There were fireworks a-plenty on recordings issued soon after Roy returned from the 1955 J.A.T.P. European tour. The new release featured recording studio duets with Dizzy Gillespie—the two trumpeters being backed by Oscar Peterson on piano and a rhythm section. A good deal of the intensity of Roy and Dizzy's cut-and-thrust

J.A.T.P. battles was captured for posterity, but despite the heat of their encounters there was no personal animosity between the two trumpeters. "Rivalry between us?" said Roy, "There never was none of that."[13] For one young trumpeter, the results of the Eldridge–Gillespie recordings were sublime. Jon Faddis told Alyn Shipton, "When I was 11 years old my sister bought me the Dizzy and Roy album, and over the next five years I wore it out completely."[14] In *Down Beat* Nat Hentoff gave the recordings a five-star review, saying, "Roy and Diz play at the top of their competitive form, creating an existing series of trumpet duels, though they're somewhat too long-drawn-out in places." Miles Davis' comments were less favorable: "They're two of my favorite trumpet players; I love Roy and you know I love Diz. It's nice to listen to for a while, but Oscar messes it up with that Nat Cole style, it could have been much better."[15]

Because Norman Granz recorded many permutations of his J.A.T.P. musicians (plus various other stars who signed for his record companies) there was an abundance of sessions by Roy Eldridge on the market from the mid-1950s onwards. Granz never lost an opportunity to speak well of Roy's work; an interview with Nat Hentoff was typical:

> Roy has that extra ounce of competitiveness, and because he's an emotional guy he rises to the heights. On the tour he changes his ballads from night to night more than anybody. Roy is completely honest, not only musically but as a person. I've never seen him not try.[16]

Roy, for his part, spoke warmly of Granz:

> Norman made sure the cats got a decent living, he was the first to break down all the prejudice, and put the music where it belongs. They should make a statue to that cat, and there's no one else in the business end of this business I would say that about.[17]

Roy regarded one particular recording session he did for Norman Granz as an important landmark in his career: this was the March 1955 date with Art Tatum. Of all the talents in jazz, Roy felt that Tatum (despite his ability to command big fees and his reputation among his fellow musicians) was never given the universal acclaim that Roy felt he so richly deserved. Roy could never understand why so few of the general public latched on to Tatum's genius, and, in one of the last conversations I ever had with him, he again raised this subject:

> How could they have missed him? Surely everyone loves great piano-playing and here was someone who was every bit as talented as the classical virtuoso players; yet people outside of jazz have very little idea who Tatum was. He was the last word in brilliance, technique, melodic sense, harmonies, rhythm—and even now players are years behind his musical ideas. I knew how great he was from the very first time I ever heard him in Cleveland when we were both youngsters. He was fantastic even then.[18]

With admiration so deep and long-standing it's no wonder that Roy approached the Tatum date with a degree or two of excitement. The recordings had originally been scheduled for January 1955, but somehow Tatum forgot to make a note of the date. The two months' delay made it even more significant for Roy, but one has to say that when the session eventually took place the music produced did not live up to the high expectations. As one reviewer put it, "Tatum is so busy in the background that he tends to restrict the soloist." However, it's not difficult to cite many other albums where Tatum was ultra-busy behind a soloist. The real disappointment isn't caused by Tatum's prominence but in the guarded way that Roy plays on most of the tracks. Roy usually described the Tatum session as "great," but he was more candid in conversation with Dan Morgenstern:

> I enjoyed playing with him. Not so much on the record we made, because once he was in that studio it was a different

thing. The minute the red light went on, man, he struck me—
we made that thing *I Can't Dance*. I could hardly play the
melody; he was flying.[19]

During this period of Roy's life his work schedule almost dropped
into a set pattern: a spring tour of Europe with J.A.T.P., festival dates all
over the U.S.A., some alongside Coleman Hawkins, a fall tour of North
America with J.A.T.P., plus club bookings in New York and Chicago to
end the year. All these various dates were interspersed with
recordings on both the East and West Coasts. The regularity of Roy's
earnings gave him and his wife Vi the confidence (in 1956) to move
from their apartment on Convent Avenue, Harlem, and to buy their
own house out in Hollis, Long Island, where they moved with their
daughter Carole. This remained the Eldridge family home for the rest
of Roy and Vi's lives. Roy, in common with many other "swing era"
stars, continued to play occasionally in various weekend Dixieland
"bashes" that were held in New York City. For some veterans these
sessions provided the main source of their income, but for Roy they
allowed him to keep his "chops" in good shape. He told Nat Hentoff,
"I think a musician who is a musician ought to be able to play
anywhere and shouldn't be limited to one style. I play Dixieland at the
Central Plaza, but if some of the modernists had to play Dixieland,
they couldn't do it."[20] Interestingly, Buck Clayton, a contemporary of
Roy, held a different point of view: "Only in New Orleans did the
black musicians take an interest in Dixieland music and I'm not too
sure they were really interested."[21] Nevertheless, Roy was happy to
make sporadic appearances at the Central Plaza and at Stuyvesant
Casino. He even occasionally led a pick-up group at these venues,
fronting line-ups that included Tony Parenti, Herb Flemming, Willie
"The Lion" Smith, Jo Jones, and Eddie Locke. Roy never knocked the
audiences at these uninhibited sessions but did say on one occasion,
"The Central Plaza crowd sure like it loud."[22]

Coleman Hawkins rarely made himself available for these shindigs
and, as Roy was kept continually busy with other projects, the

Hawkins–Eldridge Quintet was again put into storage, even though Hawk remained Eldridge's favorite musical partner. They did, however, work together at the Second Newport Jazz Festival, playing a richly improvised quintet set, with Nat Pierce on piano, Jo Jones on drums, and John Beal on bass, filling a Friday evening spot (on July 15, 1955) which also featured the blues singer, Joe Turner. Over the years, Roy played countless sets with Hawk (and dozens with Ben Webster) but, curiously enough, he never worked in a quintet format with Lester Young on club dates. Yet the two men had been friends since 1934; they shared many laughs on the J.A.T.P. tours, with Lester, who was almost six feet tall, jiving Roy by calling him "a midget motherfucker." On the road, Lester always tried to alleviate the tension that built up within Roy prior to a big concert. He'd say, "Lady Eldridge, take it easy, have a puff of your cigarette, blow your horn, then put it down and have a little sip, then take another puff."[23] But this advice rarely diminished Roy's agitation and it was not uncommon for him to chain-smoke his way through a whole pack of cigarettes before a concert. Teasing was the order of the day on these tours, with Buddy Rich often the main target, particularly when his colleagues found out that he had, as a child, been billed as "Traps– the Drum Wonder." Rich growled, "It's pretty difficult to live with a thing like that. When you come in on the job at night and everybody says, 'Hey, here comes Traps. Now, how are you Traps?' "[24]

Although Roy could no longer be classified as a trend-setter, his work was in no way dated, but still full of ingenious rhythms and forward-looking harmonies. This was underlined in 1956 when *Down Beat* published a three-part transcription of his recorded solo on *If I Had You*. It was an interesting choice, an Eldridge solo that is practically devoid of fireworks, with most of its phrases located in the middle and low registers. In the past when the magazine had published transcriptions of Roy's work, they were of spectacular performances (*Body And Soul, Rockin' Chair, High Society*, etc.) but *If I Had You* showed another side of Roy's artistry.

An unlikely musical pairing for Roy occurred in June 1956 when he shared a week's booking at the Storyville Club in Boston with Anita O'Day. The reunion was said by *Down Beat* to have been "happy"; even Roy described the proceedings as "good," but there was certainly no talk of the two working together as a regular unit. Things were amicable enough for them to share a version of *Let Me Off Uptown* after they had completed their own solo spots. Roy had retained a party piece he had developed during his stay in Europe, and amused the Boston crowd by singing the blues in fractured French. In that year's *Combo Directory* (published in *Down Beat*), Roy's entry read:

> Veteran jazz trumpeter and star of Jazz at the Philharmonic available as a single and with own trio.

Roy's agency was given as the Shaw Artist Corporation, but, to Roy's sadness and regret, the head of that organization, Billy Shaw, died in June 1956. The company continued to represent Roy with Billy Shaw's son Milton acting as President, and Jack Archer as the agency's General Manager. Billy Shaw was a rare creature—an agent who enjoyed listening to jazz. In the August 8, 1956 *Down Beat* issue, Norman Granz said of him, "He was one of the very few heads of agencies who genuinely understood and liked jazz." In that same month, Roy was touched by another death, that of trumpeter Clifford Brown, who lost his life in an automobile accident. Roy spoke with Nat Hentoff shortly after this tragic event: "Clifford Brown. I just liked—period. The way he blew his horn! As good as he was he was going to be better."[25] Roy loved the sound that Brown got, but during this conversation he was openly critical of Chet Baker's work:

> I don't dig that type of trumpet playing. It's too mild. Baker plays right in a straight line, no ups and downs, soft or loud. I don't think it should be like that. Trumpeters today, they're playing very fast, it's easier to slip over the horn like that, rather than really blowing.[26]

Roy spent part of that summer of 1956 playing in the intimate surrounds of the Café Bohemia in New York, but his next engagement underlined the immense contrast in his working schedule. He left the small New York club in August and traveled to California to play a huge concert (in front of 19,000 people) at the Hollywood Bowl. He was part of a Norman Granz line-up that included Ella Fitzgerald and several J.A.T.P. "regulars" plus trumpeter Harry Edison and Art Tatum (who was to die before the year ended). The special attraction was Louis Armstrong and the All Stars. Granz almost missed the concert—a few days earlier he'd escaped serious injury when his new Mercedes-Benz sports car crashed near Benedict Canyon. The full J.A.T.P. line-up reassembled in September 1956 for its annual national concert tour, and when that ended Roy resumed at the Café Bohemia. A highlight of this period for Roy was his appearance (with Coleman Hawkins) at two Carnegie Hall concerts (on November 10 at 8.30 p.m. and midnight) featuring Billie Holiday. The presentations, billed as *Lady Sings The Blues*, served as a publicity launch for her recently published "ghosted" autobiography. By getting Charles Graham to drive him to and fro, workaholic Roy managed to dovetail his Carnegie Hall assignment with a gig downtown at the Central Plaza.

Roy continued to take a wide variety of jobs, and as 1957 approached he guested in Washington, D.C., with Frankie Condon's fourteen-piece band prior to playing at a Long Island Dixieland club. He briefly worked again in a quintet set-up, this time with Flip Phillips, then went to Chicago to play at the Blue Note alongside another celebrated tenorist, Bud Freeman. More weekend dates at New York's rumbustious Central Plaza followed, interspersed with appearances at a brief series of late-night concerts at New York's Town Hall. A new J.A.T.P. jaunt to Europe was delayed because of Ella Fitzgerald's temporary indisposition through ill health. When the tour finally got underway the line-up was smaller than usual, consisting of Ella, Oscar Peterson, Don Abney, Ray Brown, Herb Ellis, Jo Jones, Roy, and a relative newcomer to the Granz team—violinist Stuff Smith. The troupe's six-week tour began in Sweden on April 20, 1957, and again did tremendous business. However, despite all this exposure, Roy's recordings for Norman Granz's Clef and Verve labels failed to achieve good sales figures. Roy was well aware of this: "Norman Granz has stuck by me and let me make what I wanted. I know my records don't sell peanuts, but he feels it's good music and said to keep on trying."[27]

Granz summarized his attitude toward Roy's recordings: "It has been one of my prime projects to keep his talent before the world. No matter what their acceptance."[28] There were no studio recordings by Roy on the 1957 tour of Europe, but there were plenty of opportunities for him to blow in this abridged package. Harald Grut (writing in *Melody Maker*) was enthusiastic about this reduced line-up, describing it as "a big improvement on Norman Granz's other, rather boisterous groups." Peterson, Ellis, and Brown opened the show, and were then joined by Jo Jones on drums, Stuff Smith, and Roy Eldridge. Jo Jones' playing was supreme as far as Grut was concerned. He wrote, "I doubt whether there is a better drummer alive than Jones." Roy Eldridge's work he found "less impressive, when he lets himself go, musical taste suffers."[29] The second half of the show mainly featured Ella Fitzgerald (backed by pianist Don Abney). Roy had mixed feelings about Jo Jones as a person, but always praised the drummer's talent:

> I'll tell you what I like in a rhythm section. You need a drummer like Jo Jones, that thinks when you think. A rhythm section should follow you and let you free. When an improvised solo is being taken, all the drummer should do is keep the beat.[30]

Roy was often irked by Jo Jones' eccentric behavior and mood swings. They had known one another since the 1930s, but in summarizing their friendship Roy told Dan Morgenstern, "He makes me nervous." Others felt that Papa Jo (as he was often called) became increasingly difficult as the years passed. Buck Clayton wryly summed up the situation when he said, "In the old days Jo Jones was mad, but now he's plumb crazy."[31] But late in his career Roy usually managed a chuckle when he spoke of Jo: "If he liked you he'd play for you. Every little thing you do he's right in on you. He builds with you. He can turn left on you too!"[32] Jo Jones, for his part, often cited Roy as being one of the only players left who had first-hand experience of the hardships of touring during the 1920s and 1930s.

Roy still loved to play the drums, and at the July 1957 South Bay Festival he did so with an unusual pairing of Blossom Dearie on piano and Charles Mingus on bass. Roy also took part in a drum duet with Jo Jones at the 1957 Newport Jazz Festival. This was part of a set that featured Roy on trumpet, alongside Coleman Hawkins and altoist Pete Brown. Later, the entire group went to a hotel party hosted by Norman Granz. Two days later, Roy and Jo Jones were featured with Sonny Stitt, then, together with Lester Young and Illinois Jacquet, guested with the full Count Basie Orchestra at Newport for a spirited *One O'Clock Jump* finale. On that year's J.A.T.P. national tour Roy was regularly part of Ella's accompanying group. Roy's stamina was amazing. During a stopover in Los Angeles on October 11, 1957, he recorded three separate albums (with Sonny Stitt, Russ Garcia, and Herb Ellis) all within the space of one day, as well as supervising a recording session by Stitt.

That 1957 odyssey proved to be the last national tour that Norman Granz organized in North America. Business had dwindled in certain key cities. Granz put the cause of this down to the popularity of the ever-growing number of jazz festivals, but another reason was that the format had changed little (despite the injection of new blood) in ten years, and the jam session finales now had less appeal either for young audiences or for up-and-coming musicians who worked with the troupe—they preferred to play within their own groups rather than join in what sometimes became a hurly-burly of sound.

Coleman Hawkins wasn't part of the 1957 J.A.T.P. national tour, and although Roy was always happy to work with Hawk he certainly drank less when the great tenorist wasn't around; the two soon

Roy, the teenager. Photo: courtesy of the
Institute of Jazz Studies, Rutgers University.

Joe Eldridge. Photo: courtesy of Teresa
Chilton Archive.

Leon 'Chu' Berry. Photo: courtesy of Teresa
Chilton Archive.

Rex Stewart. Photo: courtesy of Teresa Chilton
Archive.

Speed Webb and His Orchestra, 1929, featuring Roy Eldridge, Teddy Wilson, and Vic Dickenson. Photo: courtesy of the Institute of Jazz Studies, Rutgers University.

McKinney's Cotton Pickers, 1933. Directed by Billie Bowen, featuring Roy and Joe Eldridge, Cuba Austin (drums), and Prince Robinson (tenor/clarinet). Photo courtesy of Frank Driggs Collection.

Roy's Quintet in Chicago, 1941.
John Simmons (bass), Roy
Eldridge (trumpet), and Dave
Young (tenor). Photo: courtesy of
the Institute of Jazz Studies,
Rutgers University.

Roy with Woody Herman's
trumpeter Billie Rogers.
Photo: courtesy of Teresa Chilton
Archive.

Artie Shaw's Band rehearsing in Hollywood, 1944. Photo: courtesy of Teresa Chilton Archive.

Benny Goodman's group in Europe, 1950. Dick Hyman (piano), Nancy Reed (vocals), Benny Goodman (clarinet), Roy Eldridge (trumpet), Zoot Sims (tenor), and Ed Shaugnessy (drums). Photo: courtesy of Nancy Reed Kanter.

J.A.T.P. leave for Europe, 1956. (Right to left) Flip Phillips, Gene Krupa, Roy Eldridge, Ella Fitzgerald, Herb Ellis, Illinois Jacquet and Dizzy Gillespie. Photo: Popsie Randolph, courtesy of Frank Driggs Collection.

Buck Clayton and Roy Eldridge, c.1967. Photo: courtesy of Jack Bradley.

Sonny Stitt (tenor), Ray Brown (bass), Oscar Peterson (piano), and Roy Eldridge (trumpet) at Harlem's Apollo Theater. Photo: courtesy of Jack Bradley.

Joe Eldridge and Anita O'Day at New York's Half Note, 1970. Photo: courtesy of Jack Bradley.

Roy Eldridge with singer George Melly, New York, June 1979. Photo: courtesy of Teresa Chilton Archive.

Roy Eldridge c.1980. Photo: courtesy of the Institute of Jazz Studies, Rutgers University (Nancy Miller Elliott Collection).

Roy Eldridge with the author, New York, 1983. Photo: courtesy of Teresa Chilton Archive.

Dizzy Gillespie playing at Rose Eldridge's funeral service, St. Peter's Lutheran Church, New York, March 1, 1989. Photo: News photo courtesy of Charles Graham.

polished off a full bottle of brandy as they sat in their dressing-room waiting to go on stage. By himself, Roy sipped whiskey steadily but not excessively. He said, "When I'm not working I very seldom take a drink, unless there are friends around. I just have to have a little taste to quieten my nerves down."[33] Roy rarely carried marijuana with him on his travels (and never when he was going from country to country), but he was not averse to smoking a joint or two. However, he continued to draw the line when it came to hard drugs: "Drugs? I think my head's on too straight to be messed up like that. Bad enough with whisky. And I don't like needles even *for* my health, so I couldn't get bothered by that."[34]

In 1954, the Metropole Bar on Seventh Avenue near Times Square adopted a highly successful jazz policy. Although Henry "Red" Allen led the main resident group there, many other combos were needed to fulfill the tavern's seven-nights-a-week jazz policy (which included regular appearances by Gene Krupa's Trio). After a sporadic start, Roy and Hawk began appearing at the Metropole on various Sundays, Mondays, and Tuesdays whenever they had no out-of-town bookings. The excellence of their quintet soon began attracting devoted listeners, and Roy responded by expressing his pride in the group: "This is the swingingest band in town. The job's relaxed, we have all the freedom in the world, play what we want to play and Coleman is too much."[35] When Hawkins went off to play solo dates, Roy continued to work at the Metropole, sometimes with Tony Parenti and Zutty Singleton. He also occasionally went out to Sheepshead Bay in Brooklyn to guest at a club that was run by Max "The Mayor" Cavalli. Roy usually enjoyed that gig because he was always given the chance to play drums when local sitters in got onto the bandstand. Besides promoting jazz, Max Cavalli also ran a booking agency from his Brooklyn base and often obtained work for Roy during the 1960s and 1970s. Roy also played another residency at the Café Bohemia in the fall of 1957, part of which entailed working opposite Miles Davis' small group. By then Miles had been voted "Top Jazz Trumpeter" in the annual *Down Beat* readers' poll (Roy was in eighth place). Roy's contract at the Bohemia was renewed twice, and the only cloud that drifted across occurred when Roy was temporarily out of action through influenza (his place was taken by Phil Sunkel). Roy soon resumed at the Bohemia, and when his stay ended he underlined the fact that he was fully recovered by working at the Metropole with clarinettist Sol Yaged.

The big event of 1957 for Roy (and for several other jazz veterans) was their appearance on a C.B.S. television show entitled *The Sound of Jazz*. This December 1957 production remains one of the most star-studded assemblies of jazz greats ever to be televised. The informality of an authentic jam session was movingly captured as Billie Holiday, Roy, Coleman Hawkins, Lester Young, Count Basie, Henry "Red" Allen, Rex Stewart, Pee Wee Russell, Doc Cheatham, Gerry Mulligan, Vic Dickenson, and others were seen on camera. Many of the same performers took part in a recording studio session that also produced some superfine jazz. Of the television show, Nat Hentoff, one of the organizers, wrote, "During the rehearsals and blocking sessions, Roy Eldridge played with every bit of his astonishing energy."[36]

In May 1958, Roy again played in Europe with J.A.T.P., where the jazz fans' desire to see famous jazz musicians *en masse* was undiminished (one concert at the Salle Pleyel in Paris drew 6000 people). Because of a relaxing of the Musicians' Union rules the show also played in Britain, allowing their followers to see Roy, Hawk, Dizzy Gillespie, Stan Getz, Ella Fitzgerald, Oscar Peterson, and others in person. I was among the big turnout that attended the J.A.T.P.'s London press conference (held at a Mayfair hotel) and was delighted to have my first conversation with Roy Eldridge. He was seated on a sofa next to Coleman Hawkins, and was neither hostile nor over-friendly. He answered my questions with brief, noncommittal replies, inserting one joke about Hawk's advanced age. Hawkins himself barely acknowledged anyone, even people he had known well in the 1930s. To the disappointment of many of their British fans, Roy and Hawk usually only played one brief set early in the program. Roy smarted over the demotion, and his aggravation increased when he read dismissive comments by some critics, who inferred that the two veterans were has-beens, just relegated to fulfilling a subsidiary role. British clarinettist Dave Shepherd, working with a trio that featured pianist Dill Jones, was temporarily added to the package:

> My memories of Roy and Coleman Hawkins on that tour were that they kept themselves slightly apart from the rest of the musicians. We all traveled together on a band coach to each concert. They'd sit sipping a bottle of brandy as a preliminary to going on stage, but I never saw them drunk. Everyone in the line-up had a different way of preparing for the show. On the first date, at the Gaumont-State in Kilburn, London, I was amazed to see Stan Getz rushing around the dressing-room hitting the walls, the chairs, the door…with a pair of drum brushes. Although it wasn't the ideal time I asked him what it was like working with Benny Goodman. He said, "He was a genius," and carried on hitting everything in sight.[37]

Roy remained disgruntled for a long time about the subsidiary billing he and Hawkins received on that tour, and later said, "I never read what any critics had to say after they wrote that in 1958 Hawk and me were finished."[38] The consolation was that soon after the 1958 J.A.T.P. tour ended, Roy did a six-week tour of Europe, working mainly as a guest star with various rhythm sections, which meant that solo space was unrationed and prominence guaranteed. On that trip, Roy was not only featured on trumpet at the July 1958 Cannes Jazz Festival, but he also played drums as part of an all-star line-up led by Sidney Bechet. Recorded results show that he acquitted himself admirably, fulfilling his duties as percussionist with verve and swing.

Back in the U.S.A., Roy adopted a suggestion by Norman Granz that he should again work in Ella Fitzgerald's backing group for a series of tour dates to be entitled "An evening with Ella Fitzgerald, and the Oscar Peterson Trio." The money was good even if the billing was unspectacular; Roy wasn't overburdened with work, usually playing muted when backing Ella, and open for his two feature numbers.

During his absence from the Metropole, his place was taken (alongside Coleman Hawkins) by trumpeter Johnny Letman. In Roy's hearing Johnny once explained to me how big a part Roy's playing had in shaping his style, but Roy immediately barked back at him: "You are, and always were, a Louis Armstrong man." That September, Roy worked with the pianist-composer Mary Lou Williams at Carnegie Hall as part of a fund-raising concert for her Bel Canto Foundation. In January 1959, Roy and Hawk took part in another huge assembly of jazz stars (including Louis Armstrong and Duke Ellington) who gathered for the *Fourth Timex Television Show*. In this over-laden program solo space was at a premium, which meant Roy's contribution was brief on *Body And Soul* and fragmentary on a version of *Perdido*, which must rank among the most cacophonous jam sessions of all time, containing as it does chorus after chorus of massed trumpeters squeaking out their highest notes. Roy's occasional appearances on Channel 13 as part of *Art Ford's Jazz Party* were much more satisfying.

One media event that Roy enjoyed being part of occurred in August 1958, when *Esquire* magazine gathered together almost sixty famous jazz musicians for a group photograph that was taken at West 126th Street. But at the crucial moment when the main photograph was taken, Dizzy Gillespie said something that made Roy turn his head away from the camera. Nevertheless, Roy was pleased to be part of the gathering, though, as his long-time friend Charles Graham wrote, he had reservations:

> Roy was very conventional (bourgeois?) in his outlook on a not-surprising number of ordinary things. For example, when I took a large framed copy of the "big picture" (Harlem, 126th Street) over to his house to put up on his wall, he said, "Oh, yes, I remember that picture. It's nice, but that bunch of kids on the curb, they shouldn't have been there. It takes away from the seriousness of that occasion." He and I hung it on the wall, and it was still there when he died, about 15 or so

years later.[39]

It was soon time for J.A.T.P. to resume its hectic travels through Europe. For the spring 1959 trip Norman Granz devised a truncated bill that featured Ella Fitzgerald, Gene Krupa, Sonny Stitt, Ed Thigpen, Ronnie Ball, Eddie Wasserman Jimmy Gannon, Wilfred Middlebrooks, and Roy Eldridge. It seemed to Roy, in this period of his life, that he was spending more time abroad than he was in the States. On one J.A.T.P. European tour in the late 1950s, Roy took his wife Vi and his daughter Carole on the trip. Charles Graham gave the details:

> I stayed at Roy's house for the six weeks while the family went overseas with J.A.T.P. When they got back Roy said to me, "I could hear Vi and Carole in the room next to me saying, two more weeks and one day, two weeks only, one week and six days more...They couldn't wait to get home." All they saw was the inside of airports and hotel rooms. When he came back Roy asked me what he could do for me, for watching his home while he was overseas. I told him I'd come across a stock arrangement (by Edgar Battle for Robbins Music Publishers) of *Wabash Stomp*, violins, conductor, the whole bit. I asked if I could make a copy of that stock and he said, "You can have the original, I'll never use it again."[40]

When J.A.T.P. was in London, Roy was interviewed by Max Jones of *Melody Maker*, who asked him if he would be sorry to leave that city: "No" he said promptly, "I like it here but New York's my home. If I didn't live there I'd live in Chicago or San Francisco. You can have all the others, though I've never been to New Orleans in my life."[41]

Roy could be relied on to provide a candid answer when he was asked questions like that. In a conversation I had with him about the problems of eating on tour, he was emphatic in saying how much he preferred German food to British cuisine, adding, "The main meals in Germany remind me so much of the food that I used to eat when I lived in Pittsburgh."[42] Roy told Max Jones that he hadn't forgotten the wounding criticisms he (and Coleman Hawkins) had received during the previous year's tour (not from Max Jones). He then went on to discuss his attitude to concert performances and to improvising in general:

> I found out years ago that when they stop writing about you altogether is when to worry. Whether it's good or bad it's what this cat thinks. He's writing to make a living. Often he'll tell you you're good when you know you are off, so you don't set too much store by it. So many things bear on a performance when you're playing from the heart. I know for myself if I feel happy I can do about anything; if I feel a draught, I can't do nothing right. Or if it's a concert recording—well there's a dozen different things that can go wrong. You can play as you feel, which means something new each show, or repeat what you've learned off. The second is playing safe. I've worked with people who do that, heard them practice the same solo and play it day after day. They don't want to take a chance on goofing—but the truth is I couldn't go on like that. It's the reason I don't care for studio work. You'll play something at rehearsal and the director will say, "Yes, I like that Roy, keep it in." It's a drag, you have to play something you've played before. You might as well be reading music. You're supposed to be a jazzman, to be able to improvise something. Skipping around, trying things out, that's jazz, it should be impromptu, so it's meant to have a mistake in it somewhere.[43]

11

FLYING WITH
THE HAWK

During 1959 Roy and Coleman Hawkins often worked together at the Metropole, usually with a rhythm section consisting of Joe Knight on piano, Franklin Skeete on bass, and J. C. Heard on drums (later replaced by Eddie Locke). The long hours at the Metropole (the evening stint usually lasted from 9 p.m. until 3 a.m.) meant that most of the musicians involved made several trips across the street to drink at the Copper Rail bar where prices were cheaper than at their place of work. Occasionally the intake of too much alcohol stirred up an aggressiveness that lurked within Roy. Writer Stanley Dance, a good friend of Roy's, observed one of his mood changes at this musicians' gathering place:

> You know how amusingly chesty Roy could be, but a really minor argument with Buck Clayton ended when Roy declared, "I'll cut your ass." Looking down on him with an incredulous smile, in a kind of Gary Cooper fashion, Buck drawled, "You'll do what?" Roy changed the subject at once and ordered another round.[1]

Roy never grew close to Henry "Red" Allen. Coleman Hawkins, being friends of both of these trumpeters, saw that their mutual animosity might allow him to make some mischief—a practice he was not averse to. He walked across to where Red Allen was holding forth at the Copper Rail bar and joined the conversation by saying, "Gee, Red, I'm sorry to hear about your car." Red, the proud owner of a Cadillac, asked, "What do you mean ?" Hawk replied, "Well, Roy said you were having trouble keeping up the payments." Henry looked daggers at Roy, who was standing a few feet away. Hawk then sidled up to Eldridge and said something like, "Red Allen is mighty sorry to hear that you're having such trouble with your chops." In no time the two great trumpeters had thrown off their jackets and were squaring up to one another as Coleman Hawkins snuck out of the door. Fortunately, Roy and Red cooled down without a blow being struck, but a few weeks later they were involved in another spat outside the Metropole after they had finished their night's work (at this time Roy and Hawk were working in the upstairs section of the tavern, while Red functioned on the ground level). The two adversaries got into an argument as to which of them could play a solo on *Body And Soul* in the key of "A" major (a difficult task). Buck Clayton told Humphrey Lyttelton about the incident, describing the small crowd of musicians who gathered on the sidewalk to witness this nocturnal encounter. Unfortunately, Red Allen had drunk too much and got into a musical muddle. Roy immediately ripped into Johnny Green's immortal ballad, but he too was befuddled and made just as big a hash of it as Red. Neither man could see the funny side of this duel, but everyone else present fell about, convulsed with laughter.

In July 1959, Roy and Hawk appeared at the Newport Jazz Festival, which led *Down Beat* to comment, "Roy Eldridge and Coleman Hawkins showed they are as important to jazz as they ever were."[2] On one set they both greatly enjoyed backing singer Helen Humes. The pleasure of that occasion was in strict contrast with an event that took place later the same month, namely the funeral of Billie Holiday, which for Roy was a very sad occasion. Roy rarely went into raptures about any singer, but every compliment he ever made about Billie was delivered with absolute sincerity. Among others who attended the service were Gene Krupa, Red Allen, Benny Goodman, Jo Jones, John Hammond, and Joe Glaser.

Roy and Hawk took on a variety of engagements that year, including making guest appearances (for three nights) at the Bayou Club in Washington, D.C. with a band led by trumpeter Bill Whelan. They also played at festivals in Toronto, Canada, and in Monterey, California–they were later to revisit this annual festival (then in its second year). Attendances of around 6000 a day were not unusual for Monterey but, as part of the 1959 Los Angeles Jazz Festival, Roy and Hawk played a concert that drew 18,000 people. But each man continued to fulfill his individual commitments, and for Roy this meant working increasingly with just a rhythm section. During the late 1950s and early 1960s this type of quartet line-up was all the rage in many New York "supper" clubs which wanted to enjoy the huge success that Jonah Jones' Quartet had created at the Embers, 161 East 54th Street. The spin-offs for Jonah were huge record sales, regular television appearances, and an income that was estimated at around $300,000 a year. Roy, without any trace of envy, said (about a musician he had worked with thirty years earlier), "It couldn't have happened to a nicer guy," and he meant it. Jonah's music was dubbed "muted jazz," and although Roy liked to blow a muted chorus or two occasionally, he didn't like to be in a situation where managements expected him to play muted all the time. Nevertheless, he was happy to accept good money to take his own four-piece (using Joe Knight, Franklin Skeete, and Eddie Locke) into the Arpeggio Club which, like the Embers, was on the east side of Manhattan. Later, Roy's Quartet played for almost three months at the Embers. The decibels that Roy produced at the Arpeggio were considerably less than those he had created during his early successes at the Three Deuces in Chicago, a place he still looked back on with affection when he said: "I haven't any favorite clubs. The ones with bad pianos and bad sound don't really count, because you play them once and you don't go back. I think it's the atmosphere of a club that's important. The Three Deuces in Chicago for instance, they don't make them like that anymore."[3] An unusual gig for Roy occurred in late 1959 when the J.A.T.P. package made a highly publicized visit to the Apollo Theater in Harlem. Roy had many memories of playing there during his early days, and said that being back at the Apollo made him feel a young man again. He certainly played like one on his return, indulging in the fiercest of on-stage musical exchanges with saxist Sonny Stitt—every bit as lively as the recordings they made together. For Ella Fitzgerald, it was a touching return to the venue that had launched her career.

In early 1960, a film entitled *Drum Crazy, The Gene Krupa Story* was released—and generally panned by the critics; Roy's verdict was, "I went to see that picture and I thought it was very bad."[4] Roy had good reason to view it with a jaundiced eye, because, despite his enormous contributions to the real Gene Krupa story, he wasn't even mentioned in the movie. Roy knew from past experience that Hollywood movie scripts were not models of historical accuracy, but deep down he felt that Gene could have convinced the studio moguls that he should be given a cameo role, or at least an acknowledgment within the script. But Gene had no jurisdiction on how the movie-makers shaped his story, and had spoken out in vain in the past about Hollywood's tendency to use fictitious events to bolster up a bio-pic. Roy was coolish towards Gene for a while over this issue, and declined the chance to be part of an N.B.C. television program (shown in February, 1960) featuring Gene Krupa's Band and its star from the past, Anita O'Day; Roy was not displeased when *Down Beat* commented that his absence from the show "left an unbridgeable gap."[5] Happily, Roy and Gene soon resumed their warm friendship, after Gene had made the perfect peace-offering by giving Roy a new set of drums. They were promptly installed in Roy's basement "studio" at home, and used for the multi-track recordings he created for his own pleasure.

Roy's mentor and guide in the land of hi-fi was his friend Charles Graham. Charles, who was able and willing to give Roy professional advice, found that Roy was happier tinkering with radios, televisions, and amplifiers than with learning how they worked:

In the mid-1950s, when Roy was going overseas with J.A.T.P. I gave him an RCA Tube Manual, a 300-page guide to the current and recent vacuum tubes for radio and television servicemen. I marked several pages in red ink, with special emphasis on the primary parts for him to study, to read and re-read. When he got back from the tour I asked him if he'd studied the parts I'd marked. He said, "I took it with me on the whole tour but I was too busy to get to it."[6]

However, with Charles Graham's help, Roy kept abreast of all new developments in sound systems, speakers, etc., and was an early convert to stereo listening. By using his high-quality tape-recorders, Roy successfully multi-tracked his own performances on piano, drums, and a trumpet section consisting of four Roy Eldridges.

The J.A.T.P. unit that visited Europe during February and March 1960 featured Ella, Roy, the Jimmy Giuffre Trio, Paul Smith and his Quartet, and Shelly Manne and his Men. Reports that there was backstage friction between Ella and some of the other performers were quickly denied, but Ella and Roy, though greatly respecting each other's talents, were not always relaxed in one another's company. They both tended to await the start of every concert in a state of tension, which created a contagious agitation backstage. On stage everything usually went well, and no damage was done to the performance: Roy and Ella would apologize to each other and be temporarily at peace—until the next show. While in London, Roy was persuaded by Sinclair Traill (then editor of *Jazz Journal*) to comment on various jazz recordings. Roy approached this task with enthusiasm and candor, saying of Miles Davis' *Générique*, "He plays in one straight line. It's great background for a film. For myself I wouldn't want to be just sitting here listening to that sad sound." He went on to say of Miles' *Porgy And Bess*, "I don't dig that playing, it's mouse music," but Chet Baker fared worse. After hearing Baker's playing on *Chippyin'*, Roy said:

There are 10,000 trumpet players that can play like that, and I don't like any of them. I can't get with that lifeless tone so many cats produce these days. Jazz isn't supposed to be a sad thing. But a straight tone, with no vibrato, always reminds me of a brass band cornet player: no warmth, no feeling.[7]

Roy was asked for his opinion on jazz developments, particularly on what was then termed the *avant-garde* playing of Ornette Coleman (and his sidekick, trumpeter Don Cherry):

Yes, I heard that group and I know one thing, they're the bravest people I've ever seen! I went three nights in a row, sober at that, and never got the message. You really have to hear them in person and then you *really* can't understand it. I went with some young cats, modern musicians, took Paul Chambers with me. "You explain to me what's happening" I said. But he said, "Man, I don't understand it either." The group starts out with something, plays a riff on the first chorus then they leave everything and just blow. No amount of bars, nothing conventional, just blowing their horns—no melody, no kinda way. You can't say it's the blues or *How High The Moon*—or nothing.[8]

But almost in the same breath Roy admitted that he and Clyde Hart had experimented with a sort of free-form jazz many years earlier:

Clyde and I were at the Paramount Theater one time and I had a little recording machine in my bag. So we decided to play without telling one another beforehand what we were going to play. We decided in front that there'd be no regular chords, we'd announce no keys, stick to no progressions. Only once I fell into a minor key, the rest came out alright, there was a sort of melody going along there, but this stuff Ornette Coleman plays, there ain't nothing like that to it.[9]

Another later experiment which Roy completed when he was in Manchester on a tour of England involved him sitting at the piano and recording on cassette his impressions of Cecil Taylor's playing. His colleagues in J.A.T.P. listened with a mixture of amusement and admiration, and Ray Brown urged Roy not to destroy this curio. Roy not only kept the cassette but also played it as a "blindfold test" for interested listeners back home in the States:

> There was this one cat who was on a free jazz kick. So I pulled out this tape and told him there was a fantastic player in England I'd heard. This sucker really went for it, thought it was the greatest thing he'd ever heard. That kind of freedom is a licence for fraud.[10]

This stance against "free jazz" and the *avant-garde* movement wasn't a passing phase for Roy. Years later he detailed his continued dislike of these jazz developments:

> I remember Coleman Hawkins and I arrived in Monterey around 1960 [1959]. We were going to play a set with Ben Webster and a guy I wasn't familiar with called Ornette Coleman. When Ben and I got there Ornette was doing something. I turned to Bean and said, "What the hell is that?" When Hawkins and I heard the actual set we thought he was putting us on. I stayed over a day to catch another show. I wanted to see if I was losing my mind. And it was worse in the daytime than at night. Some months later I saw him at the Five Spot in New York and finally became convinced he meant what he was saying. It was a whole new language. Charlie Parker didn't surprise me because I could recognize where he came from. Ornette and Archie Shepp came out of nothing I ever knew about. I still can't get with it. There's nothing I can use there.[11]

Roy was just as candid when he spoke to bassist Richard Davis about the work of tenorist John Coltrane, saying "I know Trane is playing, but man, I just can't get with him," to which Davis replied, "You know Roy, Trane ain't waiting."[12] Ornette Coleman's versatile bassist, Charlie Haden, worked with Roy at the Half Note in New York and was asked by the trumpeter, "How can you play music with both Ornette Coleman and me?" To which Haden answered, "Easy. You're both playing beautiful music."[13]

During the early 1960s Roy's partnership with Coleman Hawkins again went through a sticky patch, which Roy believed was caused by Hawkins continuing to quote too high a price. When bassist Bill Crow asked Roy if he enjoyed working with Hawkins, Roy replied, "Yeah, but that man has done me out of a lot of work, if he don't like the bread he won't take the gig, and he don't know no word but a *thousand* dollars."[14] The situation wasn't helped by the fact that Hawkins decided to change his agency from Shaw Artists' Corporation to Woodrow Music Management (headed by Woody Herman's manager Abe Turchen). Roy decided to remain with the Shaw set-up, which meant that anyone wanting to book the quintet had to contact two different offices to establish when both Hawk and Roy were available. But even when Roy and Hawk went months without working together, they could still move effortlessly into top gear as soon as they got on to a bandstand, phrasing complex head arrangements in perfect accord. One of their most enjoyable duo dates (in June 1960) saw them flying out to California to take part in a reunion concert with Benny Carter, Rex Stewart, and Ben Webster at the second Los Angeles Jazz Festival. An evening of fine music was brought to a climax when the Benny Carter All Stars (with Jimmy Rowles on piano) backed singer Jimmy Witherspoon.

Back East, unruly youngsters created riots that caused the July 1960 Newport Jazz Festival to be canceled half-way through. The void was partly filled by a series of concerts at Cliff Walk Manor (close to the Newport site) organized by a collective headed by Max Roach and Charlie Mingus. Roy and Hawk accepted an offer to join Roach, Mingus, Eric Dolphy, Jo Jones, and others in this enterprise, which was described as the "Newport Rebels," so-called because some of the participants objected to the increasingly commercial nature of the main festival. Roy had no desire to become enmeshed in the political aspects of the situation, saying, "my fighting days are over." Nevertheless, he entered whole-heartedly into performing with disparate stylists, and later recorded with them—one of the tracks was a magnificent *Me And You* featuring Roy and Charlie Mingus. Hawkins did the festival, but claimed that contractual reasons precluded him from making the Rebels' November 1960 recordings, though it was rumored that his absence was caused by the producers failing to meet the price he required to make an album.

English-born bassist Peter Ind worked on many of the gigs that Roy and Hawk did in the New York area:

> 1 played a lot with Coleman and Roy at the Metropole, as well as at various other places. They were great friends, but they always seemed to be fighting verbally. Roy did his own thing and his strength was in that marvelous sound, a sound matched by no other trumpeter before or since. I must say that at this stage of their careers, Hawk was the greater improviser. Roy never played set solos, but what he relied mainly on by this time were phrases that he had played before. But for me it was a great experience working with these two.[15]

Both Roy and Hawk took part in a wide-ranging J.A.T.P. that left for Europe in late 1960. Ella was not part of this unit, as she was soon to undertake a series of concert dates with Oscar Peterson's Trio. The galaxy of jazz stars that crossed the Atlantic included Roy, Dizzy Gillespie, Benny Carter, Jo Jones, Coleman Hawkins, J. J. Johnson, Sam Jones, Cannonball Adderley, Nat Adderley, Louis Hayes, Lalo Schifrin, Victor Feldman, and Candido (on bongos). They were joined in Europe by two expatriates, tenorist Don Byas and altoist Leo Wright. I was able to meet up again with Roy. He half-remembered me, but if I raised a point that he didn't want to talk about he'd tilt his head back and look through the lower half of his spectacles and remain silent. However, when we got talking about various makes of trumpet he was much more forthcoming. I told him that I had tried to follow his example by playing a Martin Committee trumpet and he relaxed for the rest of our conversation. Roy's memory was always very good, and he proved this a few days later. After a J.A.T.P. concert he went to a Saturday-night party at a London apartment where a young woman thought it would be a merry idea to hide Roy's trumpet. Roy soon discovered his loss and became extremely agitated, thinking that his horn had been stolen. He was apparently close to tears, but was still in command enough to know that he needed a trumpet for the following night's performance, and realized that no instrument shops would be open on a Sunday. He remembered that I had said I played a Martin Committee, and as a result I got a telephone call (in the middle of the night) from British pianist Barney Bates, who was at the party, explaining the situation. I said I would be delighted to loan Roy the trumpet and arranged to meet up the next day. The plan was never carried out. Happily the tipsy girl came to her senses and showed a very angry Roy where she had hidden the trumpet. The incident provided a bridge that eventually led to my friendship with Roy.

During the summer of 1961, Roy, for the first time in over twenty years, played at the Village Vanguard, a 240-seat club at 178 Seventh Avenue South (in Greenwich Village), run by impresario Max Gordon. Topping the bill during Roy's residency was the sensational "new wave" comedian Lenny Bruce, whose book *How to Talk Dirty and Influence People* summarized his bold, revolutionary approach to comedy; Max Gordon called Bruce "The funniest, angriest, filthiest, most outrageous comic in the country."[16] Bruce was often in trouble with the law for including profanity and blasphemy in his cabaret act (and for using narcotics), but Max Gordon's experience told him that Bruce would be a tremendous draw at the Vanguard, and he was right. Roy had no problem in entertaining people who had come only to see Lenny Bruce. Eldridge wasn't shocked by Bruce's boldness but expressed dismay that a top-line artist appeared in denim—a rarity on stage in that era. Roy, no mean showman, liked the challenge of pulling a "non-jazz" audience round to his side. When someone remarked about the problem of performing to this type of non-jazz audience Roy was quick to air a viewpoint that he often quoted: "Look, 98 percent of the people never did dig jazz; if we could get another 2 percent on our side we'd have a jazz boom."[17] At the Village Vanguard, Roy started his set muted, gradually building up to a storming open-horn climax. Writer Ira Gitler was on hand to report, "Roy's searing horn charged along the low ceiling. He reaffirmed his stature as an exciting, lyrical player."[18] For this booking, and various other dates during the period, Roy was well supported by a rhythm section consisting of Peter Ind (bass), Eddie Locke (drums), and English pianist Ronnie Ball. Sometimes bassist Bennie Moten took Peter Ind's place, a move that allowed Roy to indulge in a humorous introduction of his musicians: "Bassman Bennie Moten from Birmingham, Alabama…and pianist Ronnie Ball from Birmingham …England."

Soon after completing the Village Vanguard booking, Roy left for a July 1961 tour of South America (Brazil, Uruguay, and Peru) as part of a package organized by promoter Monte Kay. The tour, which lasted for three weeks, featured Roy, Hawk, Zoot Sims, Al Cohn, Kenny Dorham, Tommy Flanagan, Ronnie Ball, Jo Jones, and others. Al Cohn never forgot the way Roy and Hawk went through a sort of comedy routine in the dressing-room, making salty observations about each other and devising humorous observations about various hiccups in the travel arrangements. Roy enjoyed visiting countries he hadn't been to before, and was particularly at home in the vibrant atmosphere of Brazil, but he was not slow to observe the tremendous gulf that existed between rich and poor. For him, the vexing part of the tour was that there was so little time available for sightseeing.

For Roy, Hawk, and Jo Jones, the most unusual assignment of this period occurred when they were booked to appear in a television drama series entitled *Route 66*. Their contribution to an hour-long episode entitled *Goodnight Sweetheart* (featuring Ethel Waters) involved them taking brief acting roles, but, for reasons best known to the producer, Roy played the part of drummer "Ace Gilder," and Jo

Jones became trumpeter "Lover Brown," while Coleman Hawkins was the strong, silent "Snoose Mobley." The program was shown on the C.B.S. network in October 1961, but none of the participating musicians was nominated for acting awards. During this same time, Roy and Hawk also took part in a 27-minute film as part of a small band organized by pianist Johnny Guarnieri for a pilot television show. The filming took place in Leon and Eddie's on 52nd Street and featured Roy, Hawk, Guarnieri, plus Milt Hinton on bass, Cozy Cole on drums, Barry Galbraith on guitar, and Carol Stevens on vocals. Socially things were again smoothish between Roy and Hawk, but though both were intent on changing their booking agents, neither would agree to the other's choice. Hawk decided to sign for Willard Alexander, and Roy (doing a full circle that took him twenty years to complete) signed with Joe Glaser's Associated Booking Corporation. Despite all the joshing that the two musicians indulged in, Roy indicated his respect and admiration for Hawkins in a eulogy published by *Metronome* in December 1961:

> Coleman likes the best in everything: clothes, cars, music, etc. It is a pleasure to work with a musician like Coleman. He seems to improve with age. One night you will say that he had played his best, and the next night he'll top that. In closing I would say that Coleman Hawkins is a real pro and a real classy old man plus the greatest saxophone player of all time.

The two veterans continued to work together often in the early 1960s, at various clubs and numerous festivals. They also played concerts at New York's Museum of Modern Art and worked "fill-in" dates at the Metropole. Although Roy and Hawk played concert tours of Britain as part of a package, Eldridge always felt disappointed that they were never given the chance to present their quintet format in British clubs. To the amusement of their sidemen, Hawk and Roy regularly indulged in patter worthy of a stage double act, each kidding the other about many things, especially age. Roy was always amused to point out to people that when he and Hawk were deep in conversation on stage they were not discussing music but simply talking about cooking or baseball, and this was borne out by drummer Eddie Locke:

> J. C. Heard who had played drums with them before I joined told me all about Roy, Hawk, and the talking; he said, "Don't pay it no mind if you see them talking on the bandstand. They talk all the time on and off it; they are like two old maids, not talking jazz at all, but cooking, clothes, this and that." The sport that Roy took a big interest in was baseball, he liked the Mets and he and Hawk used to talk about that too.[19]

Roy never hesitated to praise Hawkins in press interviews. He told British journalist Les Tompkins about the perpetual inspiration he got from Hawk:

> I really dig playing with Coleman, he's my man. We've worked together so long. And it's a funny thing—we could be playing some nights and wouldn't be nothing happening. Come back—maybe the third set—and all of a sudden the thing just takes fire.[20]

But lurking within each man was the feeling that musically the partnership could have been even better, or at least more enjoyable. Dan Morgenstern spoke of this: "Hawk never ever put Roy down personally, but he told me that he'd rather work with Charlie Shavers than with Roy. No matter how acrobatic and cute Charlie played, Hawk could hold his own against it."[21] And Roy, in a reflective moment, told Eddie Locke, "I played better with Chu Berry than I do with Hawk."[22]

Because of the 1960 riots there was no Newport Jazz Festival in the summer of 1961, but happily the annual pattern resumed in July 1962—and provided Roy with a good deal of merriment. The source of his amusement was Hawk's late arrival—which meant he missed playing on the first set with Roy. Eldridge said he quite understood how infirmity and forgetfulness were enemies of punctuality and reliability, and watched Hawkins, already vexed by traffic hold-ups, become increasingly annoyed. But the date ended happily with Roy and Hawk backing singer Joe Williams, and taking part in a mammoth jam session. Critic Bill Coss wrote in *Down Beat* that "Eldridge was the most outstanding performer of the Festival."[23] Not long after the success at Newport, Roy had the sad task of journeying to Pittsburgh for the funeral of his father Alexander, who died on July 22, 1962, aged 84. In his will he left several houses to Roy, but the trumpeter's work schedule meant he couldn't supervise their administration properly, and, after encountering problems with tenants and damage to the properties, he decided to cut his losses and sell the houses. Roy had seen his father earlier that year when he and Peter Ind (after playing a gig in Columbus, Ohio) made a detour to Pittsburgh on their way back to New York:

> Roy asked me if I would mind if he called into Pittsburgh as he wanted to see his father. It was a Sunday morning and Roy wanted to surprise his dad coming out of church. Sure enough, at exactly the time Roy predicted, his father emerged. Roy greeted him warmly and introduced me. I stood listening to the conversation in which Roy's dad said, "Why don't you give up music? I know of a good business opening that would suit you," but Roy just smiled and replied, "Thanks, but I've still got some wild oats to sow."[24]

On that same journey, out of the blue, Roy was stopped and questioned by a white policeman for no apparent reason. He was allowed to drive on after a few minutes of interrogation, but the incident led him to say to Peter Ind, with some bitterness, "Now do you think I'm paranoid?"[25]

Besides engagements with Hawkins, Roy also continued to guest with various "house" bands, including dates at Lenny's-on-the-Turnpike in Peabody, Massachussets, working with Billy Bauer's group at the Sherwood Inn, Long Island, and being featured with trumpeter

George Mauro's Band on the Manasquan (New Jersey) Ferryboat; he also played return dates in Canada and Chicago. One of these Chicago performances caused a critic to comment that Roy had barely made the top note that he aimed for—Roy brooded on this for ages, raising the subject again and again. Roy could never hide his exasperation when he felt he'd been unjustly slighted, nor could he mask disappointment, for instance, when his plans to work regularly in a small group featuring Ben Webster, Jo Jones, and pianist Ray Bryant failed to attract band-bookers. He said, "It's a crime to break that group up, but the agency couldn't find any jobs for us."[26] He then did a series of solo dates in Europe (not visiting Britain), and when he returned to the States he decided to accept an offer from Norman Granz to work regularly as part of Ella Fitzgerald's backing group (in which role Roy had made an album *These Are The Blues* in October 1963). The new arrangement began during a two-shows-a-night residency at the Hotel Americana's Royal Box in New York, where Roy augmented the existing line-up consisting of Tommy Flanagan (piano), Gus Johnson (drums), Les Spann (guitar), and Bill Yancey on bass (who alternated with Jim Hughart).

Roy and Ella were well aware of each other's foibles; nevertheless, after playing a successful residency at the Latin Casino in Philadelphia they felt the move was a good one. Their first major expedition together was a fifteen-day tour of Japan in January 1964, followed by a two-month concert trek around many of the major halls of Europe. They returned to the U.S.A. and again played the Hotel Americana before fulfilling a residency in Florida followed by a stint at New York's Basin Street East. These long periods of working together began to put a strain on the Ella–Roy partnership, and pre-show agitations again surfaced. Ella was the star, so Roy often had to bite his tongue to avoid an argument, but Roy's feisty nature made it difficult for him to hide his feelings, and Ella's long-time road manager, Pete Cavello, often had to smooth ruffled feathers. Pianist Paul Smith, who had preceded Tommy Flanagan in Ella's group, spoke of the trumpeter's role with Ella:

Roy played with us when I was with Ella. Roy owed Norman Granz quite a lot of money, as a lot of musicians did. When he used to do the Jazz at the Philharmonic things he would always say, "If you need any money" and advance it against salary…and in his book he'd keep track of the guys that borrowed…and at the end of six weeks there would be an accounting. Roy was one of the guys I guess who spent a lot of money on the road. He could maybe end up having a salary of, say, 6,000 dollars for six weeks, and he'd spend eight! So Norman would take him on another tour to make up the two thousand. Or he'd put him with Ella and he'd just go along and play on a harmon mute, all night behind her and maybe a solo at the top of the show. It wasn't that he was needed. In fact a lot of times it was kind of irritating to Ella. I never felt it was personal.[27]

Roy felt increasingly discontented with the subsidiary role he played, his dissatisfaction made keener by the fact that he was paying off a debt for money he'd frittered away. Early on in Roy's link-up with Ella he said, "The chick gets in a nice groove, and so it's interesting. It's like a challenge having to play for her and not try to outshine her."[28] The sentiments of this last sentence soon created problems in the working relationship. Roy, for most of his career, had been an unshackled soloist, and he always found difficulty in restraining himself in front of an excited audience. Ella (a mixture of toughness and deep uncertainties) wasn't pleased when she had to wait until the tumultuous applause for a Roy solo died down before she could resume singing. Leonard Feather summed up the great singer's problems when he wrote, "On stage, in command of an audience, she reveals little of the inner tensions that have wracked her so deeply. Off-stage she can relapse too easily into a self-concern for which there is rarely, if ever, any artistic justification."[29]

An incident that occurred during a Florida residency (at the Deauville Hotel, Miami Beach) illustrated how a trivial occurrence could get Ella extremely agitated. One evening, Roy glanced out into the audience and noticed that Frank Schiffman (long-time boss of Harlem's Apollo Theater) was part of the crowd. He let Ella know this via a stage whisper, but instead of being pleased that an old acquaintance had come to hear her, she became totally unsettled, saying, "I got so nervous I could hardly sing."[30] Apparently, back in 1938, Frank Schiffman had barred Ella from singing her hit *A-Tisket, A-Tasket* at the Apollo, on the grounds that it was too much like a nursery rhyme. Ella had so taken this to heart that she was still unnerved by Schiffman's presence thirty years later. A musician who toured with Ella spoke of her perpetual uncertainties: "Whenever she heard a crowd mumbling she feels that they are discussing her."[31] Roy's relationship with the rest of Ella's group was affable. Pianist Tommy Flanagan said, "Any friction was completely between the two of them."[32] But despite the squabbles, Roy and Ella retained enormous admiration for the other's skills. Ella said of Roy, "God gives it to some and not others. He's got more soul in one note than a lot of people could get into a whole song."[33] Ella's signed photograph held pride of place in Roy's home, on top of the television set where everyone could see it. Even so, time never smoothed out the path that Roy and Ella trod together. In 1971, at one of their occasional reunions, Dan Morgenstern observed, "Ella, never the most secure performer, seems to resent any applause going to Roy and gives him progressively less to play. If Roy got a big ovation for one of his solos you could bet that Ella would drop that number from the second show."[34] Their regular musical partnership ended in 1965, though they shared occasional concert dates for several years after that, but these reunions were not full of joy. In 1977, John McDonough wrote, "Roy never appears on stage with Ella. He is discreetly silent about the reasons for this obvious lack of rapport."[35] The big break occurred in March 1965 when Roy appeared at yet another Hotel Americana booking, this time with an augmented line-up that included trombonist J. J. Johnson and saxist Oliver Nelson. Roy was officially designated leader and conductor of this ensemble, which led to him having several touchy exchanges with the singer, each taking it in turn to light the other's short fuse. Ella became progressively more fidgety during the rehearsals, asking for endless run-throughs of routines that Roy deemed perfect. Naturally the booking was a success, as was almost every engagement that Ella played throughout the world, but Roy had had enough, and later told B.B.C. producer Steve Allen that he threw down the baton and walked out. Roy and Ella's admiration for each other's artistry lived on, but both were delighted that they had ceased working together regularly. Roy celebrated his freedom by playing a residency at the Village Vanguard from where a Sunday matinée was recorded that also featured Coleman Hawkins and Earl Hines. The other group was led by Charles Mingus, who became very vexed when Coleman Hawkins talked while the Mingus group was performing. A full-scale row was narrowly averted as Mingus ranted and raved at Messrs Eldridge, Hawkins, and Hines. For most of his stay, Roy used Oliver Jackson on drums, and either Barry Harris or Richard Wyands on piano, with George Tucker and Bob Cranshaw alternating on bass. Lucky Thompson, who was also on the bill, used Roy's rhythm section. Dan Morgenstern was again on hand to summarize Roy's performance:

> Bold, warm, passionate, pouring all his strong emotions into the horn. Roy's sound, so different from the vibrato-less (and sometimes) lifeless tone adopted by many post-Gillespie trumpeters (excepting Fats Navarro and Clifford Brown) is jazz personified.[36]

Roy moved on to work at the Five Spot Café, New York, from the end of March 1965, where he was accompanied first by Sir Roland Hanna's Trio, later by Walter Bishop, Jr. Next came a June 1965 stay at the Village Gate (again working opposite Charles Mingus' Jazz Workshop). Soon after that booking ended, Roy established a productive musical partnership with tenorist Richie Kamuca, Kamuca, born in 1930 and originally from Philadelphia, was an avowed fan of Roy's playing, describing him as "my favorite all-round musician."[37]

After enjoying considerable success in the Los Angeles studios, Kamuca moved back East in 1963 to play in the ensemble regularly seen on Merv Griffin's television show. His schedule at the New York studios allowed him time to play local gigs, and, after one particularly swinging get-together with Roy, the two decided to work together as often as possible. Their official debut as a partnership took place at a Museum of Modern Art concert in New York on July 29, 1965, soon followed by a stint at the Half Note in August. The quintet couldn't become a full-time enterprise because Kamuca had to dovetail his studio commitments with "outside" gigs. Nevertheless, he and Roy managed to play several residencies in tandem, and to record an album together. Although they displayed an admirable musical rapport and worked well together, they never became close friends. Pianist Dick Katz, who worked in the quintet, said, "They didn't really get along. There were sparks there. Some personal issues, but I don't know what they were."[38] But Kamuca enjoyed working with Roy and went out with him on all sorts of gigs including mall concerts (in New Jersey or in upstate New York). For these jobs the line-up was usually Roy, Richie, Eddie Locke on drums, and C. C. Williams on organ. The quartet was expected to play requests, and they did so willingly, even when the numbers asked for were not connected with jazz. A favorite request at this time was *Hello Dolly*, which, via Louis Armstrong's recording, had achieved Hit Parade success. Roy had no objections whatsoever to playing this tune: "It's a real swinging thing. I knew it was going to be a hit the first time I heard the record in the Copper Rail. It's not a fluke hit either. I mean it's one you can listen to. I enjoy it. It's very nice to see someone like Armstrong come through with a hit."[39] But Kamuca could play only some of the gigs offered, which Roy found frustrating. Roy always preferred working with a tenor-player in a quintet line-up, and during the 1960s shared gigs with several, including Billy Mitchell, Frank Foster, and Julian Dash.

Roy's on–off romance with the flugel horn was going through an affectionate period and he regularly doubled on it during the mid-

1960s. Some younger musicians felt more at ease when accompanying Roy on flugel horn, because he was less likely to produce what
they found to be the disconcerting "explosions" that were a regular
feature of his trumpet-playing. Canadian pianist Wray Downes (then
in his early thirties) worked with Roy in Toronto, and like other
musicians from his generation he found Roy's emotional blowing
(complete with rasping inflections and throat buzzes) almost
alarming: "He always made me nervous because he sounded as
though he was going to fall off his note, his lip was going to give out—
that's his style, but as an inexperienced player I wasn't used to it."[40]
Another pianist, Norman Simmons, who worked with Roy in Chicago
and New York, said that small incidents could temporarily throw Roy
completely off-course: "Roy is very emotional and he can get upset
and not be able to get a note out of the horn. And then he can turn
around after drinking all evening and wind up playing high F's and
G's at three o'clock in the morning, on the last show."[41] Roy
confirmed that scenario, but said, "People don't know how hard it
is to play the trumpet. Those lips, if they don't vibrate, nothing comes
out."[42] British bassist Lennie Bush, who worked with Roy in London,
said he felt almost alarmed when he heard Roy's efforts in the
opening set: "I listened and thought, 'He's really got trouble with his
chops,' but by the end of the night he was blowing like a maniac, it
was fantastic."[43]

There were no signs that Norman Granz had any plans to
recommence the J.A.T.P. tours of North America. By this time Granz
had apartments in New York, Los Angeles, and London, but spent
most of his time based in Switzerland. From there he decided to sell
his Verve recording company to Metro-Goldwyn-Mayer Inc. for a sum
reputed to be two and a half million dollars. Roy missed the money
that touring the big circuits brought, but never reserved his best
efforts for the big gigs. When he was "on song," whatever the venue,
he would play his heart out. Jo Jones commented, "Roy will work as
hard for 25 dollars as for 250 dollars."[44] Even at this illustrious stage of
his career Roy still wanted to work as often as possible, and was still

willing to take jobs that paid little so that he could blow regularly. One of his haunts at this time was the Shore Café in Brooklyn (where he played in jam sessions with drummer Sonny Greer), and another hang-out was the Bovi Town Tavern in Providence, Rhode Island. Keeping his lip in good shape was the prime objective, as he explained:

> I found out years ago that I'd never be rich, so I stopped worrying about that. So long as I can get something to eat, put gas in my car, take care of my wife and look after my animals, everything's cool. I don't want a hit record. I had all the thrills and all the glamor a long while ago. But now I just want to play and make my little bread, not too much, but enough. There are maybe only a few times a year that I play in a way that really pleases me, but those handfuls of special nights make up for everything, but if I'm not together I break into a cold sweat.[45]

To quell the restlessness that surfaced when there was nowhere to blow, Roy spent an increased amount of time in his basement studio, amusing himself by recording unusual chord progressions on piano so that he could use them later as accompaniment for his own trumpet-playing: "On the road I carry a small portable tape recorder. I put chords on it with the piano and I can sit in a hotel room and play my trumpet with it."[46] But fewer and fewer clubs encouraged jam sessions, and Roy found this frustrating:

> I've got a couple of places in Long Island where I can go and play. If I'm off and I've got a weekend gig I'll go in on a Thursday to get my chops up. But now you have to be announced and all that, and really put on a performance. So I stopped making the rounds and jamming. You come out, you pay for your own drinks, and you still have to get up there and entertain.[47]

Roy's willingness to play all sorts of gigs attracted the attention of several lesser-known bandleaders. Roy wasn't only interested in playing with "name" musicians; his main concern was the competence of those he worked with:

> I mean if the cats play good I enjoy playing with them, such as a policeman named Herbert "Herb" Meyers in New York. He plays clarinet and he's got a nice little group. I play those barmitzvahs and gigs like that with him every once in a while.[48]

Roy began 1966 by playing a two-week booking at Blues Alley in Washington, D.C., where he delighted local musicians by recalling many obscure jazz performers of yesteryear. At Blues Alley he worked alongside guitarist Steve Jordan in Tom Gwaltney's group. In his book *Rhythm Man* (written with Tom Scanlan), Jordan also recalled Roy's pessimism about the future:

> Look, I'm making more money than I ever have in my life. But the music business isn't good. There are fewer and fewer places to work. Too many good musicians out of work. And some of the places you have to work. Take the Embers in New York. When I signed the contract there I didn't notice that it included words saying that I had to use a mute all the time. I'll never work there again.

After playing another residency at the Half Note in New York, Roy began a ten-week stay at Manhattan's Embers West (where he wasn't restricted to muted playing), but any cobwebs that might have gathered there were blown away at that year's Newport Jazz Festival when Roy featured in a trumpet workshop with Dizzy Gillespie, Bobby Hackett, Ruby Braff, and Kenny Dorham. While playing at the Embers West, Roy made the important decision to accept an offer to join Count Basie's Orchestra. This meant that for the first time in almost twenty years Roy again played regularly in a big band. The instigator behind the move was tenorist Eddie "Lockjaw" Davis, who sat in with Roy at Embers West. Count Basie also visited the club and said of Roy, "I wish I had him in my band."[49] "Lockjaw" picked up on this and made the offer to Roy, who, after some deliberation, agreed to join Basie. When the news was announced, some of Basie's trumpeters called into Embers West and hailed Roy with the greeting "Hey Section," and everything seemed set for a joyful and productive association, particularly as Roy had known Basie since they were both struggling youngsters. Roy entered the Basie Band full of optimism, and told Ralph Gleason: "I'll be cool in about two months. It's been 27 years [sic] since I've been in a big band brass section," adding as an aside, "Basie used to raid my band for recruits."[50] Roy was equally upbeat when he talked to a *Down Beat* reporter:

> I'm looking forward to it. Naturally I've always dug the band, and I think it will be a good thing for me, playing-wise. One of the reasons why I'm doing this is that I'm tired of being out on the road by myself. It's not that I can't get enough work on my own, but it gets pretty lonely out there sometimes. Now I'll know I'll always have good company when I travel.[51]

But it wasn't to be. Roy's stay with Count Basie provided him with one of the biggest disappointments of his latter-day career, and some of his unhappiest touring experiences. Later he told Phil Schaap, "It was worse than being in a white band. I had buddies in the white bands, but in Basie's Band the only cat I was real tight with was 'Lockjaw.' When the band took an intermission, all the cats would split and I'd be left sitting up on the bandstand."[52]

12

FESTIVALS
GALORE

Roy might have been less bothered by the lack of closeness with his Basie Band colleagues if he had been happy musically, but he was rarely featured by Basie, and this made him extremely restless. What Basie's strategy was remains unfathomable. It was as though he was paying Roy back for something that had happened in the distant past. When Roy was eventually featured on *After You've Gone*, Basie (a master at picking a perfect tempo) beat it in at what Roy called "breakneck speed." For most of his stay with Basie, Roy was given unchallenging section parts. After Roy left the band, he claimed that Basie had deliberately not played arrangements that Nat Pierce had written especially to feature him, but Nat himself cleared up that part of the dispute by saying, "Roy had left Basie before I turned them in."[1] Despite this being pointed out to Roy, he made no effort to remove it from the pile of complaints that his stay with Basie created. On a couple of occasions, when Sonny Payne was late, Roy took over on drums, but even then things didn't work out happily. "Basie kept me up there…I could hardly play my trumpet when I got through."[2] Charles Graham spoke of this period: "Once, while he was on the road with the Basie band I went backstage and asked Jimmy Rushing, who of course had a separate dressing room,

'Where's Roy?' Jimmy told me, 'Back with the rest of the band, where else?' "[3]

Roy was particularly vexed when members of the general public accused him of taking it easy during his stay with Basie: "People were heckling me, saying 'You don't wanna play no more. You're tired of carrying the ball,'"[4] whereas Roy would have been happy to be featured on every number. Roy appeared with Basie's Orchestra at the July 1966 Newport Jazz Festival and fulfilled other East Coast dates before moving West to play in California and at Lake Tahoe—where Roy had difficulty in breathing, an early sign of the emphysema that plagued his later years. Roy soloed briefly on a September 1966 album *Broadway Basie's Way*, and took part in a Grover Mitchell small group recording as well as appearing on a television show that featured Diana Ross and the Supremes, but these events were the only highlights for Roy, who looked back and said, "I hated to come to work,"[5] which for someone with Roy's usual upbeat attitude showed how low he felt. His mood was not helped when he was accidentally hurt by one of Louie Bellson's cymbals. Louie explained the background to the incident:

> In the summer of 1966 Basie came to Hollywood and Sonny Payne got sick so Count got in touch with me and said, "Please help." So for two or three days I played with the band at Ciro's on Hollywood's Sunset Strip. Roy always sat immediately next to me on the end of the trumpet section. One night, as I was taking a drum solo, the cymbal toppled off the drum-riser and hit Roy smack between the eyes. The blood started flowing immediately and I was upset. Roy realized it was a pure accident, and later we even joked about it, with Roy saying, "Please don't try to be so dynamic in future."[6]

All in all, Roy's stay with Basie lasted for about twelve weeks (from the middle of June to early September 1966). He soon returned to New York, and within a week was back at the Embers West leading a quartet consisting of Ross Tompkins (piano), Russell George (bass), and Chuck Lampkin (drums). The booking was described as an indefinite stay, but in fact lasted only through November, at which point the club's owners decided to close the venue. Roy wasn't dismayed, as he was due to commence a tour of England in December, but the British Musicians' Union ban, which prevented overseas musicians from working in Britain unless they were part of a Union-approved exchange, was still in force. As no work permit had been ratified, the deal fell through at the last moment, much to Roy's annoyance and the disappointment of his British fans. However, these followers were consoled by the news that Roy would soon visit Europe as part of an all-star Jazz From a Swinging Era package, which was due to play in England during March 1967.

On this tour Roy shared trumpet duties with Buck Clayton, working alongside Vic Dickenson, and tenorists Bud Freeman and Budd Johnson. Altoist Willie Smith was scheduled to be on this tour, but became too ill to travel (sadly he died before the troupe flew to Europe). Smith's place was taken by Earle Warren (playing alto-sax and clarinet). Sir Charles Thompson and Earl Hines were the pianists, Bill Pemberton was on bass, and Oliver Jackson on drums. Since no overall leader had been appointed, or delegated, Earl Hines (the most experienced bandleader in the troupe) took it upon himself to fulfill that role—a decision that irked Roy. Roy, never a placid tourist, was (by my own observations) just about as tetchy and short-tempered as he could be, throughout almost the entire tour. I asked Buck Clayton for his view on Earl assuming command, and he chuckled and said, "Earl is Earl, and he is not going to change now. He's quite a nice old fellow, but he wants the show to be a success, and he loves that limelight."[7] Hines' habit of taking longer solos than anyone else was mildly irritating to the rest of the cast, but it made Roy incandescent with rage, and liable to lash out verbally at anyone close at hand. He had a bitter row with Bud Freeman over nothing in particular, and a contretemps with Vic Dickenson that almost came to blows. Buck Clayton was appalled by this fracas between volatile Roy and laconic

Vic, and said in disbelief, "I just don't understand this—they worked together in Speed Webb's Band damn near forty years ago."[8] Fortunately, I managed to stay on the right side of Roy, and during a long talk at the Manchester Free Trade Hall he was very forthcoming about his early days, but made it clear he didn't want to discuss any aspect of the Jazz From a Swinging Era tour.

The tour was organized by Harold Davison's Agency under the personal supervision of Davison's right-hand man, Jack L. Higgins. Roy and Jack had never got on well, but this tour established an implacable hatred between them. To his dying day, Roy never had a good word to say about Jack: "He hated me with a purple passion" was one of the Roy's comments, and Jack, in a 1999 pronouncement, called Roy "a most hateful individual."[9] The two men clashed head-on at a television show that the troupe recorded for the B.B.C. in the Questor's Theatre, West London, and were separated by Buck Clayton, who read the riot act to Roy. The filming took place on a Good Friday, which meant all the local pubs had closed early, so the B.B.C. provided drinks and sandwiches for the performers. Ray Bolden, later to become a firm friend of Roy, met up with him for the first time that day and was delighted to be part of an informal gathering in the bar. Roy had mellowed by then and began playing the blues on an upright piano, soon to be joined by Earle Warren, who sang a series of risqué lyrics. Buck Clayton generally held his own against Roy in their trumpet battles, and some Eldridge devotees, such as Ray Bolden, even felt that Roy came out second best on several Swinging Era dates. However, on the Easter Sunday (March 26, 1967), the group played at Ronnie Scott's Club in London, where Roy sailed into Buck and virtually took him apart. I was in the audience and couldn't help wondering about this complete reversal of form. I found out later that during the previous evening Buck had broken part of a dental bridge. He was touched and grateful that Roy had stayed up half the night while he waited for emergency treatment at a nearby dental hospital. Makeshift repairs allowed Buck to resume playing, but he was wary of applying mouthpiece pressure. However, despite Roy's friendliness in keeping Buck company through most of the night, he did his darndest to "cut" the inconvenienced Clayton on the following evening. In soccer there's a saying, "No pals on the park," and this certainly applied to Roy's attitude when he played alongside another trumpeter.

One of the group's tour dates took them to Liverpool. By this time the duets between Roy on piano and Earle Warren's vocals had become a regular feature of backstage life. Writer Steve Voce heard and enjoyed Roy and Earle's informal efforts, then, using the portable tape-recorder he had brought with him, played Louis Armstrong's *I'm Confessin'* to several of the musicians in their dressing-room. He later described the scene: "Immediately a choir of Buck Clayton, Earle Warren, Vic Dickenson and Roy Eldridge began to sing the solos and the vocal along with the tape, not one of them had forgotten a note."[10] The Swinging Era package made a double album in Paris for a British label, which involved recording manager Terry Brown flying over to help supervise the date. As a former jazz trumpeter, Terry had done his fair share of tippling, but he was stunned by the prodigious drinking that went on that day, and relieved that the simmering feelings between Roy and Earl Hines never developed into physical confrontation. The group later played in Belgium, where several of them enjoyed a happy reunion with Ben Webster (then living in Europe) when they went along to hear him at the Blue Note Club in Brussels.

Back in New York, Roy played a variety of casual dates (including some with clarinettist Sol Yaged). He also did a week at the Half Note and made a brief trip to Canada to play at the Montreal Expo 1967 as part of a Newport All Stars package organized by George Wein. The May weather suddenly changed, and the 35,000 crowd that had gathered in the open air at the Place des Nations were made well aware that a cold breeze had caused a drastic drop in temperature. Roy, instantly reminded of that traumatic childhood occasion when he had tried to play "taps" in the open air, became alarmed and kept the trumpet warm by tucking it into his coat until a second before it was time for him to play. Warmer dates in Toronto, Washington, D.C., and Cleveland followed, then a return home.

With the sounds of Roy's playing on the Jazz From a Swinging Era tour still ringing in his ears, Ray Bolden decided he wanted to hear more of the same; accordingly, he paid his first visit to New York and soon linked up with Roy in Jim and Andy's Bar, a celebrated gathering place for jazz musicians. Roy was delighted to renew the friendship and insisted on acting as chauffeur to Bolden: "He drove me back to my hotel, even though Jim and Andy's was only a block and a half away. We mounted the pavement in what was a nightmare ride—Roy's eyes were giving him (and me) problems."[11] Other people noticed that Roy's eyes were increasingly bothering him, and eventually he had to have cataracts removed from both eyes.

Roy briefly entertained the idea of working regularly with a new quintet consisting of young players: Steve Butler (drums), Larry Slezak (tenor-sax), Bernie Thompson (organ), and Billy Cable (guitar). The group's performance at the Red Garter in New York was favorably reviewed by Dan Morgenstern:

> For his local gigs Roy has been working with the musicians he brought to his recent Jazz Interaction session. All but the guitarist are very young, and he is no ancient either. Though Roy could have brought in an "all-star" line up, he preferred to bring "his people," he is proud of them and wants others to hear them. In answer to a request Roy ventured his hit from the Gene Krupa days *Let Me Off Uptown*. The band didn't know it, so there was a brief and very enjoyable on-the-spot rehearsal. They made it and Roy's vocal (including an impersonation of his erstwhile partner in the song, Anita O'Day) was a gas, so was the concluding high-note "whistles" that are Roy's private property; nobody else hits them like that.[12]

Listeners agreed with Morgenstern's assessment that the line-up was "a nice group with a nice feeling," but getting regular bookings for it was impossible, and Roy soon reverted to guesting in various cities. One week-long residency (in November 1968) saw Roy leading Jack Gregg on bass, Danny Farrar on drums, and Dick Wellstood on piano at a restaurant in Rochester, New York. Wellstood always enjoyed working with Roy, and on this occasion found that the food provided for the musicians was "great," but he added ruefully:

> The nature of the room precludes any real playing and except on the few occasions when Roy opens up, we wind up playing the depressing, familiar club-date repertoire: *Hello Dolly, Mame, Fiddler on the Roof*, etc. Even the customers are familiar club-date customers.[13]

Roy continued to play gigs occasionally with Richie Kamuca, and in late 1968 they played another residency at the Half Note, backed by Dave Frishberg on piano, Gus Johnson on drums, with Bill Takas and Russell George alternating on bass. A visitor to the club noticed that Roy was as keen as ever to blow all night, and during the intermissions he went to the back of the club to blow softly along with the house juke-box. Through Kamuca, Roy subbed briefly in the television studio band that played for the Merv Griffin show, and the two men's spirited jazz won over a young crowd when they played a Sunday concert at Fillmore East in New York's East Village. Early in 1969 Roy and Richie began yet another stay at the Half Note, this time with Sir Roland Hanna on piano, Buddy Catlett on bass, and Eddie Locke on drums, who recalled that the management kept renewing the contract: "We did thirteen weeks at the Half Note in 1969; the people lined up to get in."[14]

Roy celebrated his fifty-eighth birthday during his stay at the Half Note, and used the occasion to tell the audience that his life had consisted of "58 good summers, and 58 bad, long winters."[15] Roy and Richie were delighted to see Coleman Hawkins (by this time a wan figure) listening approvingly to one of their sets at the Half Note. Appearing opposite the quintet was Anita O'Day (with her regular pianist Alan Marlowe, who worked with Eddie Locke and Buddy Catlett to make up Anita's accompanying trio). Roy and Anita chose not to share any numbers, handing over the sets to each other with an affability that masked genuine disdain. Roy spoke of this booking:

> They thought that we would do something together, but she had no eyes for it. People would ask and she'd say, "Oh, Mr Eldridge doesn't want to play it." Which was not true. I was getting ready to go home and there were people at the bar, and they said, "Anita, why don't you do *Let Me Off Uptown?*" so she said, "Oh, Mr Eldridge is going home." I said, "Look, I don't have to go home." So I took my horn and laid it on the bar. So she went up for her set, and she never called me. I sat there until the joint closed.[16]

Some years later, after Anita's autobiography *High Times, Hard Times* had been published, Roy was vexed to learn that Anita felt there had been jealousy between them. His agitation was such that (unusually) he voiced some ungallant thoughts: "She's crazy! First of all I didn't think she could sing to start off with, so what am I gonna be jealous of? No, there was no jealousy on my part."[17]

By now most of Roy's work was done in clubs, but an occasional big concert date cropped up, as in April 1969 when Roy played at Carnegie Hall as part of a line-up that included Dizzy Gillespie and the Thad Jones–Mel Lewis Big Band. For an appearance on a Blossom Sealey concert Roy took the unusual step of playing his pocket trumpet. In March 1969, Roy's long-time agent (and occasional adversary) Joe Glaser suffered a paralyzing stroke which soon proved fatal, but the death of Coleman Hawkins two months later was a much sadder event in Roy's life. Roy summarized his admiration for the great tenorist, saying, "He knew more music than anyone else I ever played with."[18] It was apt that Hawk's last gig was with Roy. It involved them playing at a Sunday concert in Chicago, as well as recording a television show (compèred by Dan Morgenstern) for W.T.T.W. It was somehow typical of the wary friendship the two had long shared that they traveled to Chicago by different flights, just as they always drove separately to gigs. Hawk collapsed at Chicago Airport and was taken to a hospital where malnutrition was diagnosed, but he rallied enough to do both the television show and the concert. Ill though he was, he corrected Roy when he mis-announced an item, something that greatly impressed Eldridge. Next day, Hawk was put on a plane and made the journey back to his New York apartment. Sadly he was too ill to move far, and finally his family decided, much against Hawk's protestations, that he should be admitted to Wickersham Hospital, New York, where bronchial pneumonia was diagnosed. This illness proved too much for his emaciated body, and he died in the early hours of May 19, 1969.

Pianist Norman Simmons told Mark Gardner:

> I was working with Roy on the night that Coleman Hawkins died. Roy and Coleman were very close and he was very heart broken that evening. At one point we started to play *Bean And The Boys*, a line he and Bean used to play on the changes of *Lover Come Back To Me*. Roy broke down in tears on the stage and he couldn't play a note.[19]

I spoke with Roy about Hawk's demise soon afterwards; by then his mood was one of resignation. He reflected on all the fine music they had created together, but also said, "You know, even up to that very last gig we played in Chicago, he wouldn't agree to do it unless he was sure he was getting more money than I was. We had a thousand laughs, we talked about everything, cooking, women, sport, but we weren't always as close as people thought."[20] During the late 1960s Roy had seen his sidekick change from a dapper, almost fastidious, dresser into someone who couldn't be bothered to button up his shirts or have a crease in his pants. Roy watched Hawk gradually lose interest in so many things, his various desires being obliterated by a desperate need for alcohol. During Hawk's occasional visits to Roy's home he was full of praise for Vi Eldridge's cooking, but on his last dinner date there he hardly ate anything that was put on his plate. Roy was one of the honorary pallbearers at Hawk's funeral, along with Eddie Locke, Zutty Singleton, George "Big Nick" Nicholas, Zoot Sims, and Major Holley. On June 13, 1969, Roy returned briefly to Chicago, where, along with Barry Harris (piano), Truck Parham (bass), Bob Cousins (drums), and saxophonist Franz Jackson, he took part in filming material for a televised tribute to Hawk, which consisted of the April and June footage combined.

During the summer of 1969 Roy traveled to Louisiana to take part in the New Orleans Jazz Fest (organized by George Wein). Working with the festival's "house band" he played a magnificent *I Can't Get Started*, then won the crowd over with his singing of *Ain't That Just Like A Woman?* Roy was then joined on stage by Clark Terry and Bobby Hackett for a long, lively version of *Perdido*. Roy enjoyed the musical company, but had no desire to go sightseeing in what was his first-ever visit to New Orleans, and no entreaties could make him change his mind:

> My first and only time in New Orleans and you know when I left? Right after the gig. Benny Carter changed my ticket and we went right back home. And I never saw most of the city, which was a mistake. But how often do I see the Statue of Liberty? Only when I have a gig in that direction. Then, I've been coming to London for a long time and never seen Scotland Yard. I think there's always been a myth about New Orleans, and New York too. There were some great musicians in both towns but there were great musicians everywhere. I'll set the record straight, you didn't have to come from New Orleans to play jazz. I know Louis Armstrong and Sidney Bechet would have jumped on me for saying that, but it's true.[21]

The Half Note proved to be Roy's most regular place of work in 1969 and 1970. Ray Bolden, back in New York, caught the last night of an Eldridge–Kamuca booking there (with Ross Tompkins on piano,

Jimmy Garrison on bass, and Harold White on drums). Ray arrived early at the club and was surprised to find Roy warming up on an "electric" trumpet (using an amplifying device on his own horn). Roy chose not to use the attachment on the gig, but played some little tunes with it to amuse Richie Kamuca's 6-year-old daughter. As the evening wore on, a very tough-looking customer asked Roy if his Japanese girlfriend could sing with the band; Ray Bolden was on hand to observe that "nobody argued." During that summer of 1969 Roy organized a line-up of Budd Johnson, Nat Pierce, Bill Pemberton, and Oliver Jackson to play a memorial gig at the Half Note for the recently deceased Baron Timme Rosenkrantz, the well-known Danish jazz follower, who had lived on-and-off in New York for many years. That same weekend Roy and his quintet played for a gathering of the Duke Ellington Society, where Roy was amused to note that the audience clapped only numbers that had been written by the Duke. The money earned on these gigs was relatively little, but Roy was still able to top up his annual salary by playing in Europe; during his early 1970 overseas trip he took part in a "tribute to Louis Armstrong" held in Antibes. Another out-of-the-ordinary booking occurred when Roy and trombonist Kai Winding co-led an all-star band briefly at New York's Roosevelt Grill where they took over from the World's Greatest Jazz Band, who had gone to play dates in Las Vegas, a place where Roy never got the chance to lead his own group.

In 1970 Roy's working life changed dramatically when he joined the house band at Jimmy Ryan's Club at 154 West 54th Street (between Sixth and Seventh). Ryan's musical fare was billed as "Dixieland," the venue claimed to be the "Oldest Jazz Club in New York," and, though there was no cover charge, no minimum, and no music charge, the drinks were certainly expensive. Ryan's was to be the site of the longest residency that Roy ever played. He knew all about the club and its origins on West 52nd Street and had played for the club's 25th Anniversary "bash" held in November 1967. Jimmy Ryan, who started the club in 1942, was a former lifeguard and Broadway "hoofer" who died of a heart attack in July 1963, not long

after the West 52nd Street premises were demolished in a redevelop-
ment scheme. Ryan's reopened at the new site on West 54th Street (in
a building owned by John Kaveanos) where it was capably managed
by Matt Walsh, who shared the partnership with Kaveanos; some of
the waiters and bartenders had been part of the 52nd Street set-up.
Roy occasionally sat in there during the 1960s. The music played there
in that decade was mainly Dixieland, and in 1970 the usual line-up
was Max Kaminsky on trumpet, Bobby Pratt on trombone, Joe
Muranyi on clarinet, soprano-sax, and vocals, Oliver Jackson on
drums, and Claude Hopkins on piano.

There were no hard-and-fast contracts for the job at Ryan's, which
usually entailed a five-or-six nights-a-week schedule, and the resident
musicians were allowed to put in substitutes if an important job
cropped up or if they were offered a lucrative tour. Pianist Claude
Hopkins took time off from Ryan's to play a gig with Roy Eldridge at
the Glen Island Casino. When he and Roy returned to Manhattan,
Hopkins suggested they call into Ryan's for a nightcap (the club being
open until beyond 3 a.m.). Roy had a drink or two, then sat in with the
band to play and sing a few numbers. Usually at this late hour many of
the audience were drifting towards slumber or the exit, but when Roy
began to blow they perked up and ordered another round of drinks.
Matt Walsh was not slow to observe this enthusiastic response. There
and then he let Roy know that Max Kaminsky wasn't happy about
doing a full week at the club, so if Roy was interested he could split
the work-load with Max. The idea appealed to Roy, who wasn't
bothered by the club's long hours, usually from 9.30 p.m. to 3 a.m. (six
sets of thirty minutes on and thirty minutes off) He knew from fifty
years of blowing that his "chops" would hold out. Roy accepted the
deal, making sure that he too was allowed "leave" to fulfill tours and
concert dates. So in September 1970 Roy began working at Ryan's,
and (according to a *Down Beat* report), "turned the former Dixieland
outpost into a swing oasis reminiscent of 52nd Street in days of
yore."[22]

Ray Bolden was at Ryan's for Roy's opening night:

Only Ruby Braff of all the New York musicians was there to witness this epic beginning, which took place on a Tuesday night. The backbiting jazz establishment were shocked and horrified that the great Roy Eldridge could stoop so low as to play at a Dixieland club. On the first few nights Roy's lip wasn't at its strongest, he hadn't been working too regularly before the opening. Questions were immediately asked: "Had Roy lost it? Was he too old? By Friday night these questions were truly answered and on the Saturday evening I was standing with Dan Morgenstern and agent Jack Whittemore and we were terrifically impressed. Roy had settled in and even played a request for *Sugar Blues*, which he performed a la Clyde McCoy, with a wah-wah mute.[23]

The main stumbling-block for Roy and for the rest of his colleagues at Ryan's was that the budget there didn't allow for the hiring of a bass-player, even though, for a brief while, banjoist (and painter) Davis Quinn was employed there as a speciality soloist. A bonus for Roy was that his residency at Ryan's brought him into contact with numerous people who wanted to book him (and the band) for private engagements. Some of these gigs were daytime press launches held in Manhattan offices which meant that Roy took along the electric piano (that usually rested in his basement at home) so that a keyboard player could be part of the line-up. For Roy the residency also meant a reunion with Gilbert Pinkus, the doorman-cum-barker, formerly known as the "Mayor of 52nd Street." Pinkus stood outside Ryan's, shouting out exactly the same come-on patter that he had used twenty years earlier. Through Bill Weilbacher of Master Jazz Recordings, Roy was invited for the first time in ten years to record with his own line-up—all the sides he'd cut in that period were as a freelance soloist. Weilbacher gave Roy the chance to select his own sidemen and to choose the material, but the preliminary negotiations didn't go smoothly because Roy was at his most cagey. When Weilbacher approached Roy at Ryan's with the "you call the shots" proposition, he was struck by Roy's suspicious response, noting also a "certain world-weariness."[24] "It took five meetings and heaven knows how many phone calls before he decided he could believe us." However, the end results made it all worthwhile, and Weilbacher was relieved to report, "And what a time Roy had in the studio! It was his time, his date. He was exultant, and beamed from start to finish."[25]

Even on quiet nights at Ryan's, Roy was always full of enthusiasm. Drummer Eddie Locke said, "I never worked with anyone who so loved to play."[26] Coupled with this love of performing was a deep sense of professionalism, as pianist Dick Katz observed:

> He believed in being on time and taking care of business, it was a tradition he'd grown up in: the musician had an obligation to the audience. He was there to entertain them; he was totally mystified by Miles Davis' attitude to an audience.[27]

Roy found certain numbers to be audience-pleasers, and it meant a lot to him to see and hear the crowd respond, but, when he first played at Ryan's, pianist Claude Hopkins didn't go for these flamboyant presentations, as Dan Morgenstern recalls:

> Roy was always disappointed that Claude didn't or wouldn't get involved in various of the routines. Roy managed to get him to join in a stanza of something that everyone in the band took it in turns to sing, but he wouldn't do more than that.[28]

Others in the band accepted the new regime, as Joe Muranyi confirmed: "When Roy came in he brought all his big numbers, and also the novelty things like *Saturday Night Fish Fry*, which, to be honest, I didn't really have eyes for, but they were part of Roy's show."[29]

Roy's work at Ryan's was interrupted early in 1971 when he slipped over in an icy parking lot and broke his ankle. Wild Bill Davison was on hand to deputize for most of the nights that Roy missed, but Eldridge, complete with a walking stick, was soon back at work. Shortly after this hiatus there was a change of personnel at the club when Eddie Locke (who became a long-term fixture) replaced Oliver Jackson, after Freddie Moore had some trial dates that didn't quite work out. Soon afterwards, Roy, by now completely mended, took a leave of absence in March to play for a couple of weeks at Chicago's London House, using New York-based pianist Chuck Folds, and two Chicago musicians, Truck Parham on bass and Paul Gusman on drums. This was Roy's first club date in Chicago for several years; his deputy at Ryan's was Jimmy McPartland. When Eldridge and Folds returned to New York in April 1971, the pianist joined the band at Ryan's, replacing Claude Hopkins. Folds, who worked at Ryan's for over two years, gave Alyn Shipton a graphic account of the routine there.

> Roy liked to do the novelty tunes, Louis Jordan's number *Saturday Night Fish Fry*, and *Kidney Stew* we played an awful lot. We played a basic repertoire of six or eight such tunes, and six or eight Dixieland tunes. Half an hour on and half an hour off, from 9.30 p.m. until 3 a.m. The third set we played a "show set." On "show set" Roy would feature each one of us. He always wanted me to do James P. Johnson's *Carolina Shout* or *Mule Walk*. He insisted I do that and I got peeved with him, because I wanted to do other things, but he said, "Nobody else does that. There's a thousand, million guys got the right hand but they don't have that left hand." I'm glad he kept on my case; it made me a better stride piano player. Sometimes when he felt just right, towards the latter part of the night, if he got back on the bandstand first, he'd sit right down at the piano and play. He had a wonderful time. When he played the drums he kept perfect time, he was such an innately musical guy.[30]

Roy never lost his love of stride piano-playing—his all-time favorite in the style was Donald Lambert—and his enthusiasm for playing the drums never waned. He occasionally played them at Ryan's, leading

Joe Muranyi to say, "He was one of the best drummers I ever played with, he was tremendous."[31]

In April 1971, a midnight concert was held in memory of Coleman Hawkins (at New York's Manhattanville Community Center); Dizzy Gillespie was there, Duke Ellington was there, so too was Roberta Flack; but amazingly Roy was not invited to attend, something he found lastingly hurtful. Roy's main health problem at this time was caused by cataracts which were affecting his eyesight, and it was necessary for him to wear very thick lenses in his spectacle frames. In May, he underwent surgery for the condition, and consequently had to take a month off from blowing the trumpet. Jimmy McPartland again "subbed" for Roy at Ryan's. Charles Graham called Roy on the hospital's bedside telephone:

> I spoke to Roy briefly and he said he'd just had both eyes done and was feeling OK. I then told him I had a friend of his with me, and put Dizzy Gillespie on the telephone. Dizzy said to Roy, "Be sure you come back very soon, and don't die on us, because if you do, then *I'll* have to be the Senior Statesman."[32]

Roy always hated "resting" but some of his frustration was dispelled when he learned that he had been awarded a place in *Down Beat*'s Hall of Fame, sharing the honor with the late Django Reinhardt. Although Roy made a point of saying he attached no importance to winning a poll, he nevertheless displayed his various awards at home. In the run-up to Roy's cataract operations Joe Muranyi resumed working with Louis Armstrong in the All Stars; thus Joe was in the unique position of working with both Roy and Louis within a matter of days. He later gave his candid assessments:

> Louis was a much better adjusted person; sure, Louis could get mad, and he had a temper too, but with Louis it was related to a specific event, whereas Roy was so mercurial, his moods were so inconsistent. Roy and I got along, but at first

he was hostile, and on one occasion at Ryan's he said, "Come outside and we'll settle this"—he and Bobby Pratt actually had a fight on the sidewalk outside Ryan's, and Bobby loved him and he loved Bobby, but Roy just got that mad. Later Roy and I buried the hatchet, and one night when I played something pretty good he whispered to me, "You've learned a lot from me."[33]

When Louis Armstrong died in July 1971 Roy reflected on the musical debt he owed to Louis' genius, commenting that they had never played together on any after-hours sessions, sadly realizing that now they never would. A few days later Roy's sorrow was compounded by the passing of trumpeter Charlie Shavers, with whom he had enjoyed a long-standing, easygoing friendship. Charlie died of cancer of the throat, diagnosed much too late. One of the last jazz venues he visited was Ryan's, and only later did Roy realize that the visit was Charlie's way of saying goodbye. Roy, Dizzy Gillespie, Art Farmer, Jimmy Maxwell, Jimmy McPartland, and Joe Wilder were among the many ace trumpeters who attended Charlie's funeral service.

In September 1971, Roy flew out to California to take part again in the Monterey Jazz Festival. For that year's event Jimmy Lyons organized a special feature in the shape of a Sunday night salute to Norman Granz's J.A.T.P. concerts. The nostalgic recreation was split into two groups: one featured Roy with Bill Harris, Eddie "Lockjaw" Davis, and Zoot Sims, with a rhythm section consisting of Oscar Peterson, Louis Hayes (drums), and Niels-Henning Ørsted Pedersen (bass); the other consisted of Clark Terry, Benny Carter, Ray Brown, Louie Bellson, Mundell Lowe on guitar, and John Lewis on piano. Roy played an effective feature on *The Man I Love*, and was in his element during the jammed finale, but jamming was becoming a lost art, a fact mournfully confirmed by Norman Granz when he said, "Musicians like John Coltrane or Archie Shepp don't care to jam, they prefer playing with their own groups. Even Stan Getz doesn't want to jam with others."[34] But jamming remained Eldridge's favorite occupation, and in September 1971 he flew up to Toronto, Canada, to team up with another avowed "jam" master, Lionel Hampton, for a television special. After this extensive bout of traveling Roy resumed at Ryan's. He seemed to thrive on the long hours there, so much so that he often took gigs on his nights off from the club, and one of these involved playing with Balaban and Cats at New York's Your Father's Mustache club. Though he was now over 60, Roy still had energy in store after he'd finished a long stint at Ryan's. When he arrived home he'd often sit down (sometimes for hours) listening to shortwave radio programs (including the B.B.C. World Service) or tuning in to pick up neighborhood police calls.

Chuck Folds established himself as the regular pianist at Ryan's, but during his leaves of absence the group's trombonist, Bobby Pratt, often took over at the keyboard (his place on trombone was usually filled by the ex-Benny Goodman star Vernon Brown). When reed-player Joe Muranyi was absent he booked as his "subs" various players. The ex-Casa Loma clarinettist Clarence Hutchenrider often filled the vacancy, but other players who temporarily took his place were Pete Clark, Sammy Margolis, and Herbie Hall. Over the years a steady stream of jazz luminaries called into Ryan's to hear a set or two from Roy. One distinguished visitor was pianist Erroll Garner, who kidded Eldridge about early days in their home city of Pittsburgh. Another Pittsburgh personality, singer Maxine Sullivan, also visited Ryan's, leading me to remark to Roy that I thought Maxine was singing better than ever. He pondered for a while, then said, "I think she's singing *as well* as ever; the difference is she can choose what she sings, instead of being told what to do."[35] Roy liked to play for such visitors, and continued to broaden the band's repertoire at Ryan's: "We played Duke's tunes, be-bop tunes, all kind of tunes."[36] Lovers of traditional jazz were offered a New Orleans medley consisting of *South Rampart Street Parade, Just A Closer Walk With Thee, New Orleans*, and *Bourbon Street Parade*.

After Joe Glaser's death, Roy continued to retain ties with the Associated Booking Corporation, and in December 1971 accepted a trip (instigated by that agency) which took him to San Remo, Italy, where, in company with Bobby Hackett, Earl Hines, and Louis Armstrong's widow Lucille, he was a guest of honor at the unveiling of a Louis Armstrong bust. These visiting musicians, plus pianist Alton Purnell and expatriate clarinettist Albert Nicholas, took part in a recorded concert that was part of the San Remo Festival. Back in New York, Roy was honored on his sixty-first birthday at a surprise party, complete with cakes and candles, organized by Charles Graham at Ryan's. Many visitors dropped in, including his old friend and ex-colleague Jonah Jones. Each year thereafter, special celebrations (not always at Ryan's) marked Roy's birthdays. Roy was briefly out of action in February 1972 through laryngitis and was unable to participate in a concert recording organized by Charles Mingus, at which he was due to play Mingus' specially written tribute *Little Royal Suite*; Jon Faddis (then aged 18) took the principal role instead. Roy soon recovered and again journeyed West, this time to Denver, Colorado, where he was interviewed in depth by Jack Winter, revealing some candid comments about life at Ryan's:

> Where I'm working now is a Dixieland joint in New York, Jimmy Ryan's, and when I first started working there you got the older crowd, some were the people that remember, and some were people that really dig the Dixieland thing, which is not my schtick, but I just play whatever my job calls for. Well, I've been there almost two years and since I've been there more young people have been coming in, and they've been coming back. So I think if you get a chance to play before them they will dig what is happening. Recently I played a college gig with Slam Stewart in Binghampton. And I did some of those concerts with the Jazzmobile. Those are good, in fact the last one I did was a sensation.[37]

Despite having said that he would never again work with Count Basie after the 1966 fiasco, at Norman Granz's behest Roy decided to join up with a unit billed as The Kansas City Seven, which was to be part of a Count Basie tour of Europe. Basie himself, in a mood of reconciliation, called into Ryan's to reassure Roy that there was no ill feeling on his part. The tour package consisted of Basie's Orchestra plus guest stars Roy, altoist-singer Eddie "Cleanhead" Vinson, and vocalist Joe Williams. Singer Joe Turner was originally slated to be part of the tour, but he was ill with diabetes and unable to travel. On the tour (which took place in March and April 1972) Roy was usually featured in only the second half of the show as part of the septet. His speciality number was *I Surrender Dear*, but he also soloed on the four standard tunes that made up the Seven's set. The group consisted of Roy, Al Grey on trombone, Eddie "Lockjaw" Davis on tenor-sax, Count Basie on piano, Freddie Greene on guitar, Norman Keenan on bass, and Harold Jones on drums. The tour passed smoothly without any major incidents between the various performers, but the concert at London's Hammersmith Odeon was blemished by backstage officiousness which prevented invited visitors from reaching the dressing-rooms. As a result, several of Roy's fans were unable to welcome him back to London after a five-year absence. Roy was bitter about this and said, "Those prejudiced mother-fuckers spoiled my glow."[38] Writer Max Jones tried to console the trumpeter by telling him how well he had played on the concert, but Roy barked back, "Don't tell me that. I know if I've played well or not."[39] Roy was used to receiving compliments, but they never affected his own assessment of his performances. Over and over again throughout his career he stressed that there were only four or five occasions each year when he was truly satisfied with what he had played: "When it's there, nothing matters. Range, speed, sound—they just come. It's nothing I use. I can be cold sober, but from somewhere it comes. Afterwards I sit in my room trying to figure it out."[40] During this period Roy's inconsistency worried some listeners, but Louie Bellson, who was again taking part in tours organized by Norman Granz, said:

> In 1972 Roy proved to me that he hadn't lost anything. There's
> a video made in Montreux, Switzerland of a jam session with

me, Count Basie, Niels-Henning on bass, Johnny Griffin on tenor-sax, and Milt Jackson on vibes, plus Roy on trumpet, and although Johnny Griffin played on and on, showing amazing stamina in his solo, Roy just took off in a way that brought everything to a climax.[41]

When Roy visited Switzerland, he usually linked up with his old friend Johnny Simmen (whose admiration for Roy's playing went back a long way—he'd received a signed photograph from him in the mid-1930s). But over the years Johnny and his wife Liza came to realize that sitting listening to great jazz records and dining well were not Roy's favorite way of unwinding after a concert: the fact was that Roy didn't want to unwind. Johnny was made aware of this in the 1950s when Roy had promised to visit the Simmens' apartment; he then changed his mind, but was candid enough to give his reasons:

I sure appreciate your kindness, but something more exciting might happen in town tonight and, if I'm sitting with you, I wouldn't know about it and wouldn't be part of it. That's why I prefer to ball, going from place to place. Music, chicks, booze will all be handy and I won't miss anything this way.[42]

Happily Roy and Johnny's friendship stayed intact. There is no doubt that Roy found female company eased the woes of international touring. One such friend, Kitty Grime (dubbed by Roy as his "London pound cake"), spoke of Roy with affection years after their first meeting:

I first met Roy at the time the Modern Jazz Quartet were playing at Ronnie Scott's Club. Roy was talking with the M.J.Q.'s drummer, Connie Kay, in the downstairs bar. I said, "I see the wicked faces are here." Connie Kay was not amused, but Roy smiled and said, "If you weren't with someone and I wasn't with someone, we could get together." Next time we met, again at Ronnie Scott's, we hit it off immediately. Later he came to my place and cooked a really first-rate chilli con carne. He sat down and listened intently to the recordings I played, sitting in a very prim and proper way. He was the least doomy of any American jazz musician that I met; he had a complete lack of a death wish. What you saw is what you got. If he was in a bad mood then he usually stayed in a bad mood, but if he was in a good mood, nothing mattered. He was up front and didn't have an agenda. Maybe he was a bit rough tongued, and some musicians didn't like him because he spoke out if he didn't like a situation. Whatever his mood he was a jumpy person, very restless.[43]

Roy returned from his spring 1972 tour with Basie in good time to be honored by receiving the first Pittsburgh Jazz Award (and a cheque for $1000). In his home city, local musicians were eager to blow alongside Little Jazz and there was literally a queue of willing accompanists (including the ex-J.A.T.P. trombonist, Tommy Turk), all keen to back Roy for his June 17 and 18 dates at the Pittsburgh Civic Arena. June 16 was designated Roy Eldridge Day by the city. Also in June, Norman Granz decided to stage a J.A.T.P.-type presentation at the Santa Monica Civic Auditorium. For this, Roy, Harry Edison, Stan Getz, Oscar Peterson, Ray Brown, Ed Thigpen, Eddie "Lockjaw" Davis, Al Grey, Count Basie, and Ella Fitzgerald were featured. The concert brought back memories of the "old days" for the performers, so much so that when it was over, Roy rounded up Nat Pierce, Kai Winding, and others and made for the Woodland Hills district where they jammed with trumpeter Bill Berry's Band at a club run by disk jockey Scott Ellsworth. On this trip Roy met up with his former colleague Richie Kamuca, who had moved back to Los Angeles in 1971, when the Merv Griffin television show ended its New York tenure.

Roy's next gig away from Jimmy Ryan's was much closer to home, at the first "Newport in New York" Festival. Promoter George Wein programed many of the events to take place in Manhattan, where Roy took part in a Schlitz-sponsored Midnight Jam Session at Radio City Music Hall, blowing alongside Bobby Hackett, Bud Freeman, Gene Krupa, Red Norvo, Vic Dickenson, Benny Carter, and others. Two days later he guested with Lionel Hampton's Orchestra at Philharmonic Hall. Within weeks Roy was in entirely different surroundings, thousands of miles away in Lebanon, where he was part of a star-studded Norman Granz unit which presented the biggest jazz event ever held in that region. The Lebanese audience heard a galaxy of jazz stars, including Ella Fitzgerald, Dizzy Gillespie, Oscar Peterson, and the Modern Jazz Quartet. The trip was part of an itinerary that also took the Granz package into Europe for a series of dates including the Nice Jazz Festival. Some people who first met Roy during his latter-day international tours found that he could be touchy, and disinclined to take part in long conversations about jazz, whereas everyone who first met him at Jimmy Ryan's found him to be generally affable and welcoming. Ray Bolden, who saw a lot of Roy, both at home and away, had this to say: "Roy on tour was a different man, he was wary, often ill at ease and generally not at his happiest. I believe these reactions stemmed back to the Gene Krupa days when touring was a nightmare for him."[44] Pianist Dick Katz offered another reason: "I always felt Roy was pleased to get back from a J.A.T.P. tour. On them I think he felt he was one of many; people like Oscar were the big chiefs, but back in New York, Roy was himself again."[45] Dan Morgenstern frequently visited Ryan's when Roy was playing there:

> The music could be mesmerizing there, be it an inspired ballad, a fabulous *Chinatown* or, on a quite regular basis, the fantastic bridges he'd fashion on Eddie Locke's feature *Caravan*. And then there would be the extended, fanciful and humorous free-form excursions on the closing theme, *Yard Dog* (the blues, of course) in which Roy would give his impression of avant garde jazz.[46]

Even after a long tour Roy took the briefest of rests before returning to give his all at Ryan's. Eddie Locke never lost his admiration for Roy's stamina and professionalism. One night, when the club was virtually empty, Locke's mind wandered as he was accompanying an Eldridge solo: "He turned around and looked at me and said, 'What are you doing?' I said, 'Well, Roy there's nobody in here man.' And he leaned over the drums and right in my face said, 'I'm here!' That was a great lesson."[47]

13

RADIANCE
AT RYAN'S

Roy returned to Ryan's in time for Labor Day, 1972, but he was soon on the move again, playing return dates at Chicago's London House, followed by another appearance at the Monterey Jazz Festival. Despite being so busy, Roy still managed to find time to play at benefits and charity concerts, often donating his services for events organized by The Sickle Cell Disease Fund. In October 1972 Roy again toured Europe for Norman Granz, who, by this time, had ceased billing his shows as Jazz at the Philharmonic promotions. Roy, like others who toured for Norman Granz, recorded regularly for Granz's new label, Pablo (named after the impresario's favorite painter, Pablo Picasso). When Roy returned to Ryan's in late November he was delighted to learn that the management there had agreed to pay for the services of a bass-player, so Major Holley joined the other regulars: Chuck Folds, Bobby Pratt, Joe Muranyi, and Eddie Locke. During Roy's various absences his main deputy was Jimmy McPartland. Max Kaminsky continued to play at the club twice a week usually on Sundays and Mondays. Chuck Folds' place at the piano was shortly to be taken by Dick Katz; during Roy's long tenure at Ryan's, various keyboard players were featured including Claude Hopkins, Johnny Morris, Jim Andrews, Don Coates, and Benny Aronov, as well as the pianists who played during the band's intermissions, including Red Richards, Peppy Morreale, Charlie Lotsarella, and the long-serving Cyril Haynes.

On January 30, 1973, Roy celebrated his sixty-second birthday in great style at Ryan's. He was in such a good mood that he didn't even bristle when a posse of trumpeters arrived to blow tributes to him (including Joe Newman, Donald Byrd, Jimmy Owens, and John Carisi). Dizzy Gillespie dropped in, as did Howard McGhee, Milt Jackson, Percy Heath, and Budd Johnson, several of them bearing gifts. As Roy announced the last set he said, with a twinkle in his eye, that it was time for "Wyatt Earp's last battle of the night."[1] One of Roy's more unusual trips that year was a flight to Europe to record an album with the Swiss singer, Miriam Klein. Miriam gave the background to this unusual date:

> My producer and I thought it would be a great idea to have Roy Eldridge on an album I was recording as a tribute to Billie Holiday. So I found out his telephone number in New York and called him—the trouble was I hadn't allowed for the time difference and I reached him at around four in the morning. He said, "Call me back later when I've had time to think it over." Two days later I phoned him at a better time and by then I think he'd checked me out with various musicians, so he said, "Everything's fine." And it was. Roy flew over and we spent three days making the album, which also featured Dexter Gordon. Roy then invited me to sit in at Ryan's whenever I was in New York. I took him up on that offer and this led to Roy saying, jokingly, "Hey, are you trying to put me out of a job?"[2]

During that summer of 1973 Roy continued to mix club dates at Ryan's with appearances on much larger stages. For one of these bookings (on July 4) Roy and his colleagues from Ryan's played at Flushing Meadows as part of the ceremony that renamed the venue as the Louis Armstrong Stadium; the event was part of the Newport in

New York Festival and was later shown on P.B.S. Television. Roy also joined in a "Salute to Ella," which was part of that year's festival; it seemed as though both the singer and the trumpeter enjoyed the reunion. Another happy occasion for Roy was when he played an informal session at the New York Jazz Museum, where the majority of the listeners were dedicated jazz fans. At Ryan's, part of the clientele was made up of businessmen who came in for a drink or two before wending their way home. As these customers became relaxed they often asked for unlikely requests, but whether the song they wanted was familiar or testing, Roy managed to get over to them that a few dollars would lubricate the creative process involved—Roy referred to any such "tips" as "lamb's tongues." Dick Katz recalled:

> I started playing regularly at Ryan's in 1973 and at first I was amazed that they had a cup on the piano for people to put tips in, and I thought, "Surely Roy doesn't need that." But it was part of the show and Roy would make a joke of it, saying, "We don't mind playing requests, but it would be nice to see some dead Presidents in that glass."[3]

Roy called the businessmen visitors "the raincoat and briefcase guys." There was also a steady stream of out-of-town tourists who had once been "swing fans." They made a bee-line for Roy and asked if he remembered playing this or that town during his days with Gene Krupa. Roy usually managed to share a chuckle with these visitors, even if he had nothing but bad memories of the places they mentioned, but increasingly he began his reminiscences about Krupa by saying, "You know that poor Gene is pretty sick." Much of Gene Krupa's later life was filled with distress, including the death of his wife Ethel, losing all his possessions and memorabilia in a fire, and suffering a heart attack, but in the early 1970s he became grievously ill with leukemia—finally succumbing in October 1973. Some weeks later a big tribute concert in Krupa's memory was held in New York, featuring Roy and Anita O'Day plus an all-star cast that included six drummers: Louie Bellson, Roy Haynes, Mickey Sheen, Roy Burns, Lionel Hampton, and Buddy Rich. Anita and Roy had prepared only one duet, *Let Me Off Uptown*, so when the audience begged for an encore they repeated the same number, again to tumultuous applause. For some while after Gene's death there were rumors that a "ghost band" was to be formed, featuring Roy, Anita, and Charlie Ventura, but no serious backers could be found for the enterprise.

Roy's October 1973 trip to Europe included a concert at London's Hammersmith Odeon, which was marred by the fact that Oscar Peterson's stage clothes had been stolen, forcing him to appear in denim casual wear. This naturally upset the pianist and he was still agitated the next morning. Roy, ultra-sensitive to any sort of turbulence, was keen to get away from the band hotel for a while and took up Ray Bolden's suggestion that they visit a North London jazz pub The New Merlin's Cave for a change of atmosphere. I had been leading The Feetwarmers there for some while, playing Sunday lunch-time sessions (principally with Wally Fawkes and Bruce Turner). Merlin's, as it was always referred to, was very unusual in that by some ancient by-law parents were allowed to bring their children to the pub's hall even though alcoholic beverages were being consumed. Ray and Roy arrived just before the session began, and it was plain that Roy was still agitated. He walked straight up to me and said, "Don't think I've come here to play trumpet; if I do sit in I'll play drums." I said that we would be pleased whatever he played, and got onto the bandstand to start the session. Roy came and stood close by; he obviously liked the ambiance and was happy to see dozens of youngsters sitting down listening to the music. The tension which had shown on his face seemed to melt away. He unzipped his trumpet case and without more ado joined the band; he played and sang wonderfully and remained on stage throughout the entire session. Not long before that session I had written, "I've lost count of the times that I've had conversations with Roy Eldridge, but I hardly know him any better than when I first met him, fifteen years ago." Those words were washed away by the friendly spirit and ebullience which Roy showed towards me that day. Something had put our association on a totally different plane, and ever afterward we shared a happy friendship. There were, of course, times when he was moody and touchy, but these moments were outnumbered by the occasions when he was kind, considerate, and humorous. In my cups I was inclined to give uncalled-for assessments of various players of yesteryear, and actually had the temerity to say to Roy that I felt that Chu Berry was overrated. As Chu was one of Roy's all-time favorite musicians, my words were an invitation for him to jump down my throat. Instead he patiently explained a dozen of Chu's musical virtues, and summed up his assessment by saying, "What you must also realize, John, is that he was so young when he died, we'll never know just how great he might have become." I still blush when I think of my crassness, but am ever grateful for Roy's reaction.

At Ryan's, Roy went only part of the way toward observing the dictum that the customer is always right. He was affable with most of the male customers but didn't hesitate to correct anyone giving a false outline of jazz history, and he was ever watchful for any signs of condescension. He was, however, charming and friendly to almost all the females who visited the club. There were exceptions: an English visitor, John Bray, saw Roy turn salty when a woman, who had come into Ryan's with a conventioner, asked in a slurred voice if Roy could play something "sexy or romantic" without adding please or even smiling. Roy looked over his spectacles at her and said, "You don't know anything about sex and romance. Let me tell you that sex without romance is like taking your car in for a service."[4] Discussing this subject with Graham Colombé, Roy said:

> Years ago I used to have a thing about jazz and women. If I got into a club with the right piano player and the right rhythm section, a chick would be sitting over there, talking, and I could play a ballad or maybe two or three and before the third one was over she'd be looking at me and next thing you know… .[5]

In May 1974 George Melly, myself, and the Feetwarmers were booked for a series of dates in the U.S.A. which included bookings at The Bottom Line Club in New York, giving us the perfect opportunity to call into Jimmy Ryan's to hear Roy and the band. Roy could not have been more welcoming. He made sure we all got our drinks at musicians' prices, bought a double round himself and, when the session ended at 3 a.m., took us off to Cecil's Bar on the corner of 54th and Seventh for a few nightcaps (during this part of his life Roy's usual tipple was vodka). The conversation there was stimulated by the sounds coming from a juke-box that featured several of Roy's best recordings. Roy worked hard to give the impression that listening to these masterpieces was a painful and unwelcome experience, but, as he called into this bar almost every night, hearing the disks could not have been that distressing. I'd never known him so relaxed, and it seemed as though he was thinking aloud when he said:

> Time to me is the most important thing in playing jazz. It isn't being fast or playing high; it is feeling the exact pulse of the rhythm. If you know exactly where the first beat in every bar falls then all your phrases will reflect and underline the exact tempo and you'll be on your way to swinging, whether you're playing fast or slow. I've played with many musicians who were good improvisers, they had all the ideas in the world, but they didn't have time. I'll hear of a new cat that everyone is talking about and I listen to him, and the first question I ask myself is, "Has he got time?" It's the vital part of playing jazz.[6]

In September 1974 another journey to the Monterey Jazz Festival temporarily took Roy away from Ryan's, and at the festival he guested with Dizzy Gillespie's Quartet (as did Clark Terry and Harry Edison). But Roy never tarried on the West Coast; old memories lingered, as he told writer Gary Giddins after that visit:

> I still don't like California, though they treat me beautifully now, because in the back of my mind I think of working the

Palladium and having to get in my car to find a sandwich because not even the Chinese restaurants would serve me.[7]

Another painful memory for Roy was connected to the fact that soon after Pearl Harbor (in December 1941) a Japanese friend was interned on the West Coast under wartime regulations and Roy never heard from her again.

Back at Ryan's, a newcomer, Ted "Mohawk" Sturgis, was on double-bass. Ted could also play piano and alto-sax but now specialized on bass—he had first worked with Roy forty years earlier. Ted had won a long battle with alcohol, and those who knew him during his wild, drinking days had difficulty in associating the tearaway of earlier years with this quiet, courteous man who had been persuaded by Roy to join the band at Ryan's. Roy and Ted shared a close friendship, so I thought it would be fruitful to ask Ted about working with Roy in the 1930s and 1940s. Sadly, Ted didn't have much to say about those days, though he remained completely friendly throughout the questioning. Roy observed what I was doing and later called me aside and said, in a regretful way:

John, it's no good trying to get Ted to talk about those days. The memories have been totally washed away by booze. Sometimes I've tried going over that same ground, but, as far as Ted is concerned, there is just a long, totally blank gap in his recollections.[8]

Roy had the highest regard for Ted's musicianship, so he was everlastingly tolerant toward him, even on the rare nights that Ted just didn't feel like playing, which resulted in the sound of his bass dissolving into near inaudibility. Roy, of course, was immediately aware of the drop in volume, but all he ever said (half to himself) was, "Ted's playing off his lapel again." By this time, Dick Katz was firmly established as the band's pianist, and he happily recalled those days:

Roy was a hero of mine since I was a teenager, and I guess I first played with him at jam sessions in the Sunnyside neighborhood of Queens during the 1950s. They were informal sessions with Roy, Oscar Pettiford, and sometimes Al Cohn. Roy and Oscar Pettiford were somewhat similar: two headstrong guys, both very proud, sentimental men. Sort of macho, but both had their soft sides. Roy had a temper but you never felt he was hostile, it was an immature rage. He got annoyed when people requested numbers he'd done in the 1930s, things like *After You've Gone*—it was like asking a 70-year-old Tiger Woods to play a round like he did forty-five years before. Roy wasn't a bandleader as such; he was a front man—the featured attraction. At Ryan's we never rehearsed and he never wrote out changes. He'd sit at the piano to show you the harmonies for something like *Ball Of Fire*, or he'd say, "Put a shuffle beat behind this one," or something like that, and if he liked something you played he'd tap you on the shoulder and say, "Keep it in," but there was no bandleading as such. I think he was one of the most genuine, sincere people I've ever met. A lot of his generation had some kind of façade, friendly, but you never knew what they were thinking, Roy was not like that; he was very contemporary. He didn't like people to bullshit; he would look you straight in the eye and that look meant, "I know who I am. Do you know who you are?" I loved the man for that. I don't think he had close buddies among the musicians. Ted Sturgis and Eddie Locke were his friends, certainly, but Roy's had all been in the past; they were all gone—he really wept when Ben Webster died. I was a good friend of Roy's but he had another life away from Ryan's.[9]

After a slow start, Roy and Jack Bradley also became good friends:

I first heard Roy in person at the Central Plaza. I used to go into New York for the weekend, and at the Plaza they had regular all-star sessions: two bands on Friday and two on Saturday. Naturally I knew Roy's playing on record, but to hear him live was a great experience. When I moved to New York in the fall of 1958 I saw and heard him often at the Metropole. He wasn't really friendly, in fact he was a little aloof, but slowly I got to know him. Roy was a very private person. When it was intermission time at the Metropole he didn't want to be smothered with questions about records he had made; he just wanted to take it easy in the Copper Rail bar. Of course, Louis was my man, but when Louis was alive Roy didn't want to hear anything about him. This changed after Louis died, and in the 1970s when I went to Ryan's with my wife Nancy, usually during the third set when Roy was warmed up and had drunk just the right amount, he'd see us and play *Chinatown* just like Louis.

One day Louis' widow Lucille visited the Jazz Museum just before closing time and I suggested we go to Ryan's (which was only a block away). She liked the idea and as soon as we entered made for a front table—now I never sat at a table because drinks were twice as expensive there as they were at the bar. Lucille ordered a bottle of the best champagne, Roy came and sat with us and he and Lucille talked about old times, then she ordered another bottle of champagne and I got worried. We agreed to split the cost, but I only had about ten dollars in my pocket. So I had to see Matty Walsh and he agreed that I could call in next day to pay my part of the bill, which was about a hundred dollars. From then on Roy and the band always hailed me as "The Big Time Spender"—it took some while to live down. Roy often spent his intermissions standing outside Ryan's and one night, in a somber mood, he said, to my surprise, "They say the history of jazz trumpet is Louis, Red Allen, me, and Dizzy, so how come I'm working here?"[10]

Roy was re-airing a sentiment he'd expressed some thirty years earlier, but I too heard him (in a downcast mood, outside Ryan's) say with a sigh, "This is like baseball: you sink down the leagues until you get to the bottom."[11]

Roy and the rest of the band at Ryan's enjoyed a respite from the club routine when they provided the music on a cruise ship that took them to Bermuda and back. But there were minor complications, as Eddie Locke explained:

> It was a good gig, two days down there, then three days off so the people on the cruise could do their sightseeing, then two days back. Roy had his wife Vi with him, but despite this he didn't want any days off; he wanted to blow.[12]

Joe Muranyi recalled the situation:

> Roy was furious that we weren't working more on the cruise, and even went to the captain and asked if we could play some more. I think that Roy didn't want to be thought of as a little man wandering around; he wanted to establish that he was the trumpeter. Johnny Desmond, who sang with Gene Krupa when Roy was in the band, was part of the cruise. He liked Roy and Roy liked him, and when we got to Bermuda, Jimmy and Marian McPartland were there—they were friends of Roy, and he was always pleased when they came into Ryan's, but no one could pacify Roy; he couldn't relax, he wanted to work.[13]

One visitor to Ryan's was a young tenor-saxist from New England who called into the club after midnight having just finished playing nearby at a private party organized by some people from his home town of Providence, Rhode Island. He was with a girlfriend, whose presence was immediately noticed by Roy, who soon approached the couple and struck up a conversation. When he learned that the male visitor was a tenor-saxist he invited him to sit in. Roy was instantly impressed by the young Scott Hamilton's playing, and invited him to sit in whenever he was in town. Thereafter Scott Hamilton needed no excuse to go to New York as often as possible, and, as a result of these get-togethers, Roy agreed to work for a week with Scott at Sandy

Berman's Jazz Revival club in Beverly, Massachusetts, where Scott was
co-leading (with guitarist Fred Bates) a group billed as Hamilton Bates
and the Blue Flames:

> We were very enthusiastic. We didn't read music at all, but
> worked out a lot of head arrangements, which Roy was happy
> to join in with. Roy stayed at my parents' house and he was
> absolutely charming with them, but now I've grown older I
> realize that, no matter how good the hospitality is, it's better
> for musicians to stay in a hotel, they can relax more.
> Nevertheless, Roy got on well with all of us, and some time
> later he dropped in to see my parents again when he was in
> the area. I guess it would take about four hours to drive to
> Providence from Manhattan, and for the gig at Sandy's Roy
> came up in his estate wagon, with pots and pans, cooking
> utensils, etc., what he called his "survival kit." We didn't use a
> piano, and had a Fender bass in the line-up but the gig
> worked out fine. Roy was very encouraging, but also
> extremely critical; he was trying to direct me, and I welcomed
> it. He thought I would do all right in New York but said he
> could make no promises to help personally. But when I
> decided to move to New York he was very helpful and talked
> me up to various people. He recommended me Max Cavalli
> who sometimes acted as an agent for Roy, and Max got me six
> weeks at Michael's Pub with Johnny Hartman, Billy Butter-
> field, Hank Jones, and Milt Hinton. Roy also took me into
> Eddie Condon's, which was close to Ryan's; he called it "the
> enemy camp" and said, "They say they play jazz over there
> and I guess that's what it is." He told them that I should be
> booked on their Tuesday night guest night, so they booked
> me. Roy didn't sponsor many people, but luckily for me he
> loved tenor-sax-players, Zoot Sims, Budd Johnson, Illinois
> Jacquet, etc. But he had a special feeling for Coleman
> Hawkins' playing and said to me, "He was the only one that
> I didn't know what he was going to play next in his solos."
> One night when I dropped into Ryan's, Charlie Ventura was

there in the audience, he was smashed, I think he'd been recording all day. Anyway, he was loaded and sat down in front of the band. He obviously loved Roy because he pointed at him and called out, "This man played a big part in my life. He talked Gene Krupa into giving me solos and that was the turning point for me. If it hadn't been for this guy, who knows what might have happened." Charlie was full of emotion, but the audience were with him, and I guessed Roy was pleased too.

So I got to know Roy and I was often in Ryan's. At this stage of his career Roy took forever to warm up. He'd start blowing at around 8.30 p.m., but it wasn't until midnight that his chops were in, and then the high notes flowed out of him. But when people went to hear Roy in concert during those later years they were often disappointed, and they came back saying Roy had played poorly, but the reason was he hadn't had time to warm up properly. He liked to feel Eddie Locke's powerful drumming behind him; one time a "sub" came in and Roy got frustrated and pointedly took his jacket off. Roy could get upset about the slightest thing; in fact, I never saw anyone so intense. With Roy it was drama all the time, and he'd get disturbed by silly little things, but he didn't let the audience know. He said to me once, "Always make it like a house party; make the audience feel that they are at a house party." As far as other trumpeters, Roy viewed them as though it was the "old West," six shooters and all. He said, "Every time I try to relax another of them comes through the door." But he didn't give an inch, though if someone like Johnny Carisi came in, Roy knew that he only wanted a gentle work-out to keep his chops in, so they blew together relaxedly, and Roy loved it when Thad Jones dropped into Ryan's. But his attitude to some of the younger men was different. One night he invited Warren Vaché up, saying, "I'm so tired I can't make this set." He sat listening for a while, then jumped up on the bandstand and started playing with one hand in his pocket, blowing high phrases as if it were a matter of life and death. I think he liked the routine at Ryan's. After a lifetime of touring he could at last drive home every night and relax there with Vi. He said to me, "My wife saved my life," but he still liked to carry on as though he was twenty years of age, dashing to the telephone that was near the exit at Ryan's and using up stacks of coins to call up one or another of the young girl students who came into the club.[14]

Despite Roy's comments about Eddie Condon's Club (also by this time on West 54th) he often called in to listen to the resident band for a few minutes. The line-up usually featured Vic Dickenson, Connie Kay, and others, the atmosphere made cheerful by the presence of bartender Ricky, whom Roy had known since the days of Jim and Andy's Bar. Ray Bolden summarized the merits of Condon's:

> It was definitely a more social place to hear music than Ryan's. At Condon's the drinks were much cheaper than at Ryan's and people felt happy to sit and booze in a convivial atmosphere. But Roy was like the Pied Piper, as soon as he left Condon's at the end of his intermission, the people left Condon's and followed him into Ryan's.[15]

Roy continued to balance his employment at Ryan's with trips to Europe, which, in July 1975, included a highly successful appearance at the Montreux Jazz Festival, where the splendor of his set with Dizzy Gillespie, Clark Terry, and Oscar Peterson was caught on record. Kitty Grime remembered how keen Roy was to prepare for this particular encounter: "Roy warmed up for a long time below the stage. He wasn't forced to dash on; he had a chance to blow softly, and this really paid off."[16] On the same tour Roy and Kitty entered a hotel in The Hague, Holland, to discover that a jam session was being held in the foyer, featuring cornettist Wild Bill Davison:

> The crowd virtually manhandled Roy to get him to join in alongside Wild Bill, and he rightly got very annoyed at being

pushed and pulled. Someone suggested that Roy was avoiding the chance to blow with Davison, and this led him to say very forcibly, "I wiped that mother-fucker's ass thirty years ago, and I don't intend to do it again now."[17]

Having made so many trips to Europe, Roy was always well aware that record-collectors could spring out of nowhere to ask a question about an obscure session from long ago. Surprisingly, he was unusually patient when faced with these inquiries, but he was less forthcoming when his friendship-seeking conversation with a young female follower was interrupted by someone quizzing him about recordings he had made before his erstwhile companion had been born. Back home in the States, Roy was often less than willing to go over old discographical mysteries, as his work colleague Joe Muranyi discovered:

> He wouldn't talk about certain things. He didn't want to discuss his first recordings. Tom Lord (who wrote the book on Clarence Williams) sent me a tape of the titles that Roy was said to be on. I gave it to Roy to listen to. Six months went by, he didn't mention it, so in the end I asked him and he said he wasn't on those sides, that was the end of it.[18]

Tenorist Loren Schoenberg was slightly luckier with his inquiry:

> I asked him one night about this 1938 Martin Block broadcast of *I Know That You Know* with Benny Goodman, Lester Young and Teddy Wilson. He told me it never happened, that he remembered everytime he played with Lester in the 1930s. Next time I saw him I gave him a cassette of it—he listened to it and agreed that it was him and Lester, but it still never happened—what a sense of humor![19]

By late 1975 Roy was back in Europe doing a series of concerts for Norman Granz, including a date at the London Palladium, a performance that prompted Steve Voce to write, "Roy played the best trumpet I've heard him play in concert. He was intense, disciplined and carefully measured."[20] After the concert ended, Granz took the entire troupe to an Armenian restaurant in West London. This trip to Europe allowed Roy to play a season at Ronnie Scott's Club in London, alongside Zoot Sims, where they were backed by a British trio consisting of Colin Purbrook on piano, Martin Drew on drums, and Ron Mathewson on bass. In her *Melody Maker* review Val Wilmer described Roy as "Someone who puts as much into the first tune as most people of his age save for the out chorus of the closer."[21] Roy liked the sentiments expressed but wasn't enamored by the reference to his age, particularly as infirmity had nearly laid him low with an attack of bursitis which meant he could hardly move from his hotel room, except to make the journey from Kensington into Soho to make the gig. Ronnie Scott and his partner Pete King were delighted with Roy's unflagging performances and booked him to return to the club.

Roy fulfilled a pleasurable task in 1975 by playing at one of Jack Kleinsinger's long-running Highlights in Jazz concerts. This one honored Zoot Sims, one of Roy's favorite people and favorite musicians. Roy always enjoyed blowing with Zoot, but despite many invitations, Zoot rarely visited Ryan's. However, many other jazz musicians continued to call into the West 54th Street club, knowing they might hear Roy recapturing the vibrancy of his early days. Roy was no longer an ace experimenter, but, when he was on form, fresh ideas cascaded out of his horn, and, even when he was struggling to blow, every phrase was full of feeling. Clark Terry recalled:

> Dizzy Gillespie and I used to check out Roy Eldridge on 54th Street. He was still a dynamo player. When Roy found out we were there he'd pour on the juice. Diz and I used to tell Roy we came by to get our batteries charged.[22]

But very few of the visiting musicians were Roy's close friends. Joe Muranyi spoke of this: "Roy knew everybody and a lot of people dropped in to Ryan's to see him, but as for close buddies, I can't name one, and we worked together for years."[23] Eddie Locke elaborated:

> Roy didn't have too many close friends that he hung out with. He was friendly with lots of people, but he wouldn't go and seek out their company. He and Vic Dickenson talked together, but you couldn't say they were close, and Roy's relationship with Jo Jones was complex, though in some strange way they were tight. I think one musician who was close to Roy was Buster Bailey; they always seemed to drop into easy conversation when we worked at the Metropole. I know Roy liked Oscar Peterson, and he definitely was friends with Charlie Shavers; they'd go off and drink together. Roy never minded Charlie dropping in to Ryan's yet he didn't like it when trumpeters appeared who were half as good as Charlie. They would worry him and he'd get nervous and agitated. It was the same when we worked with Coleman Hawkins, and Hawk would say, "Now, what are you worried about?", but Roy couldn't change, he was so sensitive.[24]

Actor Nicol Williamson often called into Ryan's to listen to Roy or to Max Kaminsky (the two trumpeters still shared the week). Nicol was easily persuaded to sing a number or two with the band: "I remember Roy saying to me after a session, 'Did you ever make a record? You should do, you sound just like Bing.'"[25] One of the most memorable nights at Ryan's as far as visitors were concerned occurred in November 1976, following a Pablo Jazz Festival concert that Norman Granz had presented at Carnegie Hall. When the concert was over, Granz visited Ryan's and brought various musicians who had taken part, including Oscar Peterson. Peterson was soon at the keyboard, inspiring Roy to play superbly—drummer Bobby Durham and Keter Betts on bass joined in, as did another illustrious visitor, Benny Carter. Roy was almost bursting with pleasure, but Dan Morgenstern later heard that Granz, Peterson, and Carter, though delighted to see Roy, felt that Ryan's was not the place for him to show-case his unique talent. Morgenstern succinctly put Roy's case:

> Granted that Ryan's may not be the ideal environment for this giant of music, but let's face it, there are very few steady gigs of any kind around, and this one keeps Roy in shape and at home with his family. He can and does go out on major Pablo tours and other engagements when he pleases, so why should he trade in Ryan's for trips to Cleveland and other dreary places to work with local rhythm sections of doubtful merit?[26]

Roy's long stay at Ryan's permitted his life to fall into a routine. He usually arrived home at around 4 a.m., and pottered about listening to various shortwave radio transmissions on his powerful Radio Shack D. 150 receiver, occasionally listening to tapes. He still harbored the idea that he could be a television and radio repair man, and continued to seek advice from his friend Charles Graham, who was an expert; but, as in the past, when Charles lent him manuals to learn from, they remained unopened. Vi Eldridge continued to be vexed when Roy picked up other people's discarded television sets and brought them home to repair without ever actually getting around to the task. But in general, Roy's wife was a patient woman, as Dan Morgenstern observed: "Vi was rather shy, a very sweet person; they were a devoted couple. Roy may have fooled around but he really loved Vi, and Vi was always supportive, always in Roy's corner."[27]

Roy was a keen and capable do-it-yourself man when it came to household repairs, but he liked to garden in fits and starts rather than regularly. One habit he never broke was to walk his dog every day; he and Vi had owned a succession of dogs since the early days of their marriage, beginning with Wiz, who was followed by Chico, then by various German Shepherd dogs, Fang I, II, III, and IV. Roy's daughter Carole had a good knowledge of the music business, having worked in various booking offices, including one run by Mrs. Billie Bowen, who managed various singers. During her teens Carole played trumpet for four years in her high school orchestra. At first, Vi was against the idea, and told Carole that blowing the trumpet would mark her lips permanently, but Roy interceded, saying, "The only reason my lips are scarred is because I wasn't taught properly." Roy was extremely proud of Carole's musical achievements, but after she left high school she gave up playing the trumpet. The only professional musician in the immediate family was Robert Eldridge III, a successful baritone-player, who was the son of Roy's first cousin.

Roy definitely liked betting on the horses; Eddie Locke spoke of this:

> Roy wasn't a heavy gambler but he liked to play the horses. Once when we were in Toronto we went to the track there. We only put a couple of dollars on a race, but Roy became so excited, people nearby must have thought he had $500 on the result. When he moved out to Long Island he was close to the race-track and he said that it was so easy to get to the track he had to quit betting.[28]

But Roy didn't lose interest in gambling, as Charles Graham discovered:

> I visited Roy in Hollis many times, it was near the end of a subway line which terminated one or two stops beyond where Roy would meet me. It was within a block of the Off-Track-Betting parlor. Roy would sometimes tell me to find him in the O.T.B. When I got there he'd be studying the daily "Green Sheet." I never saw him actually gamble, but he was very interested in reading about the horse races.[29]

Despite not being enamored by Roy's place of work, Norman Granz never failed to champion Eldridge's playing whenever he could. In a *New York Times* interview with Nat Hentoff he spoke about meeting up with a Russian journalist:

A man from *Izvestia* wanted to know what qualities I look for in a jazz musician and, in particular, which musician typifies jazz for me. Oscar Peterson kept whispering to me, "Tatum, Tatum, tell him it's Tatum." I said, "No, It's Roy Eldridge." Everytime he's on, he does the best he can, no matter what the conditions are. And Roy is so intense about everything, so it's far more important for him to dare, to try and achieve a particular peak, even if he falls on his ass in the attempt, than to play it safe. That's what jazz is all about. And that's why it's so important to have Roy on record.[30]

14

ENDING WITH
A SONG

The presence of one visitor to Ryan's spawned a good deal of publicity and caused Roy long-lasting irritation. The caller was Lester Bowie, a stranger when he dropped into Ryan's to hear a set. He was introduced and described as a fellow trumpeter. Roy eyed him up and down, then suggested that Lester should call again and bring his horn with him. Gary Giddins, a writer for the *Village Voice*, sensed that a lively occasion was in the offing; so too did Dan Morgenstern, and both resolved to be there when the return meeting took place. The night in question duly arrived, and Roy, seeing Giddins, Morgenstern, and a third writer, Stanley Crouch, in on the same occasion (as well as a photographer from the *Village Voice*), immediately deduced that they had come to observe a "battle." Dan Morgenstern described Roy's reaction:

> Roy's famous combative instincts told him that Lester's presence was a challenge. In fact, Lester was in awe of Roy and had no intentions of entering in a cutting contest. To Roy, bless him, any person entering the premises with a trumpet in hand is an antagonist, friendly perhaps, but nevertheless to be sized up and taught a lesson.[1]

Lester Bowie was invited up during the next set and played effectively alongside Roy on a number requested by a customer: *Bei Mir Bist Du Schoen*, a theme that Bowie later said he had never consciously heard before. Roy, on flugel horn, played *Black And Blue*, with Bowie finding a suitable harmony part on the final chorus. The leader then granted Bowie the spotlight, giving him a nice introduction. Lester responded with *Now's The Time*, and Roy yielded the stand to him. In the jam that followed, Roy showed his bristles for the first time with some high notes. The two trumpeters blew *Apple Honey* and a blues to end the set. Roy began the next set by calling *Little Jazz*, which Bowie had to learn there and then; this was followed by a ballad medley, in which Bowie chose to play *Misty*. The event concluded with *Chinatown*, which featured only two soloists: Roy on trumpet and Joe Muranyi. Roy triumphantly stayed above top "C" to shape an exciting climax to his solo. Morgenstern summarized the get-together:

> After a final exchange of pleasantries, Lester Bowie took his leave. Roy had given him the respect due to a fellow pro, but I can't help thinking that the encounter would have held greater warmth if the press hadn't been so obviously on hand. The piece that Gary Giddins wrote for the *Village Voice* the following week had a nice big photograph, but his thesis—that this had been an example of the supposedly lost art of the cutting contest—is one I find it hard to subscribe.[2]

Somewhere along the line Roy developed the notion that Lester Bowie had arrived at Ryan's intending to insult and usurp him, though, for years afterwards, when Bowie was asked about the incident, he said he was surprised that anyone could take this attitude, particularly as it was Roy himself who invited him to revisit the club. Years later, Dan Morgenstern remained certain that Bowie had no antagonistic feelings toward Roy, and indeed had shown deference to Roy throughout the encounter, borne out by Bowie's comment, "My father was very proud when they put our pictures together in the *New*

York Times."[3] The aftermath of the duel provided a classic example of Roy's inability to forget and forgive. It is not an exaggeration to say that he brooded over it intermittently for the rest of his life. When I next met Roy, some months after the event, it was the first topic he began to talk about, and he was still smarting over the "Bowie" encounter a decade later, as he proved by raising the subject in radio interviews he did with Phil Schaap in March 1987 and January 1988. Even Bowie's headgear annoyed Roy, as he told Schaap:

> This cat from Chicago had a big fur hat on. I come from that old school; you don't sit down like that for nobody, wearing a big fur hat. He had to get smothered with his attitude. He couldn't get to nothing and he never came back.[4]

When Roy returned to London's Ronnie Scott's Club in 1977 he was again accompanied by Colin Purbook on piano, but this time Lennie Bush was on bass and Bobby Orr on drums. Roy's performances were enthusiastically reviewed by Chris Welch in *Melody Maker*:

> Eldridge retains that youthful, bubbling humour that refuses to be cowed by the backlog of time. Even his greatest admirers tend to be a trifle nervous about hearing Eldridge live. When he is off form Roy can suffer the terror of all trumpet players, of hearing a distorted parody of his intentions, but tonight Eldridge was blowing with care, discipline and due regard for pacing his sets. Still the greatest distinguishing factor between British and American musicians is the latter's understanding of an audience.[5]

During this tour, Roy spoke about his method of getting the best out of his accompanists. In doing so he gave signs that he was mellowing:

Like if any cat makes a mistake. I don't even say anything to him when we come off stage, but two nights later I'll say, "You know that thing you were doing there? It's supposed to go the other way around." See, I often work as a single, been doing it for a long time and one of the most important things when you're a single is getting along with the guys. You get the best out of them. If you start fighting with them, it's all uphill.[6]

These views were expressed to *Melody Maker's* Max Jones. On one of Roy's gigs at Scott's during that trip I was present at the club with Max and his wife Betty. Betty was charming and intelligent with a wide knowledge of jazz, and she and Max always got on well with Roy. On this particular occasion Roy's chops were not in tiptop shape; nevertheless, he was playing some superbly constructed middle register solos. During intermission, Betty, in making conversation at the bar, said, by way of a semi-jocular comment, "Winging it tonight, Roy?" The effect of the remark was instantaneous. Roy's eyes filled with tears and in a voice choked with emotion he said, "I never wing it. If I was dying I'd try my best." To say that a cloud descended over the gathering would be putting it mildly, and nothing anyone could say, including a profuse apology from Betty, could salvage the evening for Roy. On that tour Roy made another well-received appearance at Montreux.

In July 1977 the New York Repertory Company concert tributes to the careers of Earl Hines and Roy Eldridge took place at Carnegie Hall as part of George Wein's "Newport Jazz Festival in New York." To everyone's surprise, Roy chose not to attend the event, and played at Ryan's instead. Years later, Dick Hyman, who was the musical director for the concert, said he felt it was a question of money, with Roy holding out for more than George Wein would pay. However, the show went ahead with Jon Faddis, Jimmy Maxwell, and Joe Newman playing solos recorded by Roy and transcribed by Hyman. Roy's famous 1941 *Rockin' Chair* solo was given a new twist, with Hyman scoring it for the saxophone section. Anita O'Day sang *Boogie Blues* and *Let Me Off Uptown*, and Roy's blues composition *5400 North* ended the show. The concert was a success musically, but Roy's many fans were disappointed that the great trumpeter had declined to appear at the event. But in general, Roy was as keen as ever to blow, whatever the financial return, as Charles Graham recalls:

> Roy sometimes took little afternoon gigs in nearby Connecticut or New Jersey and took me along with him. On these occasions I told people I was his "manager" and collected the money (in the 1970s it was often just 50 dollars, plus gas money of 5 or 10 dollars). I was also his "manager" at Chicago and Washington, D.C. Festivals.[7]

Roy was saddened to learn of the death in Los Angeles of his former colleague Richie Kamuca, who died in July 1977 just before his forty-seventh birthday. Although they had an up-and-down friendship, Kamuca (twenty years younger than Roy) had definitely stimulated Eldridge's performances. Their musical association resulted in only one album of airshots, which didn't give a telling picture of the quintet they co-led. To mark Roy's sixty-seventh birthday (in January 1978), Phil Schaap at New York's Radio W.K.C.R.-F.M. broadcast a marathon 123-hour tribute, spread over six days, which contained tributes by various musicians and interviews with Roy.

Roy's work schedule at Ryan's was still being punctuated by overseas tours and other occasional high spots, one of which occurred on June 18, 1978 when President Jimmy Carter invited a number of famous jazz musicians to play at the White House. Various ensembles performed brief sets; the one featuring Roy consisted of Benny Carter, Clark Terry, Illinois Jacquet, Teddy Wilson, Milt Hinton, and Jo Jones. Roy had the original invitation framed as a memento of an event that he was proud to have attended. Another unusual booking for Roy involved him in taking part in the São Paulo Brazilian Jazz Festival held in September 1978, which also featured

Zoot Sims, Harry Edison, and Mickey Roker. That same year Roy was part of an all-star line-up brought together by Eddie Locke for an American Field Service concert. The performance was later issued on record, a release that commemorated Locke's long-time dedication to the A.F.S.

In June 1978 I played a season at Michael's Pub (on East 55th, New York) with George Melly and the Feetwarmers, so I again had the chance to see and hear Roy in action at Ryan's. As we finished playing long before Ryan's closed, it was an easy task to hear at least two sets at that club. As soon as we arrived we were warmly greeted by Roy, who was taking an intermission. He was in a jovial mood, but it was easy to see that he wasn't in the best of shape physically. His bout of bursitis had affected his mobility and he had put on a lot of weight. Nevertheless, he got back on to the stand and played a magnificent version of *I Surrender Dear*. This involved enormous effort, which seemed to overtax him; I remember thinking at the time that he might never be his old self again. During that summer the names of Roy Eldridge and Billie Holiday were implanted in the sidewalk of 52nd Street alongside similar plaques set in stone to honor players like Dizzy Gillespie, Thelonious Monk, Charlie Parker, Lester Young, etc., who had helped establish 52nd Street as a jazz haven in years gone by. Although Roy had been part of the *ad-hoc* committee that had selected the names of those to be thus honored, he complained afterward about the final listing, saying over and over again that it was all wrong that no space had been allocated to altoist Pete Brown, of whom Roy said, "He spent his life on 52nd Street." Roy himself was omitted from a 1979 Tribute to Billie Holiday which was part of that year's Newport in New York Jazz Festival, organized by George Wein. One assumes that George took the view that if Roy had been unwilling to be part of a tribute to his own career (in 1977) he was unlikely to be interested in participating in a salute to anyone else's. Roy didn't see it that way, and was particularly upset to learn that Ruby Braff had played on numbers that Roy had originally recorded with Lady Day.

My concern about Roy's health proved unfounded, and when we returned to play another season at Michael's Pub in June 1979 he had fully recovered. I walked apprehensively up the hill toward Ryan's, but my worries disappeared the moment I saw Roy outside the club. He was taking the air during an intermission and looked sprightly, many pounds lighter, and moving with total ease. The recovery showed in his playing: he soared up to top notes with no discernible effort and filled the horn with his richest sound. As I had just come from playing at Michael's Pub I had my trumpet with me, and during the next intermission Roy told me he would be offended if I didn't sit in. I said, "No, thanks" several times, having seen a familiar gleam in Roy's eyes. He tried a different tack, saying, "Oh, yes, I see. You've had some good reviews so you don't have eyes for blowing with old Little Jazz. Well, don't worry, this sort of thing has happened to me before," all this said in a down-hearted fashion. I felt ashamed of myself for turning down an opportunity to play alongside a true musical hero. I climbed on stage and listened to Roy's effusive speech of welcome. When that was completed he proceeded to cut me, slice me, and mince me into tiny fragments. He played like a demon, and being his victim was an education, though I had to keep telling myself that there was nothing personal in Roy's musical onslaught. We got off stage and had a drink together, then Roy looked over his spectacles at me and said with a chuckle, "I can still wash 'em away, eh?" I think I managed to laugh.

Roy continued to return occasionally to play in Chicago during the late 1970s, usually guesting at the Holiday Inn and at Rick's Café Americain (where he worked with his two old sidekicks Franz Jackson and Truck Parham), but his November 1979 trip to the Windy City was to take part in a television recording of a W.T.T.W. tribute to Ella Fitzgerald (organized by Norman Granz). The only daunting aspect for Roy of appearing on television was the brightness of the studio lights, and, like Ella Fitzgerald, he usually wore dark glasses throughout the various run-throughs. A reporter at the Chicago taping of the Ella tribute show wrote, "Ella was visibly tense and impatient with herself and certainly didn't appreciate Roy Eldridge warmin-up off camera."[8] However, Roy, from past experience, knew when Ella was about to explode, so he judged his moment and went to his dressing-room for a snack just as the rumblings became ominous. Some months later Roy returned to Chicago to star at the Chicago Jazz Festival, in which he was featured playing old Gene Krupa and Artie Shaw charts in a big band led by drummer Barrett Deems (formerly with Louis Armstrong's All Stars). The event was a success, with Roy's "expansive solos lifting the band into an intense and exciting performance."[9]

During one of Roy's bookings at Rick's Café in Chicago he first met young trumpeter, Spanky Davis:

> This was in the summer of 1978. Roy was working at Rick's Café, and during his stay a bass-player named Quinn Wilson died. I had done jobs with Quinn and Roy had worked with him back in Fletcher Henderson's Band, so we both attended the funeral and Barrett Deems introduced us. Roy learned that I was planning to move to New York and said, "When you get there come to Ryan's; you could do some subs for me. At the moment the band don't like the trumpeters that the club-owners like, and the club-owners don't like the people the band like." So I moved to New York in September 1978 and Roy made me welcome. I had already met Joe Muranyi and Bobby Pratt in Chicago. Some time later Bobby Pratt said to me, "Roy really likes you, and that's good because there are only six or seven people he does like." I sat in at Ryan's often, but sometimes it was a set-up. Roy would say, "I'm just too tired to do this next set." I'd get up and play and he'd dash to the pay-phone that was in the club's entrance and fix up his social schedule for the week. Roy was a sharp-shooter and he got mad when he discovered that Ryan's had put their drinks prices up without giving a raise to the musicians. He walked out one night and stayed out a few nights as a protest. Actually, Ryan's was a tourist trap. It finally closed on

December 23, 1983, and neither Roy nor Joe Muranyi were there for the send-off. Roy was a wonderful person. He could be brutally honest, but you always knew where you stood with him. He had fans from all walks of life that used to come into Ryan's. One of them, whose name was Magic Dick, was part of a harmonica act. He gave Roy a really good trumpet, maybe a gold Besson, as a gift. Roy was pleased and said jokingly, "Gee thanks, but I wish I had your name."[10]

Whenever Roy revisited Chicago there was always someone on hand to talk about the glories of the old Three Deuces (a subject that Roy never minded discussing). By the time Roy played his gig with Barrett Deems, the *Jazz Archive* label had issued some of the broadcasts that his band did from the Three Deuces in the 1930s. Happily, Roy was paid for the release of these airshots, but some record companies issued similar material without permission from, or payment to, the artists involved. Roy wasn't displeased that these mementoes of his happiest musical days were being made available to the public, but I remember his annoyance when someone mentioned that items from a house-party Roy played at in 1940 were being released. Roy made his bitterness clear:

> This isn't like someone issuing a broadcast, where you know everything was performed up to a standard, whether or not the musicians were inspired or not, but recording at a party is like sneaking up and taking something that doesn't belong to you. The musicians might be juiced or the piano way out of tune, or amateurs playing the wrong changes backing you. You can live with all that if you're having a good time at a party, but if it is recorded and issued years later as an example of your work, well, that's terrible.[11]

Early in 1980 Jack Kleinsinger saluted Roy at a Highlights in Jazz concert. A good, lively bill featuring Clark Terry, Maxine Sullivan, Slam Stewart, and Panama Francis' Savoy Sultans paid tribute to Roy's career and his musical achievements. Lee Jeske covered the concert for *Jazz Journal*:

> The last act was Little Jazz himself, looking grey and content. The Savoy Sultans joined him for his opener, *I Can't Get Started*, and Roy proved that those notes that most trumpet players need a cherry picker to reach are still within his easy, 68-year-old grasp. He is an international treasure.[12]

For the final part of Roy's set, his playing was graced by Dick Katz's piano accompaniment. Roy's enthusiasm was limitless. Gary Giddins described the finale: "Eldridge and Katz, reluctant to go home, played a 90-second duet of whimpered blasts and scatter-shoot chords."[13] Promoter Jack Kleinsinger felt that on that particular night Roy was more determined than ever to come out on top: "At that concert Roy blew so hard against the other trumpet-players he had to take a few days off from playing at Ryan's to recuperate."[14]

In October 1980 we played another season at Michael's Pub, so I was able to see and hear for myself that Roy was in good shape. He seemed more ebullient than ever, and was in fine form on the bandstand at Ryan's, but within a week he suffered a severe heart attack, and was taken to the Terrace Heights Hospital on Palermo Street near to his home in Hollis, Long Island. I spoke to Vi Eldridge on the telephone and was told that Roy was in intensive care, but was as well as could be expected. Two days later a Scandinavian friend of Roy's dropped in to Michael's bringing greetings to me from Roy: things had taken a turn for the better. Vi confirmed that there was a distinct improvement in Roy's condition; he slowly recovered as we left to return to England.

The next stage of Roy's recovery meant he had to undergo rigorous tests in hospital. Sadly the results were not encouraging, and the doctor had the ominous task of telling Roy that he would not be able to continue playing the trumpet for a living. The medical evidence was irrefutable, and there was no appeal. The doctor said that after a long period of recuperation Roy might be able to blow again, but only gently and carefully. He was warned that the sort of vigorous playing that he was famous for would prove disastrous. Roy took this somber news better than any of his family or friends could have believed. His thoughts on the matter were positive: he had never played under wraps in his life, and rather than do so he would give up playing. Roy's motto had always been "I have to play," but he heeded the warning and never did another gig on trumpet. Later, while sitting at home, he'd occasionally gently blow along with the music in various television commercials, but he hated placing himself under restraint and decided to put the trumpet away for ever. But the old combative spirit hadn't left him, and long after he'd packed away his horn for the last time he made his defiance clear to Dan Morgenstern: "How could I play and not get carried away. So I made the decision not to try and the doctor was relieved. *I Could Still Do It Though!*"[15]

Once Roy was back home after his stay in hospital, the immediate problem was getting someone as restless as he was to take it easy. Gradually he shaped a domestic routine that involved his working regularly in the garden (doing his best to grow prize tomatoes), tinkering with gadgets, buying more tools than he could ever use, adjusting and readjusting his hi-fi and radio equipment, playing the piano, reading the papers, watching television, and taking the dog for a walk. But Roy wasn't caught up in a procession of quiet days, and soon there were many outings and social occasions.

By early 1981 Roy was out and about again, and for his seventieth birthday (on January 30) Jean Bach threw a big party (which was co-hosted by Dan Morgenstern and Charles Graham) to celebrate the occasion. At the relaxed gathering, Roy and Vi listened appreciatively as trumpeter Jon Faddis (accompanied by Tommy Flanagan on piano) re-created the solos that Roy had recorded on *Heckler's Hop*. By June, Roy was well enough not only to attend a Newport-Kool concert in his honor, but was also willing and able to sing a scat duet with Ella Fitzgerald.

At this "Portrait of Roy Eldridge" celebration held at New York

Town Hall, Jimmy Maxwell did a masterful job of re-creating Roy's famous *Rockin' Chair* solo, and Dizzy Gillespie, Ernie Royal, Johnny Letman, and Jon Faddis played heartfelt tributes to a player they so admired. Jimmy Maxwell and Jon Faddis also played at a "Homage to Roy Eldridge" event held at the Roosevelt Hotel, where they joined Doc Cheatham in blowing David Baker's transcriptions of some of Roy's recorded gems. When Roy attended the various tributes he was easily persuaded to sing a number or two, and invariably glowed with pleasure at the warmth of the audience's reaction. Roy had told Charles Fox back in 1977, "Singing without my horn—I'd never want to do that."[16] But the stimulating power of the listeners' admiring responses to his vocals made him change his mind. And it wasn't only his vocal chords he exercised: at Jo Jones' seventieth birthday celebrations, held in October 1981, at the West End Café, Roy played a drum duet with Papa Jo.

Roy often called into Ryan's, where trumpeter Spanky Davis now held forth. For a regular reimbursement Roy allowed owner Matty Walsh to keep his name on the billboard at the entrance to the club. This wasn't exactly subterfuge, because Roy usually sang with the band, told jokes, and played the piano during his occasional visits, which continued until shortly before the venue closed in December 1983. Early in 1983 I was in New York on a research trip, and arranged to meet Roy in Ryan's. We listened to the band for a few numbers, then Roy said he had heard that a saxophonist was playing that night at Condon's who might be well worth listening to; we strolled over to the "rival" club, where Roy was greeted by just about everyone in the audience. But, after listening to three numbers, Roy said grumpily, "If you think I'm gonna listen to this shit all night, you're mistaken," as if I had been the one who suggested we visit Condon's. We left, and Roy drove me to a friendly bar that he knew well, but getting there was a hazard because Roy was still full of the agitation that had been caused by his first hearing of the disappointing saxophone-player. His driving that night was as combative as his trumpet-playing used to be, and everyone on the road was vehemently cursed. He gradually calmed down and we enjoyed a very pleasant evening. He was his old self again, mischievously airing the latest jazz world gossip and throwing in random details about his early days on the road.

The tributes to Roy's career continued, and at a Roy Eldridge Night held at the Blue Note, Greenwich Village in June 1984 he sang and played drums and piano, with Dizzy Gillespie looking on admiringly at Roy's triple-threat performance. Roy even sang one number when he was inducted into the Rutgers Hall of Fame in 1984, and happily took part in a tribute to Anita O'Day, sharing a version of *Let Me Off Uptown* with her. Just as surprisingly, he attended a salute to Wild Bill Davison at a New York J.V.C. Festival concert. In August 1984, Pittsburgh honored Roy by dedicating a week-long jazz festival to him. In May 1985, he was delighted to record some vocal numbers with a line-up led by Spanky Davis. Throughout the 1980s Roy did his best to hear various old friends and ex-colleagues play, making trips to the Sweet Basil Club to listen to Benny Carter, Buddy Tate, etc. Roy also effectively em-ceed a Benny Carter Celebration Concert held at Carnegie Hall. Roy made sure that he visited the Blue Note Club for Artie Shaw's 1985 visit. Shaw, who had come out of retirement to front a band led by Dick Johnson, had long ceased playing, and left all the clarinet work to Johnson, but he compèred with skill and panache. On spotting Roy in the audience, he hailed him as "one of the greatest jazz trumpeters who ever lived."[17] Roy was naturally delighted with these words, but he was less pleased when people referred to him as "an elder statesman of jazz": he still saw himself as something of a devil-may-care.

There were sad moments for Roy at the increasing number of funerals and memorial services for various of his old friends. He was present at the farewell to Paul Quinichette, and spoke movingly at Jo Jones' send-off in 1985. He spoke from the pulpit at a Resurrection Service for Lester Young in 1986 and attended a memorial service for Buddy Rich a year later. But each year, on the occasion of Roy's birthday, there was a bright beacon in the shape of the annual Tribute programs on Radio W.K.C.R., organized and presented by the indefatigable Phil Schaap. Little Jazz appeared on these programs, commenting on the records being played, discussing jazz history, and peppering the airwaves with marvelous anecdotes. One of Phil's greatest coups occurred on the W.K.C.R. Tribute to Doc Cheatham's eightieth birthday in June 1985, when he managed to assemble a magnificent array of jazz trumpeters, including Doc, Roy, Buck Clayton, Jabbo Smith, and Jonah Jones.

Roy linked up with good friend pianist Dick Katz, and sang at some summer 1986 gigs at Struggles in Edgewater, New York, where they worked with saxist Turk Mauro, drummer Ron Turso, and bassist Lisle Atkinson. Roy was also briefly part of a Swing Reunion package in which he sang and jived his way into the hearts of audiences in various cities. His performances caused Benny Carter to comment, "I'm not sure he ever needed that trumpet."[18] Roy traveled further afield to work with his former colleague at Ryan's, drummer Eddie Locke, who recalls:

> In the spring of 1986 I took a band down to Fort Lauderdale, Florida. It was a promotion for the liquor company, Seagram's, and I got a good line-up: Buddy Tate on tenor, Doc Cheatham and Spanky Davis on trumpets, Al Grey and Jimmy Knepper on trombones, Norris Turney on alto-sax, Frank Tate on bass, and Richard Wyands on piano. I booked Roy to sing with the band, and he did a great job. I kidded him and said he'd have to sit to the side of the band on stage, like a Swing Era vocalist. We had a good laugh over that.[19]

Tenorist Loren Schoenberg also spoke of Roy the vocalist:

> After he couldn't play anymore he sang on occasion backed by an ad-hoc band of mostly Ryan's vets usually led by Spanky Davis. I remember playing in this band at a concert at the Brooklyn Art Museum and receiving the same electric shock from his singing as I did from his playing.[20]

Roy was by no means forgotten by his fellow professionals ,and in April 1986 at the Village Gate he was honored by a salute from the

Jazz Musicians' Foundation of Local 802, when an illustrious quartet of trumpeters—Randy Brecker, John Carisi, Michael Mossman, and Clark Terry—played *Little Jazz* for Little Jazz. A plaque listing Roy's achievements was presented to Roy by Union President (and trumpeter) John Glasel. With a lot of help and encouragement from Phil Schaap, Roy gradually began taking part in concerts and seminars designed to introduce young children to jazz. Some of these dates also featured Eddie Locke (himself a noted jazz educator) and pianist Dick Katz. The youngsters were happy to sing along with Roy on *Jumbo The Elephant*, and the under-tens were delighted by their first hearing of *School Days*. Roy began to be regularly invited to speak about jazz, and to compère various events, including a talent show on radio. In June 1986 Roy spoke at a National Music Council's lunch held to honor Dizzy Gillespie and Morton Gould. Also present was Roy's old adversary Benny Goodman, who was greatly impressed by the way Roy delivered his eulogy on Dizzy Gillespie. Goodman said, "I think Roy should go on a national speaking tour. I think I'll book Roy Eldridge on the lecture circuit," but Goodman had no time to carry out this plan. That lunch was the last public function he attended. He died three days later on June 13, 1986. Roy met up with Dan Morgenstern soon afterwards:

> Life sure is strange. I knew Benny for more than fifty years and worked with him lots of times, but there was always something that kept us apart. But that day, we had such a nice time together, and I left him with real warm feelings, and then...it's mysterious, isn't it?[21]

In August 1986, Roy took part in Marian McPartland's popular radio show *Piano Jazz*, playing solo piano and singing, as well as talking about his career and performing keyboard duets with his hostess on various numbers. Almost a decade later the whole program was issued on a Jazz Alliance C.D. Roy's health became more variable from the mid-1980s and he suffered several recurrences of his heart problems; emphysema was also plaguing him, and as a result he became less active. He didn't rant and rave against the fates. A tone of resignation sometimes entered his voice, but he gave his views without bitterness:

> To tell the truth I don't think blacks, particularly young blacks are very interested in my music. The fact is most young blacks seem interested only in what's happening now, whatever is current. For some reason they can't relate to me or Coleman Hawkins, or others like us, in large numbers.[22]

Kitty Grime, in New York to research a book, met up with Roy at a benefit and saw how much he had changed: "He was a shadow of his old self, and seemed embarrassed by his appearance."[23] But there were no surges of grim pessimism, and pianist Chuck Folds observed, "I think he accepted what happened and rode with it."[24] Dan Morgenstern observed that Roy was not slow to praise Norman Granz for all the help he had given:

> Roy was very fond of Norman, felt that he could be trusted implicitly and in later years did not hesitate to express to friends his gratitude for Norman's help with matters medical which could have been a terrible financial burden.[25]

Roy was as mentally alert as ever, but at times he sounded world-weary. In a long interview with Whitney Balliett he said:

> I don't miss the music anymore. I've had enough fun and praise and ovations to keep me. Anyway I found out that the main doors were always locked. The color thing. Sometimes I drive over to Nassau, but I don't go into New York much anymore. It's expensive going places now, and they don't always know who you are. Anyway, all my old clothes are too big.[26]

When I was briefly in New York during April 1987 we were

scheduled to meet, but Roy had caught a chill attending Maxine Sullivan's funeral and had to call off the get-together; we had a long phone conversation, during which he surprised me completely by saying he felt that if he had learned to tongue the trumpet properly he would have been "a top player." I was astounded by this, because Roy never went in for mock modesty, and the remark seemed so out of character. Late in his life, Roy expressed a similar comment to Dan Morgenstern, saying he could have been "A hell of a legitimate trumpeter" if he had listened to his original teacher P. M. Williams. In my talk with Roy I emphasized that his position of eminence in the jazz world could never be challenged, adding that I thought he was a genius, but even these assurances didn't lock tight, and somehow Roy got the impression I was talking about Louis Armstrong, which led him to say reflectively, "Yes, Louis is a genius." But there was no melancholia in Roy that day, and he was soon sharing jazz-world gossip with me. The one thing that certainly did depress Roy was the failing health of his wife Vi, who, together with their daughter Carole, remained the central figures in his life.

But the old trouper could still emerge from his shell and sound full of his humor and sharpness during his radio interviews with Phil Schaap, or if he met up with an old confrère, and he was temporarily fired with ambition as the result of a gift from Norman Granz and Oscar Peterson, as Charles Graham explained:

Two or three years before Roy died he called me up to tell me that he had "a big electronic piano" that Norman and Oscar had sent him. He asked if I could go over and help him figure it out. When I got there it hadn't been unpacked. It was pretty imposing with a full keyboard, many controls, and a thick manual on set-up and operation. It was a fairly early electronic synthesizer. He hadn't figured out where to put it (or on what), so the next time I went out to Hollis I took my car and gave him a good general purpose stand to put it on. Meanwhile I'd taken the manual home and studied it, marking the section which told him how to use it as an electric piano.

I'm sorry to say that Roy never apparently used it. It was still in the basement on the stand I gave him, apparently unused. He never mentioned it to me again, which he most likely would have done had he started using it.[27]

Speaking about the electronic keyboard, Roy said to Phil Schaap, "So much to learn; I wish I was twenty years old." Roy added that he wanted to create sound-tracks for movies on it, but alas he never did. Roy gave away his old piano because of a problem with damp in his basement, and his drums remained packed away rom one year's end to the next. One of Roy's major plans during the last part of his life centered around his making a record devoted to children's songs, including a narration of Saint-Saëns' *Carnival Of The Animals* (with keyboard accompaniment), but unfortunately the project never materialized. Roy felt well enough to take part in a radio interview with Phil Schaap on W.K.C.R.-F.M. in January 1989, and he also attended a celebration of his life held at St. Peter's Lutheran Church on Lexington Avenue, which was conducted by the Pastor John Gensel. Dick Katz played a big part in co-ordinating the music that was performed, which included Roy's old friend and colleague Ted Sturgis playing a number on piano. Jazz musicians of all styles were there to pay homage to a great originator, including altoist Lee Konitz. Although not feeling at his best, Roy attended the Bar Mitzvah of Dan Morgenstern's son Adam on January 26, 1989, having been driven there by his relative, Robert Eldridge III. The music was provided by Keith Ingham on piano, Eddie Locke on drums, and Loren Schoenberg on tenor-sax. Loren recalled the gathering: "Roy was there, but I believe Vi was ill and he was a tad subdued. He was persuaded to sit in and sang up a storm."[28]

Sadly, Vi's condition worsened, and to Roy's utter grief she died on February 1, 1989. Charles Graham stressed that despite his immense sadness, Roy stoically made sure that all the funeral arrangements were looked after:

Vi's funeral was out in Hollis, not far from their house, and Roy was quite together, he organised things afterwards to be sure everybody had a ride back to New York City. In fact he asked me to give Phil Schaap a ride.[29]

But once these tasks had been done, Roy's spirits buckled completely. The bereavement caused him to lose all interest in life. He virtually gave up eating, and, despite Carole's loving care, he gradually abandoned the will to survive. Even his close friend Eddie Locke (who telephoned Roy every week during the last years of his life) couldn't reach him: "When Vi died, Roy just went down to his basement and shut himself off from the world. I phoned and he wouldn't answer. I spoke to Carole and she said he didn't want to speak to anyone, and that wasn't like Roy at all."[30] The parlous state of Roy's health wasn't able to stand the combination of self-neglect and immense sorrow. He was admitted to hospital but nothing could save him. Charles Graham was one of Roy's last visitors:

> During his terminal illness I visited him in the hospital. He was in bed and very frail and his arms were like matchsticks, very skinny. He seemed to have trouble seeing, or at least focussing. He was not sure who I was. Then, after we had talked for a minute or two, he suddenly said to me, "Who's that? Wasn't Charlie Graham here?" I said, "It's okay Roy, I'm Charlie Graham. I'm right here." He seemed to get more vague and confused, and then he said, "I just want to go to sleep," and closed his eyes. He didn't seem in pain, just way out there somewhere. The next day Carole called me and said, "Roy died last night."[31]

Roy's death occurred on February 26, 1989, three weeks after Vi's life ended, and on the very day of his cousin Reunald Jones' demise. Three days later, at 10 a.m. on March 1, 1989, the funeral service for Roy took place at St. Peter's, conducted by the Reverend Gensel. Dizzy Gillespie was the central figure among the many famous jazz musicians who attended the funeral. He spoke warmly of his old adversary and of their many trumpet battles, but nothing he said in his heartfelt tribute was more moving than when he stood in front of Roy's casket and played, as a requiem, a solo version of Thelonious Monk's 'Round Midnight. Then Roy made his final journey to the Pine Lawn Memorial Park in Farmingdale, New York. The most restless of men was finally still, but his remarkably vibrant life-force continues to echo through the hundreds of recordings he made during a prolific career.

ROY ON RECORD

15

1935-39

When the subject of Roy Eldridge's first recording came up, he usually avoided mentioning the freelance session he did with Clarence Williams in 1931 (soon after he moved to New York). Because he didn't solo on these sides he didn't consider them worth discussing. Roy was also reluctant to attach any importance to the brief phrases he blew with Elmer Snowden's Band in the 1932 movie short *Smash Your Baggage*. It suited Roy's character to have a spectacular start to his recording career, which is why he cited the making of *Here Comes Cookie* with Teddy Hill's Orchestra in 1935 as his actual debut. He had every right to be proud of his extraordinary performance on that piece, which was nothing short of sensational, and, brief though his solo passages were, they startled the jazz world and introduced Roy's talent to a wider public.

The arrangement of *Here Comes Cookie* wasn't a natural launching pad for unrestrained improvisation, but it was, like most of the scores that were then in Teddy Hill's music library, designed for commercial acceptance. The full band plays a four-bar introduction that could be mistaken for the beginning of an overture by a theater orchestra. This piece of musical ordinariness is followed by a four-bar solo from Eldridge's trumpet that is in a different league of artistry; Roy's choice of notes and the way he rhythmically phrases them is astonishing. The band re-enters and plays a scored 34-bar chorus that is smooth and prim, then the sax section is allocated four bars of sugary melody, which Roy adventurously answers, and the routine is repeated, allowing Roy to inject even more urgency into his remarkable high note phrases. The full band lopes through the eight-bar channel, then Roy again pulls inspiration out of the air in answering the saxophones with perfectly shaped six-bar fill-ins, rising well above top "C" to create a thrilling conclusion to his improvisations. Tenorist Chu Berry is formidably creative in his subsequent solo and trombonist Dicky Wells doesn't let the tension slacken off, but it is Roy's solo passages that make *Here Comes Cookie* a landmark recording in the saga of development in jazz trumpet-playing.

Roy's next recordings showed that he was equally adept in a much smaller line-up. The sales achieved by Fats Waller's small band recordings prompted various companies to replicate the formula of having cheerful vocals backed by jazz musicians. Pianist-singer Putney Dandridge wasn't in the same class as Waller, but his engaging vocals are easy to take. Roy and his sidekick, Chu Berry, were simply booked by Harry Grey (the a-and-r man for the session) to supply a little seasoning for the fun engendered by Dandridge. Considering the brief space available they acquit themselves well, and show that, despite their penchant for marathon improvising at jam sessions, they could create musical vignettes with the best of them. On *Nagasaki*, Roy opens proceedings by blowing a quote from *Yankee Doodle Dandy*, then slips into the background where his open phrases bubble away beneath Dandridge's vocal line. Putney takes a quaint piano chorus that almost strays into barrel-house territory, following up with scat vocal chorus reminiscent of the inspired nonsense that Leo Watson used to create. Roy then plays a series of dramatic breaks that lead into a brief, exuberant solo, which obviously galvanizes the final half-chorus of vocalizing.

Chu Berry eloquently states the melody of *Chasin' Shadows*, unaffected by a rhythm section that plods (despite the presence of the able rhythm guitarist Carmen Mastren). Roy takes the eight-bar release, demonstrating the magnificence of his open tone; both men combine well to support the vocalist without ever trying to steal the limelight. The tenor-sax and muted trumpet also offer Dandridge unobtrusive support during his vocal on *When I Grow Too Old To Dream*. Chu takes the first solo, extemporizing around the melody in short, strong phrases, and Roy (tightly muted) punches out the tune for eight bars and continues to dwell on the melody during a rich-sounding open solo, all the while imparting remarkable rhythmic momentum to what is a fairly simple tune. The jammed finale radiates a happy feeling, and Roy lets everyone know he's feeling good by rising to a bright sounding top "F." There are no revolutionary moments from Roy or Chu, but even in this cramped exposure they both demonstrate their growing individuality.

A month after the Dandridge date Roy was featured on two July 1935 sessions organized by pianist Teddy Wilson. Wilson led a pick-up septet to accompany Billie Holiday, who by this time was gaining a reputation for being one of the most expressive of all jazz-singers. On the first date the band recorded four superb performances during a single afternoon session (from 2 p.m. to 7 p.m.) in a fifteenth-floor studio at Broadway and 57th. The musicians and the singer were inspired by each other's creativity, nonchalantly tackling songs that were often completely new to them. The slow ballad *I Wished On The Moon* brings out the tender side of Roy's trumpet-playing, enabling him to create a solo that was always a favorite with his wife Vi. Roy follows this with some scorching playing on the ride-out chorus of *What A Little Moonlight Can Do*. By then the piece was already on fire thanks to Benny Goodman's unrestrained clarinet work (stoked by drummer Cozy Cole's brush work), and the infectiously joyful singing of Billie Holiday. Billie swings effortlessly, sounding as happy and carefree as at any time in her career—she later said that this was one of her favorite songs. Roy plays tightly muted on *Miss Brown To You*, then adds some fiery, open phrases to the jam session ending. Tenorist Ben Webster is suitably entrusted with the opening melody of *A Sunbonnet Blue*, and sets the mood aptly for Billie's ingeniously timed singing. Roy bursts in via a slightly haphazard trumpet break, but immediately regains his musical composure and plays an emphatic sixteen-bar solo, one that Gunther Schuller described as "unceremoniously out-of-context"[1] before returning to eight bars of concluding melody.

The next batch of Wilson–Holiday recordings relied less on inspired jamming and more on neatly scored passages for a three-piece reed section. Roy's old boss, clarinettist Cecil Scott, sounds full of energy on *What A Night*, and Roy's efforts nod in Louis Armstrong's direction as he interprets sixteen bars of melody. On *I'm Painting The Town Red* Roy airs his remarkable upper register, and on *It's Not Too Hot For Words* his introduction contains some "modern touches," as does his under-recorded solo, in which he adroitly uses substitute chords without sounding too adventurous for the occasion. Billie Holiday sings with total commitment throughout the date, but is not on the final title, *Sweet Lorraine*. Instead, a cup-muted Roy leads the ensemble during the first chorus before handing over to the graceful alto-playing of Hilton Jefferson. Teddy Wilson on piano is his usual urbane and skillful self, and Roy's subsequent solo (played into a felt hat to create a mellow effect) follows the leader's mood but overall this instrumental number is unambitiously arranged, leaving the listener regretting that Billie Holiday's artistry wasn't featured.

During Roy's residency at New York's Famous Door Club, he again recorded with his friend Chu Berry, this time as part of another Teddy Wilson–Billie Holiday session. Roy's style was still developing, and one can hear that he is exploring avenues that he rarely entered again. This is noticeable on *Eeny Meeny Miney Mo* where his 32-bar solo has more than a trace of Henry "Red" Allen's work. Roy always vehemently denied that his style had any links with Allen's playing, and though I think he firmly believed there was no influence because he felt that Red's harmonic approach was "wrong," on this title it seems that unconscious assimilation had taken place. *Eeny Meeny Miney Mo* is not an inspiring example of popular compositions of the 1930s; it's a poor song, but compared to *Yankee Doodle Never Went To Town* it is a gem. How Billie and her confrères managed to produce immortal music out of such dross is astounding. Roy's playing on *Twenty Four Hours A Day* is magnificently robust yet ingenious, and on *If You Were Mine*, inspired by a poignant vocal from Billie, he sounds tender and relaxed. Chu Berry plays well enough on this session but never comes close to establishing the rapport that Billie later shared with Lester Young. Roy's stay at the Famous Door played a direct part in his next recording date on which he "deputized" for trumpeter Wingy Manone, whose band was working alongside Roy's group at the New York Club. Manone, who was unable to take part in the recordings because of contractual obligations, attended the date in an advisory capacity, though frankly there was nothing that Wingy could tell Roy about playing the trumpet. The line-up for the date was the unusual one that Wingy had at the club, namely Carmen Mastren on guitar, Sid Weiss on bass, and Joe Marsala on clarinet—no piano or drums were used. *Swinging' On That Famous Door*, the musicians' tribute to their place of work, is a straightforward twelve-bar blues taken at an attractively "bouncy" pace. Roy is the first soloist, and blows confidently over the simple rhythmic pattern that first surfaced on King Oliver's recording of *Dippermouth Blues*. There is nothing revolutionary in Roy's lines, but they are of a higher quality than Joe Marsala's clarinet improvisation, whose rich sound and fervency are marred by his stilted phrasing. Trumpet and clarinet play long notes behind the double-bass solo; then Mastren creates two choruses of flamboyant chording. A repeat of the melody begins building towards a sturdy final chorus which resolves into a neatly effective ending. *Farewell Blues* begins with a train-like effect; then Roy improvises a solo that begins in the low register before climaxing with a series of high, searing blue notes. Sax-like phrasing plays a part in Roy's soloing, but the "hot" tone belongs to a tradition established by previous trumpet-players. His individuality is underlined by the inclusion of "unexpected" notes in his improvisations, his remarkably fast technical facility, and his extraordinary command of the trumpet's extreme upper register. Marsala again sounds vaguely jittery in his first two choruses, but then creates the sort of flowing, confident lines that his hero, Jimmie Noone, was noted for. The final ensembles reflect an energetic spirit, and in the buildup Eldridge and Marsala's phrasing fleetingly collide, indicating the general spontaneity of the session, while a fade-out ending makes an effective conclusion. Although this two-tune session consolidated Roy's reputation with jazz record collectors, it didn't prepare them for the great things in store.

A landmark in Roy's recording career became clear during his 1936 stay in Chicago with Fletcher Henderson's Band, but it wasn't the Henderson ensemble that provided the surroundings for Roy's achievements; it was a pick-up group, nominally led by drummer Gene Krupa. Krupa's musical team consisted of three African-American musicians: Roy, Chu Berry, and a young bassist Israel Crosby, plus four white musicians: Krupa, pianist Jess Stacy, guitarist Allan Reuss, and Benny Goodman (by then a famous bandleader, and Krupa's employer). *I Hope Gabriel Likes My Music* opens with some dramatic interplay between trumpet and drums, and some sensational two-bar breaks from Roy. Chu Berry plays a thoughtful, well-constructed chorus, then Goodman effortlessly improvises a solo, and Roy enters, seemingly determined to eclipse what had gone before by playing a series of stark but highly rhythmic phrases before moving to his top register for an emphatic "I'm the King of the Castle" musical proclamation which culminates with a clean sounding top "G." *Mutiny In The Parlor* is more sedate. Roy sounds admirably relaxed at this slow jog tempo, but his acrid tone and skillful half-valving ensure that sentimentality is not allowed to take over. Roy builds some of his phrases on chord extensions, but nothing he plays affects the chirpy innocence of Helen Ward's vocal. The early stages of *I'm Gonna Clap My Hands* are even more orderly, and reminiscent of the structure of a Teddy Wilson–Billie Holiday side, though Helen Ward's competent vocal doesn't measure up to Lady Day's timeless artistry. Roy creates some stirring phrases in a call-and-answer with the reeds, then both Berry and Goodman play sublime solos that seem to stir Roy into top gear. Against a somewhat unwieldy rhythm section, Roy makes a final onslaught into the top register, literally jostling Benny Goodman out of prominence.

The final number of the date, *Swing Is Here*, is fast and feverish, with Roy playing an introduction that spreads heat through his 32-bar exposition of the melody. Chu Berry opts for a series of familiar patterns for the basis of his solo, nevertheless creating a highly enjoyable romp. Goodman seems to revel in the swift pace, his phrases floating over the rapid tempo, demonstrating his vivacity and his admirable rhythmic balance. Roy's trumpet work here is full of rhythmic and harmonic daring, containing, as it does, several whole-tone strands. His ability to create a sense of urgency by flying up above top "C" is perfectly demonstrated, but the move doesn't bring musical chaos; instead it links with a series of incisive unison riffs that wind down subtly into a fade-out ending.

The music this mixed group created epitomized the new approach that musicians were taking toward jam session playing. In earlier days almost every jam session was based on a Dixieland style of ensemble, but during the mid-1930s a new approach developed that created intense interplay between the front-line players, none of them tied to set roles. Instead of the trumpet clearly stating the melody, with all the other front-line participants weaving over or under that lead, a new freedom took over that allowed any of the front line to assume the central voice in an ensemble. Occasionally anarchy prevailed, but often, as on this Krupa session, the musical give-and-take produced sublime, exciting jazz. The recordings mark the emergence of Eldridge's genius. There isn't a dull moment on the four tracks but there is an abundance of totally fresh ideas. Nothing that Roy plays here could be mistaken for the work of any of the stellar trumpeters of that era such as Louis Armstrong, Henry "Red" Allen, Jabbo Smith, Rex Stewart, etc. Roy's approach, from this point on, became a bright beacon that was to guide many young jazz musicians.

Although Roy always regarded his joining Fletcher Henderson's Orchestra as the biggest step of his early career, he did not view his entire stay with unalloyed pleasure. Nevertheless, he was able to consolidate his reputation and to work alongside top-class players, all the while creating embryo ideas that became the basis of many of his future solos. This doesn't mean that he stored away ideas to be trotted out on some later occasion; instead he was continually experimenting with new harmonic approaches, tonal effects, and making use of his low notes, as well as the ultra-high ones. He developed his breathing control to make his phrases longer, and gradually introduced more light and shade into his solos; sometimes Roy seemed overburdened in trying to set the frequently staid ensemble alight. This was not Henderson's most exciting band, and though Smack (as the leader was nicknamed) had provided Benny Goodman, and others, with the arrangements that sparked the Swing Era into life, he didn't orchestrate much for his own band during this period, leaving that task to others, including his brother Horace. The flag-wavers that had formerly been featured by Fletcher were notably absent.

Fletcher Henderson had a higher regard for Chu Berry's tenor-playing than he did for Roy's trumpet work, and accordingly he allocated more solo space to Chu. Clarinettist Buster Bailey was also a well-featured soloist. Bailey was a superb musician, ever reliable, with an admirable technique and a discerning ear, but his stiff phrases are usually delivered in a thin, pipey tone and rarely do they swing. Buster may have impressed his listeners, but he rarely moved them.

Both of these musicians took part in a septet assembled by Roy that made recordings in Chicago during 1936. The results were rejected at the time, and sadly only one title (a buoyant *Christopher Columbus*) has ever surfaced.

There are some uneven moments in the solos Roy recorded with Henderson between March and August 1936, but even the low spots are full of interest and enterprise. His high note entry on the full band's *Christopher Columbus* proved to be a gambit he often used later, but on *Stealin' Apples* his muted, middle register work has considerable appeal, containing as it did forays into new harmonic territory. Fletcher rarely took long piano solos but on this track his cosy, rather prim playing fills a whole 32-bar chorus. On *Blue Lou*, Roy skids through a patch of mispitching but quickly becomes sure-footed as he moves effectively from high to low registers. On some of the titles Roy uses a buzz mute, producing a rasping, kazoo-like timbre that is not easy to love (Roy resumed using this mute in the 1960s). Its use on *I'm A Fool For Loving You*, a commercial tune uneventfully arranged, won no hearts. Roy copes well on the challengingly swift *Jangled Nerves*, but Chu Berry sounds as though he didn't want to peddle that fast. Fletcher didn't cast much limelight on the trombonists he had in the band, but here allocates a sixteen-bar morsel to Ed Cuffee. Roy creates sixteen ingenious bars to *Do You Or Don't You Love Me* and *Grand Terrace Rhythm*, but moves up a gear for *Riffin'* where his solo gives the impression that he hadn't said all he wanted to say on that particular sequence. The buzz mute takes over for a brief solo on *Mary Had A Little Lamb*, and is evident again on *Shoe Shine Boy*, where it sounds effective and appropriate. Charming, husky but lilting vocals from Roy are a bonus on these two tracks. *Shoe Shine Boy* was originally meant to be sung by Arthur Lee Simpkins, but the arrangement was in a key that didn't suit his voice so Roy was press-ganged into performing the vocal. Apparently Chu Berry got angry because Roy got an extra $10 for singing, but they soon resumed their warm friendship. Thereafter Roy sang regularly for the rest of his career, but never really considered himself as a vocalist. He told Phil Schaap, "I never had any eyes for it. I can hardly ever remember lyrics."[2] Roy hits some powerful low notes to introduce his trumpet solo on *Sing, Sing, Sing*, reveling his way through the minor key sequence, and managing to insert some humor into his vocal on the awful song, *Knock, Knock, Who's There?* (which has the rare virtue of featuring a baritone-sax solo from Chu Berry). Roy is at his most spectacular on *Jimtown Blues*, cleanly hitting a string of notes that are way above the top "C" barrier (which in the manuals of that era was usually given as the highest trumpet note). On *You Can Depend On Me* he surpasses his previous efforts with Fletcher by playing a superbly constructed 32-bar chorus. Though no one realized it at the time, this was to be Roy's last recording with Henderson's Orchestra.

In May 1936, Teddy Wilson, temporarily in Chicago with Benny Goodman, took the opportunity to round up several ex-colleagues (by then sidemen with Fletcher Henderson). The result was four unpretentious but enjoyable jazz sides including a version of the twee composition *Mary Had A Little Lamb*. This is a jazzier performance than Fletcher Henderson's recording, containing a polished solo from Wilson and two worthy outings for Chu Berry's tenor-sax. Roy contributes a cheerful vocal and later plays an outstanding sixteen-bar trumpet solo, in which poise, and the spacing of his phrases, show ever-growing maturity; Buster Bailey's eight-bar fling cools things down, but Roy re-enters to blow a storming ending. *Too Good To Be True* is a slowish, orthodox ballad. Roy plays an appropriate introduction, then Berry gives a ravishing interpretation of the 32-bar theme, creating a performance that has strong echoes of Coleman Hawkins' 1933 recording of *The Day You Came Along*. The piano work again sounds graceful, but then Roy plays an astonishing break that heralds a series of climactic phrases perfectly supported by drummer Sid Catlett's inspiring press rolls. *Warmin' Up*, a standard 32-bar work-out devised by Wilson, has a buzz-muted first chorus from Roy. Berry and Bailey take typical solos which are followed by Roy blowing a chorus that contains a couple of his standard, highly nimble pet phrases, and sturdy riffs add another layer of excitement in the final stages. The outstanding item from the date is the slow *Blues In C Sharp Minor*, which is built on an ostinato bass figure, played by the youngest man on the date, Israel Crosby. Wilson's two choruses are elegance itself, then Roy adds another dimension by introducing a note of pathos in his solo. Buster Bailey sounds a little too precise for the occasion, but Chu Berry creates some intriguing lines. The key, rarely used for jazz performances, provides a stimulating challenge to all the musicians, though one senses that Roy twice hesitates slightly as he resolves the dominant seven during the ninth and tenth bars. Underpinning everything is the firm pattern of Crosby's deliberately repetitive bass line, which creates a rondo effect by being the first and last sounds on the recording.

The first recordings made by the dynamic band that Roy led at the Three Deuces, Chicago, give no indication of the fiery, ingenious, devil-may-care attitude for which the group was noted. Instead they provide some restrained, neat backings for the nationally established vocalist, Mildred Bailey. The white tenorist Herbie Haymer replaced Roy's regular incumbent Dave Young, but the rest of the line-up contained regular members of Roy's group. Mildred's pitching was always accurate and her diction never less than first class; she demonstrates both assets and also phrases eloquently throughout. Fireworks were not the order of the day, and the musicians' main task is to play long backing notes. Roy's best moments are on *Where Are You?*, on which he gently paraphrases the melody, gradually letting some piquant variations unfold. Herbie Haymer is far from sensational, and sounds quite nervous, whereas altoist Scoops Carry's performances make him the instrumental star of the session. His solos on *My Last Affair* and *You're Laughing At Me* show his harmonic mastery and reveal the attractive panache with which he delivered his solos.

Four days after the Mildred Bailey session, the same group of musicians, with Joe Eldridge added on alto and Dave Young resuming his place on tenor-sax, began making a sensational series of recordings. All wraps are cast off as the Three Deuces line-up create some extraordinary examples of musical team work, with Roy improvising with an intensity that placed him apart from all other jazz trumpeters. All his phrases, searing or subtle, were couched in a technique that allowed him to play higher, faster, and more daringly than any of his rivals. Only occasionally did a superfluous phrase interrupt the flow of new ideas, and he somehow managed to add a climax to every finale. But it wasn't only a question of speed, range, and experimentation; it was also the tremendous amount of feeling that Roy poured into his performances, fast or slow, that made him unique. His playing of the theme of *Wabash Stomp* displays great authority and confidence, and the three-piece sax section do their best to phrase like Benny Carter before the trumpet again commands attention. Joe Eldridge also sounds exploratory, but Teddy Cole on piano confirms, as he does throughout most of the recordings, that he was not much more than a reliable journeyman. Scoops Carry plays eight bars, offering a sound and style that soon inspired Joe Eldridge to be his *doppelgänger*; if anything, Scoops was the more sophisticated player. The rest of the recording belongs to Roy, who makes a dramatic, low-register entry that flows smoothly into an ingenious release. He then rises to the top register, using his high range as fertile ground for a series of fine ideas. Dave Young on tenor plays eight bars, and he, too, like the pianist, reveals that his heart was in the right place, even if his fingers were not, but Roy would never hear a word said against any of this group, whose team spirit and empathy became a byword in Chicago jazz circles. Dave Young's brief solo offers a respite before Roy re-enters and plays a series of phenomenal phrases, adding a slight throat growl as he movingly shades his tone in the run-up to the final high note. A second, slower take of *Wabash Stomp* confirms that the band believed in improvising wherever possible, but the solos on this version don't flow as they do on the first attempt, and it is easy to understand why it was originally rejected.

Roy makes his considerable musical presence obvious from the opening notes of *Florida Stomp*, a stark theme that is made to sound relentless by the rhythm section's emphatic on-the-beat phrasing. Many years later, drummer Shelly Manne placed this recording in his top ten of all time. Joe Eldridge plays an atmospheric solo which is interspersed by a piano interlude that does little more than mark time. Roy, sounding bold but relaxed, enters and weaves some fascinating patterns through the prevailing dissonance. Though this Eldridge composition and *Wabash Stomp* are forward-looking, they don't compare to the free-thinking on display during Roy's contributions to the up-tempo *Heckler's Hop*. Alto-sax, tenor-sax, and piano have subsidiary solos, and there is a competently strummed guitar solo, but all the pyrotechnics—and the genius—are created by Roy, whose fast fingering allows him instantly to express the ideas that are racing through his mind. His first chorus is in the lower middle register, but as he approaches the thirty-second bar he reacts like a top-class runner hearing the bell for the final lap, and he zooms into yet another amazing finale, his confidence and ingenuity bolstered by some sturdy off-beat drumming from Zutty Singleton. On paper, Singleton, a New Orleans veteran, might not have seemed the ideal man for this band, but in fact his ability to provide an array of percussive tone colors created a rhythmic drive that stimulated Roy's playing.

The most commercial offering of the date was *Where The Lazy River Goes By*, a Jimmy McHugh composition of the period, which is sung here by the Three Deuces' resident entertainer Gladys Palmer. She conveys the melody, dutifully allowing Roy to take all the honors in playing an evocative first chorus followed by a series of clever variations, which include a sudden octave leap that adds a burst of excitement to an unspectacular arrangement. *That Thing* has a somber quality that marks it as a precursor to Nat Adderley's *Blues March*, though here the feet seem a little heavier. Both alto-players are featured, and neither of them seem afraid to experiment. Cole's twelve bars on piano are uneventful; all the glories are again created by Roy's trumpet-playing, which displays the richness of his open tone, and his fascinating ideas. An austere riff concludes a piece that was (somewhat surprisingly, considering its bleak qualities) a favorite with the crowd at the Three Deuces. The final number of the date was a remarkable trumpet feature on the Creamer and Layton evergreen *After You've Gone*. Joe Eldridge's arrangement allows Roy to project the melody in fiery, emphatic phrases, then for chorus after chorus the trumpeter builds up the tension, interspersing each segment with a series of daredevil breaks—not all of them epitomize good taste, but each is worth a cheer. In between Roy's efforts the piano is given space to roam, as too is Gladys Palmer, who gives an unflattering imitation of Sophie Tucker on a bad day. Zutty's drumming marshals Roy into a coherent and effective finale, which has a trumpet and piano call-and-answer leading into an out-of-tempo ending that makes a suitable finish to a *tour de force*. *After You've Gone* became a cornerstone in Roy's repertoire for many years. It was an epic test piece for him, but he usually managed to re-create the excitement of the original.

The sales figures for Roy's brilliant Chicago recordings seemed to prove that the general public were not quite ready for such flabbergasting improvisations. It was to be almost two years before Roy's next studio session, and in the interim he had moved back to New York. There, in November 1938, alongside Chu Berry (who was the nominal leader on the date), Roy recorded for Milt Gabler's Commodore label. All four sides recorded sound as though they were part of an inspired jam session, and the quality of the improvising is breath-taking, a fact underlined by the countless variations that occur on the two versions of *Sittin' In* (which uses the chords of *Tiger Rag*), and on both takes of *Forty-Six West Fifty-Two*; the address of one of the Commodore Music Shops provided the title for this work-out on *Sweet Georgia Brown*.

Despite their close friendship, neither Roy nor Chu give an inch during a four-bar chase on *Sittin' In*. Chu takes the lion's share on *Forty-Six West Fifty-Two*, but Roy presages a device that was to feature on many of his later recordings. This involved him playing a muted chorus in which the piano is silent, and the backing is provided mainly by guitar and bass. Later Roy often took solos accompanied only by bass and drums—he devised the name "strolling" for this particular activity. *Body And Soul* has a full chorus of melody from Chu, then Roy doubles up the tempo and plays some daring chromatic runs, romping his way through the sophisticated chord sequence. Roy used to call the doubling up of a tempo "playing long meter"; it had been used before in jazz performances, one example being Louis Armstrong's brief excursion on his 1931 recording of *Just A Gigolo*, but no one had been able to exploit the possibilities as effectively as Roy does here. Roy benefits from the accompaniment of pianist Clyde Hart who, in his sixteen-bar outing, shows why he was so highly rated by the forward-looking musicians of that era. Roy re-establishes the original tempo, then hands over to Chu (at his most rhapsodic) prior to playing a worthy sign-off cadenza. *Stardust* shows Chu in ravishing form; in contrast Roy takes a bitter-sweet look at Hoagy Carmichael's theme, leaving dramatic gaps in his lines and mixing smooth runs with angular wide intervals. It is possible to detect the faint outlines of Roy's later work on *Rockin' Chair*, but this performance stands in its own right as a fine example of musical exploration.

Roy's only other visit to a recording studio during the following eleven months saw him taking part in a January 1939 Teddy Wilson–Billie Holiday session which produced the exquisite *What Shall I Say?*, on which Roy's muted solo is both supremely expressive and exactly appropriate to Billie's compelling vocal. Again the alternate takes on *It's Easy To Blame The Weather* and *More Than You Know* underline how informal and inventive these sessions were. But despite the lack of studio activity, it's possible (thanks to items Charles Graham had recorded from radio programs) to hear Roy at work with his Arcadia Ballroom Band during 1939. These airshots were taken down on what would now be considered primitive equipment (and not all the tunes are complete); nevertheless, some sensational musical moments were captured and later issued. There's a particularly fine, albeit brief, sample of Roy's then signature tune *Little Jazz*, and a vigorous *Mahogany Hall Stomp* containing dexterous lines from Roy, many of them shaped in the manner of Louis Armstrong. Roy's version, however, ends with four choruses of Prince Robinson's powerful clarinet-playing. *St. Louis Blues* features Roy playing cup-muted phrases that epitomize "time," the elusive quality of perfectly rhythmic delivery sought by all jazz musicians, but only achieved by the few. This version also has some cheerful vocalizing from Eldridge, and another salute to Louis Armstrong by way of some climactic high notes. For some years Roy chose to include Armstrong items such as *Basin Street Blues* in his repertoire, and he particularly liked to work out on the chord changes of *King Of The Zulus*. At the Arcadia, Roy was reminded by his agent, Joe Glaser, that Louis' success was achieved by blending the old and the new, but Roy's tributes to the past reach an absurd level with his version of the Armstrong-inspired *Shine* (played faster than Louis' recording). Here Roy monotonously hits dozens of top "C"s before being exhorted by his fellow musicians to spiral up to a concluding "F." Prior to launching into the gimmicky finale, Roy is heard to say, "I don't ever get tired," and he goes on to prove this in a way that gave ammunition to those critics who branded him as "tasteless." But overall, Roy's fans could only marvel at what they were hearing, and Roy, free from any of the restraints of the recording studio, takes many breath-taking chances, nearly all of which come off. Roy's brother Joe also seems to benefit from the informality of the radio shows, and solos magnificently. The only person to suffer is the band's pianist, who has to perform on the Arcadia's ancient piano. Trombone solos are few and far between, but there is one on the stock arrangement of *Woodchopper's Ball*. A truncated version of *Sam, The Vegetable Man* shows that vocalist Laurel Watson could swing on up-tempo numbers. Roy takes a light-hearted vocal on *King Of Bongo Bong* (a Don Redman arrange-ment), and *Oh Lady Be Good* promises much, but the untidy arrangement always sounds as though it's going to split at the seams. However, the full version of *Minor Jive* rates among Roy's finest achievements. Inspired by some rocking drumming, he creates a series of exciting variations without letting wildness divert the flow of his ideas; the intense playing in the final chorus is astounding.

But the studio recordings by the Arcadia Band did little to elevate the general public's appreciation of Roy's remarkable talent, and the mixed contents of the eight sides must have disappointed the steadily growing number of Roy's fans. *It's My Turn* is an ordinary, commercial arrangement, without the elements that might charm a casual listener into buying the recording. Roy plays the melody tastefully, Prince Robinson and tenorist Franz Jackson contribute eight bars of variations, and pianist Clyde Hart again reveals that he was continuing to add modernity to Teddy Wilson's style. Laurel Watson, an underrated vocalist, sings well enough, but nothing suggests that the band was likely to achieve an attractive individuality. The same applies to *You're A Lucky Guy* pleasantly sung by Roy, who also plays an adventurous solo on what is otherwise a careful rendering of a pop song of the period. However, caution is thrown to the winds on Roy and Joe's composition *Pluckin' The Bass*, an up-tempo piece that develops an almost frantic edge. Robust tenor-playing leads into flamboyant clarinet work, then Roy gives a frenetic display of his technical skills, sounding musically overwrought. Ted Sturgis on bass has brief moments of glory at the beginning (and end) of the piece, but his efforts don't prepare the listener for the turbulence that follows.

Roy shows on *I'm Gettin' Sentimental Over You* that he was continually developing the ingenious way he created "turn-around" phrases in the seventh and eighth bars of each stanza. filling these segments with harmonically interesting progressions. Roy phrases this fine song effectively, as does singer Laurel Watson, but again one feels that something is missing. The band follows a popular fad of the period in reviving a number that had long been a favorite of the New Orleans marching bands, but Roy's version of *High Society* is taken at a pace that would have caused a band to sprint at full speed down Bourbon Street. Prince Robinson (highly regarded by Roy) effectively re-creates the "traditional" clarinet solo, followed by a cleverly scored (but difficult to play) section featuring clarinets and muted trumpets, but again the performance is taut rather than swinging. Another old jazz favorite, *Muskrat Ramble*, is performed with spirit, but, of the soloists, only Joe Eldridge sounds anywhere near top form. The arrangement pays homage to Louis Armstrong by featuring a harmonized version of his original phrases, but this isn't enough to make the rendering exceptional. *Who Told You I Cared?* has a pleasant, Billie Holiday-like vocal from Laurel Watson, and some attractive muted work from Roy (using a Harmon mute with the stem in), but the paucity of the song lets everybody down. The same fault gives a weak pulse to *Does Your Heart Beat For Me?* and here the performance is further debilitated by a very ordinary arrangement. Roy's plaintive qualities lift the latter stages, but this recording could not have gained the band a single new fan.

1940–46

Wn Roy looked back on his freelance activities, his recordings with singer Mildred Bailey always occupied a special place in his affections. Originally, these elegantly arranged sides were noted more for their charm and feeling than for any monumental jazz achievements, but nowadays their merits are universally acclaimed. Roy's cup-muted work on both takes of *Wham* is neat and subtle, as is the dainty vocal he shares with Mildred. On *Tennessee Fish Fry* (a hit for Kay Kyser), Roy cheekily plays the theme of *Wabash Stomp* as the introduction, and in the instrumental section demonstrates his immaculate cup-muted intonation (those juvenile hours spent blowing into a trumpet muffled by a glove paid rich dividends). Again, Mildred's vocal is full of appeal, and on *I'm Nobody's Baby* she swings relaxedly. Roy's solo here (blown into a felt hat) is the high spot of all his work with Mildred: it's full of fat-toned new ideas, and although there are a couple of fluffs in the delivery, the recording manager wisely let them pass. Henry Nemo (a composer who enjoyed success with *Don't Take Your Love From Me* and *'Tis Autumn*) wrote the evanescent novelty number *A Bee Gizindt* to cash in on the short-lived craze for "swing slang" songs. Mildred does her best with the lyrics, and Roy plays a sixteen-bar muted solo that is well executed but devoid of anything daring. Most of his other contributions to Mildred's recordings contain the briefest of solos and fill-ins, but everything underlines his admiration for the singer. Looking back he summarized his feelings: "Maybe she wasn't a great singer but what I liked is she used to pick out the pretty songs with the pretty verses that a lot of people don't sing."[3] In this series of recordings Roy proved to the world that he could play in a restrained manner at a time when he was being described as a high-note firebrand. He had shown a quieter side on some of his recordings with Billie Holiday, but with Mildred he consistently played a subsidiary role that complemented the vocalist without igniting any upper register fireworks.

Roy used a similar approach on the 1940 sides he made with Freddie Rich's Orchestra, a big white band that on this occasion featured Roy, Clyde Hart on piano, and Benny Carter, who played alto-sax and arranged all the material. On *Till We Meet Again*, a restrained rhythm section is at work. Babe Russin plays an effective sixteen-bar tenor-sax solo, then Roy again shows his controlled muted playing as he weaves over and under the melody. He's also cup-muted on *A House With A Little Red Barn*, whose banal lyrics are entrusted to poor Rosemary Calvin. Roy isn't featured on *How High The Moon*, carefully sung by the same singer and taken at a slow–medium tempo. No one could have forecast that this tune would become an anthem of the revolutionary be-bop movement. The best arrangement by far is *I'm Forever Blowing Bubbles*, in which a boogie-ish introduction announces a whole series of interesting voicings. Here Clyde Hart's piano work is orderly rather than brilliant, but Carter's 32-bar chorus is full of grace and ingenuity; Roy contributes an open-horned eight-bar vignette.

Roy's freelance work during the first months of 1940 represented a plateau stage of his career, but the recordings he made with The Chocolate Dandies lifted him to new heights. Alongside ex-Fletcher Henderson sidemen, Benny Carter on alto-sax, Coleman Hawkins (recently returned from Europe) on tenor-sax, Bernard Addison on guitar, John Kirby on bass, and Sid Catlett on drums, Roy was playing in fast, competitive company. For all the team spirit of the Three

Deuces line-up and the camaraderie of the Arcadia Band, no one in those ensembles offered a serious challenge to Roy when it came to top-class improvising. The Chocolate Dandies' session was markedly different. Everyone involved was a notable musician, and this illustrious gathering created some of the finest jazz ever recorded. It was hoped that Fletcher Henderson would be in on the session, but his schedule made this impossible, so the group recorded without a pianist (though Carter did take over at the keyboard on one track). Carter, on alto-sax, introduces the scant theme of *Smack*, then improvises a 32-bar solo; he never sounded better and piles one ingenuity on another. Roy, perfectly supported by Catlett's lithe drumming, keeps up the formidable high standard, gliding through phrases that are truly saxophonic, a ploy made obvious, being juxtaposed between solos by two of his idols, Carter and Hawkins. After a workmanlike piano introduction from Carter, Hawkins settles down to emote the melody of *I Surrender Dear*, playing somewhat in the manner of his recent recording success *Body And Soul*. His performance here doesn't reach the same epic dimensions, but it perfectly prepares the ground for some impressively fertile playing from Eldridge, whose low register sounds at its most expressive. Roy's near tender approach to the sequence is all the more remarkable because the combined block-chording of Carter on piano and Addison on guitar is decidedly pedestrian. *I Can't Believe That You're In Love With Me* is introduced by Coleman Hawkins, who shakes the melody playfully in his mighty jaws, then, after the briefest of hesitations, launches into an improvised chorus that is both strong and cerebral. Roy follows on with two of his most admirable choruses, creating ingenious and vigorous phrases on the spur of the moment. Monumental though these efforts are, they are surpassed by an alto-sax solo by Carter that is one of the best examples of thematic development in all jazz. Carter carries a series of complex ideas to delightful conclusions, injecting them with interesting harmonies and superimposing time signatures on the four-in-a-bar accompaniment, yet still managing to swing elegantly.

The give-and-take of the final jam sessions could only have been created by master musicians.

Years after the initial issues of the Chocolate Dandies' session on 78 r.p.m., alternative takes were released on vinyl. None of these eclipse the architectural magnificence of the original releases, but the variations displayed on the "rejected" attempts are countless. Anyone doubting Roy's prowess as an improviser needs only to listen to both takes of *I Surrender Dear* (a tune that became an everlasting part of his repertoire) and to the slow version of *I Can't Believe* to be convinced that he was an ace experimenter. The session remains a landmark in jazz, and although it is possible to carp about the stolid nature of the rhythm section (despite Sid Catlett's propulsive drumming), the richly inventive solos and the complex maneuvers apparent in the jammed ensembles underline the merits of three great improvisers.

Roy continued to record with Billie Holiday in 1940 and 1941, but the impromptu approach of their earlier sides together was rarely apparent; instead most of the pieces were heavily arranged. Even those that were not fully orchestrated were sketched out on paper, with brief gaps left for improvising, and sometimes even the contours of the solos were written down. Even so, Roy was able to imprint his musical personality by deftly rearranging the melody and delivering the results in a tone that was unique; if a second (or third) take was called for, he always devised further subtle variations. A lot of his later work with Billie featured him blowing soft, cup-muted obbligatos behind the singer, but even within eight bars (as on *Body And Soul*) he could still make an incisive contribution. *I Hear Music* was one of his own particular favorites with Billie; he also liked *Falling In Love Again*, on which he creates some startling phrases. His open playing on *I'm All For You* is excellent—authoritive without being overbearing, showing that he really understood the role of an accompanist, always catching the mood of each song, as is typified by his brief but poignant contribution to *God Bless The Child*.

In May 1941, within days of joining Gene Krupa's Orchestra, Roy was being featured on the band's recordings. His first effort was on

Green Eyes, which starts out as a rumba-ish feature for singer Howard Dulaney. The vocal ends, and Roy makes a scorching entry prior to engaging in a fierce duet with Krupa's drumming. Gene plays a four-bar break, then Roy catapults his phrases into a reprise of the melody, epitomizing his ability to create instant swing. Anita O'Day sings a smooth and clever sixteen bars, rounding off an arrangement that manages to balance commercial intent with unrestrained jazz. The score was by ex-trumpeter Elton Hill, of whom Roy said that it was only his lack of confidence that prevented him from being one of the top arrangers of that era. *Green Eyes*, like most of the Krupa–Eldridge output, was accorded a second take. Roy creates a new burst of inspiration for the alternate but plays one of his rare "clinkers" just as he is about to reintroduce the melody. However, many of the second attempts were just as meritorious as the original effort, and a toss of the coin could have prompted the decision to release one version or the other. On that first session, Roy, Anita, and the band combined to create one of Krupa's hits, *Let Me Off Uptown*, a song that both Roy and Anita were regularly asked to perform throughout the following decades. A sturdy sax figure answered by the brass section's hat-muted figures sets the tone for the conversational exchanges that Anita and Roy share, then Anita swings her way through the "hip" lyrics. After another exchange with Roy she exhorts him to blow, and he readily obliges by punching out one of his trumpet trademark phrases (four quarter notes hit smack on the beat). The intensity of the trumpet breaks ensures that the excitement pulses through to the very last note of the piece. *Kick It*, by comparison, sounds too much like a Tin Pan Alley creation, with a vocal by the band being answered by Anita's singing. She phrases well on unproductive material, but Roy, in trying to energize the paucity of the composition, resorts to stock phrases. Perhaps he was girding his loins for a new version of *After You've Gone*. The arrangement was based on the one created by Joe Eldridge for Roy's 1937 recording, but it is considerably faster and more streamlined, allowing Roy to show that he was one of the most nimble jazz trumpeters of all time. Admirable though Roy's speed was, he could also imbue swing and feeling into the fleetest phrases. Some critics questioned Roy's taste, but for listeners who liked bravura performances *After You've Gone* became one of the most thrilling of all Swing Era recordings. Roy invariably said that this showcase was designed to get people clapping, but one sensed that he felt a degree of pride in pulling off such an amazing *tour de force*.

Whatever rancor existed in the personal relationship between Anita and Roy, it never interfered with the sense of enjoyment that comes through on the recordings they made together. Anita, after her vocal on *Stop The Red Light's On*, shouts out "Are you ready, Roy?" in a way that is full of encouragement. Roy responds with some blowtorch phrasing, creating patterns that are full of searing blue notes, his efforts adding merit to a fatuous song, competently arranged by Elton Hill. Roy often cited *The Walls Keep Talking* as one of his favorite Krupa recordings. It's a slowish piece effectively sung by Anita, with vocal interjections from Roy and some biting trumpet work that is highlighted by Gene's off-beat cymbal-playing. Growling downward runs mark the first sixteen bars of Roy's solo, then he belts out some high screamers that effectively pile on the tension. But Roy wasn't only used as a battering ram, and proves this during his sensitive half-chorus on *Skylark*.

Pass The Bounce is another vain attempt by composer Henry Nemo to write something banal enough to get the dance-hall crowds singing. Anita does her best with the fast–medium twaddle, and a beefy tenor-sax solo adds merit, and prepares the way for Roy's sterling but futile attempt to save the day. *Ball Of Fire* is much more satisfying, being a catchy, step-by-step minor-keyed composition by Roy and Gene. Like most of Roy's compositions it has an acrid flavor, but it provides a good vehicle for some driving trumpet-playing, some springy drumming, and a good, if unoriginal, clarinet solo. The work's third eight-bar section moves up a fourth and this underlines its repetitiousness, which nevertheless has a hypnotic appeal, and a curious aspect of the arrangement is the "brick wall" ending: sudden, surprising, and unsatisfactory. *Harlem On Parade* is a slice of wartime jingoism that doesn't quite ring true. Anita is again lumbered with some improbable lines, but she performs well, as does Roy in his effective trumpet solo. Lyrics for *The Marine's Hymn* came from the same writer (L. Z. Phillips). Johnny Desmond sings them with his hand on his heart, but the swing interlude and Roy's sixteen bars of improvisation sound out of place. However, Roy's vocal feature on *Knock Me A Kiss* is particularly worthwhile. The song was to have been recorded by Anita O'Day, but she declined to sing it, so Roy was hastily drafted in to vocalize; the arrangement was left in a key that was more suitable for Anita's range than for Roy's. Roy side-steps this problem and sings a fine, appealing vocal garlanded by his neat, cup-muted solo. The Krupa band nods in the direction of Count Basie's Orchestra during the early stages of *That Drummer's Band*, but identity is re-established by a vigorous duet between Roy and Gene, with Roy sounding buoyant and imaginative. Roy inserts some adroit harmonic ideas into his relaxed solo on *Murder He Says*, a Fields–Loesser creation that is well interpreted by Anita O'Day, but Anita really has to battle with *Massachusetts*, a state tribute song from two veteran writers Andy Razaf and Luckey Roberts, on which Roy has the briefest of solos.

Because of their shared successes in the *Metronome* annual popularity poll, both Roy and Gene took part in a recording session on the last day of 1941 which featured a batch of jazz stars who were that year's favorites, including Harry James and Cootie Williams. In the era of the long-playing record, worthwhile music might have emerged from the gathering, but with most of the participants being allocated only eight-bar solos the jittery results border on the absurd. Roy would have been better served if the second take of *Royal Flush* had been issued, but even that outcome would not have made the recording into anything special. Harry James takes the opening melody on *Dear Old Southland*, but again the arrangement turns out to be a series of fragmentary offerings from a distinguished cast. Krupa's enthusiasm is obvious, but Roy, in playing a fairly cautious solo, almost gets himself into a tangle, and it is left to Cootie Williams to storm his way up to the piece's concluding top "F."

Gene Krupa's enforced absence from the music business in 1943 caused his band to break up, and, even before that, the Musicians' Union ban on recording had come into effect, so the final part of Roy's stay with Krupa is not represented on issued recordings, though various airshots exist. Roy's achievements with Krupa present several tracks where his playing is only the topping on some fairly indigestible mixtures; however, when his talents were suitably featured he created several dazzling performances and one master-piece, *Rockin' Chair*. From the perfectly structured cadenzas of the introduction through to the sure-footed climb to the concluding top "F," the performance is awesome, containing as it does the most expressive ballad performance of Roy's career. Each phrase is perfectly weighted, with Roy sounding relaxed yet purposeful. He cleverly shades the middle eight by adding an attractive huskiness to his notes. Subsequently he fires off a salvo of phrases during the bridge passage, deliberately using dissonance to add drama to the performance, and strengthening the latter stages by playing a variation of the melody an octave up. The end is almost an anticlimax as Roy and a clarinettist swap simple phrases, but excitement re-emerges when Roy makes an exultant climb to the thrilling, finishing note. Roy did his best to improve on his first attempt, but, despite creating an array of impressive variations, he didn't quite capture the sheer presence and brilliance of take one.

Roy proved on *Rockin' Chair* that when he was granted the lion's share of an arrangement he always triumphed. He underlined this gift on his next series of recordings, made in Chicago with an augmented version of the band he led at the Capitol Lounge in 1943. Roy was on top form throughout this session, which can safely be counted as one of his most productive recording dates. His first task was to re-record *After You've Gone* (based on the Gene Krupa version). He does so with considerable panache, his efforts boosted by Harold West's spry hi-hat cymbal work. After brief saxophone solos Roy re-enters the fray and blows some formidable phrases that are punctuated by soft grunts. This sound often intruded into Roy's performances; sometimes it was a grunt of effort, but it could also denote that Roy was proud of an idea that left the bell of his trumpet exactly as he intended, and sometimes the grunt signified frustration, particularly when he had just mispitched a phrase. Roy next recorded a work-out on the chords of *Sweet Georgia Brown*, which was entitled *The Gasser*. It remains one of his greatest achievements, a performance packed with ingenious ideas and a grand passion. Roy, using a Harmon mute, "strolls" through the first chorus, accompanied only by bass and drums; the pianist then enters and gently adds some lightly played chords to the swinging patterns. Ike Quebec on tenor-sax plays a booting but highly rhythmic solo before Roy re-enters, blowing open phrases that create the perfect musical denouement, each of his linked ideas being given a telling impetus by the saxophone section's insistent riffing. *I Surrender Dear* doesn't quite match up to *The Gasser*, even though the two-chorus treatment is full of lovely ideas, and a bold high note ending. But Roy went on to create a monumental *Minor Jive*, on which his open trumpet conveys a captivating melancholic edge. Pianist Rozelle Gayle solos well enough but doesn't quite possess the co-ordination of the great keyboard artists. Against a backing consisting of dramatic on-the-beat phrases, Roy emotes without losing the incisive coherence that is the hallmark of all great jazz solos. A brilliant unaccompanied introduction sets the stage for an elegaic *Stardust* (one of Roy's own favorite recordings). The very slow tempo underlines the majesty of Roy's performance, which includes a spectacular two-and-a-half octave leap. Again he imparts an attractive cloudiness in his tone by making a cooing sound in his throat while blowing. A promising *Oh Lady Be Good* was cut short by the recording engineer, but *Jump Through The Window* was completed in all its glory. It's a stirring twelve-bar blues, on which Roy encapsulates some new, pithy ideas, all the while making use of his remarkable range.

Soon after returning to New York from Chicago, Roy was featured at the January 1944 *Esquire* Metropolitan Opera House concert: one of the most illustrious gatherings of jazz greats that has ever taken place. It was one of the rare occasions when Roy and Louis Armstrong were in the same line-up; the other participants were Jack Teagarden, Barney Bigard, Coleman Hawkins, Art Tatum, Teddy Wilson, Al Casey, Oscar Pettiford, Sid Catlett, Lionel Hampton, Red Norvo, and two great singers, Billie Holiday and Mildred Bailey. Roy creates some exhilarating moments on a small group *Tea For Two*. His cup-muted solo is a gem, but the final stages of the piece veer towards chaos as Roy takes the melody up an octave, leaving clarinettist Barney Bigard with nowhere to roam effectively. Roy plays an eloquent solo on *Stompin' At The Savoy*, and creates interesting lines on *For Bass Faces Only*, where his skill at bending notes adds a telling effect. On *Flying Home* his strategy of leaving gaps in the early part of his solo makes the transition to the fiery, whistling high notes of his second chorus all the more effective, aided as they are by the efforts of a superfine rhythm section. Roy is restrained and sympathetic while gently backing Billie Holiday, and equally attentive when accompanying Mildred Bailey, but only occasional moments on this concert match up to his recently completed Chicago recordings, and on *I Got Rhythm* he seems to be trying too hard to triumph over Louis Armstrong (despite Joe Glaser's instructions) and, whereas Armstrong, Hawkins, and Bigard solo for two choruses, Roy takes it upon himself to blow three, during which his musical thoughts gradually become more unruly. There's no doubt that the audience responded to Roy's efforts, but the manner of the cheering was like the frantic reactions that were later to be experienced at many Jazz at the Philharmonic concerts.

Harry Lim, who moved to the U.S.A. from Java in the late 1930s, became one of the most revered jazz record producers when he began operating his Keynote label. In January 1944, Roy was featured as the leader on one of Lim's early sessions. For contractual reasons, Roy (who recently signed with Decca) was billed simply as "Little Jazz" on a session that featured two other trumpeters, Emmett Berry and Joe Thomas, supported by Johnny Guarnieri on piano, Israel Crosby on bass, and Cozy Cole on drums; solos were democratically allocated between the three horns and Guarnieri on piano. Thomas and Berry both had big, mellow tones, but there was a nice contrast in their styles: Thomas' playing always exuded poise and gracefulness, and Berry had an emphatic yet nimble way of phrasing. Roy seems determined to move away from his recent tactics at the *Esquire* concert days earlier, and makes no journeys to the far reaches of the trumpet's range; a happy, co-operative spirit fills all four titles recorded. The second takes from the date reveal many variations, and although jazz history wasn't made on this occasion, those who like swinging, melodic trumpet-playing were well satisfied.

A week later, Roy again recorded for Keynote, this time as part of a quintet led by Coleman Hawkins. The session marked the historic moment when Roy and Hawk began working together in a front-line duo (one that was usually backed by a three-piece rhythm section). Here they are supported by the urbane Teddy Wilson on piano, the ex-Duke Ellington bassist Billy Taylor, and Cozy Cole on drums. Hawkins, as the leader on the session, puts himself firmly at the head of the pecking order, a not undeserved prominence since he was at this point much better known internationally than Roy. Roy willingly accepts the secondary role, and, incredible though it may seem, actually sounds lethargic on the first take of *S'Wonderful*. Lim's vast knowledge of jazz and jazz performers invariably enabled him to select the most fertile takes from a session; thus he was able to choose another attempt on *S'Wonderful*. He had three versions of *I Only Have Eyes For You* to select from, and chose take three, notable for Roy's handsome, burnished tone finale, though Hawkins' second chorus on take two is a triumphant achievement. *I'm In The Mood For Love* shows both men's mastery of ballad-playing, each of them capable of creating entrancing tonal light and shade, as well as finding new harmonic routes through a standard sequence. Roy had never been backward when it came to chordal experimentation, but working with Hawkins provided him with a new and challenging stimulation. The final side on the session, *Bean At The Met*, was based on the changes of *How High The Moon*. It was the prototype of many of the unison riff-like themes that Hawk and Roy later devised for their quintet performances.

Roy's next recordings were as a guest star with Charlie Barnet's Orchestra. Roy blows lustily throughout his long outing on a curious arrangement of Duke Ellington's *Drop Me Off In Harlem*, which is taken too fast and scored in a way that obscures a splendid melody. The Eldridge "chops" sound at their strongest during his 32-bar solo on Andy Gibson's arrangement of *The Great Lie*, but, spectacular though the physical achievement is, a sense of musical continuity is missing. Roy's brief contribution to *Gulf Coast Blues* is more effective and worthwhile, but even more satisfying is the *After You've Gone* that Roy made while guesting with Benny Goodman's Orchestra for a V Disk session. One might have thought that Roy had said all he had to say on that tune's chord sequence; however, his half-chorus on this 1944 version is a perfect miniature. Unfortunately, the big band that Roy took into the Decca studios in June 1944 had neither the precision nor the panache of the Goodman line-up. It recorded yet another version of *After You've Gone*, and, although Roy blows spectacularly and creates some new ideas, the band's performance is quite ordinary, with the saxophone section sounding wooly and the brass-players giving only an approximate reading of the score. Roy pays majestic deference to the melody of *I Can't Get Started*, and also adds intricate patterns of his own devising, but the arrangement is woeful, featuring some odd harmonic progressions, one in the fourth bar being positively wince-making. *Body And Soul* is more interesting, revealing Roy's innate sense of rhythm; his move to a faster tempo is both smooth and exciting, and his return to the original speed also demonstrates his extraordinary breath control. Roy plays almost continuously throughout the three sides recorded, but apart from his efforts there is nothing about the band's performance that was likely to attract record buyers.

Using a more distinguished personnel, Roy took a big band into the studios four months later and created two very worthwhile sides. *Fish Market*, devised by Roy and arranger Buster Harding, is a brooding, twelve-bar blues that opens with the saxophone section answering pedal notes from the trombones. Roy enters and blows a slightly understated cup-muted chorus; guitarist Napoleon "Snags" Allen takes over and plays a chorus that is a microcosm of the harmonic developments that were beginning to affect the jazz world. Joe Eldridge takes an innocuous alto-sax solo, then trombonist Sandy Williams cries out a series of phrases that confirm that he was a master of the blues idiom. Roy then powerhouses some high blue notes, and he continues to blow vigorously above a flag-waving ensemble, preparing the way for a final chorus in which three different themes intertwine. A commercially slanted band introduction precedes Roy's attractive rendering of the strong, angular melody of *Twilight Time*. The saxophones take over for the middle eight, then Roy shapes some warm sounding variations that are delightful; after sixteen bars of unadventurous arrangement, Roy re-enters to blow a series of attractive ideas that culminate in tasteful low note ending. The coupling deservedly proved to be one of Roy's best-selling 78 r.p.m. recordings.

In November 1944, a month after joining Artie Shaw's Orchestra in California, Roy made his first recordings with them, beginning by playing a featured part on *Lady Day*, Jimmy Mundy's compositional salute to Billie Holiday. Roy demonstrates the agility and accuracy of his cup-muted work, but the lion's share of the playing is taken up by the immaculate clarinet performance of the leader. This situation is repeated on many of the sides that Eldridge made with Shaw, even on numbers that seem to cry out for a burst of Roy's wizardry, such as the peerlessly arranged *S'Wonderful*, where Roy's role is restricted to section work. This rationing of exposure didn't apply only to Roy; even an up-and-coming young star like pianist Dodo Marmarosa rarely got more than an eight-bar slice of the action. However, the musical content and high level of the recorded performances deservedly maintained Artie Shaw's huge following; he was certainly never accused of "dumbing down" for his audiences. Eddie Sauter's arrangement of *Summertime* is ambitious and almost takes on the form of a concert piece, in which Roy is featured growling an emotion-charged plunger-muted solo. It was the first time Roy had been featured in such a role, and, according to Shaw, it led to a slight contretemps. Roy had been playing the plunger solo on all the band's gigs, but decided to dispense with the mute on the first recorded take. Shaw recalls, "I stopped the band, and Roy said, 'You don't expect me to do that growl? That's Cootie Williams, that's not me.'"4 But Shaw insisted, and never regretted taking that stand, saying years later that the *Summertime* solo was "one of the best things Roy has ever done."5 But even a short, restrained contribution from Roy greatly enhanced many of Shaw's recordings, including *I'll Never Be The Same*, *I Can't Get Started*, *No One But You*, and *Time On My Hands*. On the last, Shaw imparts an admirable warmth to his phrasing, and Roy ensures continuity by capturing exactly the same mood.

It sounds as though Roy drew the short straw when it came to picking someone to sing *Natch*, a woeful jive-talk opus (partly written by Artie Shaw). The melody just isn't strong enough to support Roy's singing of some decidedly awkward lyrics; he doesn't solo at all on this track. Most of Shaw's material was of a much higher standard, consisting of marvelous evergreens from distinguished composers: it was material that allowed Roy to produce some superlative rephrasings of melodies such as *A Foggy Day* and *Soon*. Roy also proves that he could still set the place alight musically by letting fly on the uptempo section of *I Could Write A Book*; he also plays an unrestrained chorus on Ray Conniff's inspiring composition, *My Lucky Number*. But nothing that Roy recorded with Shaw beats the ingenuity, artistry, effort, and improvisations he showed on *Little Jazz*, a composition by himself and Buster Harding. The piece was devised by the two men between shows at New York's Paramount Theater, and remains one of Roy's greatest achievements. The band gives inspiring support to Roy, particularly drummer Louis Fromm, and spurred on this, the trumpeter creates a series of sublime breaks, his exquisite tone sounding at its very best as he projects it like a great actor moderating his voice to convey numerous emotions. Barry Ulanov and Leonard Feather, in a joint review published in the June 1945 issue of *Metronome*, were totally enthusiastic about the release:

Little Jazz features Roy's trumpet throughout in a fine consistent groove, without any screeching and screaming, with wonderful phrasing and conception. We can't recall any more comprehensive illustration on wax of Eldridge's greatness.

Back in 1940 Shaw had startled the jazz world with a series of small band recordings that were issued as *Artie Shaw's Gramercy Five*. The immaculate playing of ingenious themes was given an extra dash of interest by the novel use of a harpsichord instead of a piano. Five years later Shaw recorded several sides with a new version of the *Gramercy Five*, featuring Roy on trumpet (muted throughout), Barney Kessel on guitar, Dodo Marmarosa on piano, Louis Fromm on drums (mostly using brushes), and Morris Rayman on bass—the harpsichord wasn't used. As before, the presentations were rehearsed to perfection, but the magic quality of the 1940 sides was missing, even though Shaw is admirably generous in his allocation of solo space. The persistent use of a clarinet and muted trumpet in harmony with the single notes of a guitar palls easily, even when they move into intricate unison passages. If there is a star on these small group sides it is pianist Dodo Marmarosa, whose work typifies the interesting threshold that existed during the period between the demise of swing and the coming of be-bop. Shaw plays immaculately throughout, but often hides his heart. Roy, for his part, adopts an almost sophisticated role, one not easily associated with his work on *Heckler's Hop*, *After You've Gone*, or *Rockin' Chair*. Extreme neatness marks the two Artie Shaw–Buster Harding compositions *Grabtown Grapple* (an up-tempo 32-bar theme) and *The Sad Sack* (a lightly disguised twelve-bar blues). Here Roy manages to inject a suitable degree of mournfulness into his solo, but the two unison choruses of an obvious (and slightly out-of-date) riff serve to cancel out his effort. The remainder of the pieces were written by Shaw (a co-composer, John Carleton, is listed, but this was a pen-name adopted by Shaw for business reasons). The most interesting is *Mysterioso*, a twelve-bar minor-keyed blues (with trimmings), which briefly creates an unusual, eerie mood. The precision of the performances on all these sides has to be admired, but Shaw's formulaic approach, and the general lack of intensity, now renders them as little more than charming period pieces.

The sides with Shaw's *Gramercy Five* are in stark contrast to recordings that Roy made at a November 1945 V Disk session, shortly after leaving Shaw and returning to New York. Eldridge's fiery, open-toned paraphrasing of the verse of *I Found A New Baby* (accompanied only by drums) is full of life and adventure, and the same spirit is maintained through to the effective fade-out ending. Roy's intense muted playing on *Roy Meets Horn* (based on the chords of *I Never Knew*) radiates the same feeling of enjoyment, proving that the trumpeter had lost nothing during his sojourn in California. *Old Rob Roy* also has a couple of choruses of muted magic. The 32-bar tune is catchy, as is the cleverly scored introduction. In later years Roy said this was a theme he'd like to revive, but he never got around to it.

During 1945 and 1946 Roy was still under contract to make big band recordings for Decca, but despite some energetic tries he could never hit any sort of sales jackpot. *Little Jazz Boogie* falls between being an out-and-out jazz vehicle and a commercial attempt to cash in on the lingering craze for the eight-in-a-bar piano style, but the keyboard solo is too brief. Roy takes three choruses, then blows some ultra-high notes against dissonantly arranged passages, but does so in a manner that suggests he was doing a duty. By contrast, his playing on *Embraceable You* is beautiful. The phrasing is sublime, and his variations on the melody can be counted among his most ingenious creations, his moving use of vibrato adding to a highly impressive performance that deservedly pleased Roy for many years after the session. This side might have been a success with both the jazz fans and the general public, but unfortunately the arrangement loses its way, and Roy's outstanding playing in the early stages is wasted. *Baby That'll Be The Day* is nowhere near as impressive, and sounds suspiciously like a stock arrangement. *All The Cats Join In* benefits from clever scoring, but Buster Harding's vocal lacks finesse. There's a stirring trumpet and tom-tom interlude, but little else to make the track stand out from the dozens of big band recordings that were being issued every week. *Poor John* is an unfortunate mixture of a neo-bop theme blended with a rehash of some of Roy's previously played licks, most of them from *Little Jazz*. *Ain't That A Shame* (a slow blues) has an expressive vocal from Roy, but the lyrics are too variable to be satisfactory. However, Roy creates some majestic blues-playing, this time using his top notes as a perfectly valid part of a passionate solo. The band vocal on *Hi Ho Trailus Boot Whip* is cheerful enough, and there's a lengthy and assured solo from Tom Archia on tenor-sax. Roy makes a powerful entry, determinedly soaring upwards through a series of modulations, but rhyme and reason somehow get lost and the arrangement collapses during the cluttered finale. *Tippin' Out* is standard big band fare: Tom Archia solos well but, despite Roy's noble opening phrases, he soon begins whistling out some difficult to play—and difficult to listen to—high notes. *Yard Dog* has two fine solo choruses, one from Roy, whose cup-muted ingenuities are captured to perfection, and the other from Tom Archia, which is relaxed and swinging. Trombones playing a jaunty melody over a two-beat rhythm make *Les Bounce* an interesting prospect, but Roy's trumpet-playing is at its most reckless. Things go off at a tangent, and unfortunately the attractive opening theme isn't repeated.

Lover Come Back To Me opens with a tastefully scored introduction; then Roy steps forward to play some superior variations on the melody, proving how sensitively he could inflect a great standard song. The trombones bustle in promisingly, but depart from the limelight after blowing some wrong notes, and things slide away from then on, so that the admirable appeal of the opening is, yet again, lost. The band and Roy tackle the task of re-recording the 1941 Gene Krupa *Rockin' Chair*. Roy does a superb job in re-creating his famous *tour de force*, but the copy doesn't measure up to the original. The long series of big band recordings ended with two ballad performances, *It's The Talk Of The Town* and *I Surrender Dear*, and Roy's playing on both is exemplary—he often said he liked playing ballads best of all, and his efforts here seem to confirm his words—but Decca officials were not overly impressed by anything the big band recorded, and some items like *I Surrender Dear* (from September 1946) were not issued until years later. Roy's contract was not renewed and it was to be almost five years before he again led a band in an American studio.

17

1947–55

One of the few examples of Roy's work in 1947 that has survived is an airshot recording of a radio show that he did with Flip Phillips for the W.N.E.W. Saturday Night Swing Session series. Flip, as ever, improvises fluently throughout and Roy is enjoyably explorative; his in-form "chops" allow him nonchalantly to take the melody of *Lover* up an octave. On *Honeysuckle Rose* Roy indulges in a scat-singing contest with Mel Tormé; goodwill is apparent but this doesn't prevent Roy from doing his darndest to come out on top. Tormé then takes over on drums for *How High The Moon* and acquits himself reasonably well, both in the four-bar chases he shares with Roy and in his ensemble efforts. Roy relaxedly imparts an engaging swing to the melody before leading the group into one of the bop anthems, *Ornithology*, which precedes a rather untidy jammed finale. *Flip And Jazz* is a 32-bar original that has both Eldridge and Phillips in grandstanding mood, with Flip's lines being more pertinent than Roy's, most of which are stock-licks wildly delivered. An April 1947 V Disk jam session found Roy in an all-star line-up along with Count Basie, Illinois Jacquet, Buddy Rich, Freddie Green, and Red Callender. The impromptu results were a mixed blessing. *Oh Lady Be Good* is full of spirit, with Roy's Harmon-muted solo sounding fierce and husky. The excitement mounts as Roy and Illinois Jacquet indulge in some scorching call-and-answer phrases that simmer down pleasingly. In comparison, *Jammin' On A V Disk*, despite having a satisfying solo from Roy, descends into chaos. Things begin to crumble when Jacquet (one of the greatest of jazz tenor-saxists) obliges those who were yelling for him to start honking and squealing. Thereafter Buddy Rich launches into a drum solo, catching his colleagues by surprise: to play or not to play is the question and uncertainty overtakes the entire cast, creating utter confusion.

Roy was gradually taking part in more and more big live concerts in which his playing was almost guaranteed to inject excitement. The very best of these occasions occurred when he managed to combine hot playing with a cool head. One such occasion took place during his 1949 trip to California, when he appeared at a *Just Jazz* concert (organized by Gene Norman) in Pasadena. Roy's partners were the young tenorist Teddy Edwards (blowing with poise and imagination) and Don Hill on alto-sax, whose ideas were projected like a mixture of confetti and hand grenades. Most of the band were obviously steeped in bop, but Roy makes no attempt to alter his approach. His playing on *Boogie And Blue*, after a quiet start, reveals a molten core, but his work on *Idaho* is full of fertile ideas, which include a remarkable series of stomping phrases in his third chorus. Over the coming years there were many opportunities to hear Roy's approach to concert-playing through his regular appearances for impresario Norman Granz. For almost three decades Granz organized star-studded gatherings of great jazz musicians, and presented them in concert venues all over the world. An early example of Roy's contribution to these concerts took place at New York's Carnegie Hall in September 1949 in a line-up consisting of Roy, Lester Young, Charlie Parker, Flip Phillips, Hank Jones, Ray Brown, Buddy Rich, and young trombonist Tommy Turk. Granz, who by this time had his own record company, was increasingly keen to make "live" recordings of his concerts. Happily he did so at this Carnegie Hall gathering, allowing later generations to marvel at the high standards these great performers maintained as they improvised in front of an excitable audience. Lester Young, sounding joyful and lithe, honks out a few low-register phrases that set the crowd baying for more, and Flip Phillips, also in fine form, teases the audience by repeating some rugged bottom notes without ever seeming to pander. The one musician on stage who does go over the top in his efforts to transmit excitement is Roy Eldridge. On *The Opener* (a medium–fast twelve-bar blues) Roy creates a musical scenario that was to become a regular part of his concert performances when he was playing on a blues sequence: an orderly (often sparse) first chorus, a second chorus that was full of swift fingering with one screaming high note (to command attention), then a gradual move up through the trumpet's registers in choruses 3 and 4, in preparation for a series of high riffs in chorus 5. Chorus 6 was usually replete with savagely played blue notes (usually flatted thirds and fifths), then a long succession of ultra-high notes patterned in the way a honking tenorist might operate (but three octaves above the reed-player's phrases). It was the structuring of these solos that was similar each time, not the content, for Roy continued to improvise avidly. The routines seldom failed to set the crowd cheering, but they also cemented a resistance to his work that already existed in some critics. Tommy Turk, a speedy and powerful trombonist with a fruity tone, also opted for excitement, but his brazen efforts were prone to run out of ideas. The performer whose talents seem to transcend any obstacle is Charlie Parker; his fleet phrases contain ideas that are bursting with ingenuity, all of them full of passion. Buddy Rich, Ray Brown, and Hank Jones made a suitable rhythm section for such an auspicious occasion, sensitive to the various needs of the front-line players. On a long version of *Embraceable You*, Roy takes the first solo, projecting an appealing sub-tone and sounding supremely relaxed, tempting one to make use of the Jekyll and Hyde comparison. Fortunately, all sides of his musical character were to be captured on the many recordings Roy made for Norman Granz.

Recordings made during Benny Goodman's small band 1950 tour of Europe featured the group playing at a concert in Sweden (only issued many years later on C.D.). The opening section of the show featured Goodman with Dick Hyman, piano, Charlie Short, bass, and Ed Shaughnessy, drums. The unit was augmented for a swinging *Air*

Mail Special, which has Roy easing his way in by playing a subtle 32-bar muted solo. Zoot Sims, cooler than usual, plays effectively, as does Toots Thielemans on guitar. Nancy Reed shares a duet (*à la* Anita O'Day) with Roy on *Let Me Off Uptown*, showing she was a fine vocalist, phrasing well and singing in tune, and on this number a storming trumpet and drum duet receives some tremendous applause. Roy gives a lively airing to some warm, full-toned, if familiar, licks on *Boogie Woogie*, but improvises redoubtably, if variably, on *I Found A New Baby*. Everyone parades good, lively ideas on *Flying Home*, which leads into the signing-off theme for this tour, *Stompin' At The Savoy*. Roy, and three of his tour colleagues, Hyman, Zoot Sims, and Shaughnessy, together with French bassist Pierre Michelot, made some studio recordings for *Vogue* in Paris that were issued as by King David and his Little Jazz. The session began with *King David*, a gentle twelve-bar blues on which Zoot Sims solos confidently without displaying the presence that he later attained. Dick Hyman plays two stylish "locked-hands" choruses that pave the way for Roy's cup-muted endeavors; by this time, "strolling" (with just bass and drums) was a regular part of Roy's performances, and he uses the ploy here to good effect. *It Don't Mean A Thing* is mainly a vehicle for some scat-singing between Roy and "Anita Love," who sounds happier scatting than singing the lyrics of the piece. Roy then creates an outstanding version of *Wrap Your Troubles In Dreams* (backed only by the rhythm section), where his "time," tone, and ideas are hugely impressive, and he revels in the art of creating clever harmonic "turnarounds" in the seventh- and eighth-bar sections of the tune. *Undecided* leans heavily on the arrangement made famous by the John Kirby Sextet, but here Shaughnessy's brushwork is magnificent; Roy again "strolls" to good effect. *Ain't No Flies On Me* is a pastiche of Roy's vocal duets with Anita O'Day, the saving grace being the rough-hewn, down-home trumpet chorus. However, *The Man I Love* is full of fine improvisations from Roy, who shows that he was well aware of the work of younger trumpeters such as Howard McGhee and Dizzy Gillespie; Zoot Sims swings effortlessly, and Dick

Hyman sounds dexterous and totally unflustered. A few days later Roy recorded in a quartet format, with the American pianist Gerald Wiggins, bassist Pierre Michelot, and Roy's former colleague, drummer Kenny Clarke. Their first effort was a fairly uneventful version of *Easter Parade*, elevated by some beautifully recorded cup-muted playing from Roy. The rougher side of his muted work is evident on *Wild Driver* (a faster version of Roy's tune *Roy Meets Horn*), and two choruses of boppish piano give way to a fiery display of open trumpet-playing. Roy's noble tone is faithfully captured on the highly satisfying *If I Had You*, complete with modern touches and a series of elegant "turnarounds." *Nuts* is an up-tempo blues given a cloak of exotic rhythms and featuring solos all around. Roy again explores the ballad world on *Someone To Watch Over Me*, but here Gerald Wiggins doesn't seem to make the most of the harmonic possibilities on offer. *Goliath Bounce* has some animated muted trumpet-playing, but overall it is poorly organized and devoid of an appropriate climax. At this period of jazz history, the use of a trumpet and rhythm section line-up was rare. Later, Jonah Jones made a huge success of the format by using skillful and ingenious arrangements, but that sort of planning was only intermittent on these French quartet sides.

In contrast, the sextet sides that Roy made with local musicians a few months later are well organized and thoughtfully arranged, particularly Roy's atmospheric composition *I Remember Harlem*. Here a bowed bass line sets the scene for a somber introduction, followed by Roy's sumptuous rendering of the theme, during which his open tone glows with feeling. *Baby Don't Do Me Like That* has Roy singing some light-hearted lyrics against a steady shuffle rhythm; trombonist Benny Vasseur plays a vigorous chorus, and this induces Roy to parade some inflammatory ideas during a long ride-out. *Une Petite Laitue* is a two-beat novelty number on which Roy's trumpet is silent, all his energies being devoted to singing in French a piece that was aimed at the commercial market—charming though the attempt is, it did not cause a stampede among record buyers. Jazz fans were happier with another "take" which included a trumpet interlude. *L'Isle*

Adam, a rehash of the *Swing Is Here* theme, is dedicated to a place on the Seine west of Paris that Roy used occasionally to visit on weekends. One imagines he was reliving happy memories by the rarin'-to-go mood he displays in his muted and open excursions. *Black And Blue* allows Roy to demonstrate his exquisite sense of timing. He sings the emotive lyrics in a way that demonstrates his admirably clear diction, and there's also an awe-inspiring trumpet interlude; the piece finishes with a trumpet coda that has an almost Bobby Hackett degree of tastefulness. The band session ends light-heartedly with Roy singing a jovial blues in French, entitled *Tu Disais*, which has good, forthright solos from Roy and Benny Vasseur. Roy himself still had more to play, but not on trumpet. His final efforts were at the keyboard where he recorded an infectiously vigorous piano solo entitled *Just Fooling*, following this blend of boogie, stride, and fun with further informal work-outs at the ivories, one of which was *List Blues* and the other called simply *Improvisation*. The oddity about this conclusion to the session is that Roy told Dan Morgenstern that he only recorded one number at the piano that day.

In January 1951, during a tour of Sweden, Roy recorded a compact version of Duke Ellington's *Echoes Of Harlem* in Stockholm, and, backed by a competent local rhythm section, he plays cup-muted throughout in a subdued performance that is nevertheless rich in feeling. Rugged boogie-woogie from pianist Charles Norman and a well-phrased interlude from a sextet line-up set the stage for Roy to reel off a lively vocal refrain on *Schooldays*, which is followed by four particularly satisfying trumpet choruses, all of them devoid of clichés. Roy, the singer, is even busier on *Saturday Night Fish Fry*, where he caps his Louis Jordan inspired vocal with another burst of forceful but ingenious trumpet work. *The Heat's On* has a good tenor-sax solo from Carl Henrik-Norir, and a brave half-chorus on bass-trumpet by Leonart Sundewall. Roy starts in low gear, but soon begins blowing with a power that almost unsettles his accompanists; he flies on and up, creating some spectacular phrases before signing off with eight bars of the theme. On *No Rolling Blues*, appropriate piano backing inspires a thoughtful vocal from Roy and some expressive trumpet stanzas. Vocal jocularity graces *They Raided The Joint*, as does the highly rhythmic cup-muted playing. The trite theme of *Roy's Got Rhythm* is soon despatched: here Sundewall's playing is more impressive, as is the Getzian tenor-playing. Roy creates a mélange of ideas, but this time the familiar chord sequence doesn't fertilize anything startlingly new. Roy's final Swedish recordings featured him leading his own Gramercy Five line-up, with Charles Norman playing harpsichord and Ove Roy clarinet. *Noppin' John* is a standard 32-bar sequence featuring cup-muted Roy in a calm and inventive mood. Lind takes a skillful chorus, followed by pianist Norman and guitarist Rolf Berg, who maintain a high standard of improvisation in their solos. *Scottie* is another look at a previous Eldridge composition, and here Roy jogs along for a while before being suddenly smitten with a burst of inspiration. The rest of the solos are tastefully swinging, making the overall result a pleasing reconstruction of Artie Shaw's celebrated small band recordings. Roy's Scandinavian sessions were originally issued on Emarcy (and on Esquire in Britain).

During the final week of his stay in France, Roy took part in some highly contrasting recordings (again for Vogue); four quintet titles were made with his fellow American, tenorist Don Byas. Although both men were great improvisers, the link-up didn't produce anything significant, and the recording quality on this date is poor. Roy's contributions are zestful, but a lack of rapport between Byas and Eldridge leads to some untidy ensembles, not enhanced by the overbearing sound of Armand Molinetti's drumming. Roy has some good moments on *Oh Shut Up* (which uses the tune and the chords of *Please Don't Talk About Me When I'm Gone*) stimulated by a lively shuffle rhythm, but neither of the Americans seem prepared to budge an inch during the ensembles. Scant co-operation also blights *I Still Love Him So*, where Byas' counter-melody played across Roy's muted line impairs the melody. *The Heat Is On* (*Très Chaud*) shows Byas in a better light, but Roy lives up to the title and almost boils over; the drumming is again irritatingly busy. Conversely, a stifling air of restraint spoils *Hollywood Pastime*, where the sound of the bowed bass rapidly becomes tedious. Surprisingly, Roy's muted playing here could almost be mistaken for Frankie Newton's work, and Don Byas, his head clear by now, blows some majestic phrases, but overall one feels that two great jazz musicians wasted a unique opportunity to record together in a quintet format. There is no lack of empathy on the duet sides that Roy recorded with pianist Claude Bolling; the results of their combined salute to Louis Armstrong and Earl Hines are outstanding. Although many of the phrases on *Wild Man Blues* have their origins in Louis' May 1927 performance, Roy doesn't create a slavish copy; instead he performs splendidly "in the manner" of Armstrong. The recording quality is first class, with the brilliance of Roy's tone captured to perfection. From the dramatic opening phrases (as per Louis) through to the "period" ending on the seventh of the tonic chord, it is a bravura performance in which Roy is nobly supported by the illustrious Claude Bolling; the second take also underlines both men's flexibility. Bolling's fluency is even more obvious on *Fireworks* (originally recorded by Armstrong in a June 1928 sextet). The pianist's ideas exactly dovetail with Roy's powerful reinterpretations, and the result is one of the finest trumpet and piano duos ever recorded. These two titles show what a lasting impression Louis' early playing had on Roy. They rounded off his year in Europe in an unlikely way because they were so different from the other sides he had made in France and Sweden. His trip to Europe wasn't a pilgrimage to find a new style, but during his stay he seems to have been deliberately honing a muted approach that was more sober, reflective, and orderly than his open-toned solos, which often contained explosions that created unmanageable fires.

Roy's first recordings after his return from Europe were a mixed bunch. On an August 1951 Clef date he partnered Buddy Tate on tenor, Clyde Lombardi on guitar, Charlie Smith on drums, and Teddy Brannon on piano. Brannon was the composer of the first number recorded, *Baby, What's The Matter?*, a twelve-bar blues with an eight-bar release tagged on. What emerges could be mistaken for one of the growing number of rhythm-and-blues records being released. There's some unison riffing, some light honking on tenor, a jokey vocal from Roy, and a helping of high, open trumpet-playing; unfortunately, the lyrics (by song-writing veteran Sam Theard) sound as though they were assembled in a hurry. Roy then revived his composition *Yard Dog*, taking it at a much swifter pace than his 1946 version. The tenor-playing and the unison figures again suggest an attempt to get juke-box plays, and, though Roy shows that his fingering was as nimble as ever, he is only parading licks from the past. A very slow *Sweet Lorraine* cools things down, without contributing any magic moments. *Jumbo The Elephant* is a light-hearted song dreamed up by Roy and agent Bob Astor. The band sings lustily, and Roy takes a series of neat vocal breaks, but the lyrics are a shade too obvious. The song found its target years later when Roy began singing it at concerts for schoolchildren. Tate and Eldridge solo efficiently and indulge in some hefty calls-and-answers, but subsequently Roy misses the final note of the piece (a very rare occurrence for him). Somehow this "clam" sums up the entire session, the first of many that Roy (as a leader) did for Norman Granz.

In December 1951, Roy fulfilled an ambition to record with strings. He teamed up with an orchestra assembled by arranger George "The Fox" Williams for four numbers. Roy later viewed the enterprise with a jaundiced eye, because he had to foot the bill for the arrangements and pay all the musicians involved. Unfortunately, the resultant royalties never covered his outlay. On *Basin Street Blues*, Roy uses a Harmon mute to play the opening verse and chorus. A flute drifts in and out of the arrangement, allowing Roy to discard his mute and play eight bars of gorgeous open trumpet, full of newly minted golden phrases. He then returns somewhat anticlimatically to the melody before blowing a fluffy-toned low register finale. Roy preferred his French recording of *I Remember Harlem* to this version with strings. He was disappointed that his part was truncated to allow for a flute interlude; nevertheless, the soulful sound of his open trumpet is effectively displayed against a background of violins. The scored introduction to *Easter Parade* is ponderously delivered, but

Roy bounces in and cleverly readjusts the time values of Irving Berlin's original melody, further livening up proceedings by some double-time playing. Roy plays throughout *I See Everybody's Baby*, creating strong, fierce sounds that contrast with the innocuous string-writing. This Roy Eldridge–Bob Astor composition concludes satisfactorily with a final cadenza from Roy, which ends on a sonorous low note. In weighing up the session it seems that the experiment didn't justify the time, effort, and money involved. A few weeks later Roy played an unobtrusive part in a studio group which assembled to back Anita O'Day on arrangements written by Ralph Burns. Anita sings a languid but appealing *Rock 'N' Roll Blues* on which Roy's brief burst of prominence is a declamatory twelve-bar solo. Cecil Payne on baritone is the only other soloist, but everyone in the band gives vocal answers to Anita's lines, then she, in turn, sings a wordless theme that replicates the arranged figures the band play. This is the only number with improvised interludes: Anita sings throughout an exotic *Love For Sale* and a fast *Lover Come Back To Me*. Roy plays an elegant cup-muted introduction on *Lullaby Of The Leaves*, but again the emphasis is on Anita's in-form voice. Roy's work (as part of the 1953 Metronome All Stars) backing singer Billy Eckstine was a much livelier endeavor. On the up-tempo section of *St. Louis Blues* he blows two bold, open choruses and answers the band's riffs with some ferocious blue notes; his half-chorus on *How High The Moon* is restrained by comparison, but just as satisfying. Second takes of both numbers show a wealth of variations on these M.G.M. sides.

Norman Granz continued to record his celebrated J.A.T.P. concerts, and despite the fact that many of the performances contain top-class solos, an analysis of all those available on record would often prove that even a formidable improviser like Roy Eldridge was prone to relay similar ideas in concert situations, rather like a politician on a whistle-stop election tour. Alyn Shipton (in his book *A New History of Jazz*, published by Continuum in 2001) wrote of the variable quality of Granz's concert recordings:

Although there are many great moments in the recorded legacy of JATP, there is an almost equal number of vapid chase choruses, with soloists vying to play louder, higher, and faster than one another—all of which may have been very exciting in a concert hall at the time, but make for extremely tedious listening today.

It seems pertinent to comment on the more unusual concert recordings than attempt to cover them all. Certainly the September 13, 1952 presentation at New York's Carnegie Hall was quite out of the ordinary. The Oscar Peterson Trio and the Gene Krupa Trio performed during the second half, leaving the first part of the show to a galaxy of famous jazzmen, including Roy, Charlie Shavers, Flip Phillips, Benny Carter, Buddy Rich, and Lester Young. All these players benefited by being accompanied by Oscar Peterson's Trio (Oscar, Ray Brown, and Barney Kessel) who begin by laying down some swinging introductory choruses on *Jam Session Blues*. Flip Phillips solos with his usual mixture of panache and consistency, and then the irrepressible Charlie Shavers steps forward and blows eight choruses covering a variety of moods and a kaleidoscope of ideas ranging from the rhapsodic to the gut-bucket, making sure that the listeners know that his range was, in every way, comparable to Eldridge's. Benny Carter's calm, flowing lines (on alto-sax) provide a striking contrast, but even this sage figure decides to stir the audience's vocal chords by reiterating the same single note, roughing it up as he does so. Guitarist Barney Kessel produces a batch of varying tone colors during his solo (some of which later became the stock "licks" of beat group players). An effete Lester Young suddenly becomes energized by the fervor of his colleagues' backing riffs and the propelling force of Buddy Rich's off-beat drumming. It was then left to the master of excitement, Roy Eldridge, to bring the long performance to an end with some fervent grandstanding (and a strained finishing note). The inevitable ballad medley has no sensational moments, and Roy suffers by not being close enough to the microphone for his so-so version of *It's The Talk Of The Town* (backed by Hank Jones on piano). The next item on the recording is a fantastic musical joust between Eldridge and Shavers, rightly titled *The Trumpet Battle*. The two adversaries set out by playing a brightly harmonized 32-bar theme; they then hand over to Young and Phillips who chug affably through a shared chorus before Benny Carter waxes lyrical for three choruses, leaving the way clear for the main bout to begin. Roy is first up, playing two choruses that are full of pyrotechnics and provocative phrases. Shavers responds with some capricious ideas, going on to air some of his set ploys, such as playing a series of descending chromatic arpeggios, but, just in case any listeners were still under the impression that Roy commanded the skies, Shavers then proceeds to play some dramatically high notes, which are every bit as spectacular as those aired by Eldridge. Next the two trumpeters engage in an eight-bar chase, playing two choruses that are full of fury and technical brilliance. In general, away from this hurly-burly, Roy's improvisations had a more epic quality than Charlie's, but cerebral plotting was not the order of the day, and the two trumpeters battle it out toe-to-toe. Good taste is sometimes in short supply but there is an abundance of excitement and a purposeful ending to what was a drawn contest.

Roy's next recordings (in December 1952) were made in the more rarefied atmosphere of a recording studio, where he was accompanied by Oscar Peterson (this time on organ), along with Ray Brown, Barney Kessel, and drummer J. C. Heard. Disappointingly, three of the four pieces were remakes of Roy's previous successes, the new item being *Roy's Riff*, an energetic work-out on the chords of *Everybody Loves My Baby*. Roy (muted) becomes increasingly volatile as the performance progresses, but Oscar, the master pianist, was still a long way from being a master organist and at times sounds quite pedestrian. Roy is totally relaxed on *Wrap Your Troubles In Dreams*, and remains untroubled by the minor fluffs that occur in his performance, the sound of his open tone again creating a rich timbre to fill the concluding cadenza. On this version of *Rockin' Chair*, Roy scat-sings the introduction, subtly alluding to his 1941 recording with Gene Krupa. The original arrangement is adhered to, but this version is slightly faster. Roy's "chops" sound in splendid shape, allowing him to hit the high notes with enormous power, deliberately holding them for longer than he did on the original. The best moment occurs during the opening chorus where Roy, seemingly on a whim, plays a long, descending run that resolves perfectly. *Little Jazz* is almost exactly on the lines of the Artie Shaw recording, though here Roy sounds a little more fiery; everyone enters into the spirit that Roy is projecting, but the sound of the organ tends to muddy up the backing on this track. The results from a similar session (four months later), with Jo Jones on drums instead of J. C. Heard, are a great deal more satisfying. After a quaint organ introduction on *Love For Sale*, Roy engagingly presents the melody, assisted by the elegant sound of Jo Jones' brushwork, then launches into some swinging variations without seeming to move into top gear. The lack of intensity is amply compensated for by Roy's seemingly unlimited store of ideas, none of which, in this instance, stray far from the melody. *The Man I Love*, taken at a very slow tempo, shows another aspect of Roy's mastery, namely his ability to play his notes at exactly the tempo of the piece being performed. Many jazz musicians give the impression of dragging the speed when playing at a very slow tempo, but Roy, with his inbuilt metronome, sounds totally at one, whatever the speed the piece is played at. Throughout this number, Roy also demonstrates the expressive depth of his open tone; Eldridge himself cited this as one of his own favorite performances. *Oscar's Arrangement* is a neatly planned 32-bar opus, the introduction of which is entrusted to the safe hands of Barney Kessel. The first 32 bars of Roy's solo are as good as anything he had recorded in years, but after a lively exchange with the drums a surge of over-excitement melts the shape of Roy's phrases and the continuity is lost. However, he recovers in time to play the final eight bars of the orderly theme. *Dale's Wail*, a salute to the Cincinnati disk-jockey Rex Dale, is a medium-paced, dressed-up twelve-bar blues; Roy (using a Harmon mute) is again the only soloist. On the opening chorus Roy is backed by guitar and bass, and this quiet start doesn't prepare the listener for the mighty efforts to come. The sounds of the organ seep into the next chorus, then Jo Jones enters to lay down a rock-steady beat. The volume increases with each twelve-bar segment, and this seems to stimulate Roy into playing some of the most intense muted work he ever recorded. One senses that eagerness to play made him forget about everything else, even the placement of the microphone, which makes his high, tensile top notes take on a wispy, distant quality. On and on he storms, for chorus after chorus, and in response Peterson on organ drops into the swinging groove that he achieved so often in his piano performances, the result being highly exciting jazz. One senses that even Roy's "leather lip" is beginning to tire at the end of this marathon solo, but he still has enough control to go over the finishing line in great style. This was an especial favorite with Roy, who said that he got so excited he just had to stop playing. His efforts on this date were described in *Jazz 1954* as "brilliant" and given the accolade "Record of the Year."

Excitement was scarcer on a session that Roy did with Oscar Peterson's group in December 1953. Peterson on piano does a masterful job in giving Roy attentive backing throughout, bassist Ray Brown is his usual majestic self, Alvin Stoller's drumming swings crisply, and guitarist Herb Ellis lays down an effective carpet of harmonic changes, but the spotlight remains solely on Roy through-out the session and for most of the time he sounds unusually restrained. Part of the problem is that half of the material consists of slow ballads, and skillful though Roy was at breathing expression into them, the format of featuring only trumpet on one slow offering after another creates a lack-luster feeling. There is plenty of creativity, but one feels that Roy is curbing his natural instincts even though he often said he preferred playing ballads to up-tempo themes. He said, "I can tell when I play a ballad whether a crowd is musical, because non-musical crowds don't dig ballads."[6] But happily, his powers of creating excitement were not totally inactive on this session, and things perk up somewhat on an Eldridge medium-paced original *Feeling A Draft* (based loosely on *Love Me Or Leave Me*). Here Roy's performance is steadfastly hot, and this same stomping mood enhances *When Your Lover Has Gone*. Unusually, Roy employs a growling delivery, apt for Duke Ellington's *Echoes Of Harlem*, but instead of blowing into a plunger he uses a cup mute to create the effect.

In September 1954 Roy continued the series of recordings with Oscar Peterson, with Buddy Rich on drums instead of Alvin Stoller; Roy seems to play with renewed zest and inspiration. The backing is unobtrusive on *Blue Moon* and allows Roy to prove that he has a great deal to say on this sequence, culminating his efforts with an effortless top "G." *Stormy Weather* begins mildly, but then lives up to its title as Roy creates some gale-force blowing. Even so, the track is less satisfying than the heartening *Sweethearts On Parade*, which has Roy blowing into a felt hat before handing over to Oscar Peterson, whose 32-bar solo combines grace, strength, and effortless invention. Two choruses from Peterson enhance *A Foggy Day*, but despite a worthwhile parade of ideas from Roy the piece never takes off, and, plaintive though Roy's open tone is on *If I Had You*, this recording doesn't measure up to the version he cut in France. *I Only Have Eyes For You* has the hallmarks of a live performance, with Roy mispitching here and there, yet still effectively getting his message across. Peterson again takes two distinctive choruses, but the haphazard final section of the piece is disappointing. *Sweet Georgia Brown* is fast and furious, with Roy happily offering a blend of old and new ideas, all of them effectively stoked by the virile rhythm section. Peterson again solos flawlessly but, after Roy and Buddy Rich swap a series of four-bar phrases, a red mist descends during the tumultuous finale, after which the muted interpretation of a loping version of *The Song Is Ended* seems tame.

A month later Roy took part in one of the most celebrated confrontations in the history of jazz trumpet-playing. His adversary-cum-musical partner was none other then his former protégé, Dizzy

Gillespie. These two giants were given the ablest of support by Peterson, Brown, Ellis, and Louie Bellson on drums, in routines that allowed the horn-players to spread their productive conflict over eight- and ten-minute versions of various standard tunes. The proceedings open with both trumpeters adopting a wary stance on *Sometimes I'm Happy*. Dizzy plays cup-muted and Roy uses a Harmon mute as they share affable interplay by passing the melody to and fro. Dizzy then offers some daunting, quicksilver phrases but Roy follows on calmly; each man keeps the melody in focus during their choruses before opening up boldly for the four-bar exchanges. Dizzy takes the honors on his own composition, *Algo Bueno*, and again both principals play muted; Peterson solos with power, ingenuity, and guts, magnificently supported by Bellson's impeccable brushwork. *Trumpet Blues* gives Roy the chance to revive one of his own themes. A greater sense of urgency enters the session with each brassman showing superb control in the upper register, and Peterson again cooks some stimulating fare. During the ballad medley, Dizzy, on *I'm Thru With Love*, dips into his lower register to great effect, and Roy counters with a warm, husky-toned *Can't We Be Friends?* and finishes the selection with *If I Had You*, where he takes a new look at a tune he'd often played. *Blue Moon* is challengingly brisk, but by this time both Roy and Dizzy were fully warmed up. Roy takes the melody, muted, supported by Dizzy's pretty counter-theme, and Gillespie goes on to unleash some brilliantly articulated ideas which Roy counters effectively. Mutes are dispensed with, and searing open phrases burst from the bells of both trumpets. The two rivals go upward like mountaineers; top "G"s are reached, then top "A"s and "B"s, each man settling fleetingly on these peaks before gradually descending in range and mood to a repeat of the opening statement.

The torrid beginning to *I Found A New Baby* consists of Dizzy and Roy playing fierce, random figures backed by Bellson's vigorous tom-tom work; the opening melody is calm by comparison. Dizzy solos first, then Roy effects a seamless takeover. Gillespie airs his spectacular technique but Roy's combative attitude pushes him to offer an appropriate challenge. Musical sparks fly in every direction, and for a time both men seem intent on screeching at each other. Fortunately, they eventually regroup and interact again with the tom-toms to wrap things up with a degree of neatness. *Pretty Eyed Baby* is a fun interlude with both trumpeters singing (in unison) a simple, catchy theme. Roy then scats a chorus, while Dizzy's muted trumpet doodles in the background, then, while Dizzy scats, Roy plays tasty fill-ins. The trumpeters blow against each other in eight-bar strips, then revamp the vocal, this time harmonized. Roy gives a restrained performance of *I Can't Get Started*, spiced with intriguing passing chords, then Dizzy begins a subdued rendering of the melody before offering some thrilling explorations that are peppered with effective dissonance. A satisfying cluster of cadenzas round off a superbly integrated performance. A very fast (and long) work-out on *Limehouse Blues* allows each man to demonstrate the amazing speed of their fingering, first playing muted then open, revealing great similarities in their method of phrasing. Again the pull of high altitude takes the two trumpeters away from the more fertile plateaux, and they begin playing a I-can-play-higher-than-you game, which unfortunately only produces a series of meaningless top notes. Roy and Dizzy had several combats on recordings supervised by Norman Granz. High on this list, from a November 1, 1955 studio session, is the *Krupa And Rich* album, which highlighted outstanding performances by the two trumpeters. A longer encounter, recorded a day later, put the two rivals in the company of a third trumpeter, Harry Edison, whose presence seemed, musically speaking, to preclude any head-on clashes between Roy and Dizzy. However, things were never entirely placid when Eldridge and Gillespie got together, though an aura of contentment seems to settle over this session, even if *Steeplechase* (a work-out on *Get Happy*) is taken at full pelt. In the manner of three top-class wrestlers taking part in an exhibition bout, the trio blow muted solos at one another without malice, but with lots of unhurried ideas. The much slower title track *Tour De Force* (written by Gillespie on the changes of *Jeepers Creepers*) has all three trumpeters playing open. Edison airs several of his favorite phrases, Roy digs a little deeper, and Dizzy blows some dazzling, double-tempoed runs without seeming to expend much energy. The other two trumpeters riff sturdily behind Dizzy, whose solo is followed by an effective piano chorus, then all three brassmen swap fours, amicably wrapping up this eleven-minute jog by returning to the well-constructed theme.

J.A.T.P. sessions continued to fall thick and fast during the 1950s. At a Chicago concert, Illinois Jacquet, Flip Phillips, and Roy set the scene perfectly for a drum solo entitled the *Buddy Rich Explosion*. All three horns create phrases that meld perfectly with the exceedingly fast tempo, with Roy's muted solo locking deftly with Ray Brown's stentorian bass-playing. The muted work is poorly amplified, but Roy saves the situation by easing the mute out of the trumpet in mid-phrase. This sudden doubling of volume created a wondrous effect that always delighted the listeners.

When Roy participated in J.A.T.P. studio sessions in 1953 and 1954 (as opposed to concert recordings), the results seemed to lack a vital spark. Johnny Hodges emerges as the leading contributor to the 1953 sides, displaying his usual muscular grace and emotive ideas, but in this instance the studio walls had a daunting effect on both Roy and Dizzy Gillespie (who stays mainly in the low register but still manages to fluff a lot of notes). Roy's contribution to the October 1954 session was even more disappointing. Honors here go to Bill Harris' devout swing and robust ideas on a curiously slow *Stompin' At The Savoy*, and to Buddy DeFranco's fleet clarinet work on *Lullaby In Rhythm*. On this title Oscar Peterson's keyboard brilliance is almost Tatum-like, but Roy plays a disjointed solo, fidgeting, it seems, at this very fast tempo. A West Coast studio date in 1955 saw Roy reunited with one of his heroes Benny Carter for an album aptly titled *Urbane Jazz*. Despite an abundance of mutual admiration, the blending of their talents at this stage of their careers didn't produce as much as it promised on paper. It seemed as though Carter, graceful and musically courteous, alongside Eldridge, unrestrained and fiery, might achieve the satisfying results that contrasting talents often produce when working together, but the disparity in approaches didn't, on this occasion, create magic. Nevertheless, the two men's individuality is never in question. Roy's pithy ideas are the highlight of Carter's composition *I Still Love Him So*. The trumpeter bursts into *The Moon Is Low*, but Carter restores calm with some elegant, perfectly balanced phrases. The two stars swap eight-bar phrases, with Roy trying, without much success, to rough-and-tumble Carter. A lively riff effectively rounds things off, pushed along by Alvin Stoller's inspired drumming. On an Eldridge original, *I Missed My Hat* (based on *I Never Knew*), Roy and Benny share the honors, and pianist Bruce McDonald shows that he is as effective a soloist as he is an accompanist. During the ballad medley, Carter reflects a suave sorrow on *I'll Remember You*, McDonald adds some effective touches to Billy Strayhorn's *Chelsea Bridge* (including a quote from *Au Clair De Lune*), and Roy gives a throaty rendering of *I've Got The World On A String*. *Polite Blues* lives up to its name until Roy emotes four choruses of up-and-at-'em blowing which seem too stark a contrast with the romanticism that was, by this time, the basis of Benny Carter's approach to playing the blues. After Roy's solo peaks, he gradually unwinds and joins Carter in a genuine attempt to find common ground. *Close Your Eyes* is something of a filler: the fast shuffle seems to suit both front-line players but the brief performance consists simply of Carter's interpretation of the melody backed by an Eldridge riff followed by the two men reversing roles. During the session both Carter and Eldridge project many worthwhile ideas, not all of them apparent on first hearing, but the flare and excitement of the great jazz partnerships is missing.

18

1956–65

The session with Benny Carter was in place of a postponed recording that was to have featured Art Tatum and Roy. Tatum simply forgot to turn up for the original date, and Roy and drummer Alvin Stoller were left to twiddle their thumbs until it was suggested that the two of them record some duets so that the studio time wasn't wasted. They agreed, and launched into a work-out on a 32-bar sequence aptly called *Where's Art?* Roy is said to play flugel horn here—if he does, he makes it sound mighty like a trumpet. Things never get frantic, and the overall impression is of a series of sketches for some future master-work. *I Don't Know* opens with some dramatic trumpet-playing from Roy that half-suggests the bullring. This uncomplicated minor-keyed sequence produces some intense playing from Roy, but again, it doesn't seem to be a finished product, whereas *Striding*, on which Roy remains Harmon-muted throughout, has an attractive shape. Stoller's brushwork is flawless on this excursion into fast tempo and Roy is again given the chance to demonstrate his mastery of playing good "time."

Wailing (a twelve-bar blues) allows Roy to enjoy the benefits of multi-track recordings, playing vigorous piano behind his lively trumpet phrases. Roy's fans were delighted with this curio and not displeased with the duo sides, but, interestingly, Roy made no attempt at experimentation with meter or harmonic frameworks during the numbers he did with Stoller. Roy was at liberty to explore musical pathways outside his usual remit but chose not to do so. Instead he worked within orthodox sequences over what was basically four-in-a-bar rhythms.

Two months later Roy's session with Tatum finally took place (with Alvin Stoller on drums and John Simmons on bass). This was an event that Roy had looked forward to for a long time, but the anxiety that sometimes overtook him before a big occasion surfaced, even though the two men enjoyed a relaxed friendship. Roy said, "Art was not an easy man to get to know, but I knew him as well and as long as anyone."[7] Even so, their recorded appearances together were limited to airshots from the *Esquire* 1944 concert and their participation in a *New World A'Comin'* radio show from that same year. Tatum's dazzling four-bar introduction to *Night And Day* sets the scene. Roy enters (muted) and plays the melody without adding variations, almost as if he were reading it from a song copy. He offers some tentative improvisations in the second chorus, but his phrases merely open the door for three choruses of utter brilliance from Tatum. Even Roy, the great competitor, knows that he has nothing in his locker to combat Tatum's genius. Roy re-enters and again clings to the melody, but manages to blow with increasing flair in the final section. Roy sounds more comfortable on one of his favorite tunes, *I Surrender Dear*; he plays flugel horn here, and although the tone isn't exquisite the solo is a worthy one, and the growls he produces offset Tatum's filigree backing phrases. On *I Won't Dance*, Roy again holds tight to the melody, this time in unison with Tatum, but in a display of gamesmanship Art decides to add a series of grace notes that even Roy's nimble fingers can't replicate. Roy plays a muted trumpet part effectively, without achieving anything sensational, whereas Tatum confirms his colossal talent by swinging mightily while playing the most intricate counterpoint, following this with a demonstration of masterful stride-playing. Tatum pays due reverence to the melody of Duke Ellington's *In A Sentimental Mood*, except for one fleeting quote from *Swanee River*. Roy takes a relatively delicate approach during the second chorus, tellingly inflecting the fine composition. Tatum then creates cascades of intricate runs that take him from one end of the keyboard to the other within a split second. Roy re-enters and decides that simplicity is the answer, which results in his sensitive interpretation of the supremely lyrical melody. Drummer Alvin Stoller discreetly ticks away in the background on *The Moon Is Low*—adding without distracting—and bassist John Simmons also deliberately keeps a low profile. Roy had recently recorded this tune with Benny Carter. It was apparently a number that Roy and Art used to play together back in 1933. Roy again makes a tentative entry, but later finds his feet, opening his second chorus with some purposeful on-the-beat playing. Roy's mood of determination carries through into *This Can't Be Love*, where he sounds inspired rather than daunted by Tatum's unique blend of adeptness and technical strength; Stoller's brushwork is perfect here, offering a cohesive Roy some superb backing. Roy plays Harmon-muted trumpet during the early stages of *You Took Advantage Of Me*, but, as throughout this entire session, the attractive timbre offered by the use of that mute isn't captured on the recording. After another daredevil solo from Tatum, Roy picks up his flugel horn and blows with great spirit through the final bars. Tatum's improvisations are absolutely monumental on *Moon Song*; Roy is again on flugel horn and his efforts on the final bridge constitute his best blowing of the session. Roy said he greatly enjoyed this session; I think he did—once it was all over. During the recordings, he only hints at his full potential on a handful of occasions. I suspect he played flugel horn so as not to be tempted to fly in useless pursuit of Tatum. When he did play trumpet on this date it was always muted; this may have been a ploy to disguise any signs of nervousness that could well have seeped into his open tone. The grunts (denoting pleasure and endeavor) which were, by this time, an almost automatic part of Roy's performance are not heard on this date.

A Clef album, entitled *Krupa And Rich*, enables listeners to compare the solo styles of two outstanding drummers and how they tailored their skills to the playing of an outstanding front line consisting of Roy, Dizzy Gillespie, Illinois Jacquet, and Flip Phillips. Perhaps because they were not billed as the stars of this studio session, Roy and Dizzy relaxedly create some deft solos, and both are close to their best on a swift version of *Bernie's Tune* (which features both Krupa and Rich). The trumpeters' dovetailing of chase phrases is admirably portrayed on the opening of the lively *Buddy's Blues*. Oscar Peterson sets the scene for a top-drawer version of *Sweethearts On Parade*, which has a muted Roy cleverly imparting new twists to an old melody; Dizzy in his solo uses a soft, effective sub-tone, effortlessly delivering a string of double-time phrases. *I Never Knew* is not quite as enthralling, but both this and *Gene's Blues* have impressive moments.

In January 1956 Roy took part in recordings as one of the Jazz Giants, a star-studded pick-up group that included Lester Young, Vic Dickenson, Teddy Wilson, Jo Jones, Gene Ramey on bass, and Freddie Greene on guitar. Greene's playing greatly pleased Roy, who especially liked to work with a rhythm guitarist. As each of the five items recorded averaged out to be eight minutes long, all the soloists were featured, but the lion's share of prominence fell to a revitalized Lester Young, who opens with a haunting recital of *I'll Guess I'll Have To Change My Plans*. Roy sounds utterly relaxed on *I Didn't Know What Time It Was*, delivering his thoughts via a handsome, open tone. Only on *Gigantic Blues* does Roy get carried away, but he soon retrieves a creative placidity that brings the best out of drummer Jo Jones. The outstanding track is *This Year's Kisses* (which Lester had recorded with Billie Holiday almost twenty years earlier); here Lester's playing is utterly absorbing. Teddy Wilson takes over in graceful style, then Vic Dickenson, laconic and guttural, ushers in a spectacular solo from Roy that unfolds like the narrative of a great story-teller. Roy introduces the melody of the medium-paced *You Can Depend On Me* as a preliminary to his robust middle register solo which is full of ingeniously timed runs. Lester Young wraps things up, with Eldridge and Dickenson softly blowing a backing riff that the trumpeter had recorded with Fletcher Henderson in 1936. At the time of their initial release, the Jazz Giants' recordings were hailed as being among the most inspired of the decade. They were not. They were, however, examples of master improvisers playing relaxedly, and being granted ample space in which to develop their ideas. Things sound just a little too comfortable at times, and adrenalin is in short supply. Like several other recordings that Roy was to take part in during the coming years, this date had "Mainstream" written on it in large letters, and while it was wonderful to hear a cluster of Swing Era veterans still performing admirably, the music they created was not likely to attract hordes of new listeners. The participants were preaching to the converted, and although Roy's individuality remained undiminished, his influence on young trumpeters was negligible by this time.

A month later, Roy undertook the challenging task of re-creating several of the successful solos he had recorded with Gene Krupa's Orchestra during the early 1940s. In order to take advantage of new recording techniques (the subsequent album was called *Drummer Man. Gene Krupa In Highest Fi*), Gene lined up an all-star band to revive a selection of his biggest hits, some of which featured Anita O'Day, who shared the vocal with Roy on *Let Me Off Uptown* as they had done so long before. Roy blows brilliantly, his tone benefiting from the clarity of the recording. He doesn't quite catch alight on *Rockin' Chair*, but he creates some nice, novel touches that compensate for the occasional missed note. Roy had not been part of the original *Opus One* recording but adds layers of excitement to this version with a series of high adventurous phrases; Anita's vocal is "hip" personified. Roy and Buster Harding's composition *Fish Market* turns up here as *Fish Fry* (credited to Gene Krupa). Gene's drums are well to the forefront on several of the arrangements (mostly rescored by Quincy Jones), but sound at their robust best on *Drummin' Man*. Roy and Gene inspire one another on *Drum Boogie*, and on the unfettered *Boogie Blues*. *Leave Us Leap* is a new show-case for Roy's playing, but he fails to elevate this version, playing some muddled improvisations, sounding (very unusually) as though he couldn't think what to play next; even so, the next piece, *Slow Down*, has a wonderfully intense solo that bristles with ideas. Roy isn't featured on *Wire Brush Stomp*, but plays a dainty, muted obbligato to Anita's vocal on *That's What You Think*, then emphasizes his presence with some sultry growling. *After You've Gone* was always a challenge for Roy. The tone sounds perfect but his phrasing lacks cohesion, and there are flurries of fingering that don't quite meld into swinging patterns. Roy tackles a revamped ending with gusto; undeterred by hitting a "clam," he carries on and belts out a ringing top note.

During the 1950s, many veteran musicians took part in the "bashes" held at New York's Central Plaza and at the Stuyvesant Casino. Most of the customers enjoyed a beer or two while listening to vintage tunes, many of which could be classified as "traditional war-horses," and the atmosphere was rowdy but good-natured. Some of the performers were Dixieland specialists, but many of the players involved had only a nodding acquaintance with that style. This didn't prevent them from effectively soloing on what were usually undemanding chord sequences, but when it came to playing a constructive role in the ensembles many of these stylistic interlopers opted for rabble-rousing and not the integrated polyphony of Dixieland at its best. It's not unfair to say that Roy, and the men he assembled for his December 1956 Central Plaza Dixielanders recordings, took the view that a hell-for-leather approach was needed on anything remotely up-tempo. Every man jack on the *Swing Goes Dixie* session was a fine jazz musician, but none was well versed in the art of Dixieland playing, except for pianist Dick Wellstood (by far the youngest member of the group). Nevertheless, things got off to a good start with *Tin Roof Blues*. Clarinettist Eddie Barefield plays with plenty of feeling, and trombonist Benny Morton is relaxed and inventive (Roy cited this as his favorite example of Morton's playing). Wellstood sounds commendably authentic and Roy shapes the trumpet choruses effectively. On *Black And Blue* Roy conveys an almost poetic somberness, finally taking the melody up an octave. So far so good, but *Bugle Call Rag* is less satisfying. The opening breaks are full of clever touches (including Barefield's quote from *West End Blues*), Jo Jones' drum solo is superb, and Roy's "strolling" solo is agile and interesting, but during the latter stages the full cast regroup and the result sounds as though all hell had been let loose. *Ja Da* is slow and pensive, with Roy playing quite majestically, without a trace of gruffness in his tone, and Barefield and Morton, seemingly inspired, perform their best work on the date. There is a slight trace of fever during the final chorus but things remain coherent. This is not the case on *Struttin' With Some Barbecue*, where brashness takes over once the solos are out of the way. Jo Jones is the first to jettison good taste and things go downhill from there. The same blight attacks the fast *That's A Plenty*, but there is one great moment when Roy demonstrates his amazing sense of timing by repeating the same note over and over again, ingeniously shading each repetition by syncopating it in a different way. Jo Jones backs Wellstood's stride-playing with skilled brushwork, then abandons sensitivity to produce some crash-bang-wallop drumming that invalidates Benny Morton's subtle lip trills. Two takes of *Royal Garden Blues* reveal almost identical ensemble collisions between Barefield and Eldridge; Walter Page's august bass solo is a redeeming feature. The group makes an onslaught on *Jazz Me Blues*, and produces jarringly disorganized ensembles, underlining Roy's admission that "Dixieland is not my schtick."[8] On almost every track the order of soloists is the same: clarinet followed by piano, trombone, and trumpet; two minutes' planning could have avoided that situation. Whatever, Roy was pleased with the date, and, looking back years later, said, "I love that record."[9]

Over the years, numerous live recordings taken from Roy's concert performances have reached the market. Few are remarkable by Eldridge's own standards, often being little more than musical snapshots of the great man in action. Typical was his appearance with Coleman Hawkins and altoist Pete Brown at the July 1957 Newport Jazz Festival in a generally disjointed session which gives little indication that Brown was once an important and influential jazz musician. At that same year's festival, Roy, Sonny Stitt, and Jo Jones guested with Oscar Peterson's Trio, creating a work-out that was entitled *Monitor Blues*; Roy's contribution was a six-chorus burst that was vigorous without being very inventive. He played a much more worthwhile part in a rousing *One O'Clock Jump* on which he guested with Count Basie's Orchestra, along with Lester Young, Illinois Jacquet, and Jo Jones. As usual, Basie sets the scene with his inimitable piano work before handing over to Lester Young, whose handful of choruses maintain his run of good form. Illinois Jacquet follows, blowing a series of powerful and stimulating ideas. Basie provides an interlude, then Roy launches into a ten-chorus effort that takes the piece to its finale. Artistically it is not one of Elridge's greatest achievements, but as an example of his stamina and spirit it is remarkable. The solo isn't overloaded with ideas, and, even though one senses that his chops are not at their most responsive, he steadfastly negotiates a long climb that spans the last few choruses, moving on to notes that resemble a high whistle. In the latter stages his playing is all but engulfed by the power of Basie's brass section, but Roy refuses to budge and manages an altissimo peep that tops the final chorus.

Roy's July 1957 pairing with tenorist Illinois Jacquet for *Swing's The Thing* beckoned an explosive confrontation: both were famous for their forays into the extreme high registers of their instruments and for their combative outlooks, but the recordings they made together proved they were extremely compatible. On *Las Vegas Blues* (an Eldridge riff) the two front-line partners show how well their tones blended, and behind them, the rhythm section drop instantly into a swinging groove, with pianist Jimmy Jones "comping" to perfection, aided by Jo Jones, Herb Ellis, and Ray Brown. Illinois and Roy each reel off six choruses, every one of them full of clever developments. They nudge each other into producing some effective call-and-answer patterns before reprising the opening riff. Jacquet is featured playing the seductive melody of *Harlem Nocturne* (an Earle

Hagen composition that echoed through countless ballrooms during the 1950s), his soulful tone perfectly linking with some acerbic trumpet-playing by Roy. Jimmy Jones demonstrates his full command of complex voicings on *Can't We Be Friends?* Roy enters with a swagger, but becomes gentler as the solo progresses. Ellis plays a neat chorus, then Jacquet blows an alluring solo that could only have been conceived by a top-class ballader; emotion without a trace of histrionics. Jacquet's tune *Achtung* (a pacey work-out on *I Found A New Baby*) is ultra-lively, with both horns blowing torrid phrases. During the four-bar exchanges Roy buzzes at Illinois like an angry hornet, but all ends happily with a fade-out of the original theme. Jacquet's interpretation of *Have You Met Miss Jones?* is magnificent, as is Roy's open solo in which he creates a strong new melody line absolutely off-the-cuff. A faster-than-usual *Lullaby Of The Leaves* has Jacquet powerhousing the tune, never resorting to the honking sounds that sometimes marred his on-stage performances. An inspired Roy shows his mastery of note placement but then decides to enter the stratosphere, which leads to the only ungainly moments on the date. Jacquet again takes command and brings an outstanding recording session to an effective conclusion. Ironic though it may seem, Roy confided to Dan Morgenstern that he didn't like Jacquet being "incurably competitive."

Even a workaholic like Roy Eldridge could scarcely have had a busier day than the one he experienced on October 11, 1957, when, within the space of twenty-four hours, he recorded three albums with three different line-ups. The enterprise began with Roy's first studio recording with altoist Sonny Stitt, whose fast-flowing style had gained him a considerable reputation. Roy relished the challenge of working with a much younger musician, and the overall results from the date were honors even. Despite the album being titled *Only the Blues*, the first theme, *The String*, is a 32-bar tune. Roy, muted, pours out a series of exhilarating ideas, then Stitt enters and effortlessly knocks off eight choruses, revealing a huge fund of ingenious phrases. Oscar Peterson creates a brief, incisive solo then the two combatants play a series of four-bar exchanges, during which Stitt appears to be calmly picking off Roy's ideas. Roy's three choruses on *Cleveland Blues* are impressively full of feeling, and his declamatory rise to the upper register sounds totally logical. Stitt counters with some old-time blues licks before giving way to Herb Ellis' thoughtful guitar solo. On *B. W. Blues* both horn-players sound stimulated by the boogie-woogie patterns created by the rhythm section during the opening stages (drummer Stan Levey's brushwork is particularly inspiring). The mood drifts away from boogie during Peterson's deft piano solo, then the alto and trumpet begin their skillful vying again. Undeterred by the run-of-the-mill *Blues For Bags* theme, Roy swings into six choruses of productive endeavor. Stitt follows up with some dexterous outpourings during which he inserts a witty quote from *A Stranger In Paradise*. Roy makes no move to counter this, and the piece ends with a bout of four-bar exchanges. One is left with the impression that the two men combined well without offering each other deep inspiration. There was certainly no ill feeling, and Roy willingly sat in the control booth and acted as a recording manager while Stitt played three numbers with the rhythm section. Roy's next session that day was with an entirely different line-up, featuring highly dissimilar material.

Despite being disappointed by his previous recordings with strings, Roy willingly took part in a session arranged and conducted by Russ Garcia, on which they recorded a dozen show tunes from the 1920s and 1930s in a manner designed, the original sleeve-note release said, for "late night listening." Improvising doesn't play any significant part in the endeavor; instead there is a respectful observance of the various composers' intentions. Roy's cup-muted playing sounds ideal on *It Never Entered My Mind* and *Cheek To Cheek*, and his cloudy open tone cuts through tellingly on *Can't We Be Friends?* and *How Long Has This Been Going On?* He is at his most poignant on *They Can't Take That Away From Me*, and his regal embellishments on *I Can't Get Started* form the highlight of an album that was designed to attract non-jazz listeners to Roy's playing. I doubt it if it did so, because even when Eldridge concentrated solely on interpreting the melody, he still imbued it with more jazz feeling than the general public could comfortably take.

Roy's final endeavor of the day featured him working under the leadership of Herb Ellis for an album that lived up to its title: *Nothing But The Blues*. The character of the recordings (made without a piano) is mellow rather than robust, though several of Roy's solo choruses contain just the right degree of intensity. Alongside him, Stan Getz's reflective improvisations strike an admirable balance, proving that the blues has many forms. The lack of a pianist puts added focus on Ray Brown's bass-playing, but he triumphs by constructing perfect bass lines that radiate a stimulating ingenuity. Ellis plays good solo guitar on *Pap's Blues*, but is at his best throughout the seven choruses he takes on *Big Red's Boogie Woogie*, to which Eldridge and Getz add some spirited riffs. Roy plays a muted solo on *Tin Roof Blues* that is both smooth and sad, and Getz (showing a strong Lester Young influence) captures the same mood. However, Ellis sees things differently and gives a slightly winsome rendering of the old New Orleans Rhythm Kings' favorite. On *Soft Winds* Getz plays some voluptuous phrases without ever sounding sentimental, and Roy counters with some economical but highly rhythmic choruses. The blending of guitar single lines with muted trumpet and tenor-sax produces an attractive tone color on the opening of *Royal Garden Blues* (a feature for Ellis' guitar). Getz and Eldridge each have a brief say, then drummer Stan Levey skillfully rattles out a Dixieland-type four-bar tag before Roy storms into a lively coda. Ellis' *Patti Cake* is a natty blues tune whose sophisticated chords bring forth a series of profound solos. *Blues For Janet* is a close relative of *Pap's Blues* (both written by Ray Brown): it's in a different key but repeats the same formula, namely guitar phrases being answered by the horns. Here Getz almost overflows with ideas, while Roy goes on to create a compelling mood throughout his four choruses (aided by Levey accenting the off-beats). The final cut of the session was a medium-paced, quirky theme entitled *Blues For Junior*.

The guitarist takes center stage for most of the time, but in brief solos Getz (ethereal) and Eldridge (almost elegant) provide the alternate highlights. The two men were never close friends, but this album proved how effectively their contrasting approaches could be in tandem. Roy later said that he thought Getz was at his very best on this album.

But it was another tenorist, Coleman Hawkins, who was the most important of Roy's musical partners throughout the 1950s and 1960s. They worked together in various line-ups, but it was their performances together in a quintet format that produced so many outstanding recordings. Rather than trawl through the enormous number of studio dates, radio airshots, and live concert recordings featuring them together, it seems wiser to concentrate on their most auspicious achievements in five-piece line-ups. Their appearances (for Norman Granz) in the fall of 1957 certainly produced some outstanding playing. Although the original mono and stereo albums were issued as *Coleman Hawkins And Roy Eldridge At The Opera House*, not all the music was recorded at the Chicago Civic Opera House. Some was taken from a subsequent concert at the Shrine Auditorium in Los Angeles. The position was further complicated in that the original stereo release had some takes that were different from the mono album, with Roy performing *The Nearness Of You* on one and *I Can't Get Started* on the other. A recent C.D. issue has helped clarify the situation. Every selection shows that Roy and Hawk were in tremendous form, backed by three members of the Modern Jazz Quartet, with John Lewis on piano, Connie Kay on drums, and Percy Heath on bass. John Lewis' comping sounds unusually tentative at times, but overall the experiment of pairing Roy and Hawk with this rhythm section paid off, and Connie Kay, who had worked with Roy earlier in the 1950s, seems particularly to enjoy the spirit of the occasion. The first version of *Bean Stalkin'* (on the chords of *Idaho*) has lucid improvisations from Hawk and Roy, but the second attempts are infinitely superior. Hawk sounds even more purposeful, and Roy's solo is a masterpiece of linked phrases. Relaxed invention glorifies the first attempt on *The Walker* (based on *Stompin' At The Savoy*); Hawk creates a wealth of new ideas on the second version but this time Roy is less fluent. Comparisons between one performance and another reveals just how much the two men improvised on stage—not just in note selection but also in the contours of the solos. The rhythm section sounds a little unsteady on *Tea For Two*, but Hawk and Roy sail through the opening, replacing the melody with the variations they called *Bean Soup* (the verse is included as a bonus). Roy strolls his way through a chorus full of scintillating ideas, then tops what he has already played by removing the mute in mid-phrase and blowing some dynamic open figures. A few shrill samples from Roy's "whistling" register punctuate his highly mobile phrasing, but in general he proves he was there to play cohesive jazz rather than to please the gallery. On *Kerry* (riffs based on *Sweet Georgia Brown*), Roy expounds new thoughts on a sequence that was very familiar to him, moving from deep, low notes to his top register via perfectly articulated three-octave arpeggios. On a version of *Stuffy* from this same period, Stan Getz and trombonist J. J. Johnson augmented the quintet line-up. Roy, stirred by Connie Kay's drumming, lights a few fireworks, but soon realizes they are superfluous, and settles down to produce a flood of fine ideas that co-exist admirably alongside consummate solos from Hawkins, Johnson, and Getz.

Later that year, Roy and Hawk were briefly featured (as part of the fifteen-piece Count Basie All Stars) in *The Sound of Jazz*, a televised extravaganza which included a plethora of great musicians. Both the sound-track and a studio date were issued on record. Roy is in fine form on both versions of *Dickie's Dream*, playing muted on the *Columbia* recording session and open on the television show. On television his phrases are in complete accord with the ultra-poignant mood created by Billie Holiday on *Fine And Mellow* (Doc Cheatham. backed the singer on the studio version). As usual, Roy's spheres of activity juxtaposed club dates with big occasions like *The Sound of Jazz*, television appearances on Dave Garroway's show, and (together with other J.A.T.P. musicians) taking part in Nat "King" Cole's coast-to-coast television show. Whatever the occasion, Roy was a model of enthusiasm, and in 1957 was featured on several meritorious airshots of broadcasts from New York's Café Bohemia, including some fertile sessions alongside Ben Webster. From the same venue he broadcast an adventurous *Sweet Georgia Brown* with the house band, and a sublime *Lover Come Back To Me* that was faded out through lack of time. Another of these Café Bohemia airshots featured Roy bravely attempting to play the Gene Krupa version of *Rockin' Chair* accompanied only by a quartet.

Early in February 1958 Roy recorded an album whose title, *Laughin' To Keep From Crying*, seemed all too apt for the occasion. It was to be Roy's final session with Lester Young, who died a year later. By 1958, Young, ravaged by alcoholism, was a forlorn figure whose debility showed in his playing. On this recording he made the extraordinary decision to resume playing the clarinet, having neglected to perform on it for years. The results need sympathetic listening, though there are some touching moments, and some moving low register sub-tone work. Lester's sparse, wistful rendering of the first bars of *They Can't Take That Away From Me* give a flickering indication of his genius, but if his reputation was judged on this recording the verdict would surely not be favorable. *Salute To Benny* is a long blues that tends to meander, despite a stellar cast consisting of Roy, Lester, Harry Edison on trumpet, Hank Jones on piano, George Duvivier on bass, Herb Ellis on guitar, and Jo Jones on drums. The pairing of Roy with another trumpeter could have resulted in a musical scrap, but here the two men are deliberately non-confrontational, as though they wanted to save the ailing Young from any hullabaloo involving vigorous blowing. On *Romping*, another twelve-bar blues, Lester reverts to tenor-sax, but his solos are no more rewarding. Hank Jones, as ever, solos ingeniously and accompanies with an almost telepathic understanding, Duvivier plays cleverly and powerfully, Ellis is in top form, and Jones' drumming is totally sympathetic, but overall the results disappoint. Edison displays considerable drive, but Roy mispitches several high notes. In an effort to save the day, the two trumpeters create some riffs, but despite not blowing at full power they come perilously close to engulfing Lester's by now feeble tone. Lester begins playing *Gypsy In My Soul* as though he had just woken up, Eldridge and Edison take muted solos, then Lester re-enters, lagging uncomfortably behind the beat. The date ended with *Please Don't Talk About Me When I'm Gone*, which was tantamount to graveyard humor. Roy introduces the melody and Edison plays an artful middle eight; he tended to use a lot of "trademark" phrases but all of them swing impressively. There are solos all round, but the rhythmic momentum displayed by Lester's colleagues makes his own sad efforts sound like a winding-down exercise.

In stark contrast, *Coleman Hawkins and Confrères*, recorded that same month, is full of vigor, imagination, and inspiration, and a *joie de vivre* surely filled the studio as Roy and Hawk created one of their finest albums. The five-piece line-up has the redoubtable Hank Jones on piano, George Duvivier on bass, and Mickey Sheen on drums. Jones' superfine introduction to *Sunday* sets things up perfectly for Roy to sketch out the melody, with Hawkins creating a supporting line that is a joy to hear. Huge toned phrases thunder out from Hawkins throughout the date, and Roy's open and muted playing is faithfully captured in praiseworthy sound quality. *Hanid* (built on the harmonic extensions of *Dinah*) is perhaps the most remarkable offering from an outstanding date, with Hawkins creating powerful, ingenious, craggy music and Roy playing highly swinging, seamless phrases. For a long time I underrated this Hawkins solo, but now realize that it was one of his monumental latter-day achievements. *Honey Flower* (written by Hawkins) illustrates the two horns working perfectly together as their rich tones blend perfectly for the long exposition of the medium-paced tuneful theme. Roy plays an almost perfectly constructed Harmon-muted solo, then Hawk, sounding bold and muscular, brings forth ingenuity after ingenuity, the neatly arranged finale wrapping up this sublime musical parcel. On *Nabob* (also by Hawkins), Roy sounds at his most relaxed, though all his phrases retain a wondrous vibrancy. There is a long bass feature and some delightful piano-playing then Hawkins again shows that he was in commanding form, and Roy re-enters for a reprise of the pleasant sixteen-bar theme. The session underlined the empathy and shared inspiration that Roy and Hawk enjoyed. Writer Nat Hentoff wisely gave his reason for the success of the partnership:

> Roy is less apt to become over-excited when with Hawk. In other company Roy often follows a string of solos, which by his criteria are lukewarm in feeling, and, almost as if by compensation, he'll explode higher and louder than he might have originally intended. But Hawkins keeps the temperature up all the way.[10]

The year 1958 was a highly productive period for Roy as far as his recording activities were concerned. Particularly satisfying were the sessions he did under Johnny Hodges' leadership beginning in April of that year. Roy had a tremendous admiration for Hodges' talent, particularly for his ability to play the blues. Roy himself never played the blues better than on these recordings with the great alto-player. There are no moments of madness or of grandstanding; instead there is a series of solos offering a fascinating mixture of joy and sorrow. Roy plays open throughout and rarely uses his top register, phrasing more sparsely than usual. Hodges is his incomparably consistent self, but also in fine form on the session were Ben Webster (expansive and heart-warming throughout) and Vic Dickenson, whose wry slant on the blues was never successfully copied by anyone. Pianist Billy Strayhorn provides sensitive accompaniment without sounding fussy, drummer Sam Woodyard never stifles the soloists and bassist Jimmy Woode plucks metronomic four-in-a-bar patterns. The recordings benefit considerably from being well planned; in this respect it was almost like the 78 r.p.m. sessions that most of the participants had taken part in years before. Proper themes were played; there were bridge passages, worked-out endings, and a level of organization that brought rich dividends in setting all the performers at ease. There was no question of having long strings of aimless solos delivered without having a cogent, arranged beginning and end; these principles of having an arranged framework on which to build improvisations make the three sessions that Roy did with Johnny Hodges so productive. The fare on Hodges' albums was not all blues, and *Just A Memory* is a splendid example of ballad-playing by Hodges, Eldridge, and Webster. Lawrence Brown (who replaced Vic Dickenson) rarely played better than he does on *Let's Fall In Love*, but it is on blues like *Preacher Blues* and *Big Shoe* that Roy conveys unfaltering passion.

Easy Now, a glowing R.C.A. session from this period, featured Roy working on trumpet and flugel horn alongside cornettist Ruby Braff. Again there are no madcap moments, each brassman generally playing a call-and-answer role to the other, or providing fill-ins to the melody, though in the jammed finish on *Someday You'll Be Sorry* there is some exhilarating interplay. Occasionally the two horns play in unison with Mundell Lowe's single-note guitar, creating a lithe, attractive timbre. Pianist Hank Jones fashions a particularly plaintive solo on *Willow Weep For Me*, showing his ability to capture the mood of every kind of song, with Leonard Gaskin on bass and Don Lamond on drums making up the six-piece line-up. Often when Roy plays muted Ruby is open-toned and vice versa, a ploy that is particularly effective on *This Is My Lucky Day*. Braff's emphatic playing of the melody of *The Song Is Ended* is countered by Roy's bold flugel horn solo, arguably one of the best he ever recorded on that instrument, full of supremely melodic ideas, delivered with enormous fluency. The rapturous spirit that fills every bar of *Give My Regards To Broadway* makes it the outstanding track. Roy is again on flugel horn, cohesively sharing a sign-off with Ruby that moves from a bustling pace into a series of out-of-tempo cadenzas, full of rich-sounding low notes that underline the emotive powers of both Roy and Ruby. Both show solemn expressiveness on Jerome Kern's *Yesterday*, but despite the profundity of Ruby's lower register and the biting sound of Roy's muted playing, the results don't measure up to the many splendid moments on the session.

During the late 1950s and 1960s, Roy and Coleman Hawkins spent a good deal of time playing at various festivals and concerts both in the U.S.A. and abroad. The results were variable, with Roy often succumbing to a sea of faces by creating riotous phrases, introducing them as a matter of course, usually after playing a smooth, quiet first chorus. Such was the case at the July 1958 Antibes Festival in France, when Hawk, Roy, and Vic Dickenson shared the front line with two French reed-players, Michel de Villers and Hubert Jospin, for a fast version of *Undecided*. Clarinettist Jospin plays two swinging, facile choruses, but de Villers seems keener on quoting snippets of other tunes than in telling his own story. Hawkins sounds tough and uncompromising, as though he were eager to be somewhere else. The final riff chorus brings confusion, with drummer J. C. Heard being caught on the hop, thinking that the band were going to repeat the main theme. The misunderstanding brings the piece staggering to a halt. Bizarrely (also in July 1958), Roy took Heard's place at the drums for a set with Sidney Bechet at Cannes, where similar confusion occurred on *Rosetta*, with the band being uncertain whether Roy was going to play a four- or eight-bar tag on drums; the result was chaos. This was a pity, because Roy had backed all the soloists sensibly and effectively, changing his drum patterns to suit various instrumentalists. He acquits himself with some adroit brush-work on *Once In A While*, and this time, after switching to sticks, plays a smooth roll to make a tidy ending. Roy's drum solo on *Sweet Georgia Brown* is full of spirit and swing, but again nobody is quite clear (even Roy, one suspects) as to its intended duration. As a result, Bechet curtails things by cutting into the drumnastics, and this time the band unites in some positive sign-off phrases.

An unusual assignment during Roy and Hawk's stay in France was their taking part (with other J.A.T.P. stars) on recordings (originally issued on French Barclay) that were used on the sound-track of the movie *Les Tricheurs*. Roy and Stan Getz revive the spirit of the *Nothing But The Blues* album on the medium-paced blues that took the name of the film, each playing three thoughtful choruses. On *Phil's Tune*, Roy is subdued but stately, playing throughout the piece in a restrained manner, but nevertheless producing phrases that have a haunting tonal quality. Hawkins has a solo track on *Clo's Blues*, and Gillespie performs on *Mic's Jump*.

But the presence of Hawkins and Eldridge did not automatically ensure that an album would be outstanding; in fact a 1959 session, *Ben Webster and Associates*, was positively disappointing. A third tenorist, Budd Johnson, was also present. All three were favorites of Roy but, despite his efforts, a desultory feeling hangs over the proceedings and eventually engulfs him. The most ingenious moments of the date come from Coleman Hawkins' four-blues choruses on *De-Dar*, but few of the other solos catch light, despite the best efforts of a fine rhythm section: Ray Brown, Jo Jones, Jimmy Jones on piano, and Les Spann on guitar. The session leader, Ben Webster, acquits himself on *Time After Time*, though his contributions are sporadic elsewhere and mostly devoid of continuity. Ben begins his three choruses on the slowish *In A Mellow Tone* in the manner of an overweight dignitary who has dined too well. The tread is a little too heavy and precise, as though he does not want us to know that he is befuddled, and when Ben (at his best a masterful musician) enters chorus two of his solo imitating the cry of a distressed seal, we know that nothing much is in store on that particular offering. This one tune lasts for over twenty minutes; every soloist has his chance but the outstanding contribution is by Budd Johnson. Budd was never a great original, but he was capable of great performances, as he proves here, always sounding as though he was enjoying himself. Roy's Harmon-muted solo goes along with the tide, and here and there he manages to inject his own brand of zest into this lethargic session. Things were livelier in October 1959 when Roy and Hawk took part in California's Monterey Festival. Part of their duties there involved them being part of the *ad-hoc* backing group that accompanied singer Jimmy Witherspoon (along with Ben Webster, Woody Herman, Earl Hines, and others). Roy and Hawk have subsidiary roles on most of the numbers, but each is given a burst of prominence: Roy on *Big Fine Girl*, where his rough-toned solo soon occupies the upper floors of his register, much to the cheers of a good-natured crowd. Hawk's moment comes on the slow blues, *When I Been Drinkin'*, where the down-to-earth start to his solo is nothing less than startling.

Happily, Roy and Hawk were featured a good deal more on two albums taken from a live appearance at the Bayou Club, near Washington, D.C., where they were accompanied by local musicians Don Wilson (piano), Bob Decker (bass), and Buddy Dean (drums). On this 1959 date the two guest stars blow chorus after chorus in order to keep things swinging, creating solos that were full of memorable jazz. Roy's feature on *I Can't Get Started* contains several new "slants," and on *Bean And The Boys* (based on *Lover Come Back To Me*) he blows with great gusto without ever losing the strong thread of his attractive ideas; Hawkins too turns in another extraordinary performance. On *How High The Moon*, Roy, not in keeping with his usual method, quotes from *The Hawaiian War Chant*, and Hawk is on to this in a flash. After amusing themselves with this fun interlude, piling variation upon variation, the two men neatly glide into the *Bean At The Met* riff; the mounting excitement produces some over-ambitious drumming but happily there's a safe landing. *Basin Street Blues* has a fine air of freshness, with Roy producing a chorus of subdued mastery and Hawkins creating some futuristic ideas. Roy has a brief attack of frenzy on *Vignette* but Hawk is again brilliant, as he is on an inspired *Body And Soul*. The two great men work their way through a program of evergreen compositions, including *Blue Lou, Soft Winds, Birth Of The Blues*, and *Just You, Just Me* in a way that exemplifies their shared inspiration. Their playing is little short of prodigious. For Roy and Hawk this was probably just another gig, but for posterity it is a remarkable example of two supremely talented jazz soloists improvising to their hearts' content.

Some months after being part of the Newport Rebels, who

performed live in July 1960, Roy became part of a Candid studio recording session that featured several of the Rebel participants, led by bassist Charles Mingus. The results proved to Roy (and the jazz world) that he could work constructively with younger musicians. Mingus, demonstrating his tone and power, plays the opening melody of *Wrap Your Troubles In Dreams*. Roy follows on, playing a muted chorus of the melody, gnawing his way around the tune before emblazoning some open-toned variations culminating in a series of trumpet cadenzas, which inspire some ingenious answer phrases from Mingus; one senses that Roy is enjoying having his musical imagination tested. The medium-tempoed *Mysterious Blues* is a two-bar motif, repeated six times. Despite its sparse content the theme establishes a fertile mood for Roy's three muted choruses. Altoist Eric Dolphy, described by Roy as "A good saxophone-player,"[11] cries out some intricate phrases, then trombonist Jimmy Knepper blows a thoughtful muted solo that doesn't contain a single superfluous note. Enter Mingus, displaying enormous energy and lively ideas couched in a consummate technique, each of his choruses containing some fresh delight. Roy, anxious to re-establish his presence, blows six open choruses using a series of rugged, high notes to good effect—this isn't gallery playing, it's pure passion. A ruminative *Body And Soul* allows Roy to share some new thoughts on a sequence that always stirred his imagination. Dolphy gives full vent to his considerable individuality, but the best moments occur on the blues *Me And You*, which has Roy's playing thriving on the carpet laid by Mingus' indomitable bass-playing, and, stimulated by Mingus' choice of notes, Roy effectively inserts some modal runs into his solo. Genuine emotion pours out of Roy, and when Mingus plays a series of recurring low tonic notes Roy responds with a fascinating mixture of primitive and contemporary ideas. Tommy Flanagan's subdued piano solo strikes exactly the right note of contrast, and prepares the way for Roy's final buildup, which climaxes in a series of almost mellow phrases shared by Mingus and Eldridge. Roy had the last word by blowing an ultra-low pedal note, which brought an appreciative "Yeah, Baby" from an admiring Mingus. Much fine music had been created at a session which Roy had approached with some trepidation. Roy beamed as he told a young trumpeter who was at the session, "We're still trying, ain't we?"[12]

The success of Jonah Jones' "muted jazz" recordings (featuring just a trumpet and rhythm section) stirred almost every prominent trumpeter from the Swing Era to make at least one attempt to move into this lucrative field. Roy's venture was issued as *Swingin' On The Town*; it contained many subtle touches but was about as restrained an album as he ever made. The rhythm section was one that he worked with regularly at this time: British pianist Ronnie Ball, bassist Bennie Moten, and drummer Eddie Locke. The team work is exemplary, but the intensity of the venture could be described as simmering rather than cooking. Roy's task is to present a lightly embellished version of evergreen songs, including a new version of *When I Grow Too Old To Dream* (one of the first pieces he ever recorded); on many of the tracks Roy uses a cup mute, but is wise enough to know exactly when his unique open tone is needed to spice up the neat, orderly arrangements. On a bouncy version of *Sweet Sue*, Roy re-created part of a Bix Beiderbecke solo (recorded with Paul Whiteman in 1928). Much was made of this by some critics, who linked Roy with the work of the late, lamented cornettist, but Roy was adamant that he had never been influenced by Beiderbecke, and on the album he simply inserted part of an arrangement he had performed with Speed Webb's Band in 1930. As if to underline his point he moves from Beiderbecke's phrases into a theme that he and Coleman Hawkins had devised on the chords of *Sweet Sue*. Roy's cup-muted rendering of *I've Got A Crush On You* is a model of sensitivity, right until the ending when he tags on what can only be described as "polite funk." On the slow ballads *Dreamy*, *Easy Living*, and *Misty*, Roy offers some delightful inflections; Ronnie Ball's tremolo-playing on *Easy Living* provides an incisive touch in what is an undemanding routine. Roy stretches out a little more on the medium-paced *But Not For Me*, blowing sturdily into a Harmon mute here and on the more exploratory treatment of *All The Things You Are*. On *Song Of The Islands*, Roy uses a straight mute, one suspects in order to duplicate the sound that Louis Armstrong created on his 1930 recording of the piece. Intentional or not, the result is reminiscent of Louis, but during a deft piano solo Roy changes to a Harmon mute and becomes entirely himself again, playing a brief series of breaks that prove the volcano was still active. The strangest of the twelve tracks is *Bossa Nova*, which, via multi-track recordings, has Roy playing plunger-muted trumpet accompanied by his own piano, fender-bass, and drum work. It's a worthwhile novelty (just) because of the generous swing that the performer generates in his various roles. Roy usually settled into a boogie-woogie or barrelhouse groove when he played piano, but here he creates an effective block-chorded solo that rocks along triumphantly.

As Norman Granz often pointed out, Roy never failed to try his utmost whenever he played the trumpet, but sometimes, no matter how hard he tried, he failed to summon the co-ordination between brain, lips, and fingers that was needed for a performance to be outstanding. The magic was certainly absent from Roy's playing on a Jazz at the Philharmonic tour of Scandinavia in November 1960, despite being part of a line-up that included Coleman Hawkins, Benny Carter, and Don Byas. Roy creates some interesting, well-spaced ideas during the early part of his solo on *Take The "A" Train*, but on *Indiana* and particularly on the fast blues entitled *Brigitte Bardot* he sounds close to desperation; however, he saves the day with a muted version of *You Go To My Head* which has tenderness and warmth. On *All The Things You Are*, Stan Getz took Benny Carter's place in the line-up, joining Hawkins and Byas in a triumvirate of immortal tenor-saxists, each of whom parades hundreds of intricate ideas on Jerome Kern's stimulating composition. Roy's task is to blow a softly muted opening melody and a restrained chorus, leaving all the glory to the saxophonists. One of the most unusual recordings that Hawkins and Eldridge made together was the April 1961 *Riverside* album on which they accompanied veteran blues singer Ida Cox. Most of the material consisted of slow twelve-bar blues, on which Roy and Hawk offered sympathetic accompaniment, helped by Sammy Price's assured, rolling piano style. Roy chose to use a buzz-mute on several of the tracks, and it certainly produced an appropriate tone color for his solo on *Death Letter Blues*. One senses that Roy is curbing his natural boldness on some of the fill-ins, blowing gently so as not to detract from the venerable efforts of the former star. *Lawdy, Lawdy* offers the most solo space for Roy and Hawk, allowing Roy to hit a satisfying groove during his two choruses, egged on by Sammy Price's virile playing.

Roy's freelance recording activities included a February 1962 Fontana session with guitarist Elmer Snowden, a bandleader with whom Roy had worked with thirty years before. The pick-up group consisted of Bud Freeman on tenor-sax, Jo Jones on drums, Ray Bryant on piano, and his brother Tommy on bass. Roy is undoubtedly the star of the session, doubling trumpet and vocals; his singing sounds at its most cheerful on Louis Jordan's 1949 hit *Saturday Night Fish Fry*—then, stimulated by an infectious shuffle rhythm, he blows some apt phrases that climax in a high note finale. The novelty piece, *Schooldays*, follows a similar pattern, vocal followed by a dramatic trumpet solo from Roy that oozes presence. Elmer Snowden is featured on *Basin Street Blues*, and although his improvised lines are satisfactorily shaped, they are delivered in a sound that suggests Nashville, Tennessee. Ray Bryant plays an authoritative piano solo, then Bud Freeman, who has to contend with a heavy-footed rhythm section, blows two lusty choruses followed by Roy's two proclamatory segments. Unusually, Roy indulges in some plunger-muted playing on *Loveless Love*; Ray Bryant is superb, then, using a buzz-mute, Roy improvises ingeniously before stamping out the melody on the final chorus. The session ended with Roy singing and blowing effectively on *One For The Money*. Again his vocal is full of spirit and humor and his trumpet work is strident but exciting.

A few days later Roy began recording another album with Illinois Jacquet. Their previous collaboration, made five years earlier (relying mainly on informal head arrangements), had been a triumph, one of the best albums Roy ever made. The 1962 creations, for the Epic label, relied heavily on written arrangements and a bigger line-up. The orchestrations (mostly by Jimmy Mundy) are pleasant to listen to, but the spirit of inspired abandon that benefited the previous release is missing. Roy has brief outings on a brace of Jacquet blues compositions, on each occasion taking the one chorus low, one chorus high option. *Indiana* is remarkable, not only for its fast and furious pace, but also because Jacquet switches to alto-sax for four compelling choruses. Roy's strolling ploy comes into operation, but not, on this occasion, to great advantage. The person who emerges with honor throughout is Sir Charles Thompson, whose piano accompaniments are perfect.

Roy is accorded an eight-bar muted solo on *How Now?*, which he fills without achieving glory, but on *Satin Doll*, in a solo of the same length, he creates the perfect miniature, easily his best work on the entire date. As one of Herb Ellis' All Stars, Roy took part in a June 1962 session that produced four tracks for *The Midnight Roll* album (on Epic); trumpeter Frank Assunto is on the rest of the recording. This was a genuinely relaxed affair, with Ellis sounding close to his best, being part of a well co-ordinated rhythm section consisting of Ray Bryant, Gus Johnson on drums, and Israel Crosby on bass (sadly this was Crosby's last ever session; he died shortly after completing it). Roy's colleague in the front line was Buddy Tate, who always seemed able to settle down quickly in varying musical surroundings. Here he relaxedly produces muscular, swinging phrases couched in a deep "Texas tenor" tone. Tate's placidity proved to be infectious, and Roy goes through the four numbers without incinerating a single solo, all the while producing lively, interesting jazz. His paced solo on *Broadway* soon moves up a gear or two, and he adds a guttural edge to his tone without attempting to force the pace artificially. Roy is perhaps a little too laid back on *Gravy Waltz* (a tune by Ray Brown), but he inserts a host of fresh, lively ideas during his four choruses on *Roy Showed*, his swinging endeavors being helped on by Gus

Johnson's assertive drumming. The almost eerie sound of Roy's buzz-mute opens proceedings on *It Don't Mean A Thing*, and later he plays hot and open for two choruses, creating fervent phrases that stay on track. Ray Bryant follows on, masterful as usual, then Roy shares a fade-out ending for an album that was satisfying without being sensational.

During Coleman Hawkins' August 1962 booking at New York's Village Gate, he was joined by two guests: Roy Eldridge and Johnny Hodges on alto-sax, the three front-line players being accompanied by Hawk's usual trio: Tommy Flanagan on piano, Major Holley on bass, and Eddie Locke on drums. The one day get-together was recorded with great success. A loose version of *Satin Doll* has a round of top-class improvisations from the entire cast, with a last chorus that is built on Roy's ability to blow thrilling high notes. Roy's clear, open tone blows the melody of *Perdido*, and Johnny Hodges, the master of graceful strength, follows on to blow a series of choruses all of which have a magical quality, combining poise and passion. The warm phrases flow ceaselessly, all seemingly perfect examples of musical form. Roy only half-succeeds in replicating this strategy, but runs into several layers of clichés. Hawkins blows some robust ideas, then a succession of eight-bar exchanges between the front-line musicians underline the class of all the performers. There were no weaknesses in Hodges' armor but his strongest suit was the blues. His work on *The Rabbit In Jazz*, a slow twelve bar, displays his consistency, his abundant feelings, and his glorious tone. Roy makes his approval clear by shouting encouragement before creating a loquacious solo that begins on his lowest notes. This time he climbs sensibly onward and upward to the highest rungs of his remarkable top register, never once faltering. Few musicians could have followed this solo effectively, but Hawkins is on hand to reaffirm his genius. One wishes that this front line had recorded together more often.

Roy worked regularly in Ella Fitzgerald's accompanying group during the early 1960s, and during this period (in October 1963) made an album entitled *These Are The Blues*. Roy played only a subsidiary part on various eight- and twelve-bar sequences, often sounding distant enough to be in the next parish. However, his solos have plenty of feeling and the right degree of boldness, and he makes his identity inimitable even in eight-bar outings on *How Long Blues* and *Cherry Red*. He takes an evocative solo on *Jail House Blues* and is unfalteringly passionate throughout his double chorus on *Heah Me Talkin' To Ya*, well supported by Gus Johnson on drums, Wild Bill Davis on organ, Herb Ellis on guitar, and Ray Brown on bass. No one can doubt Ella Fitzgerald's supreme artistry, but the blues were not her forté, and her magnificent voice never quite captured the stark simplicity that is at the root of all great blues performances. As for Roy's work with her, no matter what the occasion, ranging from a European concert in 1957 (that produced *It Don't Mean A Thing*) to a 1972 presentation in Santa Monica, the trumpeter never sounded at his best when sharing the stand with Ella. At Santa Monica, a *C Jam Blues* featured Ella scatting light-heartedly in turn with Al Grey, Stan Getz, Harry Edison, and Lockjaw Davis, but when Roy finally joins the exchanges he doesn't seem quite comfortable, and even his usually formidable tone sounds pinched and thin. One of Roy's more torrid contributions to an Ella Fitzgerald recording took place at the 1965 Juan Les Pins Festival, where he blew a scorching eight-bar solo on *Just A Sittin' And A Rockin'*, but the brevity of his contribution underlines the restricted role he was required to fulfill.

Those who attended the Sunday afternoon Limelight/Xanadu recording session that took place at New York's Village Vanguard on March 14, 1965 describe it as a memorable affair, but the sound picture created by Roy, Coleman Hawkins, Earl Hines, Oliver Jackson on drums, and George Tucker on bass makes for rather disappointing listening. *C Jam Blues* has its moments, but not many. Roy sets the ball rolling by blowing nine muted choruses, creating some interesting, jagged edges without building up to a telling climax. Hawkins gets a big hand from the lively audience for presenting a mixture of complex patterns and unelaborate riffs—Hines plays magnificently without attempting to take over the session. The great pianist swings into *Sunday*, one of Roy's favorite tunes; the trumpeter is in good form, producing a series of lip trills that make a good impression on the friendly crowd. Roy introduces the melody of *Take The "A" Train* and zips out three choruses that promise much but then dissolve into a near freakish display of his highest notes; he makes up for the aberration by playing a contemplative *The Man I Love*. Earl Hines plays an effectively romantic introduction for the Gershwin melody and backs Roy carefully for a while, but then becomes overemphatic in his chording, creating phrases that resemble martial music. Roy solos throughout a poorly balanced *Blue Moon*, creating a nice feeling of understatement, but, on *Undecided, I Can't Get Started*, and *Blues For Old N's* he is accompanied by only bass and drums (Roy referred to this line-up as his "Hungarian Trio"). Jackson and Tucker lay down a firm rhythmic background, which Roy acknowledges with shouts of encouragement, but on *Undecided* his muted work is off-microphone, and this makes things sound lopsided. Roy discards the mute and plays some chase phrases with the drummer, but his lip starts to weary and he flounders slightly in trying to reach an altissimo final note. *I Can't Get Started* produces a rather sketchy performance from Roy, but he blows with more intent and enterprise (both open and muted) on the blues. From this same period, his long exposition on *Now's The Time*, recorded at the Tenth Annual Charlie Parker Memorial Concert, underlines his ability to present endless variations on the twelve-bar blues format. The recording, made at Carnegie Hall in March 1965, was originally issued on Limelight.

19

1966–85

Excerpts from two club sessions (issued on Pumpkin) provide the only recorded mementoes of the Roy Eldridge–Richie Kamuca Quintet which flourished intermittently during the 1960s. The first (from August 1965) gives a clear picture of the two co-leaders creating relaxed improvisations that were neither combative nor rancorous on a set of tunes that were "Mainstream" faithfuls. Roy launches *Sweet Sue*, repeating the solo from his Speed Webb days that he'd aired on record a few years before. Kamuca's tenor-sax style contained echoes of the work of several jazz greats, but at his best he created lots of original ideas, and though he had a formidable technique he rarely went in for braggadocio displays. As a result Roy never felt he was in a contest with Richie, and musically they hit it off well. On *Comin' Home Baby*, a 24-bar minor-keyed theme, the bass and drums set up a fast Charleston beat which creates a dramatic introduction. Kamuca sounds ethereal at the onset of his solo, but his airy phrases gradually take on a bulkier form. Roy, in turn, starts almost aimlessly but gradually builds up a head of steam, making valid and exciting use of his top notes. *Hackensack* (built on the chassis of *Lady Be Good*) has Kamuca gliding through the changes. Roy matches the tenor-saxist's velocity, then, after a compact piano solo, plays a series of uninhibited exchanges with drummer Eddie Locke. Roy's open tone sounds at its richest on *Stompin' At The Savoy*, and

Kamuca's deliberately laconic answers gell perfectly with Roy's phrases, inspiring the trumpeter to blow three of the most fertile choruses he produced throughout this entire era. Kamuca creates light and shade, maintaining a flow of satisfying ideas, and this spirit is carried on in Dick Katz's polished piano work, supported by Tommy Potter's apt bass-playing. The group's second session (from March 1966) is nothing like as enjoyable. The two tunes recorded were both associated with Duke Ellington's Orchestra, but neither Roy nor Richie sound at all inspired, and at times are beset by tuning problems. Neither of these classy players disgrace themselves, but their lightweight endeavors are made more obvious by pianist Dick Katz's two bewitching solos.

During Roy's brief 1966 stay in Count Basie's Orchestra, he recorded an album in a sextet led by Basie's trombonist Grover Mitchell, which was later issued under Roy's name and entitled *The Nifty Cat Goes West*. Basie's Eric Dixon played tenor-sax and flute on the date and also did the arranging, Norman Keenan was on bass, Bill Bell on piano, and Louie Bellson on drums. This studio session took place in July 1966 during the period when Basie's Orchestra was working at the Basin Street West club in San Francisco, and it provided Roy with more solo space than he got during any of his evenings with Basie. One senses the pleasure Roy got from the freedom the date offered. He's thoughtful and relaxed on *I'm Beginning To See The Light*, admirably reflective on *Willow Weep For Me*, and full of spirit during his exchanges with Louie Bellson on *Blue 'N Boogie*. On *Oh Gee* (a subtle twelve-bar theme by Matthew Gee), Roy devises some new twists, determinedly seeking new routes through old territory. None of the solos on *Things Ain't What They Used To Be* is particularly revealing, but Eric Dixon on tenor-sax (sounding like a heavyweight Paul Gonsalves) is pleasingly explorative on *A Wong Came Herb*, and Roy, in his three-chorus solo, takes the opportunity to release some of the frustration that had built up during his tribulations with Basie. Roy's 32-bar solo on *Satin Doll* is the high spot of the album; there isn't a single wasted phrase in this beautifully crafted chorus, which benefits from the mood set by Eric Dixon's graceful flute solo. This one album is the only recorded item of merit from Roy's stay with Basie. The sides he made with the full Count Basie Orchestra are hugely disappointing, not because Roy played badly but because he is allocated only minimal exposure. On *Basie Goes Broadway* his task is simply to play the melody of *Mame* for sixteen muted bars before answering the saxes with some open phrases. He stages a high note finish in an attempt to make something happen, playing the final phrases in a shared coda with Basie. On *It's Alright With Me*, Roy plays a soft, muted melody, then takes a carefully played open half-chorus. Roy said that the only number of the batch that gave him any pleasure was *Here Comes That Rainy Day*, where his emotive open tone relays the evocative melody. These meager allocations were all that Roy got, but on another album with Basie, backing the Alan Copeland Voices, his role is even more subsidiary, being restricted to wispy, tightly muted fill-ins. By comparison the space afforded to Roy on recordings he made for Jackie Gleason during the mid-1960s is bountiful, even though the arrangements are commercial in the extreme. Roy and Charlie Ventura (on tenor-sax and bass-sax) were booked to spice up what may be classified as elevator music, even though the album was released as *For Lovers Only*. Roy doesn't play on every track but provides muted melody on ballads such as *Love Is Here To Stay* and *A Taste Of Honey*; understandably he sounds half-hearted on *Call Me* but provides a glimmer of excellence on *It All Depends On You*. Roy never seemed to want to talk about this date, or one on which he guested with Ray McKinley's Orchestra, though he did go so far as to say that he liked what he played on a version of *Nobody's Sweetheart* that he made on a freelance date with the Casa Loma Orchestra.

Roy's playing is given ample prominence on the Fontana double album he made in Europe with the touring *Jazz From A Swinging Era* package in the spring of 1967, but his efforts on this trip rarely showed him at his best. The overall achievements of a star-studded line-up consisting of Roy, Buck Clayton, Bud Freeman, Budd Johnson,

Vic Dickenson, Earle Warren, Sir Charles Thompson, Oliver Jackson, Bill Pemberton, and Earl Hines were impressive, causing Buck Clayton to say that the double album they made in Paris was "the best mainstream session ever recorded." That was going too far, but fine solos were certainly created within the various permutations of the illustrious musicians on that tour. Roy sounds rather fidgety during his three-chorus outing on Buck Clayton's composition *Into The Blues Bag*, and he is no more relaxed on Buck's *Night Cap*, where his phrases seem reluctant to leave the trumpet smoothly, creating an effect reminiscent of a great tennis-player temporarily losing co-ordination while serving. Roy takes a well-calculated chorus on *Indiana*, but when he starts to become more expansive his tone develops a sort of gurgle. On this number Roy and Buck share a vigorous chase; Buck begins urbanely, but still Roy counters wildly. Buck remains relaxed and inventive, then suddenly ambushes Roy with some thrilling phrases that seem to increase Roy's agitation. At the end of the piece, Buck cooly but emphatically hits a clean top "G," as if to prove a point to Roy. Roy and Buck also duet on the Eldridge composition *Très Chaud*, using mutes to play the theme in harmony. Roy articulates more cleanly here, but the ideas he produces are tried-and-true ones from his past repertoire; however, he plays an interesting and daringly timed 32-bar chorus on *Swingville*. Roy adds a few novel touches to *I Can't Get Started*, a feature he had played countless times. All goes quite smoothly until Earl Hines begins his solo with a display of keyboard pyrotechnics that threaten to obscure Roy's achievements. Roy responds with a demonstration of power and passion that regains the limelight; a few wrong notes are created in the process, but some exciting phrases take shape. Concert recordings from various locales on that long tour show Roy in better form but still not at his best. On a date in Stuttgart, Germany, his determination pays off on another version of *Into The Blues Bag*. Despite Buck having problems with his teeth on that trip, he often plays higher than Roy, creating many valid phrases in the top register. Roy tries to use his "whistling" high notes as a rejoinder, but although he hits them he doesn't hold them, and on a concert version of *Indiana* he again sounds ill at ease after Buck's three fierce choruses. Roy balances things up with a masterful ballad recording of *Body And Soul*, but definitely overstretches himself in trying to whip up a storm at the conclusion of Earl Hines' piano feature on *St. Louis Blues*.

It was to be almost four years before Roy again recorded in a studio session. Amazing though it now seems, there was no demand from record producers for Roy's services as a sideman or as a leader (in fact, it had been almost a decade since Roy had taken a band of musicians selected by himself into a recording studio). Roy had been over-recorded in the 1950s and a lot of those issues were still in the racks, unsold. There was a hardy minority of "Mainstream" jazz fans for whom Roy had gained a special place of esteem, but overall the jazz-buying public's tastes were changing drastically. Roy was no longer thought of as a jazz experimenter, but rather as a jazz patternist, whose solos were based on the thousands of phrases he'd devised in the past. He was certainly still a formidable trumpeter, but many of the mainstays of his work, such as the sudden forays into his top register, now lacked the element of surprise; instead, an esoteric phrase from Miles Davis was what many jazz fans found more satisfying. Roy wasn't scuffling for work but the lack of recording sessions was, he felt, symptomatic of a general lessening of interest. It was in this climate that he decided to work regularly at Jimmy Ryan's club, much to the surprise of some of his fans.

Shortly after Roy began his long stay at Ryan's he was again given the opportunity to make recordings as a leader, able to choose his sideman and the numbers they were to record. For this November 1970 New York date, Roy used only drummer Oliver Jackson from the line-up he worked with at Ryan's. The rest of the sextet consisted of Nat Pierce on piano, Tommy Bryant on bass, and two of Roy's old friends, Benny Morton on trombone and Budd Johnson (who did the arrangements) on tenor- and soprano-saxes. The results were an enjoyable middle-of-the-road session, without a trace of Dixieland. Roy wrote five out of the six numbers, the sixth being *Ball Of Fire*, which he had co-composed with Gene Krupa almost thirty years earlier. Nat Pierce plays eclectic, often vigorous piano throughout the session, and Budd Johnson offers a wide gamut of tonal effects on both tenor- and soprano-saxes without ever sounding as though he was in top form. It was a mixed session too for Benny Morton, his efforts ranging from an effective buildup on *Ball Of Fire* to a rather meandering solo, marred by intonation lapses, on *The Nifty Cat* (the title track of the *Master Jazz* album). However, on *Cotton*, a tune of Roy's that suggests a blending of *Summertime* and *Yesterdays*, Benny creates a beguiling effect by playing tightly muted, soft, simple lines. Roy's best moments occur on *Wineola*, a blues he regularly sang, the stanzas of which had a variety of pedigrees. He delivers nine light-hearted vocal choruses with obvious relish, and the blues choruses he plays at the beginning and at the end have an incisive, authentic feel. On the fairly somber *Jolly Hollis* Roy gets his message across without any grandstanding, and plays flowing open trumpet on *5400 North* (the address of a Chicago studio). He skips through his first 32-bar chorus on *The Nifty Cat* before emitting a few obligatory squeaks on the second, and that done he resumes his spate of creativity. Roy's solo on *Ball Of Fire* begins brilliantly but then tapers away somewhat, yet still retains all the hallmarks of Eldridge's unique individuality. Thus Roy was once again on record, in good form as he entered a new decade. The compositions could have been stronger, but the trumpet-playing offers a fine memento of a jazzman who refused to be thought of as a veteran. Writer John McDonough listed *The Nifty Cat* among the top three albums Roy ever made.

In December 1971, Roy took leave from Ryan's to play at A Tribute To Louis Armstrong concerts held in San Remo, Italy. Also on the bill were Bobby Hackett, Earl Hines, Albert Nicholas, Alton Purnell, and some talented European musicians. Roy gave a sensational performance on *The Man I Love*, creating what was possibly one of his top ten ballad recordings. First he curls up against the melody, gradually developing a passionate exposition of Gershwin's masterpiece, moving inexorably through variations of the tune, aided by pianist

Guido Monusardi's confident accompaniment. Roy uses his high notes to great effect, hitting them with a bell-like clarity. After the piano solo Roy builds architecturally on the chords of the middle sixteen, then swoops to play the melody an octave up, climbing to a difficult high note finish without a trace of uncertainty. The vocal on *Wineola* is cheered by the appreciative crowd, Roy's enthusiasm giving no clue that he sang this song every time he ever played at Ryan's. The jam session on *Perdido* opens with a chorus of chaos as the seven-piece front line jockey for a position somewhere near the melody. Roy makes sure he is heard by soaring above everyone else during the middle eight; the soloists then blow two choruses apiece with varying degrees of success. Albert Nicholas' dignified contribution on clarinet has a quaint old-world air of politeness, but others attempt to batter their way into the audience's heart. Roy sounds almost desperate to succeed, whereas Bobby Hackett's two choruses are full of graceful melodic ideas that obviously please the audience. A confused ensemble, as much like a traffic jam as a jam session, ends a recording that has some bleak moments but also a minor masterpiece in the shape of *The Man I Love*. The results were issued in Europe on C.B.S.

Under Norman Granz's auspices Roy spent a good deal of 1972 touring Europe, taking part in various concert recordings including one in Sweden with The Jazz Giants, which consisted of Benny Carter, Eddie "Lockjaw" Davis, Al Grey, Oscar Peterson, Louie Bellson, and Niels-Henning Ørsted Pedersen on bass. On the slowish *Jim Dog's Blues* Roy sounds happy and inventive, responding enthusiastically to the bass and drum figure that backs his first two choruses. Less satisfying is Roy's contribution to *Undecided*. He plays two well-paced choruses, full of deft ideas, but then it's showtime, and high wails and whistles pop out of his trumpet bell. But, yet again, he gives a divine rendering on his featured ballad: *Cherry*—a tune he had never previously recorded. His one-and-a-half chorus routine is full of delightful inflections delivered in a fat, warm-sounding tone. He enters the high register only in the latter stages in order to underline a musical point, but then moves gracefully downwards to end on a low, sensuous trill. During that same year, as part of The Kansas City Seven, Roy took part in a Pablo-recorded German concert that also featured Count Basie, Lockjaw Davis, Al Grey, Freddie Greene, Norman Keenan on bass, and Harold Jones on drums. On a fast medium *In A Mellow Tone*, Roy sets the ball rolling, giving a debonair edge to some swinging phrases, but during the second chorus he begins an ascent into cliché land where he stays to blow some familiar figures. On the fast twelve-bar blues title track *Loose Walk* Al Grey adopts a powerhouse approach and Davis (so familiar with Basie's backings) plays at his most uninhibited. Roy and Basie play musical tag for a chorus, then Roy leaves the chase and shapes some supple lines, unusually inserting quotes, one from *Yankee Doodle Dandy* and another from *Il Travatore*. The version of *I Surrender Dear* wasn't among the best of Roy's achievements, but the most curious aspect is Basie's piano introduction, which sounds as though he were trying to recapture the time he spent accompanying silent movies. However, Basie comes into his own on Roy's *5400 North*, beginning with typical single note interjections and ending with three choruses of stride-playing that rocks along mightily. Overall, this was a more successful concert than the group's efforts at the Salle Pleyel in Paris (where Eddie "Cleanhead" Vinson was also featured). A heavy two-beat feel on *Broadway* seems to preclude the prospects of any easy swing, and Roy, in trying to arouse the audience, hits a spate of mispitched notes.

A curio from this period is a blues recorded at an all-night session in Pescara, on the Adriatic coast of Italy. The get-together followed a July 1972 concert that Roy had played in Najadi. Roy agreed to attend the informal gathering, but politely and firmly declined the chance to play because he had to catch a plane at 7 a.m. However, as had happened so often in the past, once he heard the live music, he got out his trumpet and blew until dawn. Part of this informal session featured a long, slow, atmospheric blues in which Roy's relaxed phrases, rarely moving out of the middle register, are clad in a not unattractive rasp. Other solos by John Lewis on piano, Charles Mingus on bass, and Charles McPherson on alto-sax are also highly expressive. This unusual memento of a summer night's blowing was issued on *Philology*.

After Roy, Basie, Al Grey, and Lockjaw Davis returned to the States they took part in an August 1972 concert in Santa Monica, California, working this time with Ray Brown and Ed Thigpen, together with guest stars Stan Getz and Harry Edison. The selection of tunes (*In A Mellow Tone, Loosewalk*, and *5400 North*) was the same as that featured in Europe, with Roy repeating *I Surrender Dear* but garlanding this version with many new, emotion-laden ideas. Getz, as ever, is full of ingenuity, but detached at times, whereas Davis seems determined to make his physical presence felt. Al Grey takes a similar approach, but too often reveals that his store of phrases is limited. Harry Edison plays a witty *She's Funny That Way*, and keeps up with Roy for every move of the way on *5400 North*, sharing Roy's ability to imbue every phrase with "time"; Oscar Peterson replaced Basie on this number. Finally, Ella Fitzgerald scatted for chorus after chorus on *C Jam Blues*. Roy, Lockjaw Davis, and Al Grey played concerts together, including working as The Carnegie All Stars, but they never built up much rapport as a front line. It was as though they couldn't be bothered to work out any themes, or even establish the phrasing of the melody when they played in unison. The ensembles on *Somebody Loves Me* (from the July 1973 Newport Festival) are woeful, and on *Avalon* even a long, rambling drum solo seems an act of mercy. Roy's valiant approach wins the plaudits of the crowd, but his best moments occur during his delicate rendering of *Stardust* (complete with verse).

In June 1973, Roy took part in a neatly arranged session (for Chiaroscuro) led by Buddy Tate, which featured an all-star cast: Mary Lou Williams (piano), Steve Jordan (guitar), Milt Hinton (bass), Gus Johnson (drums), Illinois Jacquet (tenor-sax), plus Tate and Eldridge. The two tenor-saxists are kept apart except for a four-bar chase on *Sunday*, but each produces absorbing results in their various solos. Roy plays well enough, without ever moving into top gear. Even so, his improvisations have a lucid, searching quality. He enjoyed the four-in-a-bar style of Jordan's guitar playing and responds on *Rock-away* with some ingenious non-frantic blues choruses, later creating some fast-moving, sweet-and-sour phrases that sit well on the chords of *Medi-2* (composed and arranged by Mary Lou Williams—who is in admirable form throughout the date). Roy leads off on *Sunday* with a sprightly cup-muted solo and returns to play the concluding chorus, which culminates in a rather directionless finale—conversely, his solo on *When I'm Blue* is notably well structured. Overall it was a friendly and musicianly session in which the talented participants only occasionally touch the heights of which they are capable. Two months later Roy made one of his least satisfactory albums on a date he shared with tenorist Paul Gonsalves. Paul was in poor health and died within months of this session; at times he seems to be struggling to get through the date, and this must have affected Roy, who shared an easy friendship with the tenor-saxist. It sounds as though Roy was unable to warm up properly on this occasion and, although he contributes some cutting phrases to *I Cover The Waterfront* and *Body And Soul* by judiciously using his "froggy" tone, there are few noteworthy moments from the trumpeter. Roy's husky vocal on *Somebody Loves Me* offers some entertainment, and his two trumpet choruses show that he was trying hard to dig out a nugget or two, but the final, improvised ensemble proves that, despite their friendship, Roy and Paul were uneasy musical partners on this occasion. A lack of cohesion also blights (yet another version of) Roy's blues *5400 North*. The clever counter-melody that Roy and Paul play alongside Cliff Smalls' piano solo on *Body And Soul* adds a novel touch, as does Roy's variant of *The Hucklebuck* which he uses as a second part to the melody of *C Jam Blues*, but these are fleeting glimpses of inspiration. Smalls' on piano, Eddie Locke on drums, and Sam Jones on bass contribute power and guile in their backings, but Gonsalves seems, at times, unable to get in synch with them; however, the tenor-saxist conveys some magic via the stark soulfulness of his opening chorus on *I Cover The Waterfront*. Nobody stops trying, but no enduring music emerges from a session that was finally issued on Fantasy some years after it was made.

Roy's brief trip to Europe to record for M.P.S. with Swiss singer Miriam Klein resulted in the aptly named *Lady Like* album, on which Miriam often sings uncannily like Billie Holiday. There's no question of caricature; the vocals have their own validity, being fine examples of adept phrasing and accurate pitching. Roy doesn't play an enormous part in the proceedings, but makes his inimitable presence felt during several solo interludes within the loosely scored arrangements. His muted 32-bar solo on *Comes Love* is restrained but effective, and his tone sets the scene perfectly on *You've Changed*, which contains a superlative solo from tenorist Dexter Gordon. *What A Little Moonlight Can Do* has a long piano solo from Vince Benedetti, but Roy plays a telling obbligato without attempting to relive the excitement of his original recording with Billie Holiday. Roy gives a plaintive account of the opening melody of *The Man I Love*, leaving the principal solo spot to trombonist Slide Hampton. He does, however, move into top gear on his *Fine And Mellow* solo, opening with a dramatic, perfectly articulated high note that presages a moving exposition of the blues. On *I Cried For You*, taken more swiftly than Billie's version, Roy and Dexter Gordon each take highly creditable solos on the least swinging number of the set. Roy emphasizes the appropriate mood in his muted backings on *Body And Soul*, but is close to his best on *Yesterdays*, where he creates an impeccable solo that is both dark and tender.

In 1974, Roy did two contrasting sessions with singer Joe Turner, one with the Trumpet Kings (Roy, Dizzy Gillespie, Clark Terry, and Harry Edison); these produced four tracks that illustrate the togetherness that is regularly forged when vastly experienced jazz musicians work with one another. None of the soloists reach their peak, but the improvisations and the singing are generally satisfying. But Roy's recorded meeting with Joe Turner in June 1974 (for the Pablo label) produced musical results that, at times, border on the ludicrous. The album's issue undoubtedly dented Big Joe Turner's massive and deserved reputation. Roy's role in the musical mayhem is a subsidiary one: he simply co-exists alongside the sounds of an electric organ, a powerful guitar, and some pulverizing off-beat drumming; Roy is only heard in the distance, as is Al Grey on trombone. Roy's big moment is his eight-bar solo on *Morning Glory*. The accompanists get the chord changes nearly right for the trumpeter's brief excursion (on the middle eight), but unfortunately get the chord sequence hopelessly wrong for the main theme. Joe Turner, for whom that song was a triumph on his *Boss Of The Blues* album, chose not to get involved in any disputes and sings his lines, seemingly untroubled by the laughable mangling of the changes. Joe was in a strange mood that day, and on the title track *Life Ain't Easy* offers some stream-of-consciousness lyrics, issuing his brand of philosophy in unconnected stanzas—none of which makes any sense. Roy plays a bold introduction, then hangs around briefly to see if there is any direct route out of a muddled mess. Having got away with singing whatever came into his head, Joe decided to try the same tactics on *For Growin' Up*, and makes unresolved comments about various people including his grandparents, linking these observations with mundane thoughts about nothing in particular. Roy gladly blew the concluding riff, took his money, and went home.

A happier occasion took place late that same year when Roy played on one of a series of duos that Oscar Peterson recorded with various trumpeters. Oscar, perhaps mindful of the success of *Dale's Wail* years earlier, decided to play organ on five of the seven tracks, but although his organ-playing had greatly improved in the intervening time, nothing that he and Roy recorded matches that 1953 creation. Nevertheless, there is some astonishing playing from both Roy and Oscar on a swift version of *The Way You Look Tonight*, with Roy unreeling skein after skein of eighth notes, all brimming with jazz feeling, doubtless encouraged by a barrage of adroit piano chords. In his solo Peterson gives a remarkable demonstration of stride-playing, then each man plays unaccompanied for half-chorus thrusts; unlike many of Roy's "combats" these exchanges suggest team work and a friendly spirit. Each of the numbers has its moments, but the swinging, carefree feeling on *Between The Devil And The Deep Blue Sea* (on which Oscar produces a daring solo on organ and Roy blows spirited open trumpet) is an outstanding track, as is the gentle *Bad Hat Blues*, which is full of invention. Happily, Roy's "chops" stayed in fine fettle throughout the date.

In April 1975 Roy and the regular line-up he worked with—Joe Muranyi on clarinet and soprano-sax, Bobby Pratt on trombone, Eddie Locke on drums, Major Holley on bass, and Dick Katz on piano—made an album entitled *Roy Eldridge And The Jimmy Ryan's All Stars*. Roy produced the album, which presented a selection of the most popular numbers the band played at the club; unfortunately, no ballads were included, but apart from that, the album offers an accurate picture of the sextet's work. *Wineola* is naturally included, but Roy sounds almost too anxious to please during the first two choruses. He then settles down to sing nine verses that bewail life's pay-outs; in this version there are no climactic trumpet phrases. *Cute* is a feature for Eddie Locke's impeccable brushwork, *Bourbon Street* has a lively Joe Muranyi vocal, and *All Of Me* show-cases Major Holley singing and bowing simultaneously (*à la* Slam Stewart). Roy sings during an effective, if rather showy, arrangement of *St. James Infirmary*, and also vocalizes on *Black And Blue* (both titles have eloquent soprano-playing from Muranyi). The all-round strength of the band is apparent on a neat but spirited version of *Beale Street Blues*, on which everyone solos. *Sing, Sing, Sing* doesn't quite come off, though Roy creates electricity during his fierce opening exchanges with Locke's buoyant tom-tom work. Roy's best moments occur on *Between The Devil And The Deep Blue Sea*, where, following some neat clarinet-playing, he blows two ingenious choruses, adding light and shade to his phrases very effectively, and the final ensemble uses a riff that Roy had created during his days with Teddy Hill forty years before. Roy is magnificent on an impromptu blues, *Last Call At Jimmy Ryan's*, where he blows a handful of exquisitely subdued choruses, increasing his volume as the other two front-line players enter to back him with long notes. The album has a few uneven moments, but then, so did most nights at Ryan's.

To ring the changes for Roy's next release on the Pablo label, Norman Granz offered him the chance to record an album that featured Roy's vocals. Roy was delighted to accept, particularly as the June 1975 recordings were to be made in New York, which allowed Roy to use Eddie Locke on drums, making up a rhythm section comprising Oscar Peterson, Ray Brown, and Joe Pass on guitar. Pass solos well and plays elegant fill-ins, and Peterson never fails to provide Roy with rolling splendors, full of rich harmonies. Roy's singing radiates his irrepressible spirit, but sometimes his pitching is a little suspect and his vocal range stretched—overall a case of too much of a good thing. Roy follows the lively vocal on a fast version of *Sweethearts On Parade* with three choruses of muted trumpet that unfortunately sound slightly sour, Joe Pass' two choruses are polished and mellow, and Peterson marshals the rhythm section perfectly. Roy's best vocal efforts are on *Willow Weep For Me* and on *Gee Baby Ain't I Good To You?* (where his Harmon-muted solo achieves artistic understatement). Roy and Ray Brown duet on the opening chorus of *All Of Me*, and Roy goes on to improvise a rampant chorus before singing a cheerful vocal; Peterson's piano solo is momentuous. *I Want A Little Girl* is purely vocal, but there is some determined trumpet-playing on *I Can't Get Started* and *On The Sunny Side Of The Street*. The only blues, *Stormy Monday*, sounds a little too light-hearted to be truly effective, and *Let Me Off Uptown*, where Roy gruffly sings his own role and then imitates the rejoinders that Anita O'Day recorded, survives simply as a novelty offering, one that is redeemed by some fiercely blown trumpet.

From the various tracks that Roy recorded at the July 1975 Montreux Jazz Festival in Switzerland, two performances stand out. The first is a version of *Sunday*, with Benny Carter, Zoot Sims, and Clark Terry, on which Roy produces three free-flowing choruses which profit from the powerful swing of Bobby Durham's drumming, using the full drum kit to great advantage. Clark Terry takes the melody in the final chorus, allowing Roy to blow a piccolo part that ends on a strong high note. The other high spot is *Collection Blues* where Roy is teamed with Count Basie, Louie Bellson, and Niels-Henning Ørsted Pedersen, plus Johnny Griffin on tenor-sax and Milt Jackson on vibes. Roy plays ten resolute and stirring choruses; many of the ideas are from his past, but they are structured and delivered with such feeling that they all sound brand-new. Johnny Griffin plays with soul and speed but doesn't quite wrest the "top dog" spot from Roy; the two combine for a stirring couple of sign-off choruses, Griffin playing riffs and Roy belting out a strong counterpoint.

Roy's January 1976 recordings, issued as *What's It All About?*, was an album of which he was justifiably proud. This Pablo session was well thought out; it shows Roy in good shape, albeit a little less daring than usual. His paraphrasing of the melody of Benny Carter's composition, *I Still Love Him So*, is quite ingenious. Roy revives his own composition *The Heat's On*, leaving the biggest slice of solo space to Budd Johnson on tenor-sax, who delivers with panache and skill. Norris Turney also solos splendidly, adding to the Carter-like touches he showed on *I Still Love Him So*. Roy delves deep into his treasure chest of compositions and brings out *That Thing* (originally featured by his 1937 band). Here Turney's tone sounds quite Hodges-like, but the insistent phrasing is all his own. Norman Lester seems introspective at the onset of his solo, but, via a series of well-voiced block chords, builds some interesting patterns. Roy returns to his buzz-mute and blows some well-spaced lines that are in keeping with the hypnotic theme—a lack of high notes is not missed. *Recado Bossa Nova* brings a delightful change of pace, with Eddie Locke providing an exhilarating Latin American beat. Turney takes a brilliant flute solo and Roy seemingly glides from one fine phrase to another. Vibes-player Milt Jackson, a last-minute addition to the line-up, strikes some lyrical tone colors, well supported by Ted Sturgis' masterful bass lines. The final track, *Mélange*, is actually another name for Roy's 1944 *Fiesta In Brass* composition. Here Milt Jackson's sophisticated mallet work creates an effortless swing, which brings the best out of Budd

Johnson. Roy again sticks mainly in the middle register, and although he doesn't manage to summon full power the solo is a gem.

Unfortunately, Roy's next album for Pablo (made in November 1976) was much less successful. The leader on the session was Jo Jones, who makes no effort to hog the proceedings and instead allocates solos all round the distinguished line-up, which consisted of Roy, Harry Edison, Lockjaw Davis, Tommy Flanagan, Vic Dickenson, and Sam Jones. The only participant who doesn't solo is Freddie Greene, who kept up his lifelong habit of concentrating on playing rhythm guitar. The only drum feature is *I Want To Be Happy*, presented almost like the routines devised to feature tap-dancers, only here it is the neat, swinging sounds of Jo Jones' brushes that fill the gaps left by the band. Jones' muscular but svelte stickwork is heard at length on *Ol' Man River*, *Metrical Portions* (a clever composition by Budd Johnson), and *Ad Lib*. This last named, a slender theme that leads into a twelve-bar blues, has a nine-chorus excursion by Roy which must rank among the poorest solos he ever recorded. Few of his phrases link coherently, and, try as he may, he can't build up any excitement; almost uniquely he trails off at the end of his efforts. Roy plays more convincingly on the slow *Goin' To Chicago*, but is still a long way off top form, his plight being made all the clearer by his blowing being sandwiched between a delightful, growling solo from Vic Dickenson and the unhurried exposition of some fine ideas from Lockjaw Davis. Roy's fellow trumpeter, Harry Edison, lives up to his reputation for consistency, and blows his phrases with aplomb and firm-toned accuracy. Tommy Flanagan supplies the best moments of the session during his solo on *Metrical Portions*, presenting a stream of crystal-clear ideas, conveying them in perfectly voiced, skillfully harmonized phrases. Edison's effortless extended solo on Buck Clayton's arrangement of *Dark Eyes* contrasts strongly with Roy's brave attempts to produce something worthwhile. Roy knew that this was a low spot and said, "I don't think I played well at all on the Jo Jones *Main Man* session. Awful bad, Terrible. For me it was a lost night, although Jo played beautifully."[13]

An April 1977 Sonet session under the leadership of Tiny Grimes was slightly more successful, producing a good-natured album that featured several songs by Grimes and a boogie-ish instrumental (dedicated to Phil Schaap) entitled *West End Phil*. Grimes sings his own rather unadventurous lyrics over familiar chord sequences, but also contributes some nicely relaxed guitar solos. Frank Wess on tenor-sax shares the relaxed mood but Roy doesn't. His chops were not in good shape; in fact he struggles through most of the date sounding distinctly rusty, though his two choruses on *Downtown Sound* (a good, old-fashioned, slow B-flat blues) are full of feeling. Roy sings *Tain't What You Do* with infectious enthusiasm but his brief solo is very disappointing. Pianist Lloyd Glenn (then working in New York with singer Joe Turner) plays effectively, and Eddie Locke binds together a rhythm section that contains the Modern Jazz Quartet's bassist Percy Heath (in his honor Grimes quotes from the *Golden Striker* on *Food For Thought*).

Roy's playing on the sessions with Jones and Grimes could have led one to believe that his great days were over, but during the following July he triumphed at the 1977 Montreux Festival by performing an amazing set with Oscar Peterson's Trio (Niels-Henning Ørsted Pedersen and Bobby Durham). Peterson came off stage (wringing wet) at the end of the performance and said it was the best set he had ever played with Roy. Producer Norman Granz underlined the pianist's sentiments by affirming, "I honestly don't think Eldridge has played this well in the past ten years."[14] The splendors commenced with a bright version of *Between The Devil And The Deep Blue Sea*. Roy relays some choice ideas during his four choruses, stimulated by Pedersen's powerful bass notes, Durham's energetic drumming, and Oscar's backings (which are eager without being pushy). Roy trots out his well-worn penultimate riff, then returns to the melody, shaping up as if to add a simple tag, but suddenly a surge of inspiration flows through the performers on stage, and the original plan is abandoned so that Roy can blaze a trail of phrases that induce a whirlwind of excitement. This extraordinary mood overflows into each of the six numbers on the album. Peterson's rocking boogie patterns introduce the fast twelve-bar blues *Gofor*. Roy tackles the opening choruses brilliantly, and never lets up. Ideas, intensity, swing, and a feeling of exultation gird the solo, so much so that when Roy finishes his efforts one senses his total fulfillment. *I Surrender Dear* begins with almost a minute-and-a-half of wistful trumpet cadenzas (gently punctuated by piano chords), then Roy starts a passionate rendering of one of his favorite melodies, doubling up the tempo before handing over to Peterson, whose fusillade of lively ideas is countered by a nimble bass solo. Roy reasserts the original tempo, pouring his heart out as he takes the melody up an octave, yet still sounding in full command. His out-of-tempo phrases climax in a fierce high note, and he boldly rises up a third to fashion a sensational ending. Pedersen's ostinato bass line introduces *Joie De Roy*, and gets the audience clapping (most of them on the off-beat). Roy follows up with five unrestrained blues choruses that provide an impetus for Oscar's locked-hands solo, then storms into the final choruses, proving that his chops were at their strongest and surest. Roy rips into an impeccable solo on *Perdido*; the piece is taken at a fast clip but Roy's fingers remain perfectly co-ordinated. Everything falls into place on *Bye Bye Blackbird*, with Roy's open tone sounding at its most wondrous (he doesn't use a mute at any time in the set), and when he hits a high note to announce his third chorus, it rings out like a bell. Throughout the set the rhythm section gave Roy non-pareil backing: Bobby Durham took only brief solos, but together with Peterson and Pedersen he helped maintain a flow of excitement that had the audience cheering and hollering for more.

It would have seemed almost too poetic if Roy's final recordings were of the triumphant music he created at Montreux; however, he returned to play at Ryan's, which led to his taking part in a session organized by his friend and colleague Eddie Locke. This was a May 1978 concert recording of an afternoon of jazz performed for patrons and friends of the American Field Service, featuring an all-star line-up consisting of Locke, Eldridge, Budd Johnson, Vic Dickenson, Major

Holley, and Tommy Flanagan. Although the audience for this *All That Global Jazz* album wasn't as effusive as the Montreux crowd had been, their response was warm and vigorous. The band responded by playing a spirited *Lady Be Good*, with Roy contributing three open choruses that are a model of thoughtful middle register playing. Sensitive restraint is also the main ingredient of his muted feature *There Is No Greater Love*. Eddie Locke performs magnificently on *Caravan*, other individual features being Budd Johnson on *Yesterdays*, Vic Dickenson on *Manhattan*, and Tommy Flanagan on *Like Someone In Love*. The full band regroups for an absorbing version of *Satin Doll*. Roy's chorus is a mixture of bright, clear notes and stifled sounds, but every bar is packed with endeavor and jazz feeling. During the final ensemble Roy plays like an ace lead trumpeter, blowing the melody in a way that typified his ability to transmit emotion in his top register. In its own way this final burst of spirit represents a fitting farewell to the talent of a trumpeter who could not resist a challenge and who rarely gave less than his utmost.

Roy made one more album after ill health forced him to give up playing the trumpet. At a May 1985 Vineyard Theater session, headed by trumpeter Spanky Davis, Roy appeared as a guest vocalist. He puts his heart and soul into this concert performance (issued on Challenge), scatting enthusiastically on *Kidney Stew*, then imparting a slow, infectious swing to a revival of his fractured French offering *Une Petite Laitue*. Finally, with all the bounce and verve of a young rock star, Roy intones his version of Wynonie Harris' light-hearted hit *Don't Roll Those Bloodshot Eyes At Me*. Roy's super-showmanship and his ability to charm an audience shine through every number he performed, and his good humor didn't waiver when Spanky Davis asks, "Do you mind if we play *After You've Gone?*" Roy replies with a chuckle, "Be my guest. I can't play it!" Sadly this was all too true: Roy's days as a trumpeter were definitely over, but happily he left an enormous legacy in the shape of so many momentous recordings featuring his irrepressible ingenuity; he was someone who never stopped trying, a man who always shared his emotions with his listeners.

NOTES

1 SMOKETOWN

1 Conversation with the author.
2 Ibid.
3 Kitty Grime, *Jazz at Ronnie Scott's* (Robert Hale, London, 1970).
4 Conversation with the author.
5 Ibid.
6 Ibid.
7 *Melody Maker*, May 27, 1972.
8 Chuck Folds interviewed by Alyn Shipton, Ascona, 1998.
9 Conversation with the author.
10 Ibid.
11 Conversation with the author, and letter to the author, April 9, 2001.
12 Conversation with the author.
13 National Endowment for the Arts interviews conducted by Dan Morgenstern, 1982 to 1983. Available through the Institute of Jazz Studies, Rutgers University, Newark, New Jersey.
14 Conversation with the author, plus radio interviews conducted by Phil Schaap (Station W.K.C.R.-F.M., January 30, 1988) and Charles Fox (B.B.C. radio, August 29, 1977).
15 Conversation with the author.
16 Nat Shapiro and Nat Hentoff, *The Jazz Makers* (Peter Davies, London, 1958).

17 Dan Morgenstern interviews.

18 Les Tompkins interview, *Crescendo*, April 1967.

19 Charles Fox (B.B.C. radio).

20 Ibid.

21 *The Jazz Makers*.

22 Conversation with the author.

23 Arthur Smith interview, *Artists and Influences* (Hatch-Billops, New York, 1981).

24 Burt Goldblatt, *Jazz Gallery I* (Newbold Publications, New York, 1982).

25 *Metronome*, December 1949, and *Music and Rhythm*, March 1941.

26 Dan Morgenstern interviews.

27 Ibid.

28 *Down Beat*, October 1936.

29 Dan Morgenstern interviews.

30 Ibid.

31 *Down Beat*, September 19, 1956.

32 Conversation with the author.

33 *The Jazz Makers*.

34 *Artists and Influences*.

35 *The Jazz Makers*.

36 Dan Morgenstern interviews.

37 Ibid.

38 Conversation with the author.

39 Count Basie, *Good Morning Blues: The Autobiography of Count Basie as Told to Albert Murray* (Random House, New York, 1985).

40 Conversation with the author.

41 Dan Morgenstern interviews.

42 Conversation with the author.

43 *Down Beat*, September 19, 1956.

44 Phil Schaap (W.K.C.R.-F.M.).

45 Dan Morgenstern interviews.

46 Ibid.

47 Ibid.

48 *Down Beat*, October 1936.

49 Dan Morgenstern interviews.

50 *Down Beat*, October 1936.

51 Dan Morgenstern interviews.

52 Bill Coleman, *Trumpet Story* (Macmillan, London, 1990).

2 TERRITORY BAND TRAVELS

1 Dan Morgenstern interviews.
2 Conversation with the author, 1971.
3 Ibid.
4 *Storyville*, Issue 46.
5 Duncan Schiedt (publ.), *The Jazz State of Indiana* (Pittsboro, Indiana, 1977).
6 Stanley Dance, *The World of Swing* (Scribner, New York, 1974).
7 Dan Morgenstern interviews.
8 Dan Morgenstern interviews and Charles Fox (B.B.C. radio).
9 Dan Morgenstern interviews.
10 *Down Beat*, May 1, 1958.
11 Conversation with the author.
12 *Melody Maker*, November 8, 1975.
13 *Metronome*, October 1943.
14 Conversation with the author.
15 Ibid.
16 Ibid.
17 Ibid.
18 Ibid.
19 *The World of Swing*.
20 Conversation with the author.
21 *Down Beat*, October 1936.
22 Charles Fox (B.B.C. radio).
23 James Doran, *Herman Chittison* (I.A.J.R.C., Bel Air, Maryland, 1993).
24 Conversation with the author.
25 Dan Morgenstern interviews.
26 *The Jazz State of Indiana*.
27 Conversation with the author, 1982.
28 Stanley Dance, *The World of Earl Hines* (Scribner, New York, 1977).
29 Teddy Wilson, Arie Ligthart, and Humphrey van Loo, *Teddy Wilson Talks Jazz* (Cassell, London, 1996).
30 Dan Morgenstern interviews.
31 Ibid.

32 Morroe Berger, Edward Berger, and James Patrick, *Benny Carter: A Life in American Music* (Scarecrow Press, Metuchen, N.J., 1982).
33 Matthew Bruccoli, C. E. Frazer Clark, Jr., and Richard Layman Knauss, *Conversations with Jazz Musicians* (Gale Research Co, Detroit, 1977).
34 *The Jazz Makers.*
35 *Jazz Journal*, November 1963.
36 *The Jazz State of Indiana.*
37 Dan Morgenstern interviews.
38 Charles Fox (B.B.C. radio).
39 Dan Morgenstern interviews.
40 Phil Schaap (W.K.C.R.-F.M.).
41 Conversation with the author.
42 Ibid.
43 Dan Morgenstern interviews.

3 A BITE AT THE BIG APPLE

1 Conversation with the author.
2 Ibid.
3 Dan Morgenstern interviews.
4 Burt Korall, *Drummin' Men* (Schirmer Books, New York, 1990).
5 Rex Stewart, *Boy Meets Horn* (Bayou Press, Oxford, 1991).
6 *Jazz Record*, Issue 56, June 1947.
7 Phil Schaap (W.K.C.R.-F.M.).
8 Dicky Wells, *The Night People* (Robert Hale, London, 1971).
9 *Crescendo*, April 1967, and conversation with the author.
10 Ibid.
11 Marian McPartland radio interview, 1986.
12 Dan Morgenstern interviews.
13 *Storyville*, 17.
14 Dan Morgenstern interviews.
15 Bill Crow, *Jazz Anecdotes* (Oxford University Press, New York, 1990).
16 Phil Schaap (W.K.C.R.-F.M.).
17 John Hammond, *John Hammond on Record* (Ridge Press, New York, 1977).
18 Phil Schaap (W.K.C.R.-F.M.).
19 *Jazz Anecdotes.*

20 Dan Morgenstern interviews.
21 Ibid.
22 *The World of Swing.*
23 Mike Hennessey, *Klook: The Story of Kenny Clarke* (Quartet, London, 1990).
24 *Jazz Anecdotes.*
25 *Klook.*
26 Conversation with the author.
27 Ibid.
28 Ibid.
29 Lowell Holmes and John Thomson, *Jazz Greats* (Holmes and Meier, New York, 1986).
30 Conversation with the author.
31 Stanley Dance, *The World of Count Basie* (Sidgwick & Jackson, London, 1980).
32 Red Callender and Elaine Cohen, *Unfinished Dream* (Quartet, London, 1985).
33 Conversation with the author.
34 Dan Morgenstern interviews.
35 Warren W. Vaché, Sr., *Pee Wee Erwin: This Horn for Hire* (Scarecrow Press, Metuchen, N.J., 1987).
36 *Into Jazz*, February 1974.
37 *Trumpet Story.*
38 *The Night People.*
39 *Boy Meets Horn.*
40 Dan Morgenstern interviews.
41 Ibid.
42 Phil Schaap (W.K.C.R.-F.M.).
43 *Melody Maker*, August 31, 1935.
44 Conversation with the author.
45 Dan Morgenstern interviews, and conversation with the author.

4 CHICAGO BANDLEADER

1 *Melody Maker*, September 10, 1949.
2 Arthur Smith interview, and Phil Schaap (W.K.C.R.-F.M.).
3 Dempsey J. Travis, *An Autobiography of Black Jazz* (Urban Research Institute, Chicago, 1983).

4 Dan Morgenstern interviews.

5 *Music 1969, Down Beat* Yearbook.

6 Charles Fox (B.B.C. radio).

7 Dan Morgenstern interviews.

8 Ibid.

9 Ibid.

10 Ibid.

11 *Down Beat*, July 28, 1966, and *Metronome*, September 1946.

12 Dan Morgenstern interviews.

13 *Metronome*, February 1936.

14 Charles Fox (B.B.C. radio).

15 *Music and Rhythm*, September 1941.

16 Phil Schaap (W.K.C.R.-F.M.).

17 *Jazz Monthly*, August 1963, and Walter C. Allen (publ.), *Hendersonia* (Highland Park, N.J., 1973).

18 *Jazz Journal*, June 1972.

19 *Crescendo*, April 1967.

20 *Drummin' Men*.

21 Whitney Balliett, *American Musicians* (Oxford University Press, New York, 1986).

22 *Down Beat*, July 1935.

23 Milt Hinton and David G. Berger, *Bass Line* (Temple University Press, Philadelphia, 1988).

24 Dan Morgenstern interviews.

25 Ibid.

26 *Music and Rhythm*, September 1941.

27 Conversation with the author.

28 Truck Parham interviewed by Alyn Shipton (Ascona, June 1998).

29 Phil Schaap (W.K.C.R.-F.M.).

30 *Jazz 1950, Metronome* Yearbook.

31 Letter to the author, November 10, 1998 (from Helen Oakley Dance).

32 *An Autobiography of Black Jazz*.

33 *Metronome*, December 1949.

34 *The Jazz Makers*.

35 Sleeve-note, *Laughin' To Keep From Crying*, Verve 2304 487.

36 Buck Clayton, *Buck Clayton's Jazz World* (Macmillan, London, 1986).

37 Phil Schaap (W.K.C.R.-F.M.).
38 *An Autobiography of Black Jazz*.
39 Charles Fox (B.B.C. radio).
40 *Down Beat*, March 1936.

5 SETTLING IN NEW YORK

1 *Metronome*, May 1937.
2 Dan Morgenstern interviews.
3 *Metronome*, December 1949.
4 Dan Morgenstern interviews.
5 Ibid.
6 *Jazz Anecdotes*.
7 *Swing*, December 1940.
8 Dan Morgenstern interviews.
9 Conversation with the author.
10 *Jazz Anecdotes*.
11 *Pittsburgh Courier*, January 28, 1939.
12 Charles Fox (B.B.C. radio).
13 Franz Jackson interviewed by Alyn Shipton, Ascona, June 1998.
14 Ibid.
15 Phil Schaap (W.K.C.R.-F.M.).
16 *The World of Swing*.
17 Conversation with the author.
18 Ibid.
19 Alyn Shipton interview.
20 Sheila Tracy, *Bands, Booze and Broads* (Mainstream, Edinburgh, 1995).
21 *Metronome*, December 1961, and conversation with the author.
22 *Into Jazz*, February 1974.
23 *Band Wagon*, April 19, 1940.
24 Ibid.
25 Conversation with the author.
26 *Metronome*, October 1943.
27 *Melody Maker*, October 22, 1938.
28 Arthur Smith interview, 1981, and *Coda 173* interview with Jack Winter, 1980.
29 Phil Schaap (W.K.C.R.-F.M.).
30 *Melody Maker*, July 13, 1940.

31 Ira Gitler, *Swing to Bop* (Oxford University Press, New York, 1985).
32 *Chicago Defender*, August 3, 1940.
33 *Jazz Journal*, June 1960.
34 *Swing*, September 1940.
35 Conversation with the author.

6 CRUSADING WITH KRUPA

1 *An Autobiography of Black Jazz.*
2 *Crescendo*, April 1967.
3 *Melody Maker*, April 27, 1957.
4 *Down Beat*, January 31, 1963.
5 *Coda*, April 1977.
6 Ira Gitler, *Jazz Masters of the 40's* (Macmillan, New York, 1966).
7 *Down Beat*, May 1, 1941.
8 *Cadence*, March 1986.
9 Dan Morgenstern interviews.
10 *Coda*, March 1974.
11 *Chicago Defender* (Al Monroe article), May 3, 1941.
12 *Music and Rhythm*, June 1941.
13 *Coda*, March 1974.
14 Conversation with the author.
15 Ibid.
16 *Drummin' Men.*
17 *Metronome*, June 1941.
18 James Lester, *Too Marvelous for Words: The Life and Genius of Art Tatum* (Oxford University Press, New York, 1994).
19 *Metronome*, October 1943.
20 Nat Shapiro and Nat Hentoff, *Hear Me Talkin' to Ya* (Peter Davies, London, 1955), and *Jazz Journal*, May 1972.
21 Conversation with the author.
22 *Swing to Bop.*
23 *Unfinished Dream.*
24 Dizzy Gillespie and Al Fraser, *To Be or Not to Bop* (W. H. Allen, London, 1980).
25 *Jazz Anecdotes.*
26 *Klook.*
27 Joachim Berendt, *The Jazz Book* (Granada, London, 1983).

28 Steve Jordan and Tom Scanlan, *Rhythm Man* (University of Michigan Press, 1991).

29 *Cadence*, March 1984.

30 *Down Beat*, September 19, 1956.

31 Charles Fox (B.B.C. radio).

32 *Down Beat*, October 1979.

33 *The World of Count Basie.*

34 *Jazz Journal*, June 1972 (Steve Voce feature).

35 *Metronome*, July 1941.

36 *Rhythm Man.*

37 *Music and Rhythm*, November 1940.

38 *Coda*, March 1974.

39 *Down Beat*, December 15, 1977.

40 Conversation with the author.

41 *Drummin' Men.*

42 *Down Beat*, June 12, 1958.

43 *Drummin' Men.*

44 Bruce H. Klauber, *The World of Gene Krupa* (Pathfinder Press, California, 1990).

45 *Music and Rhythm*, November 1940.

46 Brian Priestley, *Mingus: A Critical Biography* (Quartet, London, 1982).

47 Phil Schaap (W.K.C.R.-F.M.).

48 Sleeve-note, Pablo 2310–869.

49 *The World of Gene Krupa.*

50 George T. Simon, *Big Bands* (Macmillan, New York, 1971).

51 *Down Beat*, September 1941.

52 *Music and Rhythm*, December 1941.

53 Teddy Reig with Edward Berger, *Reminiscing in Tempo* (Scarecrow Press, Metuchen, N.J., 1990).

54 *Metronome*, February 1942.

55 *The World of Gene Krupa.*

56 Arthur Smith interview.

57 Charles Fox (B.B.C. radio).

58 Sleeve-note, Pablo 2310–869.

59 Conversation with the author.

60 Ibid.

61 Anita O'Day and George Eells, *High Times, Hard Times* (Putnam, New York, 1981).

62 *Metronome*, November 1942.

63 *Metronome*, October 1948.

7 STARRING WITH SHAW

1 Arthur Smith interview.

2 Ibid.

3 Ibid.

4 Conversation with the author.

5 Dan Morgenstern interviews.

6 *Metronome*, May 1943.

7 John Wesley Noble and Benard Averbuch, *Never Plead Guilty: The Story of Jake Ehrlich* (Farrar, Strauss & Cudahy, New York, 1955).

8 *Coda*, March 1974.

9 Ibid.

10 *The World of Gene Krupa*.

11 Ibid.

12 Ibid.

13 *Jazz Journal*, February 1990.

14 *Down Beat*, August 1, 1943.

15 *Metronome*, February 1944.

16 *Down Beat*, September 19, 1956.

17 *Down Beat*, July 15, 1944.

18 Ian Carr, *Miles Davis* (Quartet, London, 1982).

19 *Jazz Journal*, February 1975.

20 Dan Morgenstern interviews.

21 *The Jazz Makers*.

22 *Metronome*, June 1944.

23 *Crescendo*, April 1967.

24 *Metronome*, August 1945.

25 *Metronome*, April 1944.

26 *Metronome*, November 1944.

27 *Metronome*, December 1944.

28 Conversation with the author.

29 W. Royal Stokes, *The Jazz Scene* (Oxford University Press, New York, 1991).

30 Brigitte Berman (film), *Artie Shaw: Time Is All You've Got* (1984).

31 *Jazz Monthly*, June 1969.

32 Arthur Smith interview.

33 Vladimir Simosko, *Artie Shaw: A Musical Biography and Discography* (Scarecrow Press, Lanham, Maryland, 2000), and *Sunday Telegraph*, March 4, 2001, article by Michael Freedland.

34 Jean Bach (film), *A Great Day in Harlem* (1994).

35 *The Big Bands.*

36 *Down Beat*, February 15, 1945.

37 *Down Beat*, May 18, 1951.

38 Ibid.

39 *American Musicians* and *New Yorker*, September 11, 1989.

40 *Down Beat*, May 18, 1951.

41 Arthur Smith interview.

42 *Artie Shaw: A Musical Biography and Discography.*

43 *New Yorker*, September 11, 1989.

44 *Metronome*, November 1953.

45 James T. Hershorn, *Let Freedom Swing: Norman Granz and Jazz at the Philharmonic, 1944–1957* (George Mason University, Fairfax, VA, 1996).

8 JAZZ AT THE PHILHARMONIC

1 *Pittsburgh Courier*, May 18, 1946.

2 Conversation with the author.

3 *Down Beat*, December 16, 1946.

4 *Jazz Notes*, January 1947.

5 *Chicago Defender*, October 24, 1946.

6 *Metronome*, January 1947.

7 Conversation with the author.

8 *Down Beat*, June 4, 1947.

9 Charles Fox (B.B.C. radio).

10 *The Jazz Makers.*

11 *Melody Maker*, June 4, 1977.

12 *Down Beat*, August 13, 1947.

13 *Down Beat*, September 19, 1956.

14 *Metronome*, December 1949.

15 *Jazz Monthly*, April 1970.

16 *The Phoenix Gazette*, February 15, 1969.

17 *Coda*, March 1974.

18 *Metronome*, December 1949.

19 *Coda*, March 1974.
20 *Down Beat*, October 21, 1949.
21 *Into Jazz*, February 1974.
22 *Metronome*, March 1951.
23 *Down Beat*, January 13, 1950.
24 *Swing to Bop*.
25 *Down Beat*, September 19, 1956.
26 Ibid.
27 Conversation with the author.
28 Letter to the author, September 5, 1998 (from Dick Hyman).
29 *Down Beat*, May 16, 1951.
30 *Melody Maker*, April 29, 1950.
31 *Down Beat*, May 18, 1951.
32 Letter to the author, May 20, 1999 (from Nancy Reed).
33 Conversation with the author.
34 Ibid.
35 Ibid.
36 Letter to the author, September 5, 1998 (from Dick Hyman).
37 *Melody Maker*, May 27, 1950.
38 Conversation with the author.
39 *Down Beat*, May 18, 1951.
40 Conversation with the author.
41 *Melody Maker*, June 17, 1950.
42 Conversation with the author.
43 *Down Beat*, May 18, 1951.
44 *Jazz Journal*, March 1980.

9 INTERLUDE IN PARIS

1 *Down Beat*, March 19, 1959.
2 Phil Schaap (W.K.C.R.-F.M.).
3 *Melody Maker*, August 26, 1950.
4 *Metronome*, October 1950.
5 Ibid.
6 Conversation with the author.
7 *Melody Maker*, November 25, 1950.
8 Letter to the author, September 25, 1998 (from Claude Bolling).
9 Ibid.
10 Ibid.

11 *Down Beat*, May 18, 1951.
12 *Coda 173* (1980).
13 *Melody Maker*, December 3, 1950.
14 *Jazz Journal*, May 1972.
15 *Melody Maker*, April 14, 1951.
16 Ibid.
17 *Down Beat*, March 19, 1959.
18 Ibid.
19 *Down Beat*, July 21, 1960.
20 *Down Beat*, January 13, 1950.
21 *Down Beat*, May 18, 1951.
22 Ibid.
23 Ibid.
24 *Down Beat*, June 15, 1951.
25 Dan Morgenstern interviews.
26 *Down Beat*, July 13, 1951.
27 Ibid.
28 Ibid.
29 Dan Morgenstern interviews.
30 Marian McPartland radio interview, 1986.
31 *Down Beat*, January 25, 1952.
32 Ibid.
33 Charles Fox (B.B.C. radio).
34 *Into Jazz*, February 1974.
35 Frank Buchmann-Møller, *Lester Young: You Just Fight for Your Life* (Praeger, New York, 1990).
36 *Down Beat*, June 4, 1952.
37 *Down Beat*, September 29, 1956.
38 *Drummin' Men*.
39 Conversation with the author.
40 Mel Tormé, *Traps: The Drum Wonder* (Oxford University Press, New York, 1991).
41 Gene Lees, *The Will to Swing: Oscar Peterson* (Macmillan, London, 1989).
42 Conversation with the author.
43 *Swing to Bop*.
44 *Jazz Journal*, March 1964.
45 *American Musicians*.

46 *Melody Maker*, February 22, 1964.

47 *Down Beat*, June 17, 1953.

48 *Down Beat*, August 12, 1953.

49 Dan Morgenstern interviews.

50 *Tribute to Roy Eldridge* pamphlet. U.S.A., no date.

10 TOURS AND TRIUMPHS

 1 Charles Fox (B.B.C. radio).

 2 *Metronome*, August 1954.

 3 *Down Beat*, August 11, 1954.

 4 *Coda 173* (1980).

 5 *Let Freedom Swing*.

 6 *Down Beat*, October 20, 1954.

 7 *Down Beat*, September 19, 1956.

 8 B.B.C. radio interview, April 19, 1999.

 9 Phil Schaap (W.K.C.R.-F.M.).

10 *The Will to Swing*.

11 Conversation with the author.

12 *Melody Maker*, February 26, 1955.

13 *Down Beat*, September 19, 1956.

14 B.B.C. Radio 3 interview, September 15, 1999.

15 *Down Beat*, September 21, 1955.

16 *The Jazz Makers*.

17 *Let Freedom Swing*.

18 Conversation with the author.

19 Dan Morgenstern interviews.

20 *Down Beat*, September 19, 1956.

21 *Buck Clayton's Jazz World*.

22 Conversation with the author.

23 Ibid.

24 *Metronome*, April 1956.

25 *Down Beat*, September 19, 1956.

26 Ibid.

27 Ibid.

28 *Melody Maker*, May 16, 1959.

29 *Melody Maker*, May 4, 1957.

30 *Down Beat*, September 19, 1956, and *Melody Maker*, August 26, 1950.

31 Conversation with the author.

32 Phil Schaap (W.K.C.R.-F.M.).

33 Charles Fox (B.B.C. radio).

34 *Jazz at Ronnie Scott's*.

35 *Melody Maker*, May 16, 1959.

36 Nat Hentoff, *Listen to the Stories* (HarperCollins, New York, 1995).

37 Conversation with the author.

38 Ibid.

39 Letter to the author, August 21, 2000 (from Charles Graham).

40 Ibid.

41 *Melody Maker*, May 16, 1959.

42 Conversation with the author.

43 *Melody Maker*, May 16, 1959.

11 FLYING WITH THE HAWK

1 Letter to the author, November 10, 1998 (from Stanley Dance).

2 *Down Beat*, August 6, 1959.

3 *Down Beat Yearbook*, 1958.

4 Charles Fox (B.B.C. radio).

5 *Down Beat*, March 17, 1960.

6 Letter to the author, August 21, 2000 (from Charles Graham).

7 *Jazz Journal*, June 1960.

8 Ibid.

9 *Jazz Journal*, June 1960, and *Metronome*, December 1949.

10 *Down Beat*, February 4, 1971.

11 *Down Beat*, December 15, 1977.

12 *Down Beat*, January 18, 1973.

13 *Down Beat*, September 1987.

14 *Jazz Anecdotes*.

15 Conversation with the author, and *Jazz Journal*, June 1996.

16 Max Gordon, *Live at the Village Vanguard* (St. Martin's Press, New York, 1980).

17 Conversation with the author.

18 *Down Beat*, July 20, 1961.

19 Conversation with the author.

20 *Crescendo*, April 1967.

21 Conversation with the author.

22 Ibid.

23 *Down Beat*, August 2, 1962.
24 Conversation with the author.
25 Ibid.
26 *Rhythm Man*.
27 Stuart Nicholson, *Ella Fitzgerald* (Gollancz, London, 1993).
28 *Melody Maker*, March 28, 1964.
29 Leonard Feather, *From Satchmo to Miles* (Stein and Day, New York, 1972).
30 Jack Schiffman, *Uptown: The Story of Harlem's Apollo* (Cowles, New York, 1971).
31 *From Satchmo to Miles*.
32 *Ella Fitzgerald*.
33 *The Jazz Makers*.
34 *Down Beat*, February 4, 1971, and conversation with the author.
35 *Down Beat*, December 15, 1977.
36 *Down Beat*, May 20, 1965.
37 *Down Beat*, October 6, 1977.
38 Conversation with the author.
39 *Melody Maker*, March 28, 1964.
40 Mark Miller, *Jazz in Canada: Fourteen Lives* (University of Toronto, 1982).
41 *Jazz Monthly*, December 1980.
42 Charles Fox (B.B.C. radio).
43 Conversation with the author.
44 *Down Beat*, March 19, 1959.
45 *Melody Maker*, March 28, 1964, and June 4, 1977.
46 *Crescendo*, August 1967.
47 Ibid.
48 Ibid.
49 *Jazz Journal*, July 1966.
50 *New York Post*, July 30, 1966.
51 *Down Beat*, July 28, 1966.
52 Phil Schaap (W.K.C.R.-F.M.).

12 FESTIVALS GALORE

1 *The World of Count Basie*.
2 *Jazz Anecdotes*.
3 Letter to the author, August 5, 2000 (from Charles Graham).

4 Phil Schaap (W.K.C.R.-F.M.).

5 Ibid.

6 Conversation with the author.

7 Ibid.

8 Ibid.

9 Ibid.

10 *Jazz Journal*, May 1967.

11 Ray Bolden Memoir, 1998.

12 *Down Beat*, January 25, 1968.

13 *Down Beat Yearbook*, 1970.

14 Conversation with the author.

15 *The Phoenix Gazette*, February 15, 1969.

16 *Coda 173* (1980).

17 Dan Morgenstern interviews.

18 Steve Voce (Radio Merseyside, 1974).

19 *Jazz Monthly*, December 1970.

20 Conversation with the author.

21 *Melody Maker*, May 27, 1972.

22 *Down Beat*, November 26, 1970.

23 Ray Bolden Memoir, 1998.

24 Sleeve-note, New World Records N.W. 349.

25 Ibid.

26 Conversation with the author.

27 Ibid.

28 Ibid.

29 Ibid.

30 Alyn Shipton interview.

31 Conversation with the author.

32 Letter to the author, August 5, 2000 (from Charles Graham).

33 Conversation with the author.

34 *Down Beat*, June 15, 1967.

35 Conversation with the author.

36 Phil Schaap (W.K.C.R.-F.M.).

37 *Coda 173* (1980).

38 *Melody Maker*, May 27, 1972.

39 Ibid.

40 *Metronome*, December 1949.

41 Conversation with the author.

42 Letter to the author, 1972 (from Johnny Simmen).
43 Conversation with the author.
44 Ray Bolden Memoir, 1998.
45 Conversation with the author.
46 Letter to the author, April 9, 2001.
47 *Allegro*, February 2001.

13 RADIANCE AT RYAN'S

 1 *Down Beat*, March 15, 1973.
 2 Conversation with the author.
 3 Ibid.
 4 Ibid.
 5 *Into Jazz*, February 1974.
 6 Conversation with the author.
 7 *Village Voice*, June 16, 1975.
 8 Conversation with the author.
 9 Ibid.
10 Ibid.
11 Ibid.
12 Ibid.
13 Ibid.
14 Ibid.
15 Ray Bolden Memoir, 1998.
16 Conversation with the author.
17 Ibid.
18 Ibid.
19 Letter to the author, October 23, 2000 (from Loren Schoenberg).
20 *Jazz Journal*, November 1975.
21 *Melody Maker*, November 8, 1975.
22 *Jazz Gallery* I.
23 Conversation with the author.
24 Ibid.
25 *Daily Telegraph Magazine*, May 19, 1994.
26 *Jazz Journal*, January 1977.
27 Conversation with the author.
28 Ibid.
29 Letter to the author, August 21, 2000 (from Charles Graham).
30 *New York Times*, February 8, 1976.

14 ENDING WITH A SONG

1 *Jazz Journal*, March 1977.
2 Ibid.
3 *Down Beat*, September 1984.
4 Phil Schaap (W.K.C.R.-F.M.).
5 *Melody Maker*, June 4, 1977.
6 Ibid.
7 Letter to the author, August 21, 2000 (from Charles Graham).
8 *Down Beat*, January 1980.
9 *Down Beat*, December 1980.
10 Conversation with the author.
11 Ibid.
12 *Jazz Journal*, March 1980.
13 Garry Giddins, *Rhythm-a-Ning* (Oxford University Press, New York, 1986).
14 Conversation with the author.
15 *Jazz Times*, September 1986.
16 Charles Fox (B.B.C. radio).
17 Letter to the author, March 2, 2000 (from James Hogg).
18 *Jazz Times*, September 1986.
19 Conversation with the author.
20 Letter to the author, October 23, 2000 (from Loren Schoenberg).
21 *Jazz Times*, September 1986.
22 *Down Beat*, December 15, 1977.
23 Conversation with the author.
24 Alyn Shipton interview.
25 Letter to the author, April 9, 2001 (from Dan Morgenstern).
26 *American Musicians*.
27 Conversation with the author.
28 Letter to the author, October 23, 2000 (from Loren Schoenberg).
29 Letter to the author, November 10, 2000 (from Charles Graham).
30 Conversation with the author.
31 Letter to the author, November 10, 2000 (from Charles Graham).

15-19 ROY ON RECORD

1 Gunther Schuller, *The Swing Era* (Oxford University Press, New York, 1989).

2 Phil Schaap (W.K.C.R.-F.M.).
3 Ibid.
4 *Artie Shaw: Time Is All You've Got.*
5 Ibid.
6 *Down Beat*, September 19, 1956.
7 Dan Morgenstern interviews.
8 *Coda 173* (1980).
9 Phil Schaap (W.K.C.R.-F.M.).
10 Nat Hentoff sleeve-note, H.M.V. 7EG 8625.
11 Phil Schaap (W.K.C.R.-F.M.).
12 Nat Hentoff sleeve-note, Candid SMJ-6187.
13 *Down Beat*, December 15, 1977.
14 Norman Granz sleeve-note, Pablo 2308 203.

SUBJECT INDEX

Bold type within a sequence of page numbers indicates a more significant section.

INDEX OF SELECTED RECORDINGS